Richard Shane

GRAIN MARKETING ECONOMICS

GRAIN MARKETING ECONOMICS

Editors

Gail L. Cramer
Montana State University
Bozeman, Montana

Walter G. Heid, Jr.
U.S. Department of Agriculture
Manhattan, Kansas

**John Wiley
& Sons**

New York
Chichester
Brisbane
Toronto
Singapore

Library of Congress Cataloging in Publication Data
Main entry under title:

Grain marketing economics.

Includes indexes.
1. Grain trade—United States.   2. Grain trade.
I. Cramer, Gail L.   II. Heid, Walter George, 1932–
HD9035.G73   1983   380.1′4131′0973   83-1205
ISBN 0-471-88894-X

Printed in the United States of America

10 9 8 7 6 5 4 3 2 1

*Dedicated to
Blaine C. Hardy
Outstanding Teacher
Wapato, Washington*

PREFACE

Grain has an ever-present influence in our daily lives, persisting at every meal, either directly or indirectly. It is involved in your breakfast cereal, toast, eggs, bacon, or rolls. At lunch, grain is a part of your soup, sandwich, and glass of milk. For dinner, it is embodied in your red meats, poultry, seafood, spaghetti, appetizers, cocktails, and after-dinner drinks. Grain is, indeed, a staple in the diets of all the world's people.

This book gives the student an opportunity to learn about the world grain industry at a time when there is an unusually high degree of unrest and change. It gives the student a glimpse into the future, into a time when some traditional trading practices may give way to new approaches to marketing. The decade of the 1970s brought forth many new concerns in the grain trade. The first real test of its effectiveness in handling new demands was met but not without severe strains and a great amount of self-evaluation. Many questions arose concerning ownership and control of grain and the ability of the industry to distribute greater quantities of grain throughout the world. Specific concerns centered on a broad array of topics including cartel arrangements with other major grain exporting countries, deregulation of trucks and railways, national and international grain reserves, and inventory disclosure policies.

The U.S. grain industry is part of a worldwide system, charged with servicing markets throughout the world. It is faced with stiff competition that often is motivated by a different set of values and trading strategies than those experienced within our own system. To further complicate the new image, the large grain marketing firms operating in the United States are, in several instances, multinational corporations. A large share of their transactions often involves a single state agency or board that is serving as a nation's sole buyer of grains and grain products. The complexity of this situation alone makes it difficult to administer national trade policy. Students are encouraged to study the ramifications of these emerging changes and to compare the effectiveness of alternative marketing systems.

The volume of grain handled by the U.S. grain industry will escalate in the coming decades if world population, incomes, and animal numbers grow as expected. This, of course, assumes an ability to continue improving crop yields, and an opportunity to compete in the growing international market. Evolving life-styles and diets, developing foreign agricultural systems, and the economic well-being of certain grain importing countries that have been hard hit by escalating energy prices and inflationary pressures will also exert their influences.

For the student who is interested in understanding how our grain marketing system functions, or may hope to be employed somewhere within the system, it is important not only to understand the marketing process but also to be aware of the system's ancillary services. This latter dimension, sometimes overlooked by students, includes all the activities involved in financing grain inventories, advertising and promotion, research (both public and private), education, public policy efforts of commodity associations, methods of handling risk and uncertainty (insurance and hedging), and the development and execution of government policies. Students should also be particularly aware of the vast amount of administrative-type work that must be performed as grains and their products flow through the system.

Although we have a free enterprise system whereby individual grain firms may privately sell to foreign buyers—usually state trading agencies—these firms are required to meet certain federal regulations, such as reporting large-volume sales, honoring embargoes, and other domestically imposed requirements. Grain firms must also negotiate with labor unions, be aware of diplomatic relations, and handle special shipments involving grain moving under government programs. Activities of the U.S. grain industry are also affected by such agencies as the Federal Grain Inspection Service, Environmental Protection Agency, Occupational Safety and Health Administration, and the Federal Trade Commission, to name a few. To meet the standards of these regulations and regulating agencies is time consuming, costly, and disruptive for decision makers but it is also apparently deemed necessary; these standards have been developed and imposed by the democratic process of law.

The complexity of our grain trading system far exceeds the lines of a flow diagram, or even the discussion in the following chapters. Therefore, this book can only whet the student's quest for knowledge. Serious students should be encouraged to take field trips and educational tours through grain-related facilities. At some universities, extra credit may be earned if the student participates in a field trip to a major grain trading center. Field trips enable students to gain first-hand knowledge, and a chance to observe the real world in action. On such field trips, visits often are arranged by or with a board of trade, grain terminals, grain brokers, flour mills, baking plants, or other processors. Students farther away from major trade centers may take advantage of other grain-related facilities, visiting port terminals, quality testing laboratories or USDA research centers. Other students may have the opportunity to travel to foreign countries to study the operations of other marketing systems. At the same time, a large number of foreign students and grain trade teams visit the United States each year to learn more about the U.S. system. One may go to Manhattan, Kansas, and visit the Grain Science Department of Kansas State University, which offers a concentrated curriculum for training students at the university level for careers in feed manufacturing, flour milling, and baking; the American Baking Institute; and the U.S. Grain Marketing Research Laboratory.

This book blends a descriptive, institutional, and analytical approach. The overall plan allows the student to follow the movement of the major grains—corn, wheat, and soybeans—from farm production to final consumption. This includes all intermediate steps, such as assembly, storage, grading, transportation, processing and merchandising channels, including international trade channels. Accompanying these chapters are treatments of supply and demand relationships, pricing, futures trading, sources of market information, and government policy.

The coeditors of this book greatly appreciate the dedicated and cooperative spirit of the contributing authors. Working with professionally oriented people has been an interesting and rewarding experience for us. But this book would not have been completed without the assistance of Dr. Clarence W. Jensen of Montana State University. A great amount of his time was spent in rechecking and updating tabulated and factual information and making other changes in the text to better serve each author's purpose in writing. Clarence devoted much final editing effort toward achieving a more uniform style of writing, and he is responsible for the added quality of this book.

Finally, we wish to express our appreciation to Dianne DeSalvo, Janet Logan, and Evelyn Richard for their skills and resourcefulness in typing and proofing the final manuscript.

Gail L. Cramer
Walter G. Heid, Jr.

CONTENTS

UNITED STATES AND WORLD GRAIN PRODUCTION

UNITED STATES AND WORLD GRAIN PRODUCTION*

CHAPTER
1

Many factors contribute to the efficiency of American agriculture. One is an abundance of productive cropland that responds well to commercial fertilizers. In 1980, over 245 million acres were planted to grain crops and oilseeds (Table 1-1). This amounted to about 24 percent of the acres classified by the U.S. Census of Agriculture as "land in farms."

It is interesting to note that land in farms has been declining steadily. This is due to several factors including encroachment by highways, industrial development, and the city-suburban sprawl on farmland. It is also interesting to note the increase in acres planted to grain, a reversal of the land in farms trend. The trend in area planted to grain may be attributed both to world supply-demand conditions of the 1970s and the profitability of grain production relative to livestock and other agricultural enterprises.

Much of our abundant land resource is organized into large productive units. Large fields that can be farmed by capital intensive methods add to the efficiency of U.S. production. The Great Plains perhaps best typifies this characteristic, although large-scale farms also exist in other parts of the nation.

The second factor is climate. The temperate climate of the Northern Hemisphere is conducive to high-yield production. In many areas, the growing season is long enough to permit complete plant development. Average annual precipitation occurs at levels sufficient to foster healthy growth, and rainfall tends to occur at critical times in the plant maturity process. Some grain-producing areas possess adequate soil and topographical characteristics for continuous cropping, while other areas are limited by a dry climate. In places of inadequate rainfall, farmers either turn to irrigation or a crop-fallow system. A crop-fallow system is called strip farming where the producer normally plants one crop every other year, or two crops every three years, depending on soil moisture. By following this farming method soil moisture is conserved, resulting in more optimal grain crop productivity. Generally these drier areas of the United States are devoted to small grains such as wheat or barley.

*Michael V. Martin, Assistant Professor, Department of Agricultural and Resource Economics, Oregon State University, Corvallis, Ore., and Stephen C. Schmidt, Professor, Department of Agricultural Economics, University of Illinois, Urbana.

Table 1-1   U.S. Land in Farms and Acres Planted to Feed
and Food Grains (in thousands of acres)

Year	Land in Farms	Planted to Feed Grains	Planted to Soybeans	Planted to Food Grains	Total Grains and Soybeans
1967	1,123,456	100,008	40,819	61,386	202,213
1968	1,115,231	96,436	42,265	58,114	196,815
1969	1,107,711	94,342	42,534	50,565	181,441
1970	1,102,769	98,399	43,082	46,806	188,287
1971	1,097,300	105,303	43,476	51,254	200,033
1972	1,093,017	92,607	46,866	50,171	189,644
1973	1,089,530	101,026	56,549	57,273	214,848
1974	1,087,788	98,614	52,479	68,683	219,776
1975	1,086,025	103,511	54,550	72,938	230,999
1976	1,084,046	105,398	50,226	73,972	229,596
1977	1,081,293	106,159	58,760	69,159	234,078
1978	1,072,341	104,509	64,383	60,907	229,799
1979	1,049,063	101,232	71,632	66,528	239,392
1980	1,046,713	101,656	70,087	74,812	246,555

Source: U.S. Department of Agriculture, *Agricultural Statistics,* 1980.

The third factor is related to technology. Research and development have provided American farmers with sophisticated machinery and equipment. A wide range of chemicals for fertilization and pest management, and hybrid seeds in the case of corn and wheat, have helped to increase productivity. These technological advances and applications result from a strong commitment to basic research, the willingness of agricultural input suppliers to invest in new products and product lines, and the desire and capability of U.S. farmers to adopt these new inputs.

American farm operators have high levels of technical and managerial skill, a fourth factor influencing efficient production. Decisions concerning production practices tend to be made on the basis of a large amount of information, with some farmers relying on computer-derived solutions. Applications of new and existing technology tend to be appropriately handled within the constraints of investment capital. Near optimal input use has allowed U.S. farmers to maintain a leadership role in supplying basic grain products.

U.S. GRAIN PRODUCTION

Grains are usually classified into one of three broad categories according to their end use. Grains that are used primarily in products of direct human consumption are referred to as food grains. These generally include wheat and rice. Grains utilized primarily as feed for livestock are called feed grains. Feed grains, which include corn, barley, sorghum, oats and rye, are sometimes referred to as coarse grains. Finally, related seed crops such as soybeans, sunflowers, rapeseed, and flax (which are grown both for their oil and high protein meal), are referred to as oilseeds.

While this method is common in delineating grains, remember that in most cases grains have more than one use and may, for some purposes, be considered to be in more than one category. For example, wheat is sometimes fed to livestock and corn is used extensively for corn meal and syrup as well as for livestock feed. Similarly, a large amount of barley is used by the malting and brewing industries.

About 85 percent of the more than 245 million acres planted to grain (including oilseeds) are planted to three major crops—corn, wheat, and soybeans. As shown in Table 1-2, the harvested acreage of each of these major grains increased after 1970. The acreage of sorghum and sunflowers has also increased. At the same time, however, the acreage of some of the minor feed grains (barley, oats, and rye) decreased. These minor feed grains compete for land area primarily with wheat. As long as wheat is more profitable, and its acreage is not limited by government programs, farmers prefer to grow this more profitable crop.

U.S. farmers can increase production of specific crops in two ways: through increasing acres or increasing yields. Farmers' ability to change acreages from minor crops to added acres of corn, soybeans, or wheat is limited by the availability of suitable cropland as well as the demand for the minor crops. Similarly, only a limited amount of cropland is, in any given year, idle or used for pastureland.

Table 1-2 U.S. Acreages Harvested and Production of Corn for Grain, Wheat, and Soybeans, 1970 to 1981

Year	Corn for Grain		Wheat		Soybeans	
	1000 Acres	*Million Bushels*	*1000 Acres*	*Million Bushels*	*1000 Acres*	*Million Bushels*
1970	57,358	4,153	43,564	1,350	42,249	1,128
1971	64,047	5,643	47,674	1,616	42,705	1,174
1972	57,421	5,576	47,284	1,546	45,683	1,270
1973	61,894	5,645	53,869	1,708	55,667	1,548
1974	65,357	4,666	65,613	1,798	51,341	1,217
1975	67,222	5,795	69,641	2,138	53,579	1,548
1976	71,300	6,267	70,771	2,144	49,358	1,288
1977	70,872	6,428	66,461	2,100	57,612	1,763
1978	69,970	7,081	56,839	1,950	63,343	1,850
1979	72,400	7,939	62,454	2,134	70,566	2,268
1980	73,030	6,645	70,984	2,374	67,856	1,792
1981	74,624	8,201	80,948	2,793	66,688	2,030
Average	67,125	6,170	61,341	1,971	55,554	1,573

Source: Statistical Reporting Service, *Crop Production, Annual Summary,* USDA, CrPr 2-1, January 15, 1982.

The ability of U.S. farmers to increase their total cropland acreage or shift from one crop to another is, at most, a short-run option. When the acreage of one crop is increased the acreage of another crop usually is decreased. This offers no solution toward increased productivity. The option for bringing additional land areas into crop production is more readily available in some foreign countries than it is in the United States. In the long run the growing world demand for grains and oilseeds must be met with increased yields, an avenue for increasing production that is limited by the human ability to generate new technology.

Production and Consumption Regions

A characteristic of grain marketing that differentiates it from the marketing patterns of many other products is the geographic relationship between production and consumption regions. Primary production regions are generally separated from consumption regions by considerable distances.

The bulk of U.S. grain is produced in the Great Plains and Corn Belt states. When individual grain crops are analyzed, more precise subregional patterns are revealed. Note in Figure 1-1 that the primary wheat production regions are in the central and upper Great Plains and Pacific Northwest.

Climatic conditions require that certain subregions specialize in a particular class of wheat. For example, hard red winter wheat is grown

Figure 1-1. Leading wheat-producing states, 1980.

Figure 1-2. Leading corn-producing states, 1980.

principally in the Great Plains states (Kansas, Nebraska, Oklahoma, Texas, Colorado, and Montana). Hard red spring and durum are produced in the upper Plains states of North Dakota and Montana and soft white wheat is produced in Washington, Oregon, and Idaho. Soft red winter wheat is produced east of the Mississippi in Illinois, Indiana, Ohio, and the Atlantic Seaboard states.

Historically, a large portion of U.S. flour milling activity took place in the Midwest near wheat farming areas. However, transportation pricing has made it more economic to transport wheat rather than flour. Consequently, some millers have found it profitable to move their mills out of the Midwest to Eastern and West Coast consuming areas. Thus, over time, wheat production and milling locations have become further separated, geographically.

Corn is grown in the same general regions as wheat. The dense corn farming area, known as the "Corn Belt," includes Ohio, Indiana, Illinois, Iowa, Minnesota, Missouri, and Nebraska (Figure 1-2).

The primary domestic market for feed grains is the livestock industry. Most of the nation's cattle are fed in the Midwest near sources of production. Nevertheless, some of the nation's largest feed lots are located nearer consuming areas, particularly in Texas and California, necessitating long movements of feed grains. On-farm feeding still accounts for about 40 percent of total disappearance.

The expanding soybean production area generally lies in the eastern Corn Belt states and the Southeast. In addition to the top four states—all Corn Belt states—Arkansas, Mississippi, Louisiana, and

Figure 1-3. Leading soybean-producing states, 1980.

Tennessee were included in the top 10 producing states in 1980 (Figure 1-3). This production area corresponds closely to the location of the soybean processing industry and explains why much of the U.S. soybean exports are shipped from the Gulf Port via the Mississippi River and other inland waterways.

U.S. Grain Production Trends

U.S. production of corn, wheat, and soybeans shows a general increase in both total production and yield per acre over the past 10 years (Figure 1-4 and Table 1-3). These increases have resulted basically from a shift of farm acreage to grain production and from technological changes that have improved grain yields. It is worth noting that a longer time series of yield averages would show the impact of improved technology for all three crops even more dramatically. In the late 1940s, the development and introduction of hybrid corn seed contributed a substantial yield increase. New technologies to control weeds and pests further elevated yields in the late 1950s and early 1960s.

Increased production has resulted from technological advances beyond that from improved seed varieties. Over the last few decades, grain farming has moved rapidly toward mechanized production, and capital investment has risen substantially. For example, the average value of production assets (farm buildings, equipment, machinery, and vehicles) per farm increased from $55,822 in 1970 to $199,080 in 1980. Asset value per farm worker increased from $86,904 to

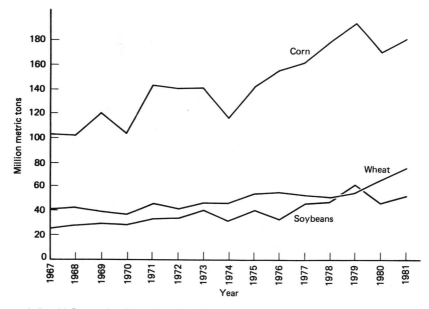

Figure 1-4. U.S. production of grain, 1967 to 1981.

$311,712 over the same period. Even when adjusted for the effects of inflation, it is clear that farming has become capital intensive.

As with mechanization, chemical fertilizers and pesticides have become basic productive inputs. The utilization of fertilizer by the grain farming sector increased by more than 28 percent between 1970 and 1979. Herbicide use increased by almost 100 percent, and insecticide application increased nearly 70 percent over the same period.

The introduction of new technology has resulted in three other significant changes in farm operations. First, the demand for farm labor has declined due to the substitution of capital for labor. Grain output per man-hour has risen by more than 50 percent between 1970 and 1979.

Second, and more complicated, the use of high technology in production requires advances in farm management skills. In general, management has responded to the challenges of modern grain production. The level of scientific management skills among American farmers has risen continually.

Third, increased capitalization has been accompanied by an increase in farm size. Between 1967 and 1978, average farm size increased from 355 acres to 400 acres. It appears that the application of new technology has created economies of scale in grain farming that encouraged expansion of the individual production unit. Larger farms require increased capital investment, inducing further expansion of farm size.

Table 1-3 Average Yields for U.S.
Grains, 1967 to 1981 (bushels per acre)

Year	Corn	Wheat	Soybeans
1967	80.1	26.3	24.5
1968	79.5	25.8	26.7
1969	85.9	28.4	27.4
1970	72.4	30.6	26.7
1971	88.1	31.0	27.5
1972	97.0	33.9	27.8
1973	91.3	32.7	27.8
1974	71.9	31.7	23.7
1975	86.3	27.4	28.9
1976	87.9	30.7	26.1
1977	90.8	30.3	29.6
1978	100.8	31.6	29.5
1979	109.4	34.2	32.2
1980	91.0	33.4	26.4
1981	109.9	34.5	30.4

Source: U.S. Department of Agriculture, *Agricultural Statistics,* 1982.

U.S. production of all grains (shown in Figure 1-5) was highly variable from 1961 to 1980, deviating from the expected trend by over 10 million metric tons nearly one-third of the time. Deviations of this magnitude cause numerous shock waves throughout the grain marketing system. Worldwide adjustments in the marketing systems are especially great when corresponding deviations, either plus or minus the trend, are experienced.

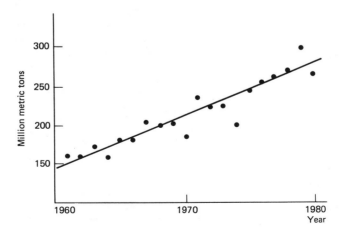

Figure 1-5.   U.S. production of all grains, annual and trend, 1960 to 1980.

Cost of Grain Production

Changes in U.S. production technology have led to changes in the level and composition of production costs. Costs of machinery, chemicals, and seed make up a larger share of the total per acre costs of grain farming now as compared to, say, 30 years ago.

The USDA has estimated production costs by component for ma-

Table 1-4   Estimated Grain Production Costs, 1979

	Wheat	*Barley*	*Corn*	*Oats*	*Soybeans*
	Dollars per Acre				
Variable	44.97	55.68	111.89	42.65	64.09
Seed	4.97	4.92	12.41	4.76	9.14
Fertilizer	10.01	12.89	37.95	7.61	6.50
Lime	.16	0.07	1.18	.85	1.00
Chemicals	2.16	3.58	13.67	.82	13.09
Custom operations	2.59	1.50	4.49	3.03	2.56
All labor	8.73	12.21	11.68	10.66	13.69
Fuel and lubrication	7.63	10.05	11.13	7.20	8.90
Repairs	6.30	7.75	8.17	6.04	6.69
Purchase of irrigation water	0.20	1.12	0.08	—	—
Drying	0.07	—	6.90	—	—
Miscellaneous	0.07	0.15	—	0.75	—
Interest	2.08	1.44	4.23	0.92	2.52
Machinery ownership	28.15	34.01	37.91	26.75	31.57
Replacement	16.23	19.36	21.26	15.20	18.19
Interest	9.59	11.78	13.37	9.29	10.77
Taxes and insurance	2.33	2.87	3.28	2.26	2.61
General farm overhead	7.95	8.89	7.92	7.49	8.34
Management	8.11	9.86	15.77	7.69	10.40
Total excluding land	89.18	108.44	173.49	84.57	114.43
Land allocation: Composite with:					
Current value	60.30	65.72	107.38	68.28	93.48
Average acquisition value	31.31	31.36	58.89	26.75	54.61
	Dollars per Bushel				
Variable	1.38	1.16	1.03	0.83	2.01
Machinery ownership	0.87	0.71	0.35	0.52	0.99
Farm overhead	0.24	0.18	0.07	0.15	0.26
Management	0.25	0.21	0.14	0.15	0.33
Total excluding land	2.74	2.26	1.59	1.65	3.59
Value of pasture	0.14	0.11	—	0.64	—
Land allocation: Composite with:					
Current value	1.86	1.37	0.98	1.33	2.93
Average acquisition value	0.96	0.65	0.54	0.52	1.17

Source: Economics, Statistics, and Cooperatives Service, *Cost of Producing Selected Crops in the United States—1978, 1979, and Projections for 1980,* for the Committee on Agriculture, Nutrition, and Forestry of U.S. Senate, July 1980.

jor grain crops. Table 1-4 provides a breakdown of these costs for 1979 on a per acre and per bushel basis.

A comparison of costs between grains reveals some information about the nature of production. For example, corn is clearly the most fertilizer intensive of the major grains. The cost of fertilizer per acre of corn is estimated at $37.95, almost four times as high as for wheat. Corn is also the most machinery intensive crop. In total, the cost per acre of corn is nearly twice as high as that for wheat. However, since corn yields per acre are much higher than those of other grains, the cost per bushel of corn is lower than for all other grains except oats.

In appraising land values for the various grains, it is interesting to note that current land values for soybeans exceed most other grains. This, at least in part, reflects the profitability of soybeans relative to other grains and suggests that soybean income potential has been capitalized into land values.

Grain farming in the United States has felt the impacts of inflation in much the same way as other sectors of the economy. Table 1-5 illustrates the change in per acre and per bushel costs of producing, wheat, barley, corn, and soybeans between 1974 and 1979. On a per acre basis, costs increased by between 44 percent (corn) and 91 percent (barley). Note that per acre costs of production increased at a more rapid rate than costs per bushel. As a matter of fact, the bushel costs of corn production actually declined between 1974 and 1979, with yield increases between 1974 and 1979 accounting for the difference.

Economic theory suggests that output will decline when costs of production increase, especially if prices are relatively low and unstable. However, some evidence suggests that when increased costs are largely the result of increases in costs of fixed inputs (or those viewed as relatively fixed) farmers may actually attempt to expand production so as to spread these fixed expenses.

Table 1-5 Costs of Grain Production in the United States, 1974 and 1979

Crop	Costs per Acre[a]			Costs per Bushel[a]		
	1974	1979	Change	1974	1979	Change
Wheat	$55.35	$89.18	+61%	$2.03	$2.74	+35%
Barley	$56.76	$108.44	+91%	$1.59	$2.26	+42%
Corn	$120.46	$173.49	+44%	$1.62	$1.59	−2%
Soybeans	$62.20	$114.43	+84%	$2.89	$3.59	+24%

[a]Excluding land costs.

Source: Economic Research Service (Economics, Statistics, and Cooperatives Service), *Cost of Producing Crops in the United States*, the Committee on Agriculture, Nutrition, and Forestry of the U.S. Senate, 1975 and 1980.

Off-Farm Grain Sales

Traditionally, nearly all grains have entered marketing channels during the fall harvest period. As a result, prices tended to dip in the fall, and rise through the winter, spring, and summer. In recent years, farmers have had a sufficient amount of storage capacity to alter this pattern, influencing seasonal price variations. Figure 1-6 shows the percentage of the 1976/77 wheat crop marketed by month over a 13-month span. While 49 percent was marketed during the harvesting period (June, July, August, and September), enough storage space existed to hold the remaining 51 percent for distribution over a 9-month period. One result of this expansion in on-farm storage is the decreased reliance on commercial storage to provide the inventory function in grain marketing.

Of course, other factors also affect the distribution of grain inventories, as well as annual carry-over levels. The size of the grain crop both in the United States and internationally is very significant. The nature and effectiveness of government programs is an important variable influencing on-farm carry-over. Commercial storage capacity and private firm marketing strategies may impact on the volume of annual carry-over. Also, recent past, current and expected conditions in the grain farming sector are important. If the previous year (or several years) was favorable to farmers, their inclination and ability to hold a

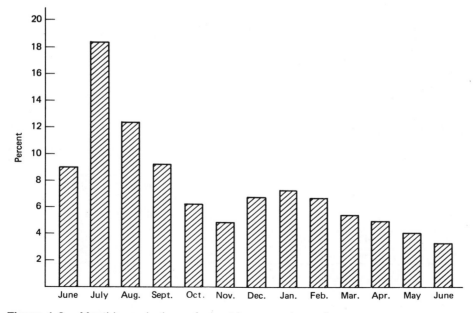

Figure 1-6. Monthly marketings of wheat by percentage of 1976/77 crop.

part of their crop for speculatory purposes may be strengthened. On the other hand, if the previous year (or years) has left farmers in somewhat tentative financial positions, cash flow requirements may force a return to traditional seasonal marketings of grain.

The size of the on-farm carry-over has important implications for all grain marketing activities. The demands for peak period transportation, storage, handling, financial, and logistical services are affected by on-farm carry-over stocks.

WORLD GRAIN PRODUCTION

In 1981/82, the world produced a record grain crop (including rice but not soybeans) of 1497 million tons (Table 1-6). This was about 670 million tons or 81 percent greater than the 1960/61 output. On an annual basis, the increase implies an average gain of 32 million tons

Table 1-6 World Land Area, Yields, and Production of Food and Feed Grains, 1960 to 1981[a]

	Annual Averages					
Grain	1960/61	1961–65	1966–70	1971–75	1976–80	1981–82*
Corn						
Area	103.0	99.4	105.7	114.0	124.0	130.5
Yield	1.9	2.2	2.4	2.7	3.0	3.4
Production	198.1	216.1	250.5	305.8	374.6	438.0
Wheat						
Area	202.9	209.7	216.6	217.0	229.5	236.5
Yield	1.2	1.2	1.4	1.6	1.8	1.9
Production	239.4	251.8	311.9	354.3	419.2	452.6
Rice (rough)						
Area	122.4	124.1	128.5	141.5	142.8	144.0
Yield	2.0	2.0	2.2	2.4	2.6	2.8
Production	239.7	253.2	276.9	349.1	372.1	406.0
Coarse grains[b]						
Area	328.2	330.5	328.7	337.1	348.1	344.0
Yield	1.4	1.4	1.7	1.9	2.1	2.2
Production	451.2	465.1	555.4	634.7	721.9	769.4
Total grains[c]						
Area	653.4	664.3	673.8	697.0	761.3	725.7
Yield	1.3	1.5	1.7	1.9	2.0	2.1
Production	825.5	970.1	1144.2	1337.8	1400.6	1496.6

[a]Area in million hectares; yield in metric tons per hectare; production in million metric tons.
[b]Includes corn, barley, oats, millet, rye, and sorghum for grain.
[c]Includes wheat, coarse grains, and milled rice.
*Forecast.

Source: Foreign Agricultural Service, *Foreign Agriculture Circular—Grains*, USDA, FG 5-82, February 16, 1982.

per year over the 21-year period. The growth in production during this period was the result of both greater area devoted to grain production and yield improvements. Most of the gain in grain production is due to yield improvements that rose an average of 2.3 percent compounded annually in the reference period. Over the same period, the area seeded to all grains has risen from 653 million hectares[1] to 726 million, an overall increase of 11.2 percent.

Type of Grain Production

Coarse Grains.   Coarse grains generally account for over half of world grain output.[2] The remaining production was about equally divided between wheat and rice during the 1960s but wheat production has consistently exceeded rice production since then. Currently, wheat production represents about 30 percent of world grain output and rice about 27 percent.

The combined output of coarse grains advanced from 451 million tons in 1960/61 to 769.4 million tons in 1981/82. Most of the increase in production is attributed to the rise in yields rather than the extension of grain area. World coarse grain yields have risen at an annual rate of 2.6 percent while the area was increased by only 0.8 percent.

Corn.   The most important coarse grain by far is corn, constituting more than half of the world production in recent years. World production of corn was 438 million tons in 1981/82, produced from 130.5 million hectares, with a yield average of 3.4 tons per hectare. World corn production has shown the second fastest growth rate among the coarse grains—3.8 percent annually. The significant feature of this growth is that it rests largely on yield improvements. While planted areas rose at a rate of only 1.1 percent annually, average yields rose by 2.8 percent, reflecting the adoption of hybrid varieties as well as increased levels of fertilizer and other inputs.

Wheat.   World wheat production reached 453 million tons in 1981/82, exceeding the previous record output of 438 million tons set in 1978/79. A notable feature of world wheat production is that it has grown at a faster pace since 1960/61 than either rice or coarse grains. The increase in production was the result of both larger plantings and improved yields. Higher yields, however, contributed more to the expansion in wheat production than did increased acreages.

Soybeans.   World oilseed production, being led by soybeans, is steadily increasing (Table 1-7). Soybeans represented 51 percent of total

[1]One hectare equals 2.47 acres.
[2]Coarse grains, in addition to feed grains, include rye.

Table 1-7   World Production of Oilseeds,
1977/78 to 1981/82 (million metric tons)

Oilseed	1977/78	1978/79	1979/80	1980/81	1981/82*	Percent of 1981/82
Soybeans	72.16	77.39	93.62	80.93	88.32	51.2
Cottonseed	25.00	23.94	25.03	25.60	27.55	16.0
Peanuts	16.41	17.61	16.94	15.98	18.18	10.6
Sunflowerseed	12.88	12.90	15.43	13.25	13.85	8.0
Rapeseed	7.88	10.71	10.08	11.44	12.01	7.0
Copra	5.16	4.57	4.71	5.09	5.39	3.1
Flaxseed	2.94	2.44	2.63	2.10	2.10	1.2
Other[a]	4.54	5.04	5.11	4.81	5.05	2.9
Total	146.97	154.62	173.55	159.20	172.45	100.0

[a]Includes sesameseed, safflowerseed, castor beans, and palm kernel.
*Forecast.

Source: Foreign Agricultural Service, *Foreign Agriculture Circular—Oilseeds and Products,* USDA,
FOP 3-82, February 1982.

world oilseed production in 1981/82. Soybeans are also the leading source of protein meal, providing nearly two-thirds of total protein meal output. Soybean oil accounts for about one-third of the world's edible vegetable oil production.

In the period from 1960/61 to 1981/82, world soybean production increased from 27.3 to 88.3 million tons. Lower yields and smaller acreage in 1980/81 reduced output below the record 93.6 million tons achieved in the previous year. The increase in production has come mostly from an expansion of acreage in the United States, Brazil, and Argentina with some increase (46 percent) in yield. Average yields of soybeans have increased rather slowly everywhere and were lagging behind most other crops.

Expansion in soybean production has been stimulated by growing demand for both soybean meal and soybean oil. Soybean meal is a valuable high-protein concentrate used in feeding of livestock and poultry. It is particularly suited in feed formulations for monogastric animals such as hogs and poultry because of the inability of these animals to utilize large quantities of fiber.

Soybeans, because of their high protein content (around 40 percent on a moisture-free basis), have a decided advantage over other oilseeds as sources of protein foods. There is much interest worldwide in the manufacture of edible protein, particularly soyflour and grits, and extruded, textured soy protein. These edible soybean products may be used as a meat extender or as a meat analog. Edible soy protein is important in the diets of people of the Far East. A variety of uses for soybean oil (and other edible vegetable oils) have developed in recent years.

Geographical Distribution

Wheat. The overall increase in wheat production conceals contrasting trends among regions and countries (Figure 1-7A). The USSR occupies an important position in the world wheat economy as the largest country producer, accounting for between one-fifth and one-fourth of all wheat produced. The 1978/79 Russian wheat harvest reached a record 121 million tons, representing 27.6 percent of the world total. While the Russian crop has declined somewhat from this record, it remains a major producer. Asia, including the People's Republic of China, is the largest wheat-growing region in the world, producing about 30 percent of the total world output in recent years. The Asian outturn in 1981/82 was forecast at 133 million tons, some one-half million tons short of the record 1979/80 crop. There was an impressive 4.6 percent growth per year in aggregate wheat production in Asia during the 1960/61–1981/82 period. Increased production in China and India was largely responsible for boosting the regional output to the current high level, accounting for more than three-fourths of the total Asian increase of 82 million tons during the reference period.

China is the largest Asian wheat-growing country. Production in China has shown an upward trend, rising to a record 62.7 million tons in 1979/80. The 1980/81 crop declined by 8 million tons primarily due to poor weather conditions.

North America produced 104 million tons in 1981/82, and is the third-ranking wheat-producing area in the world. Wheat production shows wide year-to-year variations attributable primarily to U.S. land retirement and set-aside programs in effect throughout the period.

Western Europe is the fourth-largest wheat-producing region, supplying 15 percent of world output. Output rose steeply in 1980/81 reaching 64.6 million tons for all of Western Europe; the European Community (EC) accounted for 52.1 million tons in that year, with France being the EC's major wheat producer.

High EC support prices with no differentiation as to quality have stimulated the expansion of high-yielding wheat varieties with poor baking qualities. Because of their low quality these high-yielding varieties are exported primarily for food uses.

To discourage further expansion in production of high-yielding wheat varieties the EC support price (intervention) for these feed-quality wheats was lowered to the level for feed grains. The support price for bread quality wheats is now about 13 percent above that for feed-quality wheats.

Corn. North America is the world's largest corn-producing region accounting for around half of total production. The United States predominates not only in the region, but also on a global basis (Figure 1-7B). U.S. corn production reached an all-time high of 208 million tons

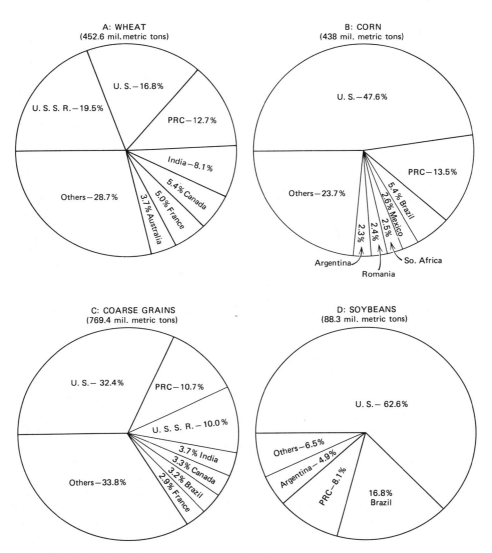

Figure 1-7. World's major producers of grains and soybeans, 1981/82. (*a*) Wheat (452.6 million metric tons). (*b*) Corn (438 million metric tons). (*c*) Coarse grains (769.4 million metric tons). (*d*) Soybeans (88.3 million metric tons).

in 1981/82 due mainly to near-record yields. This output represented 48 percent of world corn production on only 23 percent of the total area planted to corn. In 1980/81, U.S. corn production declined to 169 million tons resulting from poor growing conditions. The U.S. share of world output has increased somewhat over the past two decades.

U.S. corn production over the 1960/61– 1981/82 period increased at an average annual rate of 3.6 percent, which is only slightly below the world rate of 3.8 percent. The slower U.S. production growth reflects the small increase in corn area, with the growth in production due mostly to improved yields. Wider use of improved hybrid varieties, heavier fertilization, higher plant populations, and other improved cultural practices have raised U.S. corn yields well above those in the rest of the world. The record 1981/82 U.S. corn yield of 6.9 tons per hectare was more than double the world average, and triple the average of non-U.S. areas.

Asia is the second largest regional producer of corn with almost one-fifth of world output in 1981/82. Aggregate production of the region increased at a faster rate than world production, resulting in a modest improvement in Asia's share of the total. China is the dominant producer of corn in Asia, supplying 71 percent of the region's output in 1981/82. Actually, China is the second largest corn producer in the world, after the United States, producing almost 14 percent of total world corn output.

China's production of corn increased at about 7.6 percent per year over the 1960/61–1981/82 period. This rate of growth can be ascribed to both improved yields and expanded plantings. Yields rose by about 4.7 percent per year over the period, and area planted increased by about 2.5 percent. Despite this sizable yield improvement, Chinese corn yields are below the world average. Thus China appears to have considerable potential to increase its production of corn.

Coarse Grains.   The total world output of coarse grains amounted to nearly 770 million metric tons (Figure 1-7C), a substantial increase over the 448 million tons harvested in 1960/61.

In spite of the more widespread utilization of coarse grains throughout much of the world, the United States has long maintained a strong position as the world's largest producer with an increase of about 3 percent per year since 1960/61. The U.S. crop of coarse grains in 1981/82 was almost one-third of total world output, and more than half again as much as the combined output of the next two output leaders, mainland China (10.7 percent) and Soviet Russia (10 percent). These three nations ordinarily produce more than half of the world's total coarse grains.

The seven leading nations, including India (3.7 percent), Canada (3.3 percent), Brazil (3.2 percent) and France (2.8 percent), produce about two-thirds of all coarse grain output. One hundred-twenty other nations account for the remaining one-third. Of that group of nations, 46 produced in excess of 1 million tons of coarse grains in 1981/82. Those nations averaged 5.2 million tons, accounting for 32 percent, with the remaining 74 nations producing about 2 percent of total coarse grain output.

Soybeans. World soybean production is concentrated in a few countries with three—the United States, Brazil and China—normally accounting for around 90 percent of total production (Figure 1-7D).

The United States has long been a leader in world soybean production and supplied more than 60 percent of the world output with its 1981/82 crop of 55.3 million tons. The U.S. share averaged 70 percent of world output during the 1960s. Not surprisingly, then, world production has generally followed that of the United States. The U.S. output increased from 15.1 million tons in 1960/61 to a record 61.7 million tons in 1979/80, but declined the two following years because of both fewer acres planted to soybeans and less favorable growing conditions. The growth in production was due principally to a 5.4 percent per year increase in seeded area. U.S. soybean yields rose at an average annual rate of 1.3 percent, with the record yield being 2.06 tons per hectare in 1977/78. Much of the change in the area devoted in soybeans was due to the diversion of acreage previously used for producing other crops.

Brazil, the second largest soybean producing country, is a relative newcomer to the world soybean picture. As a newcomer, however, its entrance has been quite remarkable and its role today is a very important one. Brazil's production increased eleven-fold over the 1970/71–1981/82 period. In 1981/82 Brazil produced 14.8 million tons of soybeans and accounted for 17 percent of world output. Most of the growth in soybean production is attributable to a 19.6 percent per year expansion in acreage. The soybean buildup started by double cropping soybeans with wheat, followed by the opening of new lands not previously used for agriculture as well as switching from other annual crops to soybeans.

China has long been a major producer of soybeans and until 1973/74 was second only to the United States. China's 1981/82 output of 8.1 million tons was below that harvested in 1960/61. In China, soybeans have tended to be replaced by the higher-yielding cereals.

Argentina also has been increasing production and, with an output of 4.3 million tons in 1981/82, has been the world's fourth-ranking soybean producer since 1975/76. The soybean boom is linked to many factors ranging from the possibility of double cropping with winter crops to favorable soybean-corn price relationships.

Summary

Grain farming in the United States is one of the most productive and efficient in the world, giving the nation a comparative advantage in the production of both food and feed grains. This advantage results from the United States' relatively abundant supplies of the production factors required for modern, high-yield grain farming.

Dense production regions for grain in the United States are located in the Corn Belt and the Great Plains; the principal domestic consumption regions are in the urban centers on either coast for food consumption and in the Corn Belt for livestock feeding. The general trend is for a separation of grain production and consumption centers.

The nature and cost of grain production in the United States has changed considerably over the past few decades. Capital and technologically intense farming have replaced the more labor intense methods of the past. As a result, the level and composition of production costs have also been altered.

Technological advances and increased demand have stimulated growth in grain output in the United States and throughout the world. The growth of coarse grain and oilseed production has been particularly strong as a result of increasing world demand for livestock products.

World grain production patterns of the past decade clearly show yield improvements as the primary source of growth. Key factors in yield improvement are associated with new technologies, improved resource inputs, and economic incentives. Increases in area cultivated have played a relatively minor role in the growth in world grain production.

Coarse grains generally account for over half of world food and feed grain output. Wheat represents about 30 percent of world grain output and milled rice about 18 percent. Corn is the principal coarse grain, and the United States is the dominant world producer. Soybeans represent more than half of world oilseed production and provide nearly two-thirds of total protein meal output. Soybean production is concentrated within a few countries to a much greater extent than other major grains. The United States, Brazil, and China have recently accounted for about 90 percent of world soybean output, while the United States alone contributes more than 60 percent.

Most projections suggest that world grain supply will continue to grow at an average rate of 1.5 to 2.0 percent annually through the 1980s. This represents a slowing of recent production growth rates due largely to lower prices, limited opportunities for adaption of new technology, and a relatively small expansion of cropland.

Selected References

Heid, Walter G., Jr. and Mack N. Leath, *U.S. Barley Industry,* Economics, Statistics, and Cooperatives Service, USDA, Agricultural Economics Report No. 395, Washington, D.C., February 1978.

Heid, Walter G., Jr. *U.S. Wheat Industry,* Economics, Statistics, and Coopertives Service, USDA, Agricultural Economics Report No. 432, Washington, D.C., August 1979.

U.S. Department of Agriculture, *Agricultural Outlook,* August 1981.

U.S. Department of Agriculture, *Agricultural Statistics,* 1982.

U.S. Department of Agriculture, *Crop Production,* 1979 Annual Survey.

U.S. Department of Agriculture, *Farmline,* Economics Research Service, Statistical Reporting Service, Vol. II, No. 7, August 1981.

U.S. Department of Agriculture, *Feed Outlook and Situation,* various issues.

U.S. Department of Agriculture, *Wheat Outlook and Situation,* various issues.

U.S. Department of Agriculture, *Agricultural Statistics,* various issues.

U.S. Department of Agriculture, *Crop Production,* various issues.

U.S. Department of Agriculture, *Fats and Oils Situation,* various issues.

U.S. Department of Agriculture, *Feed Situation,* various issues.

U.S. Department of Agriculture, *Wheat Situation,* various issues.

U.S. Department of Agriculture, *Foreign Agriculture Circular, Grains,* various issues.

United States Senate, *Costs of Producing Selected Crops in the United States 1978, 1979, and Projections for 1980,* prepared by the Economics, Statistics and Cooperatives Service of the USDA for the Committee on Agriculture, Nutrition, and Forestry, July 1980.

GRAIN SUPPLY AND UTILIZATION

GRAIN SUPPLY AND UTILIZATION*

CHAPTER 2

Once a simple system where much of the farmer's grain output was fed to the livestock on that farm, grain distribution in the United States has evolved into a complex marketing system. A large percentage of farm production is now marketed off farms. Some of this grain is processed into food and feed for domestic uses. Other grain is disposed of as whole grain, primarily in overseas markets. With the growth in importance of foreign demand, the U.S. market for corn, soybeans, and wheat has assumed a worldwide dimension. An understanding of this emerging grain supply and utilization situation as it relates to traditional marketing institutions and practices should provide a better understanding of the total U.S. grain marketing system.

The U.S. marketing system has adjusted to meet the new foreign dimension by transmitting additional demand signals to sources of supply. U.S. exports of a particular grain may increase or decrease as much as 50 percent or more from one year to the next because of the greater variability of foreign demand. Such upswings and downswings in demand are largely due to the vagaries of weather and to the import policies of a number of countries throughout the world. They add much more stress on the U.S. marketing system than when the system was primarily serving the domestic market. Both U.S. production policy and marketing institutions are adapting to this expanded market. Nevertheless, the marketing system has experienced difficulties in responding to the variability of foreign demand.

Foreign demand for grain and oilseeds has grown tremendously since World War II. U.S. exports as a percent of production for wheat, soybeans, and corn were less than 15 percent in 1950. Thirty years later, 45 percent of the total U.S. output of those crops was distributed overseas.

With the growth in foreign markets, the estimation of foreign demand for U.S. grain has become a complex job, one that cannot be forecast on the basis of traditionally predetermined variables. Total demand for these commodities is now determined by trade agreements as much as by disposable income, by tariffs as much as by popu-

*Walter G. Heid, Jr., Agricultural Economist, National Economics Division, Economic Research Service, USDA, stationed at the U.S. Grain Marketing Research Laboratory, Manhattan, Kan. Information in this chapter represents the opinions of the author and not necessarily the views of the U.S. Department of Agriculture.

lation, and by diplomatic relations as much as by preference. And weather variability continues to be a major factor affecting world grain production.

SUPPLY AND DISTRIBUTION

In the marketing process, buyers and sellers are brought together for the purpose of negotiating transactions, with price as the confirming mechanism. At times when the quantity supplied greatly exceeds the quantity demanded, various government programs may complement cash markets to move products. For example, wheat may be distributed through cash sales, short-term credit at commercial rates, long-term concessional credit, or Public Law (PL)-480 donations.

Supply normally includes annual production and carry-over from previous crops, plus imports, if any. Thus the term *supply* refers to the quantity of an economic good available per unit of time for distribution in the market at alternative prices, all other things being equal.

Demand is defined as the amounts of a product that buyers are willing to purchase at alternative prices per unit of time, all other things being equal.

According to economic theory, demand indicates the differing amounts of a product that *will be* purchased at differing prices. However, in a world filled with hungry people this statement does not adequately describe the basis for distributing the supplies of grains and oilseeds. Even a more precise term, *effective* demand, does not totally explain what takes place in the market. Effective demand is the desire of the consumer backed with purchasing power. Effective demand explains the quantity that people are *able* to acquire. Although most commodities are purchased at a price, some are accepted as a donation, on credit, or through other arrangements.

The people of Egypt, for example, both need and desire many things—more wheat, better clothing, better homes, and so on. However, the Egyptian demand for all these goods is very limited, since they do not have the purchasing power to satisfy their needs, let alone their wants. Part of the Egyptian needs are met through receipts of PL-480 wheat from the United States. Many other countries receive similar aid from the United States as well as economic aid from other developed countries.

Supply Factors

Many factors cause supply to increase and decrease. Some factors such as production decisions or weather may affect total supply. Other factors, such as embargoes, may affect the available supply for general export or to a specific country.

With a large percentage of U.S. grain production finding its way into foreign markets, the world supply has become an important factor affecting U.S. prices. Knowledge of world supplies is often less than perfect, making marketing and government policy decisions tenuous. Improvements in this information may, however, soon be forthcoming, through the use of satellite photography and improvements in USDA crop information collection and data analysis.

Grain supply is affected by both nature and man. It is affected by government action and by the independent decisions of several million farmers. The supply is also affected by the buying and selling decisions of those who take title to it in the marketplace.

So many factors influence supply that its control has heretofore eluded the best of efforts to maintain a balance between supply and demand. In the United States, as well as worldwide, grain supplies historically have oscillated between periods of shortages to periods of abundance.

Nature.   Perhaps weather more than any other single factor explains the problem of year-to-year variation in total output. Weather may affect planting intentions, yields, and harvest. Droughts, hail, and floods often claim large acreages of crops. Conversely, ideal weather conditions often contribute to bumper crops. In addition to weather, insects and diseases may affect production. In 1970, for example, the U.S. corn supply was hit by the southern leaf blight. Yields were reduced by 13.5 bushels per acre, or 17 percent.

The larger the crop yield, the larger the variation in total production. Usage of commercial fertilizer and new and improved seeds have greatly increased yields, especially of corn and wheat in the United States as well as rice in other parts of the world. Weather, crop diseases, and insects have no respect for large yields. Damages or losses in high-yielding fields are often much greater than in low-yielding fields. The history of U.S. wheat production serves to illustrate this point. Yields increased from less than 15 bushels per acre in the early 1900s to over 30 bushels in the late 1970s. U.S. wheat yields deviated from the trend line by less than 2 bushels 88 percent of the time from 1900 to 1932. However, from 1933 to 1977, yields varied from the expected by 3 bushels or more 18 percent of the time. Assuming 70 million harvested acres, this degree of variation results in a 210 million bushel variation in production in about one year in five.

Acreage Control and Subsidies.   Government programs have affected the level of wheat and feed grain production since the Great Depression. In 1932, realized net farm income dropped to less than one-third of what it had been in 1929 and farm prices had fallen more than 50 percent. In an effort to correct farm economic problems associated with the Depression, the Agricultural Adjustment Act of 1933 was passed. Among other provisions, the Act authorized the Secretary of Agriculture to secure voluntary reductions in the acreage of basic crops. This included corn and wheat. Except during World War II, the Korean War, and in much of the 1970s, most farm legislation has been designed to limit grain supplies.

The Act of 1933, and successive farm legislation that introduced the term "parity," sought to bolster farm prices as well as control supplies. Ironically, the provisions that strengthened farm grain prices actually encouraged larger supplies at the same time that other provisions of the farm programs were designed to reduce acreages.

Except during World War II, and the 1970s after the large U.S.S.R. grain sale, overproduction has been a major farm problem. Beginning in 1955, the United States commenced a long period of national wheat acreage allotments. The 55-million acre wheat allotment in 1955 reduced wheat acreage 7 million acres below the 1954 level.

The Agricultural Act of 1956 established a conservation reserve and an acreage reserve system. The purpose, again, was to bring about adjustments in supply. Under the conservation reserve, known as the Soil Bank, farmers designated certain cropland for the reserve and put it into a conservation use—usually some type of grass. Many farmers placed their entire farms in the Soil Bank. On July 15, 1960, there were 28.6 million acres of cropland under contracts for a maximum of 10 years.

Under the acreage allotment program, farmers reduced the cropland planted to basic crops to an established allotment, diverting their remaining acres to conserving uses and receiving payments for the diversion.

Except for a brief period in the mid-1970s when "fence-to-fence" production was encouraged, farm programs throughout the 1960s and 1970s were designed to reduce corn and wheat supplies and to support prices. By contrast, the government has never attempted to control the supply of soybeans to maintain a reasonable balance between supply and demand.

Embargoes.   A grain embargo may effectively limit supply for various reasons. In the 1970s, the U.S. government imposed several embargoes. The first imposed by President Nixon in 1973 was on soybean and related products exports. Its purpose was to check U.S. food price inflation. The second was imposed on Poland in 1975 by President Ford to prevent transshipment of grain (reselling imported grain) to the U.S.S.R. The third embargo, imposed by President Carter in 1980, sharply reduced the sale of corn and wheat to Russia in protest to that country's involvement in Afghanistan.

Embargoes impose a financial hardship on farmers who are the first to feel the depressing effect of the sudden loss of a market. Also affected are given merchants as well as the suppliers of farm inputs.

The effects of embargoes are felt over time, both for the country embargoed and the one imposing the embargo. An embargo creates an immediate shock and then shock waves. The effects of the 1980 embargo on Soviet livestock production and U.S. farm input purchases came months after the initial shock.

Within the international grain trading system, leakages occur in two ways. First, transshipment of U.S. grain exports to the embargoed nation can occur through third countries. Second, the actions of multinational trading firms cannot be completely controlled. Perhaps an even greater reason for long-run ineffectiveness are other countries that have no quarrel with the embargoed nation who also wish to expand their own export markets.

Embargoes are trade sanctions. When trade policy is politicized, trade relationships are restructured. Within one year after the 1980 embargo both the United States and the U.S.S.R. had reestablished markets with other nations. Restructuring of markets can have both advantages and disadvantages. If an importing country is forced to go elsewhere for its supply of grain, it may be forced to choose an undependable supplier. This, of course, could have long-run ramifications.

The economy of an exporting nation, on the other hand, may be highly dependent on exports. The 1980 embargo forced the United States to cultivate other markets. In the long run, this forced activity could prove beneficial as it opened new markets.

Former markets often are recaptured once embargoes are lifted. A notable exception however, occurred as a result of the 1973 soybean embargo. As a result of this embargo, heavy investments and government policy changes were made in the Brazilian soybean industry. In less than a decade, the Brazilian soybean industry was flourishing and Brazil had become a major exporter.

Grain as a Weapon. Grain is increasingly being used as a political weapon. Embargoes are only one example. "Food for Crude" became a popular slogan in the 1970s when the United States was experiencing shortages of crude oil. The act of withholding grain supplies from developed countries and other major exporting countries is, in some respects, a harmless wargame. But the act of withholding grain supplies from underdeveloped countries can have dire consequences. Limiting or denying supplies of food to some underdeveloped nations can quickly result in starvation. Poor nations may have neither the capability nor the economic ability to move rapidly enough to locate and obtain supplies from alternative sources before starvation begins. Yet it is becoming increasingly common for food suppliers to keep the fate of the hungry in developing countries linked to food aid decisions.

Grain Reserves. Grain held in reserve for use in times of critical shortages in world production may reduce the effective supply. Grain designated for use under the Food for Peace program is an example. If, by law, a quantity of grain is set aside for donation it is, for all practical purposes, removed from the normal market. It is no longer responsive to the pricing system. Usually such reserves account for only a token percentage of the total supply.

Bilateral Supply Agreements.   Unlike politically motivated grain distribution, bilateral supply agreements are long-term commitments. Bilateral agreements are products of world food insecurity, an opportunity to capture a long-term market. Proponents claim that long-term agreements introduce stability into the market, enhancing supply management at the production level. Opponents discount the importance of stability suggesting that these agreements take away flexibility of the system to respond to short-term needs. They contend that one bilateral agreement opens the way for others, and soon the situation arises where the government controls demand. Opponents of bilaterals also claim that they erode confidence in our system of projecting a reasonable return on commercial investments, whether the proposed investment be for production inputs—fertilizers and agricultural chemicals—or market activities such as investments in storage and transportation.

In an 18-month period, 1980 to mid-1981, the United States announced 19 long-term agreements, nearly all for corn, soybeans, or wheat. These agreements ran for three to five years and involved many tons of grain.

As world population and livestock and poultry numbers increase worldwide and the supply for grain and oilseeds tightens, more importing countries can be expected to request bilateral agreements, becoming steady, or preferred, customers of exporting countries. Countries that are considered "most favored nations" and those that can best afford grain will be first in line for available supplies.

Planning Horizons.   Grain supplies are also affected by decisions made by farmers and members of the grain trade. These decisions—crop production, allocating supplies through alternative marketing channels, and distribution for specific uses—are based largely on economics; the use of scarce resources.

Time plays an important role in these decisions. Regardless of the planning horizon (short run versus long run), decisions made on the farm and in the marketplace affect both the volume of supply and its availability in terms of place, time, form, and price. Specifically, time-based decisions can affect supply as follows.

1. In the short run, storage costs, seller's need for cash, the price offered, and market outlook may influence sellers to sell their product.

2. In the intermediate period, farm production costs may change, causing, for example, a cutback in commercial fertilizer usage and, in turn, lower yields. Or in the

marketplace, changes in grain price levels or competition may affect the volume of supply.

3. In the long run there may be changes in production facilities as well as changes in all of the factors mentioned in (1) and (2). For example, agricultural land may be taken out of production for industrial development, or marginal land may be brought into production. Additional processing capacity may be added, or changes in technology may occur, increasing plant efficiency and available supplies of processed products.

Distribution Factors

In the U.S. economy, the pertinent marketing question has always been "How much will be bought at a specified price?" and not "How much will be needed or desired?" However, as producers, policy makers, and social scientists begin to think of the world as one large market, more attention is being given to humanitarian concerns. Especially since World War II, greater concern with the economic well-being of people in foreign countries has been reflected in the total demand for U.S. farm products. Distribution programs such as the Marshall Plan, PL-480, Food for Peace, Cooperative for American Relief Everywhere (CARE), and the Catholic Relief Services (CRS), are examples. U.S. involvement in relief-type programs has varied. CCC credit and PL-480 programs accounted for 78 percent of total U.S. wheat distribution in foreign markets in 1964/1965, and for 20 percent in 1977/1978. Over a recent-25 year period, 30 percent of the U.S. wheat exports were shipped under a government program. The tendency has been to distribute more commodities under relief programs when U.S. supplies are large than when they are short.

Just as the existence of charitable forms of distribution blur the use of recognized economic theory to explain and predict utilization patterns, so have they clouded the role of the United States in feeding the world. The United States is viewed by some countries as the grocery store of the world—the world's breadbasket. While it is true that the United States, *physically,* has a production capacity far exceeding domestic needs, it does not have unlimited capacity *economically* to feed the world. Without sufficient reward to cover their production costs, farmers will not endlessly produce. Similarly, the movement, processing, and storage of products at all stages of the marketing channels entail costs; and the commodities cannot freely be given away. The need for charitable types of distribution have persisted over time and will likely increase in the future. Marketing systems must handle volumes of grain being distributed under relief programs in addition to normal commercial activities. Although this type of activity has a long history, areas of responsibility are still ill defined. Who should bear this burden? The role of the United States versus other exporting countries servicing needy countries remains uncertain at this time, although some progress is being made through the United Nations sponsored World Food Conferences.

The debate concerning the morality of attempting to feed the world is in its infancy. In the quarter century from 1950 to 1975, the United States contributed $25 billion in food aid around the globe. This gesture of charity met with a diversity of opinion. On one side, there were those who said the United States should have given more to poor nations. On the other side, there were those who complained about too much food being given away. The debate centered around the burden on U.S. taxpayers, the effects on domestic and foreign food prices, a desire for higher farm prices, and the U.S. balance of payments versus humanitarian concerns. In essence, the debate was over the effects of food aid on the U.S. economy.

Opponents of food aid adopted the philosophy that efforts by rich nations to feed the world's poor are self-defeating. Such efforts were believed to compound the problems of the Malthusian food/population equation by keeping the poor alive to spawn more people who in turn make increasing demands on the world's food supply. This philosophy, termed "lifeboat ethics," suggests that rather than continually trying to save the world's poor from starvation, the United States and other food-exporting nations should tend to matters in their own "lifeboat" and let famine, floods, and pestilence keep the world population under control.

Another similar philosophy is the theory of triage. The World War I medical practice of dividing the wounded into several categories in order to concentrate medical resources on those that could truly benefit from them and to ignore those who would likely die even with treatment was suggested as a means of selectively distributing food. Proponents of food aid counter these two theories by claiming that it is well within the power of humanity to produce and distribute enough food to prevent masses of people from starving.

Unfortunately, this debate over food distribution has no simple solution. The rich cannot afford to give food away and the poor cannot afford to pay. It is a debate that will continue to surface whenever short food supplies or high prices cause widespread hunger or economic depression.

Marketing, in the traditional sense, is defined as the performance of all business activities involved in the flow of goods and services from the initial producer to the final consumer.[1] It is the task of those engaged in marketing to move products to the right place, at the right time, and in the right form. For marketing wheat, corn, and soybeans, this means that crops that are harvested in a 2- to 3-month period must be marketed over a 12-month period of time. This means matching a given supply with demand. This means storage, transportation and

---

[1]Richard L. Kohls, *Marketing Agricultural Products,* Macmillan Co., New York, 1955, p. 7.

handling, processing, manufacturing, wholesaling and retailing, financing, risk-bearing, research, and advertising—the ancillary services that accompany the marketing process. To accomplish these tasks, people in charge of marketing must have knowledge of the factors affecting demand—population, incomes, prices and quantities. This information provides the basis for projecting future demand trends. It serves as the basis for production and marketing decisions and related agricultural policies.

U.S. Population. Population is by far the most important factor in explaining food utilization. The Bureau of the Census projects the U.S. population somehere between 246 and 283 million by the year 2000. Although the annual rate of increase has declined, the total increase from 1970 to 1980 alone was over 10 percent. An assessment of the U.S. population structure shows several trends besides an increase in numbers which will affect future food consumption. These include:

Migration to warm climate states.

Shift in racial and ethnic groups.

Increasing urbanization.

Increasing number of families with single head of house.

Shift in age groups.

Increasing number of meals eaten away from home.

As a consequence of these trends, consumers may not increase their intake of total food, but their tastes and preferences for specific foods do change over time. As shown in Table 2-1, per capita consumption of corn meal, syrup, sugar, and margarine is increasing while the per capita consumption of wheat cereal, corn cereal, corn starch, and shortening is either constant or decreasing. There is some evidence that the downward trend in wheat flour consumption may be reversing itself.

Disposable Income Spent for Food. As disposable incomes increase, people tend to demand more expensive foods. In the United States, the consumer has gone two steps further, demanding, first, prepared foods, and second, the ultimate—restaurant prepared foods. Away-from-home food expenditures changed little until the inflationary period of the mid to late 1970s. Increases in away-from-home food expenditures are reflective of a viable economy. A slowing economy would likely contribute to a shift to greater home preparation of food.

The percentage of disposable income spent for food varies greatly, both in the United States and throughout the world. In the United

Table 2-1 Per Capita Civilian Consumption of Wheat, Corn and Soybean Products, United States, 1968 to 1979

	Wheat			Corn						Soybeans		
	Total Consumed (Million Bushels)	Per Capita Consumption (pounds)		Total Consumed (Million Bushels)	Per Capita Consumption (pounds)					Total Consumed (Million Bushels)	Per Capita Consumption (pounds)	
Year		Flour	Cereal		Meal	Cereal	Syrup	Sugar	Starch		Margarine	Shortening
1968	510	112	2.9	210	7.4	2.3	14.8	4.7	1.9	946	10.8	16.3
1969	513	112	2.9	215	7.4	2.3	15.4	4.9	1.9	1230	10.8	17.1
1970	510	110	2.9	220	7.4	2.3	15.8	5.0	1.9	1268	11.0	17.3
1971	513	110	2.9	225	7.4	2.3	16.2	5.0	1.9	1203	11.1	16.8
1972	517	109	2.9	240	7.4	2.3	18.7	4.8	1.9	1285	11.3	17.7
1973	524	109	2.9	261	7.5	2.3	21.7	5.2	1.9	1463	11.3	17.3
1974	517	106	2.9	280	7.6	2.3	25.0	5.3	1.9	1192	11.3	17.0
1975	534	107	2.9	305	7.7	2.3	28.5	5.5	1.9	1496	11.2	17.3
1976	554	111	2.9	330	7.7	2.3	32.0	5.5	1.9	1432	12.2	18.1
1977	542	107	2.9	345	7.7	2.3	34.0	5.5	1.9	1706	11.6	17.5
1978	578	114	2.9	365	7.7	2.3	34.7	5.5	1.9	1736	11.4	18.2
1979	596	116	2.9	369	7.7	2.3	34.7	5.5	1.9	a	11.5	18.9

[a]Not available.

Source: U.S. Department of Agriculture, *Agricultural Statistics*, and data compiled by the Economic Research Service.

Table 2-2 U.S. Food Expenditures in Relation to
Disposable Income, 1970 to 1980 (in millions of dollars)

Year	Disposable Personal Income	For Use at Home[a]		Away from Home[b]		Total	
		Amount	Percent of Income	Amount	Percent of Income	Amount	Percent of Income
1970	685,935	91,839	13.4	26,778	3.9	118,617	17.3
1971	742,811	94,250	12.7	27,774	3.7	122,024	16.4
1972	801,299	100,562	12.5	30,064	3.8	130,626	16.3
1973	901,663	112,852	12.5	33,911	3.8	146,763	16.3
1974	948,627	128,425	13.0	38,442	3.9	166,867	16.9
1975	1,084,359	140,801	13.0	43,961	4.0	184,762	17.0
1976	1,184,400	149,500	12.6	49,600	4.2	199,472	16.8
1977	1,303,000	161,400	12.4	55,600	4.3	217,000	16.7
1978	1,462,900	177,700	12.1	61,700	4.2	239,400	16.4
1979	1,641,700	187,700	11.4	67,500	4.1	255,200	15.5
1980	1,821,600	211,200	11.6	76,600	4.2	287,800	15.8

[a]Includes purchases for off-premise consumption and produced and consumed on farms.
[b]Includes food furnished commercial and government employees and purchased meals and beverages.

Source: U.S. Department of Agriculture, *Food Consumption Expenditures,* March 1978; Economics, Statistics, and Cooperatives Service, *National Food Review,* Summer 1979; and Economics and Statistics Service, *Agricultural Outlook,* March 1981.

States, the most wealthy spend less than 5 percent of their disposable income for food and the poorest spend well over 50 percent. Food expenditure data show that, on the average, U.S. consumers have spent less than 20 percent of their disposable income for food since 1960. In the decade of the 1970s food expenditures as a percentage of disposable income leveled off at about 16.5 to 17 percent (Table 2-2). In 1980, 15.8 percent of disposable personal income was spent for food in the United States. Of this, 26.6 percent was spent in away-from-home sites. In most foreign countries the percentage is over 25, with nearly 100 percent of disposable personal income being spent for food in some developing countries. Americans with average or above incomes have a great deal of choice as to the type of food item purchased—a choice based on desires and willingness to pay. In contrast, the choice of poorer U.S. consumers is based more on necessity—on what they most need and on what they are able to pay.

World Population. The growing world population has a very pronounced effect on the demand for U.S. grains and oilseeds. Beginning in 1960, more wheat was exported than was utilized within the United States. Most of the U.S. wheat exports, as well as some corn and soybean products are exported for human consumption. By the mid-

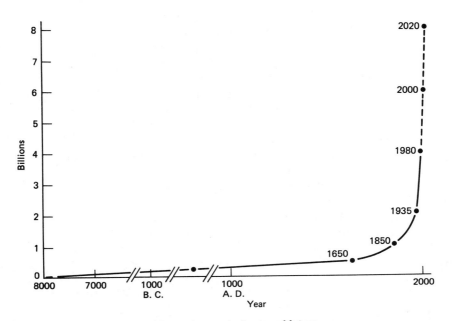

Figure 2-1. World population growth—an indicator of future grain and oilseed needs. (*Source:* Adapted from Norman Borlag, "The Human Population Monster," presented at the Landon Lecture Series, Kansas State University, Manhattan, Kansas, March 20, 1979.)

1970s, foreign demand accounted for approximately 60 percent of total disappearance.

World population may exceed 6 billion people by the year 2000 and possible reach 8 billion by the year 2020 (Figure 2-1).[2] On January 1, 1978, the world population stood at about 4 billion. U.S. population may grow by 30 to 50 million people by the year 2000; world population by 2 billion. The continued growth of world population will make foreign markets even more important in the future. Most of the population growth is expected in the developing countries. Some increase in food production will also occur in these countries, but will not likely keep pace with their population growth. Even if the rate of food production parallels the rate of population growth, the potential for famine exists in many countries.

Adverse weather can cause problems in major exporting countries as well as in importing countries. Poor weather in one or more of the major food producing countries or in more than one year in succession can cause a crisis. The world experienced a serious food crisis from

[2]Norman Borlag, "The Human Population Monster," Landon Lecture Series, Kansas State University, Manhattan, Kan., March 20, 1979.

1972 to 1974. Although this situation was soon corrected, it shed light on the types of problems that can occur when the quantity of grain demanded outruns the quantity of grain available. The major problem was related to food and income distribution—the countries that needed food the most could afford it the least. The 1972–1974 crisis brought forth questions concerning the moral issues of distributing food to people who could not pay for it, and the need for a long-term food reserve. The crisis also prompted the convening of the World Food Conference in Rome in November 1974, a conference that dealt with important issues of food production and distribution, including fertilizers and energy supplies, postharvest losses, and methods of expanding food production in developing countries.

Optimistically, the world's people will be fed. There are millions of acres of land in the United States and other parts of the world that are suitable for cropland but are not presently cropped. In many areas, land must be cleared or drained before it can be cropped. Also, the technical knowledge necessary to obtain big increases in yields must be spread to all corners of the earth. Thus while the Malthusian theory— that population is capable of increasing faster than the means of subsistence—should not be ignored, it would appear that with better communication and cooperation, more ingenuity, and the will to survive, the world can and will take the necessary steps to follow a rational food policy.

Livestock and Poultry Numbers and per Capita Consumption. Changing livestock and poultry numbers and production have a major effect on the demand for feed grains and high protein meal. Feed conversion ratios change little in the short run. In the 1970s they varied from just over 2 pounds for broilers up to 5 pounds or more of feed per pound of gain for beef production.

In the 10-year period from 1970 to 1980, U.S. livestock and broiler numbers changed as follows.

	Millions of Pounds	
	1970	*1980*
Cattle	112	111
Hogs	65	65
Sheep	20	12
Broiler hatch	2799	3964

In the 1970s, no trend developed in the per capita consumption of red meat. Throughout the decade, per capita meat consumption ranged from 143 to 157 pounds (Table 2-3). The consistency of upper consumption levels suggests that consumers' red meat demand has

Table 2-3 Per Capita Consumption of All
Red Meat and Poultry, 1970 to 1980
(pounds)

Year	All Red Meat[a]	Poultry[b]
1970	151.2	48.5
1971	156.8	48.8
1972	153.5	50.9
1973	142.6	49.2
1974	152.5	50.0
1975	145.5	49.2
1976	155.4	52.5
1977	153.7	54.1
1978	149.7	56.8
1979	147.6	61.7
1980	151.4	61.7

[a]Retail weight.

[b]Includes chickens and turkeys.

Source: U.S. Department of Agriculture, *Agricultural Statistics*; Economics, Statistics, and Cooperatives Service, *Livestock and Meat Situation*, and *Poultry and Egg Situation,* various issues.

leveled off at about 150 pounds. Domestic consumption of poultry (broilers and turkeys) increased rapidly toward the end of the 1970s having more than doubled since the end of World War II.

In view of past growth patterns in livestock and poultry production, it appears that the future domestic market for feed grains and high protein meal will be determined largely by three factors, U.S. population growth, the increasing domestic demand for poultry products, and the steadily growing foreign demand for U.S. red meat and broilers. In the long run, these three factors could be very important; but in the short run, the price of grain and high protein meal is the biggest factor. The domestic feed use of corn, for example, may be reduced by as much as 10 percent in one year if its price is high relative to the price of feeders and finished cattle.

Worldwide, numbers of both livestock and poultry are increasing as economic conditions improve. However, increases in numbers are not always accompanied by sufficient increases in feed grain production, resulting in deficit situations. For example, the rapid growth of Japan's livestock and poultry industries in recent years has led to that country's increased imports of feed grains and soybean meal. At times, substantial quantities of low protein U.S. wheat will also be demanded by foreign countries. The U.S. share of these markets will depend on competition as well as political considerations.

SUPPLY AND DEMAND RELATIONSHIPS

Changes in demand and supply result in equilibrium price changes. Figure 2-2 shows the effect on equilibrium price of four possible changes in supply and demand.

In each of these cases, either supply or demand is held constant while the other is allowed to change. An example of a supply decrease-demand unchanged situation is a government program that limits crop acreage in some manner, as shown in Figure 2-2d. Such programs theoretically should result in smaller quantities produced and increased farm prices. Whether farmers are better or worse off with an acreage limitation program depends on the elasticity of the demand

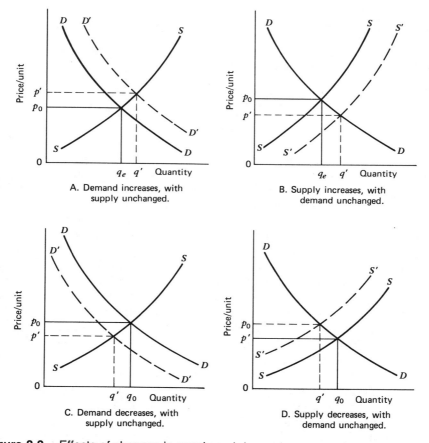

Figure 2-2. Effects of changes in supply and demand.
(a) Demand increases, with supply unchanged.
(b) Supply increases, with demand unchanged.
(c) Demand decreases, with supply unchanged.
(d) Supply decreases, with demand unchanged.

curve. If the demand for the grain products being limited is inelastic rather than elastic, as is the case with most agricultural products, then a program of crop reduction will result in higher total receipts to farmers.

Many more complex cases might be illustrated. You may wish to diagram the following situations and list the factors that could cause these shifts.

1. Supply and demand change in *opposite* directions.
   (a) Supply increases and demand decreases.
   (b) Supply decreases and demand increases.

2. Supply and demand change in the *same* directions.
   (a) Both supply and demand increase.
   (b) Both supply and demand decrease.

Elasticity of Demand

Elasticity measurements can serve as decision-making tools for individual firms and for those people involved in government policy. Price elasticity of demand is computed as the percentage change of quantity demanded divided by the percentage change in price. The computed coefficient thus measures consumers' responsiveness of quantity demanded to a price change.

Income elasticity is computed as the percentage change in quantity purchased divided by the percentage change in income. Measurement of income elasticity requires knowledge of the relationships between changes in the potential buyers income and the quantity taken.

For most purposes, both price and income elasticity are measured between two points on a curve. Such measurements are termed *arc elasticity*. This is the type of elasticity generally used when researchers or policy makers are concerned with farm programs designed to affect the price of agricultural products. Elasticity can also be measured at a specific point on a curve, thus the term *point elasticity*.

Price Elasticity.   Arc price elasticity, as previously defined, may be computed using the following formula:

$$E_d = \frac{(Q_1 - Q_2)/(Q_1 + Q_2)}{(P_1 - P_2)/(P_1 + P_2)}$$

The numerator of this formula represents the percentage change in quantity demanded. The denominator represents the percentage change in price.

Figure 2-3 assists in illustrating this method of calculating price elasticity. By substituting the values shown in the figure into the formula we can compute the price elasticity as follows.

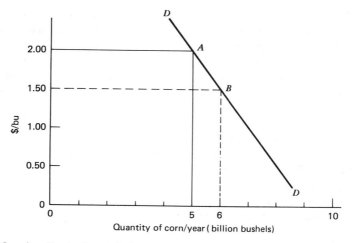

Figure 2-3. An illustration of the price of elasticity of demand.

$$E_d = \frac{(5 - 6)/(5 + 6)}{(2.00 - 1.50)/(2.00 + 1.50)} = \frac{-1/11}{.50/3.50} = \frac{-1}{11} \times \frac{3.50}{.50} = -.64$$

Thus, the price elasticity of demand between points A and B in Figure 2-3 is −.64. The elasticity of any straight line demand curve will vary according to the segment of the curve being measured.

For most goods, the elasticity coefficient sign will be negative because price and quantity demanded change in opposite directions. When the elasticity coefficient is less than 1, as in the preceding example, demand is termed *inelastic*. When the coefficient is greater than 1, the demand is termed *elastic*. When the coefficient is exactly 1, demand is termed *unitary*.

Price elasticities of demand vary greatly, both at the farm level and at different stages of the marketing process. For example, the approximate price elasticity of demand at the farm level for cattle is −.68; for hogs −.46; for eggs, −.23; and for fluid milk, −.14.

The elasticity of demand at the farm is usually less than the elasticity at the retail level. The price elasticity of demand for cereal (baking products) at the retail level is about −.15, whereas at the farm level it is generally about −.02 for wheat and about −.07 for corn.

Since farmers generally receive far less than 50 percent of the consumer's dollar for their grain products, the percent of price change at the farm level (the denominator in the elasticity formula) is greater than at the retail level. Thus, the elasticity of demand at the farm usually is less than at the retail store. In other words, the wider and more stable the margin between farm prices and retail prices, the less elastic is the demand at the farm compared to the demand at the retail store.

Factors influencing elasticity include (1) the availability of close substitutes for a commodity, (2) the number of uses to which a commodity can be put, and (3) the price of a commodity relative to the consumer's disposable income.

An example of the elasticity of substitution is related to classes of wheat. The elasticity of substitution between soft red winter and hard red winter wheat, when compared with that for soft red winter and white wheat, suggests that soft red winter can be substituted for hard red winter more easily than it can substitute for white wheat.

Income Elasticity.   Buyers will purchase more of most goods as their incomes increase, but not necessarily in direct proportion with the income increase. In the case of food, the quantity purchased increases as income rises, but at a decreasing rate (Figure 2-4*a*). Conversely, in the case of nonfood goods, the quantity increases at an increasing rate as income rises (Figure 2-4*b*).

Arc income elasticity, as previously defined, may be computed using the following formula.

$$E_i = \frac{(Q_1 - Q_2)/(Q_1 + Q_2)}{(I_1 - I_2)/(I_1 + I_2)}$$

Just as for price elasticity of demand, the numerator in this formula represents the percentage change in quantity demanded. How-

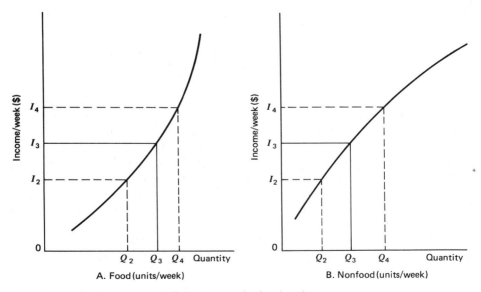

Figure 2-4.   An illustration of Engel curves for food and nonfood goods. (*a*) Food (units per week). (*b*) Nonfood (units per week).

ever, in this formula the denominator represents the percentage change in income along a segment of the curve.

Figure 2-4a provides an illustration for calculating the income elasticity of demand coefficient using the consumption of food as an example. With I_2, I_3, and I_4 representing weekly incomes of \$200, \$300, and \$400 respectively, and Q_2, Q_3, and Q_4 representing 28, 38, and 45 units of food purchased at those three income levels, the income elasticity of demand between weekly incomes of \$300 and \$400 is measured as follows.

$$E_i = \frac{(38 - 45)/(38 + 45)}{(300 - 400)/(300 + 400)} = \frac{-7/83}{-100/700} = \frac{7}{83} \times \frac{700}{100} = .59$$

In this hypothetical example the income elasticity of demand is .59, meaning that a 100 percent increase in income results in a 59 percent increase in the quantity of food purchased. If the income elasticity of demand had been measured at a lower level of income, say a change from \$200 to \$300 per week, the elasticity would have been .76.

Cross Elasticity.   Economists use a concept called the "cross elasticity of demand" to measure the extent to which commodities are related to each other. Consider, for example, the commodities X and Y. The cross elasticity of X with respect to Y equals the percentage change in quantity of X taken divided by the percentage change in the price of Y. This can be expressed mathematically by:

$$E_{xy} = \frac{(Q_{x1} - Q_{x2})/(Q_{x1} + Q_{x2})}{(P_{y1} - P_{y2})/(P_{y1} + P_{y2})}$$

If the computed cross elasticity coefficient is positive, the two commodities are termed *substitutes*. Butter and margarine are examples of close substitutes. If the price of one increases, the demand for the other increases and vice versa. High cross elasticities indicate close relationships—substitute goods in the same industry. If the computed cross elasticity coefficient is negative, the two commodities are termed *complementary*. Canning jars and lids are examples of complementary products. If the price of jars increases, the quantity of jars demanded decreases and the demand for lids also decreases. High negative cross elasticities indicate strong complementary commodities. Low cross elasticities, coefficients close to zero, indicate remote relationships— goods in different industries.

Elasticity of Supply

The concept of supply elasticity is similar to that of demand elasticity. The computed coefficient is always positive since a change in price will bring about a change in quantity in the same direction when the supply curve slopes upward and to the right.

Commodities that are very responsive to price changes have elastic supply curves and those that respond little to price changes have inelastic supply curves. For grain products, time is an important factor in determining supply elasticity. After crops are seeded, the quantity cannot be changed greatly regardless of price changes; the supply is largely fixed, depending on the weather and certain other factors. However, in the longer run, grain supplies are responsive to price and price forecasts as farmers respond to changes in the relative prices of alternative crops.

CORN SUPPLY AND UTILIZATION

The United States is the world's major corn producing country, producing nearly 50 percent of the world total. In world trade, the United States accounts for about 75 percent of the total. World corn production generally has maintained a safe margin over consumption, although in three consecutive years from 1972 to 1974 consumption pulled world stocks to uncomfortably low levels.

Supply

Except for occasional years of dry weather or widespread crop disease that limited production, the U.S. production of corn rose steadily from 1940 to 1980. Total supply (current production plus carry-over) reached 8 billion bushels in 1978 and over 9 billion bushels in 1979.

Production. Production of corn for grain reached new record levels of 4 billion bushels in 1963, 5 billion bushels in 1971, 6 billion in 1976, 7 billion in 1978, and 8 billion in 1981 (Table 1-2). Part of the production increases can be attributed to acreage shifted to corn, and part to yield increases. In 1981, corn was harvested from a record 75 million acres. Average yields reached 100 bushels per acre for the first time in 1978, and 110 bushels per acre in 1981 (Table 1-3).

Carry-over. Historically, corn carry-over has been highly variable both in terms of total volume and relative to total supply. The largest carry-over occurred in 1961 when it surpassed 2 billion bushels, or 36 percent of the total supply.

In the late 1950s and 1960, the Commodity Credit Corporation (CCC) owned over a billion bushels of corn annually. The market was glutted. Supply control measures, coupled with the opening of new export markets, reduced the burdensome carry-over to manageable proportions. At the same time, CCC activity lessened. A decade later, the government no longer took ownership, and stored no corn. The carry-over function was assumed entirely by the industry.

During the 1970s, carry-over of corn was much lower, ranging from a low of about 360 million bushels in 1976 to a high of 1.6 billion bushels in 1980. The latter figure accounted for only 17 percent of the total supply, a relatively small percentage when compared to the first billion bushel carry-over in 1955 that accounted for 26 percent of the total.

Utilization

In the quarter century from 1955 to 1980, total demand for U.S. corn more than doubled, increasing from about 3 billion bushels to about 7.4 billion bushels. Corn is used primarily for domestic purposes (Figure 2-5), including livestock and poultry feed, wet and dry processed products, alcoholic beverages, and seed. The export market grew rapidly through the 1960s and 1970s. Exported corn is largely in the form of whole grain although lesser volumes of cornmeal and other products are also shipped overseas. As the corn industry entered the 1980s, exports accounted for approximately one-third of total disappearance.

Feed. The largest use of corn is for livestock and poultry feed, as it has been throughout U.S. history. However, tremendous changes have occurred in corn marketing methods, especially in the 1970s. During

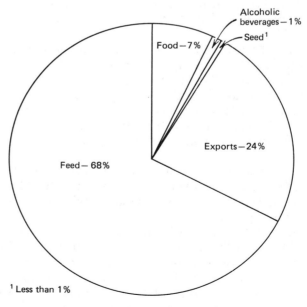

Figure 2-5. Relative importance of U.S. corn markets, 1970 to 1980.

the period 1970 to 1980 the percentage of total corn supply fed dropped to 49 percent, while exports amounted to 26 percent.

In the early 1940s, less than 25 percent of production was sold off farms. The primary demand was for livestock feed on the farm where it was grown. By the 1950s and 1960s, about 30 to 40 percent of production was sold off farms. A large percentage of this volume eventually made its way back to farms or feedlots. In the 1970s, still another change occurred. Nearly two-thirds of production entered marketing channels and nearly half of this volume was exported.

The following figures show total volume and percentage of corn supply utilized domestically for feed from 1940 to 1980:

Year	Million Bushels	Percent of Total Supply
1940	2258	72
1950	2771	71
1960	3092	54
1970	3592	70
1980	4139	50

Food. Domestic food uses increased nearly 50 percent during the 1970s, accounting for about 7 percent of total disappearance during the period. Corn, used for food, was either wet or dry processed. Wet processed products included starch, dextrin, syrup, and various other by-products. Other corn was distilled into alcohol and distilled products. Dry processed products included corn oil, corn meal, and grits. Per capita consumption of corn syrup increased rapidly, nearly tripling in the 1970s. The wet mill grind increased about 60 percent from 1970 to 1980. As the industry entered the 1980s, per capita consumption of wet corn products was as follows: syrup, 34.7 pounds; sugar, 5.5 pounds; and starch, 1.9 pounds. Per capita consumption of dry processed products was increasing only slightly. Consumption of meal, the major dry corn product was about 7.7 pounds per capita. Consumption of corn products as a breakfast cereal held at a constant 2.3 pounds per capita with no reported change since 1967.

One of the most significant developments in wet corn milling is the increase in high fructose corn syrup use. Rising demand for corn sweeteners is reflected in the per capita consumption figures shown in Table 2-2. In terms of actual volume, U.S. corn sweetener production increased from 4.0 million dry pounds in 1970 to 9.3 million pounds in 1980. High fructose corn syrup accounted for 33 percent of the total sweetener market in 1980, up sharply from 1970. In addition to capturing a larger share of the market in 1980, the industry was processing an improved product, having higher solids, lower dextrose, and a more favorable polysaccharide content. These characteristics have allowed it to compete successfully as a replacement for medium invert sugar, historically the major sweetener used by the soft drink industry.

It is also used by the baking, canning, dairy products, and confectionary industries as well as several nonfood industries. Production of high fructose corn syrup is expected to continue to increase as industry capacity is expanded and so long as the price of competing sweeteners remain high.

Alcohol and Distilled Spirits.   The utilization of corn by the alcohol and distilled spirits industries accounted for just over 1 percent of total disappearance annually in the 1970s. The use of corn for distilled liquors declined while its use for fermented malt liquors increased. Corn products—grits, flakes, and refined starch—are used as supplementary carbohydrates in the manufacture of beer. Within certain quality tolerances these adjuncts can be substituted for malt. Until the popularization of light beers, the brewing industry had steadily increased the use of grains in their brewery operations. Just over 10 pounds of corn were used per barrel of beer in the period from 1951 to 1976. The introduction of light beer has resulted in less demand for corn products, and carbohydrates (other than malt) are being supplied by dextrose rather than by grains.

Seed.   Seed corn accounted for less than 1 percent of total utilization. However, hybrid seed should not be considered along with other uses when studying the marketing system. Hybrid seed is not handled in the same marketing channels as other corn dispositions. Hybrid seed is a farm output and is distributed by hybrid seed companies to their farmer customers through a network of hybrid seed dealers.

Exports.   U.S. corn exports grew steadily after World War II but increased most rapidly in the 1970s. Exports accounted for 33 percent of the total utilization in 1980 compared to less than 12 percent in 1970. U.S. corn exports passed one billion bushels for the first time in 1972 and have exceeded that amount in each succeeding year. By 1980, U.S. corn exports reached 2.4 billion bushels and accounted for nearly one-third of total disappearance.

Year	*Million Bushels*
1940	15
1950	117
1960	292
1970	517
1980	2355

The United States exports corn to about 60 countries. However,

Table 2-4   Average Annual Imports of Corn by 25 Largest
Markets and U.S. Market Share, 1972/73 to 1976/77

| Importing Country | Rank | Average Annual Imports (thousand metric tons) | | U.S. Market Share (Percent) |
		From U.S.	Total	
Japan	1	6,181	7,468	83
U.S.S.R.	2	4,776	5,416	88
Netherlands	3	4,065	4,766	85
West Germany	4	3,563	4,889	73
Italy	5	2,575	4,862	53
Spain	6	2,440	3,475	70
United Kingdom	7	1,464	3,040	48
Mexico	8	999	1,257	80
Poland	9	905	915	99
Portugal	10	891	988	90
Canada	11	759	759	100
Greece	12	717	721	99
Belgium-Luxembourg	13	679	1,496	45
Taiwan	14	614	1,260	49
South Korea	15	596	645	92
China	16	543	702	77
Egypt	17	410	410	100
Romania	18	244	244	100
Peru	19	235	260	90
Israel	20	228	228	100
Jamaica	21	127	127	100
Czechoslovakia	22	121	162	75
Iran	23	117	150	78
France	24	116	293	40
East Germany	25	106	107	99
Total, 25 countries		33,471	44,640	75
Average total world exports		34,813	48,728	72

Source: Foreign Agricultural Service, *Foreign Agricultural Circular—Grains,* USDA, FG 5-78,
March 1978.

25 countries accounted for about 92 percent of the total market in the
mid-1970s (Table 2-4). The U.S. share of these 25 markets averaged
75 percent compared with its 71 percent share of all world markets,
dominating the rapidly growing world corn trade.

SOYBEAN SUPPLY AND UTILIZATION

Until the 1970s, the United States and mainland China produced most
of the world's soybeans. The United States accounted for over 90
percent of the volume of beans and meal traded in world markets.

During the 1970s, world production of soybeans increased at an
annual rate of 12 percent. In most years, demand kept pace with
production, a situation envied by the corn and wheat industries.

Supply

Compared to corn and wheat, soybeans are a new crop in the United States. Production was less than 100,000 bushels prior to World War II. After 1950, soybean production increased faster than that of any other major grain or oilseed. Total production reached 1 billion bushels in 1966. Thirteen years later, in 1979, it reached 2.3 billion bushels.

Production. The volume of U.S. soybean production increased largely because of increased acreages. From 1967 to 1978, for example, soybean acreage increased from 39.8 to 63.0 million acres, while soybean yields accounted for only a small percentage of the production increase. Using the same years of reference, yields were 24.5 and 29.5 bushels per acre. By 1979, soybean acreage had surpassed 70 million acres, nearly matching the cropland area devoted to corn or wheat.

For the period 1965 to 1979, U.S. soybean yields increased only 0.4 bushel annually. A trend line statistically fitted to these 15 years of yield data suggest U.S. soybean yields of 32 bushels per acre in 1985 and 34 bushels by 1990.

In view of the rapid increase in world demand and production and the small increase in U.S. yields, the U.S. share of world production and trade is likely to decline. Unless yields are increased, additional supply must be derived from added acreage. This situation presents an interesting case for the marketing student. From where do the added acres come? Will the soybean market be strong enough—profitable enough—to entice farmers to plant, say, soybeans instead of corn? Or will cropland acreages not presently cultivated be planted to soybeans?

Carry-over. Soybean carry-over was of little consequence prior to the 1950s and in the 30-year period from 1950 to 1980 it exceeded 200 million bushels only four times. Each time, these larger than normal volumes of carry-over occurred following years of exceptionally large production. Each time, the soybean industry was able to handle those minor gluts without the need for government supply management programs.

Utilization

Soybean disappearance, led by domestic uses, increased as follows after 1950.

Year	Million Bushels
1950	298
1960	580
1970	1258
1980	1901

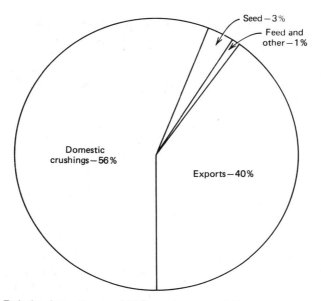

Figure 2-6. Relative importance of U.S. soybean markets, 1970 to 1980.

About 96 percent of all soybeans are either crushed domestically or exported as whole beans (Figure 2-6). The remainder is used for seed or feed as whole beans.

Crushings. During the 1970s, soybean crushings accounted for an average of about 56 percent of total disappearance. Crushings yielded about 11 pounds of crude soybean oil and 47 pounds of 44 percent protein meal per bushel. Of the meal produced, 74 percent was utilized domestically and 26 percent exported. Of the oil produced, 83 percent was used domestically and 17 percent exported.

Soybean meal is used in the U.S. feed industry, especially for poultry and hogs. Increases in U.S. livestock and poultry feeding rates are boosting soybean meal consumption, although in the case of livestock this is partially offset by decreasing numbers. During the early 1970s, protein feed accounted for about a tenth of all concentrate feed. By the late seventies, protein supplements accounted for 14 percent. This change is explained by the fact that rising feed costs encouraged the industry to adopt more efficient feeding practices.

Soybean oil is used largely in foods and competes with other oils such as coconut, palm, and peanut. Despite competition from these oils, soybean oil accounted for a record two-thirds of all oils and fats utilized in food products in the 1970s. Over 90 percent of domestic soybean oil production was used in the manufacture of shortening, margarine, cooking and salad oils, and other edible products. The remainder was used in such nonfood products as paint and varnish, resins, plastics, and other oil-based products.

Exports.   In the 1970s, soybean exports averaged close to 40 percent of total disappearance. The total volume of U.S. exports grew, as it did in the rest of the market.

Year	Million Bushels
1950	28
1960	130
1970	434
1980	760

The chief reason for this rapid growth in exports during the 1960s and 1970s was the increasing demand for high protein meal for livestock feed in Western Europe and Japan. These areas imported oilseeds and processed them into oil and meal. Developing countries tended to import edible vegetable oils primarily as oils since they did not have oilseed processing plants to produce their own oil and meal.

Soybean oil, the most important edible vegetable oil accounted for about a third of the world's total oil production. World demand for soybean oil increased at an annual rate of 9.2 percent during the 1970s, up 3 percent annually from the rate a decade earlier. Major producers were the United States with 65 percent of the market, Brazil with 15 percent, China with 10 percent, and Argentina with less than 5 percent.

At the end of the 1970s, the major exporter of soybean oil was the United States with about 80 percent of total soybean oil exports. About 75 to 80 percent of total U.S. exports of soybeans oil was marketed as soybeans and not as oil.

Although the United States dominates world production and trade of soybeans, South American countries have become more competitive. Brazil, the major South American producer, increased its production from 1.3 million metric tons in 1970 to about 15 million tons in 1980. Brazilian policy is to crush soybeans at home and export the products—mainly meal. Only about 10 percent of the crop was exported as beans.

Throughout the 1970s, Brazil increased its crushing capacity. By 1980, trade estimates placed the country's processing capacity at 19 million tons and the country crushed more than 85 percent of its soybean production.

Japan and Western Europe dominated soybean oil imports. The European countries consumed a portion of the oil that they crush and exported the remaining oil. The Netherlands and Spain, for example,

Table 2-5 U.S. Soybean Exports:
Average Annual Imports by 15 Largest
U.S. Soybean Markets, 1972/73 to
1976/77 (thousand metric tons)

Importing Country	Rank	Soybeans[a]
Japan	1	2,953
Netherlands	2	2,587
West Germany	3	1,534
Spain	4	1,163
Italy	5	770
Taiwan	6	667
Canada	7	406
Israel	8	365
Denmark	9	342
France	10	321
Belgium-Luxembourg	11	297
Soviet Russia	12	289
United Kingdom	13	280
Norway	14	204
China	15	154
Total, 15 countries		12,332
Average total U.S. exports		13,397

[a]Does not include exports of meal and oil.

Source: Foreign Agricultural Service, *Foreign Agriculture Circular—Oilseeds and Products,* USDA, FOP 1-78, January 1978.

were the world's third- and fourth-largest exporters of soybean oil in the 1970s.

Major markets for U.S. soybean oil were India, Pakistan, Iran, China, and Peru. The major importers of U.S. soybeans in grain form were Japan and the Netherlands (Table 2-5). During the 1970s, 92 percent of the U.S. soybean exports were marketed in 15 countries.

Although the export demand grew 75 percent in the 1970s, continuation at this pace is uncertain. As the U.S. soybean industry approached the 1980s, competition was increasing on at least three fronts: (1) increased world production, (2) expanded processing capacity in foreign countries, and (3) growing competition by substitute oilseeds such as sunflowerseed and palm oil.

WHEAT SUPPLY AND UTILIZATION

The United States accounts for 14 to 16 percent of the total world wheat production and often accounts for a larger percentage of total supply because of its capacity to store wheat. As demonstrated in the past, many countries depend on the United States for their wheat supply. By the end of the 1970s, exports accounted for approximately 65 percent of total U.S. wheat disappearance. The United States was the major wheat supplier in world trade accounting for about 40 to 45 percent of the total traded.

In the three decades following World War II, the U.S. wheat industry endured recurring periods of market surpluses. Neither the industry nor government were able to anticipate the effects of weather and changes in foreign demand.

Supply

The total supply of U.S. wheat rose steadily, tripling from 1940 to 1980. Total U.S. wheat supply surpassed the 3 billion bushel mark for the first time in 1977 and set an all time record of 3.3 billion bushels in 1980.

Production.   The wheat acreage harvested after reaching a record 75.9 million in 1949 was sharply reduced over the next quarter century. Still the market prices reflected a general glut on the market. Between 1949 and 1970, wheat production increased 23 percent even though total wheat acres were reduced by 43 percent.

Although acreage was much lower, production remained at or above war-ending levels. In 1970, the U.S. wheat yield averaged 31 bushels per acre. Harvested acreage was 43.6 million acres less than for any year since 1934. Production totaled 1.4 billion bushels, and nearly 1 billion bushels of old wheat was carried into the new marketing year. What looked like the recurrence of the long-running surplus problem of the 1950s and early 1960s, was, in fact, quite short lived. Four years later, in 1974, carry-over was at its lowest level in 22 years. With their first chance since World War II to test their capacity to produce, farmers responded. The next year, 1975, a total of 69.6 million acres of wheat were harvested and the 2 billion bushel production mark was exceeded.

Spurred by exports in excess of 1 billion bushels, the U.S. wheat industry produced an average of more than 2 billion bushels annually from 1975 to 1980. Once again carry-over climbed above the 1 billion bushel mark.

The preceding scenario typifies the performance of the U.S. wheat industry throughout much of the twentieth century. It is in this highly unstable environment that the U.S. marketing system has had to function.

Because the upper limits of U.S. wheat production have been only slightly tested its ultimate capacity is unknown. The world demand for wheat grew at an annual rate of over 3.5 percent from 1960 to 1979. Almost certainly, the demand for wheat will continue to grow in proportion to world population growth.

If production is to keep pace with demand, yields must be improved. For the period 1933 to 1977, a statistically fitted trend line shows a U.S. wheat yield increase of 0.5 bushels annually, and suggests yields of only 35.8 bushels per acre in 1985 and 38.2 bushels per acre in 1990. At the beginning of the 45-year study period, the annual rate of yield increase was 5 percent. However, by the end of the period, a yield increase of 0.5 bushels per acre represents only a 1.6 percent annual increase. Furthermore, from 1974 to 1980, yields reached trend line expectations in only 2 years.

Carry-over.   Excess supplies have often been the center of agricultural policy debate in the U.S. Congress, especially when taxpayers were called on to pay the cost of storing excess supplies. Stocks exceeded the volume of wheat used domestically in 12 consecutive years in the 1950s and 1960s, reaching more than double the domestic use level from 1959 to 1963. Stocks were at a record high in 1961. At that time, they amounted to 1.4 billion bushels, an equivalent of 231 percent of domestic needs. In contrast, the volume of carry-over was low in both 1952 and 1974, less than 50 percent of our domestic needs.

These extremes in carry-over are reflective of continual stresses placed on the wheat industry and grain markets in general. In times of rapid stock drawn down, the industry often operates well above normal capacity. In periods of stock buildup storage capacity may be fully utilized, but day-to-day operations are sometimes slow. The transportation system, particularly, is under pressure to perform in periods of extreme surpluses or shortages.

Utilization

The utilization of wheat consists of two major components, domestic and export (Figure 2-7). Domestic uses include flour products, breakfast cereals, livestock feed, seed, and industrial uses. Exported wheat is largely in the form of whole grain, although lesser volumes of flour and bulgur are also shipped overseas. In the quarter century from 1952 to 1977, total demand for U.S. wheat more than doubled. In the late 1970s, U.S. exports were as large as total disappearance in the early 1950s.

Food.   Flour is the major product derived from wheat. About 45 pounds of flour are extracted from each bushel of milled wheat. Wheat flour is used to manufacture bread, cookies, crackers, cake mixes, macaroni and spaghetti, and other products.

Each class of wheat has its own distinct characteristics in terms of milling quality and end use value. Flour milled from hard red spring wheat is high in protein and used primarily for baking bread and rolls. This class of wheat is often blended with lower protein hard red winter wheats for making bread. Soft red winter and soft white wheats are

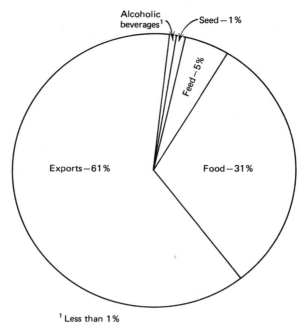

Alcoholic beverages[1]

Seed—1%

Feed—5%

Exports—61%

Food—31%

[1] Less than 1%

Figure 2-7. Relative importance of U.S. wheat markets, 1970 to 1980.

lower in protein content and used primarily in the manufacture of pastries, crackers, biscuits, and cakes; some of these wheats are used as feed in years of excess supply and low prices. Durum, a high-protein wheat, is generally processed into semolina, which is then used to produce macaroni, spaghetti, and other pasta products (Figure 2-8).

In 1980/1981, the USDA estimated the following breakdown of utilization by class as follows.

	Percent Domestic	*Percent Exported*
Hard red winter	33	67
Soft red winter	34	66
Hard red spring	48	52
Durum	47	53
White	20	80

These percentages by class will vary greatly from year to year depending on world production, carry-over, and other factors that affect relative prices. Some substitution among classes is possible when supplies and prices dictate. However, the amount of substitution for domestic food uses is limited because of end-product quality considerations.

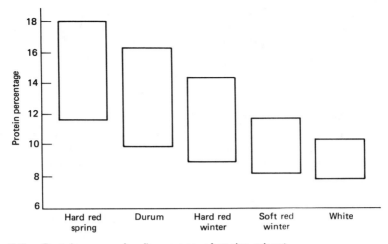

Figure 2-8. Protein range for flour uses of major wheat classes.

Per capita consumption of wheat products steadily declined for many years reaching a low of 106 pounds per capita in 1974. Then, due to diet changes, it was showing a slight increase as the U.S. wheat industry entered the 1980s. Nevertheless, U.S. consumers were still expressing their preference for prepared products and non-wheat-based foods as opposed to their purchase of flour itself.

During the 1970s, over one-half billion bushels of wheat were used for domestic food purposes annually. Food uses accounted for about 31 percent of the annual disappearance. Over time, food uses exhibit one of the most stable aspects of the entire grain industry as follows.

Year	Million Bushels
1940	492
1950	493
1960	497
1970	517
1980	605

Seed. Seed use varies with planted acreage which, in the case of wheat, is often affected by farm program changes. Seed use during the 1970s ranged from 62 to 99 million bushels or about 3 percent of total utilization.

Feed. The demand for feed wheat is quite variable. It was generally higher in the 1970s than at any time since World War II, accounting for about 5 percent of total disappearance. The practice of feeding wheat in the United States is largely related to price. Compared with corn, the feeding value of wheat is generally higher, but the amount of wheat that can be included in feeding rations is more limited. Usually the price of good quality wheat precludes its use as feed. When it is fed, it may be fed on the farm where produced. Therefore, feed wheat does not enter marketing channels to any significant amount.

Industrial Uses.   During the 1970s, hard and durum wheats accounted for 85 percent of the milled wheat products used for industrial purposes. Normally, the industrial use of wheat is limited to second clears, a by-product of flour milling. Also, some whole wheat is wet processed to produce starch and gluten products. Specific industrial uses include plywood and composition board, laminating adhesives, industrial starch for laundries, textiles, billboard and wallboard pastes, paper additive, and alcohol. Wheat is also used in making whiskey, beer, cosmetics, fertilizer, paving mixes, and certain polishes. Historically, industrial uses account for only about 0.5 percent of total wheat utilization. In the future, however, the percentage could increase, depending largely on the economic feasibility of gasohol, a fuel product that can be derived from any grain. Given current prices, however, barley, milo, and corn would probably be used to make gasohol, rather than use hard wheats.

Exports.   The volume of wheat exports expanded following World War II, but did not show phenomenal growth until the 1970s.

Year	Million Bushels
1940	41
1950	366
1960	662
1970	738
1980	1525

U.S. wheat exports reached 1 billion bushels for the first time in 1972/1973. Since that time, exports have accounted for over 50 percent of total disappearance. Exports were the fastest-growing market for U.S. wheat as the 1980s approached. A comparison of the two major channels of disappearance, domestic uses and exports, shows that from 1950 to 1980 the domestic demand increased 21 percent and the export demand increased 317 percent.

During the 1970s, the United States exported wheat and flour to about 120 countries. However, 35 countries accounted for more than 89 percent of the total (Table 2-6). The U.S. share of these 35 markets averaged 47 percent compared with 45 percent for all world markets, a much smaller share of the world wheat market than its share for corn or soybeans.

Table 2-6 Average Annual Imports of Wheat and Wheat
Flour by 35 Largest Markets and U.S. Market Share,
1972/73 to 1976/77

Importing Country	Rank	Average Annual Imports (thousand metric tons)		U.S. Share of Market (percent)
		From U.S.	Total	
Soviet Russia	1	4,007	7,282	55
Japan	2	3,205	5,539	58
India	3	2,525	3,879	65
South Korea	4	1,683	1,724	98
Brazil	5	1,316	2,694	49
China	6	1,055	4,392	24
Egypt	7	1,028	3,286	31
Netherlands	8	955	2,042	47
Iran	9	831	965	86
Algeria	10	680	1,429	48
Pakistan	11	659	1,112	59
Bangladesh	12	641	1,428	45
Venezuela	13	631	674	94
West Germany	14	565	2,308	24
Taiwan	15	540	668	81
Peru	16	525	791	66
Poland	17	477	1,162	41
Chile	18	455	838	54
Mexico	19	441	449	98
Israel	20	437	456	96
Morocco	21	433	924	47
Nigeria	22	427	474	90
Philippines	23	421	601	70
United Kingdom	24	408	3,608	11
Italy	25	403	2,265	18
Indonesia	26	355	793	45
Colombia	27	348	368	95
Portugal	28	248	333	74
Saudi Arabia	29	238	455	52
Iraq	30	215	582	37
Turkey	31	207	293	71
Ecuador	32	182	182	100
Sri Lanka	33	152	640	24
Yugoslavia	34	151	200	76
Belgium-Luxembourg	35	145	973	15
Total, 35 countries		26,489	55,809	48
Average total U.S. exports		29,633	65,345	45

Source: Foreign Agricultural Service, *Foreign Agricultural Circular—Grains,* USDA, FG 5-78,
March 1978.

Summary

The U.S. grain marketing system does not stop at the country's borders: it extends worldwide. Production uncertainty in foreign countries and, in turn, variability in foreign demand has led to periods of large surpluses followed by periods of short supply. These surpluses and shortages place much greater stress on the U.S. marketing system than if the system were to serve only the domestic demand. Nevertheless, the U.S. grain production and marketing system has performed exceedingly well when called on to increase its capacity for storage and handling, even on short notice.

The demand for corn, soybeans, wheat, and their products grew tremendously in the 1960s and 1970s. Exports became an important channel of trade for U.S. grain and oilseeds. They will likely be of even greater importance in the future. Projected world human population and livestock numbers suggest that world demand for all grain will continue to grow. To meet this growing demand some additional cropland will be brought into production. There is concern that this added cropland may be less productive than that presently in production. At the same time, there is concern over the loss of cropland presently in production due to erosion, industrial expansion, and urban sprawl. In the long run, increased yields must be forthcoming to prevent world hunger and starvation.

Projected trends, both in human population and livestock numbers, suggest a challenge to the U.S. grain marketing system and an opportunity for it to serve these growing markets for food grains, feed grains, and oilseeds. By the year 2020, according to some population projections, the world may be inhabited by 8 billion people. Optimistically, production can be doubled to meet this anticipated demand. If so, then the marketing system must be expanded accordingly to handle the distribution of supplies. In view of this outlook, challenges abound for plant breeders, farmers, grain merchandisers, grain processors, and all others associated with the grain trade. What appears as problems necessitating market growth can be turned into opportunities for improvements in marketing channels, facility design, trading procedures, and pricing methods.

Selected References

Bakken, Henry H., *Theory of Markets and Marketing,* 1st ed., Mimir Publishers, Inc., Madison, Wis., 1953.

Baumol, William J., *Economic Theory and Operational Analysis,* 4th ed., Prentice-Hall, Inc., Englewood Cliffs, N.J., 1977.

Brandow, George E., *Interrelations Among Demands for Farm Products and Implications for*

Control of Market Supply, Agricultural Experiment Station Bulletin No. 680, Pennsylvania State University, University Park, Penn., August, 1961.

Cramer, Gail L. and Clarence W. Jensen, *Agricultural Economics and Agribusiness,* 2nd ed., John Wiley & Sons, Inç., New York, 1982.

Heid, *Walter G., Jr., U.S. Wheat Industry,* Economics, Statistics, and Cooperatives Service, USDA, Economics Report No. 432, Washington, D.C., August 1979.

Leftwich, Richard H., *The Price System and Resource Allocation,* 6th ed., Holt, Rinehart and Winston, New York, 1976.

Whittaker, Edmund, *A History of Economic Ideas,* 4th ed., Longman, Green, and Co., New York, 1947.

MARKETING CHANNELS
AND STORAGE

MARKETING CHANNELS AND STORAGE*

CHAPTER
3

Individual grains are produced seasonally and are harvested over a relatively short period of time in locations that generally are quite far removed from the consuming areas. As grains and their products move through the market channels, they are bought and sold many times. In the handling of these goods, a variety of important economic functions are performed by the marketing system. Grain and grain products are moved from the raw products producers, processed into desired forms, delivered to the desired locations and, through the storage function, made available to consumers at the desired time.

MARKETING CHANNELS

Grain marketing channels are the various agencies or institutions through which grain or grain products flow from the producer to the final consumer. In these marketing channels, decision makers solve the problems of time, form, and location through storage, processing, and transportation, respectively.

When grain producers harvest their crops, they are faced with making a decision between two alternatives: store the grain for use or sale in the future or sell the grain immediately to some marketing agency. Producers who decide to store their grain may store that grain on the farm and incur costs of doing so or pay a storage charge to a commercial facility for storing the grain. If the decision is to sell, the producer must decide whether to sell that grain to a local farmer, country elevator, subterminal elevator, terminal elevator, processor, or an export marketing agency.

Agencies in the Marketing Channel

Before going further in the discussion of marketing channels, several terms used to describe agencies in the marketing channel need to be defined.

Off-farm sales include all whole grain sold from farms. These

*Robert Oehrtman, Associate Professor, Department of Agricultural Economics, Oklahoma State University, wrote the Marketing Channels sections; L. D. Schnake, Agricultural Economist, National Economics Division, Economic Research Service, USDA, stationed at the U.S. Grain Marketing Research Laboratory, Manhattan, Kan., wrote the Grain Storage section of this chapter. Information in this chapter represents the views of the authors and not necessarily the views of the U.S. Department of Agriculture.

sales of grain may be to other local farms, country elevators, subterminal elevators, terminal elevators, processors or export marketing agencies.[1]

Country elevators refer to grain establishments that receive a majority of their whole grain from farmers. Grain is normally delivered by the producer to local country elevators by farm truck, or by commercial trucking services.

Country elevators fall into three general classes:[2] (1) independent or privately owned elevators, (2) farmers' cooperative elevators, and (3) line elevators.

Independent, or privately owned elevators, refer to single-unit firms owned and operated by individuals who provide their own capital and usually operate the elevators themselves.

Elevators owned by farmers include two types of organizations. The first is a cooperative elevator organization established by its farmer members, has its own capital structure, and returns savings to the member patrons as dividends on the basis of their patronage. The second type of farmer-owned elevator is governed by a directorate elected from and by the stockholders with profits distributed as dividends on stock ownership rather than on the basis of patronage.

Line elevators are multiunit chains of elevators with two or more establishments owned by a grain company, usually located along a railroad system. Line-elevator operators receive instructions regarding buying prices and operating practices from the parent company, a corporation, cooperative, or an independent firm. These may be flour mills, grain processors, or grain import/export firms.

Subterminal elevators refer to establishments that receive over one-half of their supply of grain from other elevators, usually country elevators.[3] Subterminal elevators are typically located near metropolitan areas. They often are the only large grain-handling facility in the immediate vicinity that does not buy the majority of their grain directly from the farmer. The manager of a subterminal elevator merchandises grain directly to terminal elevators, processors, and exporters rather than selling to interior dealers or a commissioned broker.[4]

Subterminal elevators primarily, and to some extent river elevators, serve as "surge tanks" in locations outside the traditional terminal elevator markets. They provide functions such as blending to achieve greater uniformity of grain and to facilitate marketing the grain. Storage at these intermediate points in the marketing channel facilitates

[1]Walter G. Heid, Jr., "Grain Marketing—A General Description,"*Marketing Grain,* Proceedings of the NCM-30 Grain Marketing Symposium at Purdue University, North Central Regional Research Publication No. 176, January 1968, p. 16.

[2]Lloyd Besant, Dana Kellerman, and Gregory Monroe, eds., *Grains,* Board of Trade of the City of Chicago, 1977, p. 58.

[3]Heid, op. cit., p. 17.

[4]Besant, op. cit., p. 66.

the ability to move grain quickly to the final position when needed. Thus, subterminal and river elevators have a year-round demand for their services.[5]

Terminal elevators refer to establishments that receive over one-half of their supply of grain from other elevators. Terminal elevators are located in major terminal markets and railroad centers such as Chicago, Kansas City, Minneapolis, Hutchinson, Des Moines, Enid, and Fort Worth. Certain of these markets, such as Chicago, Minneapolis, and Kansas City provide a futures market as well as a cash market for grain.[6]

Terminal elevators provide many types of marketing functions, such as assembly, storage pricing, grading, conditioning, and financing. They vary in capacity from a few hundred thousand bushels to more than 50 million bushels. However, it is the location of the elevator rather than its physical size that determines its classification.

Terminal elevator operators buy grain from cash grain merchants, subterminal elevators, river elevators, and country elevators. Depending on the location and facilities of the terminal elevator, grain may be received by truck, rail, barge, or boat. Grain is sold from the terminal elevator to processors, millers, distillers, feed manufacturers, exporters, and occasionally to elevators in other parts of the country.[7]

Much as for country elevators, terminal elevators are classified according to ownership: independent, cooperative, and integrated. Independent and cooperative elevators are similar in organization to country elevators. An integrated terminal elevator company may own line country elevators, river houses, and subterminals, and be engaged in exporting, leasing rail equipment, and may also own barges and boats. While overall policy, such as financing of the integrated terminal company may be provided by the home office, day-to-day merchandising activities are carried on by the individual manager at each terminal location.[8]

Terminal agencies refer to business organizations that facilitate the assembly and distribution of grain but do not have physical facilities for handling grain. Terminal agencies may or may not take title to grain. Included among these agencies are wholesale dealers, car lot receivers, commission merchants, and brokers.[9]

Port terminals refer to establishments that receive over half of their supply of grain from other elevators, and have facilities to load

[5]L.D. Schnake and James L. Driscoll, *Number and Physical Characteristics of Grain Elevators,* U.S. Department of Agriculture, Economics, Statistics, and Cooperatives Service-22, May 1978, p. 2.

[6]Walter J. Wills, "Organization of the Grain Industry," *An Introduction to Grain Marketing,* The Interstate Printers and Publishers, Inc., Danville, Ill., 1972, p. 29.

[7]Besant, op. cit., p. 75.

[8]Ibid.

[9]Heid, op. cit., p. 17.

oceangoing ships. The major marketing functions performed by port terminals include buying, selling, short-time storage, financing, risk taking, and assembling and blending grain in shipload volumes to accommodate the specification of foreign grain buyers. Examples of typical locations of port elevator facilities are Chicago, Duluth-Superior, Toledo, Philadelphia, Baltimore, Norfolk, Mississippi River locations, Gulf Coast locations, Columbia River, Puget Sound, San Francisco-Oakland, and Stockton.

Economic Integration of Marketing Agencies.   Marketing channels have changed in recent years because of economic integration. Economic integration is the process of combining the management function of two or more economic activities and may be thought of as a fusion or coordination of business units. Integration tends to reduce the length of marketing channels and to increase the economic control, or marketing power, of those firms involved. Market power is achieved by producers or marketing agencies banding together through economic integration for the purposes of achieving a common objective. Like most other processes, economic integration exists in varying degrees.

Integration may take place in the form of ownership or contractual agreements. It may be established by acquisition, merger or consolidation, and by coordination, cooperation, or contract. The degree to which economic integration exists depends on the advantages of integration and the human motivation of management.

Vertical integration occurs when a firm combines activities that are unlike but are sequentially related to those that it currently performs.[10] Vertical integration can then be interpreted as the process of combining management functions by moving forward or backward in the marketing channel.

Forward integration refers to a business tie with another firm that is located one step closer to the final marketing stage, while backward integration refers to a business tie with another firm that is located one step closer to the source of the raw product or a business tie with a farm operation itself.[11]

Horizontal integration occurs when a single management gains control either through voluntary contract or through ownership over a series of firms performing similar activities at the same level in the production or marketing sequence.[12] Horizontal integration, then, is the process of combining the management function of two or more firms at the same level of the marketing channel. For example, if a processor wants to expand, but does not want to take on additional

[10]John W. Goodwin, *Agricultural Economics,* Reston Publishing Company, Reston, Va., 1977, p. 285.
[11]Heid, op. cit., p. 44.
[12]Goodwin, op. cit., p. 285.

marketing functions, another processing firm may be purchased. This may be accomplished by negotiating a contract to combine the management functions of these two or more firms without changing the legal ownership of the firm.[13]

In some cases firms will be involved in both horizontal and vertical integration. This is referred to as dual integration. Dual integration refers to a network, or combination, of both vertical and horizontal integration within one company. Decisions leading to involvement in vertical integration, horizontal integration, or both may be based on expected technological gain. Decisions to integrate may also be based on increased efficiency in coordinating market decisions, the gain of market power over competitors, more control over production resource supply, improved financial position, greater use of managerial know-how, or simply the drive for power and control.

Cash Grain Merchandisers

The term cash grain merchandiser, or cash merchant, describes any person or firm dealing in the buying and selling of a cash commodity. A cash grain merchandiser operates in the cash market, acting as both a buyer and a seller of grain, with margins or spreads in the price or basis generating that person's income.[14]

The cash grain merchant may locate in a deficit grain-producing area, or in a surplus grain-producing area, buying grain in the surplus area to supply to the deficit area. The cash grain merchandiser in surplus areas operates between the country elevator, exporter, processor, miller, and other buyers of grain.

One of three types of cash grain merchandisers is the country merchandiser. A country merchandiser is generally located in a rural area, buying grain from country elevators and selling it to terminal markets, to grain processors, and to exporters. The country merchandiser takes title to the purchased grain but does not operate storage facilities. Shipping instructions are given to the country elevator for shipment of the grain. The operation consists primarily of making bids and offers and giving shipping instructions by telephone. A merchandiser seldom sees the grain that is bought and sold.

Another type of cash grain merchandiser is the terminal market merchandiser. This merchandiser is located in terminal market areas, buying grain from country positions to be shipped to terminal markets such as Portland or Minneapolis. Like the country merchandiser, the terminal market merchandiser takes title to the grain that is bought but does not operate storage facilities.

The third type of cash grain merchandiser is the terminal elevator

---

[13]Rawlins, op. cit., p. 152.
[14]Besant, op. cit., p. 69.

company, involved in similar merchandising operations as other cash grain merchandisers, which also operates terminal and subterminal elevators for storage as well as merchandising.[15]

Commission merchants are also merchandisers, but they differ from cash grain merchandisers in that they do not take title to grain. They function strictly as agents, bringing the buyer and the seller of the grain together. When terms and conditions of the sale are mutually agreed on, the brokerage service has been completed. Commission fees earned by the broker are usually paid by the seller of the grain. Commission brokers are important in the marketing of fats and oils (lard, soybean oil, cottonseed oil, etc.), mill feeds, protein meals, and by-products of various processing operations.[16]

Since country elevators must compete with other country elevators for farmers' grain, the most important service performed by the cash grain merchandiser is in locating the highest bidder for country grain. Country elevators find it useful to utilize the services of cash grain merchandisers in order to compare bids of alternative outlets for grain, even though some country elevators sell directly to processors or terminal elevators.[17]

The cash grain merchandiser specializes in meeting the needs of country elevator managers. This includes providing shippers with information on the availability of grain, arranging shipment of grain, financing, and the outlook for cash and futures prices. The cash grain merchandiser may also handle their futures market transactions for country elevator managers.[18]

GRAIN STORAGE

Individual grains are harvested during a relatively short period of time but are consumed at a rather uniform rate throughout the year. It is storage that makes grain available at the desired time. Storage is the marketing function that matches production patterns with consumption patterns over time.

The Location and Types of Storage Facilities
Storage facilities are located at all stages in the grains complex: on farms; off farms at country, subterminal, terminal, and port elevators; and at milling and processing plants.

Grain is temporarily stored in piles on the ground when adequate local storage facilities are not available to hold the grain. The grain is

[15]Ibid.
[16]Ibid.
[17]Ibid.
[18]Ibid.

kept on the ground until adequate transportation facilities are available to move it to storage at other points in the grain marketing system. The losses from short-term ground storage are usually small but nevertheless greater than if proper storage were available.

On-farm facilities include woodbins, round metal bins, specially lined silos for storage of high-moisture grain, corncribs, and flat storage facilities, which may include machinery sheds for temporary storage. On-farm storage serves two purposes. It preserves grain for later use as feed on the farm where produced and it holds the grain for later sale. Most wheat and soybeans fall into the latter practice. Corn and other feed grains are stored on farms for both purposes.

On-farm and off-farm storage capacity for 1960 to 1980 is given in Table 3-1. January 1 on-farm grain stocks are used as a proxy to indicate relative on-farm storage capacity.

Off-farm storage facilities are usually referred to as elevators whether they are country elevators, subterminal or terminal elevators, or storage facilities of grain processors. Elevators are so called because the grain is elevated and poured into bins or transport vehicles.

Elevator facilities include older, steel-covered wood country elevators, large round steel bins, silos of steel or concrete construction, and flat storage. Flat storage facilities are built wider and lower than conventional silos with minimal handling equipment to provide low-cost storage space for grain. Sometimes flat storages are simply a shed-type roof over a floor connected to the side of an elevator. Flat storage facilities are built to provide relatively low-cost storage space during periods of grain surplus and expected low turnover rate. Since power shovels, augers and/or mobile power loaders may be required to move the grain from flat storage, such storage space is used to provide safe storage for grain not expected to be handled or moved immediately.

Grain Storage Capacity

Yields of corn, wheat, and sorghum have increased significantly and rapidly since World War II. The period of harvesting has been shortened with adoption of high-speed harvesting equipment. These developments have called for increased storage volume not only for increased production but also to meet peak demand.

High moisture harvesting of corn, sorghum, and soybeans and field shelling of corn since World War II have led to the development of storage-drying-cleaning systems. Storage of ear corn in cribs has greatly decreased and storage of shelled corn in bins has greatly increased.

Grain storage capacity is needed for each year's production and carry-over stocks. In addition, storage space is needed for "pipeline" stocks of processors, and storage space is needed by grain handlers for receiving, blending, cleaning, conditioning, and loading operations. This latter space is often termed working space.

Table 3-1   Off-Farm Grain Storage Capacity and
On-Farm Grain Stocks, 1960 to 1981
(thousands of bushels)

Year	Rated Off-Farm Storage Capacity	On-Farm Stocks as of January 1[a,b]
1960	c	4,585,732
1961	4,993,280	4,847,472
1962	5,472,160	4,665,368
1963	5,471,230	4,592,394
1964	5,438,150	4,848,071
1965	5,435,160	4,268,736
1966	5,463,160	4,844,925
1967	5,496,190	4,631,338
1968	5,446,100	5,204,624
1969	5,538,980	5,405,744
1970	5,636,990	5,557,920
1971	5,696,738	5,788,164
1972	5,694,880	5,603,721
1973	5,809,760	5,668,808
1974	5,884,620	5,245,927
1975	5,918,230	4,124,369
1976	6,102,880	5,062,780
1977	6,310,307	5,142,371
1978	6,635,420	6,256,973
1979	6,984,960	7,049,744
1980	7,090,480	7,490,916
1981	7,183,530	6,289,035

[a]Includes wheat, rye, corn, oats, barley, sorghum, and soybeans.
[b]On-farm storage capacity was first reported in 1978. These data are presented as a proxy for minimum on-farm storage capacity.
[c]Data not reported prior to 1961.

Source: U.S. Department of Agriculture, Grain Stocks, various issues.

Historically, grain storage capacity in the United States has adjusted with the trend of increased production. Changing volumes of carry-over have, at times, resulted in either shortages of space or excess space. Government programs have played a significant role in the steady expansion of storage capacity, especially at the farm level. They have been used since 1933 to stimulate expanded storage in conjunction with crop loan programs. In 1938, the Commodity Credit Corporation (CCC) acquired its first storage bins to handle corn in default of government loans. Farm storage was encouraged in 1941 by an advance CCC payment of seven cents per bushel to farmers to construct or repair farm facilities for storage of grain placed under loan.

Government programs also played a significant role in providing off-farm capacity during and after World War II. CCC-owned bin capacity reached 300 million bushels in 1942 with the construction of 100 million bushels capacity of prefabricated wooden bins that year. This capacity was reduced to 45 million bushels during World War II by sales to farmers and use as building materials to relieve a general shortage.

Bins were purchased by the CCC again from 1949 through 1957 except for 1952 and 1953. By June 20, 1957, CCC-owned bin capacity peaked at 990 million bushels. All CCC-owned bins were sold to farmers or private individuals by the mid-1970s. Most of the bins remained in use for grain storage.

Storage facility loans to increase storage capacity were made available to farmers by the CCC, at the direction of Congress, starting in 1949. This program continued until 1962. In 1977, the government again initiated storage facility loans to farmers. Favorable interest rates were offered to encourage program participation, and the programs were well received by farmers.

Government programs to increase storage capacity were directed toward private investment in off-farm commercial storage facilities in the 1950s. Off-farm storage capacity expanded significantly during this period. Government actions to stimulate building off-farm storage capacity included providing occupancy guarantee programs for commercial grain facilities, amending the Farm Credit Act to permit the Bank for Cooperatives to loan up to 80 percent of the cost of newly constructed agricultural storage facilities by farmer cooperatives, authorizing Small Business Administration loans for the purpose of constructing grain storage facilities, and amending the Internal Revenue Code of 1939 to permit rapid depreciation (20 percent per year) of newly erected storage facilities.

At times, the government has also provided temporary storage for grain: from 1949 to 1951 and 1954 to 1962 through CCC lease of Maritime Commission ships and leasing of military buildings in 1950 and 1951.

Government action to stimulate increased grain storage capacity has not been the only factor in expanded U.S. grain storage capacity. World population continues to increase. Many developed countries are continuing to increase meat consumption and decrease human cereal consumption. Net gains in grain consumption have occurred from animal feeding. In addition, there have been substitutions among cereal grains, for example, the dietary shift from rice to wheat in Japan. Developing country governments, in many instances, have taken action to improve the diets of their population through the use of cereals. These factors and others have increased world demand for grains.

In response to these new and changing demands, storage capacity was increased accordingly.

The export market has become a major market for U.S. grains. Efficient operators in the U.S. system have seen profit opportunities in this development and have responded to the economic incentive. Economic incentives associated with the export market have led to the expansion and greater utilization of grain storage space required for orderly foreign marketing. The majority of U.S. grain storage capacity is in areas of concentrated grain production, particularly in the Corn Belt states and wheat and sorghum states in the Plains. Since the dramatic expansion of exports in the early 1970s, the greatest expansion in storage capacity has occurred in areas of heaviest production density, particularly the Corn Belt states of Iowa, Indiana, and Illinois.

Government actions, such as the soybean embargo of 1973 and the partial embargo of U.S. grains to Russia in 1980, create marketing uncertainties that have also influenced some farmers to build additional storage to "weather unexpected marketing storms."

Size of farming operations has increased significantly in the United States since World War II. Many operators in their desire for more control over the physical product have taken on increased marketing responsibility. Farm storage capacity has been increased to gain the control desired.

Typically, storage capacity of grain processors has tended to increase at the rate of industry growth. Most processors have storage space and working space to accommodate a 30- to 45-day inventory of raw materials. Most processors also have space, usually flat storage, for processed products. This space, however, is not included in government grain storage statistics. Yet it is a part of the total pipeline, serving the function of storing grain and grain products as they move through the grain marketing channels. In recent years, storage capacity of wet corn processors has increased faster than for most other processors. This unique trend is expected to continue for several years because of technological changes in corn sweetener production.

Although grain storage capacity has expanded at all stages in the U.S. grains complex in recent years, the greatest growth in capacity has been near the point of production. The closer that storage is to the point of production, the greater is the flexibility in making final market choices.

Data on off-farm capacity have been reported annually since 1961 by the USDA. The first survey of on-farm storage capacity was reported by the USDA for 1978 and revealed that on-farm storage exceeded off-farm storage, the ratio being approximately 1.5 to 1.

Costs of Storage

The costs of grain storage, regardless of the position of the storage in the marketing channel, may be classed as fixed and variable. *Fixed costs* must be met whether or not grain is stored. *Variable costs* are incurred only if grain is stored.

Fixed costs are related to the storage facilities themselves as a result of ownership. Each item included in this category relate to the storage facilities and not the grain or oilseed in storage. They include depreciation, maintenance, interest on capital investment, insurance on structures and equipment, and property taxes.

Variable costs are related to the grain stored. They include insurance and taxes on grain stored, loss from quality deterioration, costs of quality maintenance, interest income on the grain investment foregone while the grain is in storage, labor, transportation expenses due to the storage operation, and costs of shrinkage.

The costs of grain storage vary depending on position in the grain marketing channel, the individual storage operation, the particular year, and general business conditions. Economies of size favor commercial off-farm elevators in grain drying and storage, however, on-farm drying and storage capacities are expanding more rapidly. Explanation of this phenomenon, which seemingly contradicts the least cost principle of economics, encompasses several factors that are mentioned in detail in the following section.

PRODUCER DECISION MAKING

Farmers' decisions concerning grain storage are basically (1) whether or not to store, (2) how much to store, (3) where to store, and (4) how long to store.

Seasonal price changes provide the incentive for storage, thus the first question involves a comparison of costs of storage with possible gains from a price rise later on. Differences in seasonal prices, however, present problems in selecting a marketing strategy. The ability to predict future short-term price disturbances and market response limits the success of any strategy to minimize risk and income variability or maximize average value received per bushel.

Factors that influence how much to store are needs for on-farm processing and feeding, distance to the elevator, and income tax management.

Where to store is a question with no absolute answer. Profitability of grain storage is not the same for all individuals in the grains complex. Each individual faces a unique set of circumstances. A farmer who does not already have farm storage capacity, has a weak equity position, and high capital requirements elsewhere in the operation, would be better off to not worry about on-farm storage.

On-farm storage affords the producer direct control over the physical commodity and gives farmers greater flexibility. It frees them from having to deal with only one local elevator, giving them time to shop around for the best bid. In some production areas, farmers can avoid waiting in line to unload at harvest time. By placing grain in farm storage bins the speed of harvest can be increased, so expensive farm machinery and equipment are not idled and valuable time is not wasted.

Government programs that offer farmers the option to store grain on the farm with specified storage rates, possibly in addition to other payments, may influence on-farm storage decisions. In some instances, off-farm storage charges may be higher than on-farm costs. This may be because of elevator operator uncertainty, and incomplete information on farmer response to price changes and the investment in on-farm facilities based on past elevator charges.

How long to store would normally be based on marketing strategy, and whether the added benefits exceed added storage costs. However, this marketing strategy may be influenced by government grain loan or reserve programs. If grain is stored under a government program, the conditions for release from storage will be specified, thus the storage time may be fixed or variable, depending on the specific program.

Quality Maintenance of Grain in Storage

Grain can be durable or highly perishable while it is being held in storage. Good storage practices can prevent quality deterioration by controlling moisture and temperature, and prevention of attack by insects, microorganisms, rodents, and birds. Durability of the stored grain can be promoted by using proper storage facilities and good storage practices. For quality maintenance, on-farm storage structures should do the following.[19]

Hold the grain without loss from leaks and spills.

Prevent rain, snow, or soil moisture from reaching the grain.

Protect grain from rodents, birds, objectionable odors, and theft.

Provide safety from fire and wind damage.

Permit effective treatment to prevent or control insect infestation.

Provide headroom over the binned grain for sampling, inspection, and ventilation.

Be easy to clean and inspect.

Be equipped with an aeration system to cool the grain, minimize moisture migration, facilitate fumigation, if needed, and limit insect development.

The ease or difficulty in achieving quality maintenance may begin with the farmer's selection of a given grain variety. Some varieties are more resistant to insects while in storage than others.

[19]Charles L. Storey, Roy D. Spiers, and Lyman S. Henderson, *Insect Control in Farm-Stored Grain*, USDA, Science and Education Administration, Farmers' Bulletin No. 2269, December 1979.

Upper limits on storage quality may be set during harvest. Inspection and cleaning of harvesting equipment prior to harvest will eliminate residues that contaminate newly harvested grain with insects and microorganisms. Chaff, weeds, weed seeds, and other foreign matter that affect grain drying and provide a good environment for insect and mold development in stored grain can be eliminated by proper combine adjustment. Proper combine adjustment will also minimize cracked and broken kernels that contribute to insect and mold problems, dustiness of grain, and ultimately to grain grade reduction.

Control of temperature and moisture in grain is a prerequisite to grain quality management. Harvesting grain as nearly as possible to a safe storage moisture level minimizes drying costs and storage losses. Harvesting grain too wet provides an environment for insect development and storage fungi invasion and development. Fungal spores can be distributed throughout the stored grain by migrating insects.

Management techniques that can reduce grain moisture for conventional storage include drying with or without heat, dryeration, aeration, stirring, or cooling. Use of acid preservatives, high-moisture storage facilities, and plastic covers may be used for high-moisture grain preservation.

Maximum moisture content for safe storage up to one year for aerated good quality grain is considered to be 14 percent for corn, 13 percent for wheat, and 12 percent for soybeans. For longer storage, the moisture content should be lower.

The proper application of insecticide during farm binning operations or later fumigation in conjunction with other good storage practices is an effective management practice to protect grain from insect damage for about one storage season.

Proper preparation of on-farm storage bins for newly harvested grains is a necessity for grain quality maintenance. All leftover grain should be removed: walls, ceiling, sills, ledges and floors should be thoroughly swept and sweepings destroyed; needed repairs should be made; walls should be treated inside and outside with an approved residual insecticide; and trash and litter should be removed from outside the bin area. Grain should be leveled and bin surfaces treated with an approved insecticide after binning is completed to help prevent insects from entering or feeding on the grain surface. Since grain temperature is a good indicator of grain condition, temperature should be checked at least once a month and more often during summer and early fall months when temperatures are conducive to insect development.

Temperature sensor cables installed in the storage bin provide an excellent means of temperature monitoring. A thermometer attached to a stick and inserted into the grain can also be used to measure temperature in farm bins.

Proper control of the two life-sustaining elements, temperature and moisture, is fundamental for stored grain quality maintenance. When grain temperature is over 60°F, checks should be made for insects and mold. If checks also reveal high moisture, grain may require drying to control or prevent mold growth. However, in both cases, control of temperature and moisture by aeration may be all that is necessary. If checks indicate the presence of insects, fumigation may be necessary. Fungi increase both temperature and moisture content by their growth. Temperatures of more than 60°F are required by most stored-grain insects to develop damaging populations. Many species require 70°F or higher temperatures.

Applicators are required to take special training and to be certified before they can purchase and use chemicals for grain fumigation, since the chemicals are classified as restricted pesticides by the Environmental Protection Agency. As a result of government regulation, it may be safer and more economical for some farmers to hire commercial applicators to fumigate.

The quality of grain received by a country elevator determines where it will be binned at the elevator. Moisture content, test weight, and dockage are usually checked before binning. Checks are also made for insect damage and live, stored-grain insects.

Grain may be sampled by several methods, not all of which are officially accepted by the USDA. Some elevators take samples by obtaining a random "coffee can" of grain from the top of the grain load or by inserting the can in the grain stream emptying from the delivery vehicle; some probe the grain using a mechanically or hand-operated probe; some use Pelicans, Ellis cups, or Woodside mechanical samplers; and some use diverter-type mechanical samplers installed to traverse the grain stream in the elevator. If diverter samplers are used they must be approved and operators licensed before the sample can be considered an official sample for official grades. The coffee can method and certain probing devices are not approved to obtain samples for official grades, yet these methods are often used both to determine the bin in which to store a lot of grain, and as a basis for making payment to the farmer.

Infrared reflectance devices became generally available in the decade of the 1970s and made possible for the first time rapid determination of protein, moisture, and oil content of grains. Elevators can use these devices advantageously in binning grain into homogenous lots excluding moisture variation and in other grain handling and load-out operations.

Moisture is highly variable, but not a serious problem as long as the moisture content is not too high and the grain is turned often, or aerated. It can vary as much as 4 percent within a few feet in a grain field. Such moisture variations continue to exist in any lot of grain, rail car, truck, or bargeload. Thus, it is difficult to obtain a precise moisture content reading for a large lot of grain since the moisture content of individual kernels in a sample varies, and precise segregation of grain by moisture content at the elevator is impossible because no elevator would have enough bins. As a result, an elevator bin may contain truckloads of grain of varying moisture contents. If the grain is properly handled, this variation presents no problem as the wet and dry grain will reach a moisture equilibrium within two or three days after being placed in storage. Temperature differences of the various loads will cause air currents and moisture movements in the grain. Spoutlines develop when grain is poured into an elevator. A spoutline is a core of fine particles that accumulates at the peak of the grain pile and fills the spaces between kernels as a bin fills. Whole kernels slide down the incline of the pile. The diameter of the core is proportional to bin width and the percentage of fines in the grain. The center of the core is a dense mass that impedes or may prevent air circulation or escape of heat in the grain.

Temperature cables or probes are necessary for regular checks on grain temperature in large commercial bins. Recording devices exist that allow readings to be recorded at various points in the grain mass automatically in the elevator office.

Prior to 1950, and the adoption of aeration, it was common practice in the elevator industry to "turn" grain as a part of quality maintenance programs. Turning is a process of emptying a grain bin, elevating the grain and rebinning and possibly blending with another bin. There was a certain amount of ventilation of the grain in the turning process as well as dilution or dispersal of trouble spots. This process was expensive in terms of equipment operation (particularly energy) and maintenance. It also increased the number of broken kernels and the dust content of grain. Turning creates dust, a concern in the grain industry because of its role in elevator fires and explosions, and its link to lung diseases in elevator employees. Consequently, turning grain as a routine quality control measure is now practiced mainly at older facilities where aeration systems have not been installed.

Once grain loses quality it can never be improved. However, poor quality grain and superior quality grain can be blended to raise the overall grade of the lots of grain. Whenever possible, elevator operators will blend so that the lots of grain meet the minimum of specific official grade. This practice permits such grain to move through marketing channels to end uses where quantities of lower quality grain are not objectionable. For the grain elevator manager, it is a profitable practice. However, this practice necessitates grain quality surveillance at all points in the grain marketing system to prevent quality decline, particularly from hidden insect infestation and storage fungi.

Finally, grain can be damaged in handling due to elevator equipment design and operation and speed of operations. Artificially dried corn is more subject to breakage in handling due to brittleness and stress cracks. The more times grain is handled, the more that breakage occurs and the more susceptible the grain is to deterioration.

WAREHOUSE REGULATIONS

Little thought to factors other than shelter from the elements may be given by farmers who store grain at public warehouses. Perhaps of greater importance, too little thought may be given to the qualifications of people who weigh, sample, or determine quality factors on which price will be determined. The farmer may have little, if any, knowledge about the financial responsibility of the warehouseman. Questions should be answered to the farmer's satisfaction concerning warehouse storage. Why are the products being placed in storage? What is expected to be returned? Is the warehouseman financially responsible? Does the warehouseman have adequate storage and handling facilities and competent employees to care for the grain while in storage? Will a warehouse receipt be given and, if so, what will be its terms? Will it show the correct weight and grade? Will the warehouse receipt constitute a definite, enforceable contract? If the warehouseman does not want to give a warehouse receipt, should grain be entrusted to him or her? How much will it cost to store? What are the terms of the warehouseman's tariff? Is the warehouseman bonded, by whom, for the benefit of whom, in what amount, and with whom is the bond filed? Is the warehouseman subject to supervision, and the warehouse and contents subject to inspection by the appropriate government agency? What is the supervision?[20]

The need to protect the interests of producers and other grain owners who store grain with public warehousemen was the driving force that brought state and federal government units to regulate grain warehouses many years ago. States have been regulating public grain storage for over 130 years and the federal government since 1916.

Warehouse Licensing

The regulation of public grain storage begins with operating license requirements. The license is granted to a firm with its owners and responsible officers identified, thus a transfer of ownership of storage facilities requires a new license to operate the same facilities.

There are two types of licenses, state and federal. Many states have laws requiring licenses while federal licenses are voluntary.

License requirements vary from state to state. Generally, states require new application for licensing each year. Bonding and insurance requirements vary from state to state. Inspection of facilities prior

[20]U.S. Department of Agriculture, *The Yearbook of Agriculture—1954, Marketing.*

to licensing depends on the state. Reports required and reporting frequency are also variable. Inspection of operations after licensing depends on state regulations.

To qualify for a federal license under the U.S. Warehouse Act, a warehouseman must have a suitable and properly equipped warehouse, determined to be so by a review of facts gathered on an inspection by a federal warehouse examiner. The warehouseman must submit a complete current financial report on a prescribed form, and have a good business reputation. A minimum net worth of $10,000 is required, computed according to elevator capacity.[21] A suitable bond is required with the amount based on licensed storage capacity and net worth between $20,000 and $500,000, except under specified circumstances. A new bond is required each year after licensing.

Qualified personnel, with knowledge of how to weigh, inspect, and grade grain are required. Inspectors and weighers must be licensed under the Warehouse Act. Their license is valid only for carrying out the requirements of the U.S. Warehouse Act, not for complying with the U.S. Grain Standards Act.

WAREHOUSE RECEIPTS

Federally licensed warehousemen must have adequate equipment to properly weigh and grade grain. They must post a tariff or schedule of charges for receiving, loading out, storage, insurance, conditioning, and all other warehouse services. The tariff must be furnished to the USDA and is subject to disapproval. Initial inspection and license fees must be paid at the time of application.

Federally licensed warehouses are monitored by unannounced warehouse examinations, as often as twice a year. Such examinations are also common in some states. The office, books, records, papers, and accounts relating to the warehouse, as well as the contents of the warehouse, are examined. When minor discrepancies or adverse conditions are found, the warehouseman is required to bring operations into compliance within a specified time period. Serious violations may lead to license suspension. Improprieties in connection with warehouse receipts, inspection, or weighing, carry penalties of imprisonment and fines.

Grain in storage is much like money in a bank. The depositor has a legal right in both cases to get back in kind and value the thing deposited. If grain is stored with identity to be preserved, the owner is entitled to get back the identical product stored.

When money is deposited at a bank, the bank is required to give the depositor a deposit slip. And if the bank teller fails to give a deposit

---

[21]Warehouse Division (Agricultural Marketing Service), U.S. Warehouse Act, as Amended—Regulations for Grain Warehouses, USDA, January 1980.

slip to the depositor, the depositor will not likely forget to demand a copy. However, when farmers deliver grain to an elevator they may not be offered a warehouse receipt for their grain and they may not think about the receipt unless they want to borrow money on the grain: then it may be too late. As a matter of good business practice, warehouse receipts should be demanded anytime the ownership of delivered grain has not been transferred. Also, the owner of the grain should see a copy of the warehouse tariff. The tariff, or schedule of charges, sets forth charges for specified warehouse services.

A warehouse receipt is formal acknowledgment by a warehouseman of grain received for storage. A scale ticket, which gives weight, and may give such other information as test weight, moisture, protein, and grade, is not formal acknowledgment of receipt for storage and is not a legal document of title. Scale tickets (Figure 3-1) and warehouse receipts (Figure 3-2) are not synonymous and should not be confused. The following items are typically stated on the face of a warehouse receipt: location of the warehouse in which the grain is stored, date of issue of the receipt, the rate of storage charges, description of the grain (quantity, grade, kind), facts of ownership, any lien(s) which the warehouseman claims, consecutive number of the receipt, and the signature of the warehouseman.

The warehouse receipt may provide for delivery to (1) a specified person, (2) a specified person "or his order," or (3) to the "bearer." The latter two forms are considered negotiable and can be transferred with all rights of property from one party to another without notice to the warehouseman. All rights to property of the original depositor go with the transfer.

The Uniform Commercial Code, adopted by the American Bar Association in 1952, and by all states except Louisiana, supersedes the Uniform Warehouse Receipts Act that was adopted voluntarily in all states to facilitate the easy transfer of warehouse receipts, which in turn facilitates financing and risk-bearing functions in grain marketing. Under the Uniform Commercial Code, a warehouse receipt is a certificate of title for agricultural products stored in a warehouse. Some states require registration of warehouse receipts in lieu of or in addition to sending a copy of the warehouse receipt to state authorities.[22]

---

[22]The bankruptcy proceedings in 1981 of an Arkansas firm with grain elevators in Arkansas and Missouri brought national attention to grain warehouse receipts. Delay in delivery of grain, or payment for grain stored in a Missouri elevator owned by the firm, was clouded by two issues. The primary issue was conflict in jurisdiction: Did a state regulatory agency in Missouri or the bankruptcy court in Arkansas have jurisdiction? The ruling was that the bankruptcy court had jurisdiction. A subsidiary issue was, "Was a warehouse receipt a title document?" Legislation has been proposed by both houses of Congress (S-1365, passed by the Senate) with the main intent to establish that grain held in storage for somebody else is not a part of an elevator's assets and should be promptly distributed to the owners in species or in kind.

FARMERS GRAIN STORAGE
ANYTOWN, USA

No.

INBOUND

Load of ____________ Date ____________

From ____________

Gross ____________ lbs. Test ____________ Moist. ____________ Grade ____________

Price ____________ Per Bu. / Per Cwt. Amt. $ ____________

Tare ____________ lbs.

Driver ____________ On ☐ Off ☐

Net ____________ lbs. Bushels ____________ Weigher ____________

Approved by Any State G.I.D.

Figure 3-1. A typical scale ticket.

The contents of the federal warehouse receipt are essentially those set out in the former Uniform Warehouse Receipts Act and now covered in the Uniform Commercial Code. In markets requiring registration of warehouse receipts, all federally licensed warehouses in that market comply with the local regulation. The federal warehouse receipt is uniformly dependable and acceptable in financial circles as reliable collateral for loans. Bankers who deal with warehouse receipts from several states prefer receipts from federally licensed facilities over state-licensed facilities because of uniform administration of federally licensed warehouses.

LICENSE NUMBER

RECEIPT

The undersigned Warehouseman Claims A Lien on Said Grain For Charges and Liabilities As Follows:

LICENSED AND BONDED UNDER THE UNITED STATES WAREHOUSE ACT

ORIGINAL NEGOTIABLE WAREHOUSE RECEIPT FOR GRAIN

RECEIVED FROM: ____________ OF ____________

For storage in the above-named warehouse in the course of Interstate or Foreign Commerce, grain of the quantity, kind, and grade described herein for which this receipt is issued subject to the United States Warehouse Act, the regulations thereunder for grain warehousemen, and the terms of this contract. Grade, according to U.S. official standards, and weight are as determined by an inspector and weigher licensed under said act. Said grain is by the undersigned warehouseman against loss or damage by fire, lightning, inherent explosion, tornado, cyclone, and windstorm unless otherwise stated hereon. Said grain is accepted upon condition that the depositor or holder of this receipt shall demand delivery not later than one year from the date of this receipt. The undersigned warehouseman is not the owner of said grain either solely, jointly, or in common with others unless otherwise stated hereon. Upon return of this receipt properly indorsed and payment of the warehouseman's lein claimed hereon, said grain or grain of the same or better grade will be delivered to the above named depositor or his ORDER.

Elevation Chgs. Prepaid Per Bu. Date Storage Pd. Through

Date Issued	Kind of Grain	Grain & Sub Class	Dock. %	Lbs. of Gr. Incl. Dock.	Gross Bushels	Net Pounds	Net Bushels	In @ ¢	Out @ ¢	Mo.	Day	Yr.

ISSUED AT

BY ____________

Handling and other accrued charges according to the tariff of the company. Full amount of charges furnished on request.

The Issuance Of A Fraudulent Receipt, Or Illegal Conversion Or Removal Of The Products Represented By This Receipt Is Punishable By A $10,000 Fine Or Imprisonment For 10 Years Or Both.

SUPPLEMENTAL INFORMATION *For purposes of the Uniform Grain Storage Agreement only (Not part of Warehouse Receipt)*										Date Received			Received By			FOR CCC USE ONLY			
Test Wt. Lbs.	Moisture %	Protein % Splits or Sounds	TD %	HD %	FM %	Shr. Brok. %	Tot. Def. %	Other Quality Factors	Car Initial And No.	Mo.	Day	Yr.	Trk.	Brg.	Rail	Chgs.	Type Stg.	Area	Loan/Purchase No.

Figure 3-2. A warehouse receipt.

Commodity Credit Corporation Influence on Warehousemen

Government influence on warehousemen includes requirements of CCC storage contracts with warehousemen. The statutory obligation of the CCC, as owner of and lender on large quantities of grain from time to time, has led to a body of rules that must be met by warehousemen storing grain under CCC ownership or loan.

The contractual arrangement which the warehouseman enters into with CCC to store grain is known as a Uniform Grain Storage Agreement (UGSA), Rice is covered by the Uniform Rice Storage Agreement (URSA).

The CCC does not license warehouses that store CCC-managed grain but it does require compliance with its contract terms that are comparable to those for licensing in many states. A warehouse must be examined by a person designated by CCC before being approved by CCC for storage or handling of grain.

The basic standards for CCC warehouse approval require a net worth that is the greater of $25,000, or 10 cents per bushel times the maximum storage capacity that the elevator can accommodate in the customary manner. The net worth need not exceed $250,000. If the calculated net worth requirement is greater than $25,000, any deficiency between $25,000 and the calculated minimum can be satisfied by bonds acceptable to and meeting CCC requirements, or by cash and negotiable securities, or with a legal liability insurance policy, providing the policy contains a clause or rider making the policy payable to CCC.

The warehouseman must also have sufficient funds available to meet ordinary operating expenses, maintain accurate records of inventory and operations, and use only prenumbered warehouse receipts and scale tickets. In addition, a work force and equipment must be available to complete loadout within approximately 30 working days for that quantity of grain for which the warehouse is or may be approved under a UGSA, and within approximately 90 working days for that quantity of rice for which the warehouseman is or may be approved under the URSA. The warehouseman, officials, or supervisory exmployees in charge of the warehouse operations must have experience, organization, technical qualifications, and skills to provide proper storage and handling services. These personnel must also have a satisfactory record of integrity, judgment, and performance and no prior suspensions or debarment under CCC regulations.

The warehouse must be of sound construction, in a good state of repair, and adequately equipped for grain handling and storage operations. The warehouse must be under the control of the contracting warehouseman at all times, and not subject to greater than normal risk of fire, flood, or other hazards. Adequate and operable firefighting equipment for the type of warehouse and grain must be available.

Also, a warehouseman with a Certificate of Competency issued by the Small Business Administration will be accepted by CCC for basic standards pertaining to net worth, operating funding, adequate work force and equipment, qualification of personnel, and suitability of the storage facilities. If a warehouseman with the required minimum $25,000 net worth fails (or if the warehouse fails) to meet one or more of the CCC standards, the warehouse may be approved if CCC determines the warehouse services are needed and satisfactory protection can be provided for the grain. Additional bond coverage will be prescribed by CCC in such cases that must be made by CCC-approved instruments.[23]

Payment for storage and handling services of CCC grains was made according to set schedules of payment until July 1975. These schedules were adjusted periodically to reflect changes in costs. Since July 1975, CCC has used an offer-rate system that introduced flexibility into payment for storage and handling services.

CCC requires that U.S. grain standards be used to establish the quality of grain received. States generally require warehousemen to accept grain in storable condition up to licensed house capacity. Under the UGSA, however, the warehouseman is not obligated to accept any specific quantity of CCC-managed grain.

Summary

Storage is the marketing function that matches production patterns with consumption patterns over time.

Grain storage facilities are located on farms and off farms. The types of on-farm grain storage facilities include woodbins, round metal bins, specially lined silos used for high-moisture grain storage, corncribs, and flat storage facilities that may include machinery sheds when needed. Off-farm storage facilities, referred to as elevators, include steel-covered wood elevators, large round steel bins, silos of steel or concrete construction, and flat storage.

Grain storage capacity is needed for each year's production and for carry-over stocks. Storage space is also needed for working stocks and for receiving, blending, cleaning, conditioning, and loading operations. U.S. grain storage capacity has increased with the trend of production. Government programs have been used quite effectively to stimulate increases in both on-farm and off-farm capacity.

A well-built, well-prepared storage facility does not guarantee sound quality grain. Grain must be properly conditioned and checked regularly to maintain its quality. Temperature and moisture are basic

---

[23]U.S. Department of Agriculture, *Standards for Approval of Warehouses for Grain, Rice, Dry Edible Beans, and Seed,* Commodity Credit Corporation Handbook I-IM, Part 1421—Grain Warehouse Standards.

elements of life that must be controlled in stored grain to prevent loss of quality from insects and molds.

A sound storage facility may protect grain from physical deterioration or loss, but safe grain storage is more than protection of the physical commodity. Safe storage also protects the owner's investment in the grain. The warehouse receipt, like a bank deposit slip, is formal acknowledgment of receipt of a deposit. Warehouse receipts, other than those made out for delivery to a specified person, are considered negotiable and can be transferred with all rights of property from one party to another. Warehouse receipts should always be demanded when grain is deposited in a public warehouse. Similarly, warehouse receipts should not be confused with scale tickets that are not negotiable, are not formal acknowledgment of receipt and do not transfer any property rights.

As farming operations continue to increase in size, and farmers become more marketing conscious, on-farm storage capacity will increase relative to off-farm storage capacity.

Finally, it is likely that the need for grain storage in the United States will increase as world population grows and the demand for cereals increases.

Selected References

Besant, Lloyd, Dana Kellerman, and Gregory Monroe, eds., *Grains,* Board of Trade of the City of Chicago, Chicago, Ill., 1977.

Carr, Camilla A., Keith E. Jackson, Darlene Logsdon, and David R. Miller, *Grain Elevator Bankruptcies in the U.S.: 1974 Through 1979,* Illinois Legislative Council Memorandum File 9-197, March 1981.

Christensen, Clyde E., *Storage of Cereal Grains and Their Products,* American Association of Cereal Chemists, Inc., St. Paul, Minn., 1974.

Commodity Credit Corporation, *Standards for Approval of Warehouses for Grain, Rice, Dry Edible Beans, and Seed,* USDA, Handbook I-IM, Part 1421—Grain Warehouse Standards, Washington, D.C.

Goodwin, John W., *Agricultural Economics,* Reston Publishing Company, Reston, Va., 1977.

Harris, Troy G. and John Minor, *Grain Handling and Storage,* Ag Press, Manhattan, Kan., 1979.

Heid, Walter G., Jr., "Grain Marketing—A General Description," *Marketing Grain,* Proceedings of the NCM-30 Grain Marketing Symposium at Purdue University, Lafayette, North Central Regional Research Publication No. 176, January 1968.

Hill, Lowell D., and P. J. Van Bickland, "Grain Marketing," *Advances in Cereal Science and Technology,* American Association of Cereal Chemists, Inc., St. Paul, Minn., 1976.

Rawlins, N. Omri, *Introduction to Agribusiness,* Prentice-Hall, Inc., Englewood Cliffs, N.J., 1980.

Schnake, L. D. and James L. Driscoll, *Number and Physical Characteristics of Grain Elevators,* ESCS, USDA, Agricultural Economics Report No. 22, Washington, D.C., May 1978.

Sinha, R. N. and W. E. Muir, eds., *Grain Storage: Part of a System,* AVI Publishing Company, Inc., Westport, Conn., 1973.

Sorenson, L. Orlo and Donald Anderson, *The Marketing Operations of the Commodity Credit Corporation Through 1962,* North Central Regional Research Bulletin No. 167, North Dakota State University, Fargo, September 1965.

Storey, Charles L., Roy D. Spiers, and Lyman S. Henderson, *Insect Control in Farm-Stored Grain,* USDA, Science and Education Administration, Farmers' Bulletin No. 2269, Washington, D.C., December 1979.

U.S. Department of Agriculture, *Yearbook of Agriculture—1954, Marketing,* U.S. Government Printing Office, Washington, D.C.

U.S. General Accounting Office, *More Can be Done to Protect Depositors at Federally Examined Grain Warehouses,* CED-81-112, Washington, D.C., June 19, 1981.

Warehouse Division (Agricultural Marketing Service), *U.S. Warehouse Act as Amended—Regulations for Grain Warehouses,* USDA, Washington, D.C., January 1980.

Wills, Walter J., *An Introduction to Grain Marketing,* Interstate Printers and Publishers, Inc., Danville, Ill., 1972.

Working, Holbrook, "The Theory of Price of Storage," *American Economic Review,* Vol. 39, No. 5, December 1949.

GRAIN TRANSPORTATION

GRAIN TRANSPORTATION* **CHAPTER 4**

Transportation is an integral part of the marketing system for grains. Movement is an essential function of the system but, in addition, costs associated with movement help to determine geographic price relationships, availability of markets, and locations of production, processing, and storage.

The transportation system is used to move goods from locations of less intense need to locations of greater need. If sufficient buying power exists in the areas of greater need, market value of goods will be greater at the destination site than at the origin, hence market value is increased by transport. Demand for transportation is thus derived from the demand for commodities at locations other than where they are produced. Market price at destination must be enough higher than at origin to offset the cost of transportation for the movement to be rational in a profit-maximizing market economy. Greater usefulness of the product, as reflected by a higher price at the destination, is the sense in which place utility is created.

Creation of time utility is also credited to transportation because of elapsed time in moving from origin to destination. However, time utility is a by-product of transportation and not a primary product. Occasionally, slower means of transport and circuitous routings are selected to keep goods in transit a longer period of time in order to avoid costly static storage. But such deliberate creation of time utility through storage in transport vehicles only shifts the burden of storage to transport firms and may increase the real cost of storage.

THE DOMESTIC TRANSPORTATION SYSTEM

The U.S. domestic transportation system includes five major modes or types of transport: railway, highway, inland waterway, pipeline, and airway. Domestic transportation of grain and grain products principally uses railways, highways, and inland waterways. Each mode of transport has unique cost and service dimensions largely determined by varying characteristics of system components, that is, differences in

*Orlo L. Sorenson, Professor, Department of Agricultural Economics, Kansas State University, Manhattan, Kan.

way (highway, waterway, railway), in terminals, and in vehicles (trucks, barges, or trains).

System Components

Ways.   Highways are the most ubiquitous of the three principal grain transportation modes. In 1981, there were approximately 3.8 million miles of roads and streets in the United States, including the 42,000-mile national system of interstate highways. The quality of roads varies throughout the system. Rural roads may be low surface with low weight-limit bridges allowing passage of small trucks or farm-trailer loads only. High-surface roads allow larger loads and continuous vehicle movements where highway entry and exit are controlled in a way that avoids intersecting traffic. All highways have size and weight limits that control maximum vehicle dimensions and vehicle weights. Weight density of whole grain and carrying capacities of trucks normally permit grain loads that exceed legal weight limitations of highways.

Railway mileage in the United States has declined from its maximum of 254,000 miles in 1916 to under 190,000 miles in 1981, and continued decline is likely as unprofitable lines are abandoned. Railways are not of uniform quality, with significant portions of rail lines having serious weight and speed limitations because of neglected roadbed, bridge, and track repair. Portions of the system were not built to carry gross rail car weights associated with movement of fully loaded covered-hopper cars. Other portions of rail line will carry trainloads of hopper cars at high speeds without difficulty.

Waterways are, of course, limited to developed and maintained navigation channels on rivers, canals and intracoastal waterways. The total length of navigable waterways in the United States (excluding open water navigation on the Great Lakes) with a 9-foot channel depth or greater is 15,675 miles. Waterways with a 6- to 9-foot channel depth provide an additional 3516 miles of navigable water.

Waterway depth and navigation characteristics cause waterway carrying capacity to vary significantly by waterway segment. Standard grain barges (195 by 35 feet) can load approximately 5485 bushels per foot of grain depth. At 7-foot grain depth, a standard barge will carry 38,395 bushels. A barge with 10-foot grain depth will load 54,850 bushels.

The St. Lawrence River-Great Lakes Seaway system permits ocean vessels to load grain at Great Lakes ports as far west as Duluth, on the western tip of Lake Superior—a distance of about 2200 miles from open water at the mouth of the St. Lawrence River. The major restriction in the Seaway system is at the Welland Canal between Lake Erie and Lake Ontario. The canal has a depth limit of 27 feet, which is too shallow for many fully loaded ocean vessels. Larger vessels will load grain to maximum Welland Canal depth and "top-off" at Montreal or other lower-river loading points before entering open water.

Terminals. Transportation terminals are provided for loading, unloading, transferring, assembling, classifying, grading, and routing shipments of grain and grain products. Terminal activities are significant time and cost factors in rail transportation of grain, especially when grain is moved in single-car rail shipments requiring frequent reassembly into new trains or transfer to connecting railroads. Grading of grain in rail cars also causes delays at terminals. Frequently, grain is unloaded for storage or processing at terminal sites and reloaded for subsequent rail movement to consumers. Rail-carrier terminal costs arise from investment in terminal facilities, terminal operation, and delays of road equipment.

Terminal activity for barges is primarily at loading and unloading points but may also occur at "fleeting" points where barges are reassembled into larger or smaller tows as required by channel conditions. On the Mississippi River system, barges are frequently assembled into larger tows where river tributaries enter the main stem of the river. Fewer enroute service stops occur for barges than for railroads, hence, enroute terminal costs are lower for barge than for rail movement.

For trucks, terminal activities are normally limited to loading, sampling for grade either at origin or destination, and unloading. Terminal delays are minimal except in periods of high-volume movement when truck unloading delays may occur.

Vehicles. The third major component of each system is the vehicle. Vehicles include power units (locomotives, towboats, and tractors) and mobile containers for grain or grain products (rail cars, barges, and highway trailers). Only in the case of straight trucks is the container and the power source contained in a single unit. Proper and expeditious assembly of container units and power units is important to minimizing transport costs and transit time for rail carriers and barge line operators. Trucks normally move from origin to destination without intermediate stops for assembly or equipment exchange.

Capital Investment—Private Versus Public

All forms of transportation are capital intensive when all costs (public and private) are considered. Truck and barge transportation are less capital intensive than rail when only private investment is considered because of greater public investment in ways and terminals. Public investment in highways and waterways is justified by (1) general public benefits (national defense, interregional communication, etc.), (2) extreme lumpiness of the investment, and (3) long gestation period before payoff occurs. The level of investment in ways would likely be inadequate if left totally to the private sector.

Historically, with minor exceptions, railroad tracks and terminals, as well as operating equipment, have been privately owned. Railroads in the United States reported operating revenues in 1978 of $20.1 billion and a net investment of $28 billion—a capital turnover ratio of 0.72. Hence, rail costs encompass a major element of fixed costs associated with large private capital investment that significantly affects rate making and service behavior of the carrier.

Waterways and river terminals have been provided at public expense—waterways and navigation aids normally by the federal government and port facilities by state and local governments. Historically, barge operators have not been required to pay user charges for river navigation facilities. Costs of barge operations for private operators have been limited to barge and towboat ownership and operation. Beginning in October 1980, barge operators are required to pay 4 cents per gallon tax on fuels used in barge transport, with the tax rate to be graduated upward to 10 cents per gallon by 1985. Proposals to further increase waterway user taxes are being considered by the federal government.

The largest public investment in any mode of transportation is in highways. Highway users, including truckers, provide funds for highway construction and maintenance through gasoline taxes, excise taxes on vehicles, tires and parts, license fees, and other assessments. Such charges, however, convert the user's highway investment and maintenance responsibility from fixed to variable costs. Motor carriers can adjust capacity quickly as changes in demand for services occur, avoiding prolonged excess capacity or shortages that frequently exist in the railroad industry. Truck rates, in the absence of economic regulation, strongly reflect operating costs.

Operating Cost Economics

Carriage of grain or grain products may be by private or for-hire carriers and by various transport modes. Regardless of the type of carriage, certain loading and transport conditions reduce unit vehicular costs. To reduce private transportation costs, or to negotiate effectively with for-hire carriers, grain and grain product shippers can benefit by an understanding of physical conditions affecting shipment cost.

Product Weight and Density. Weight of product per unit of space affects the ability to load to the rated capacity of the vehicle. Transport cost per unit of weight is lower when product density permits loading to maximum allowable weight before the volume limit of the vehicle is reached. Reaching the volume limit is not normally a problem with whole grains but may be a problem with milled grain by-products. For example, weight per cubic foot of wheat flour is approximately 80 percent that of whole wheat, hence, a lower maximum weight of wheat flour than of wheat can be loaded on a vehicle of a given size.

Optimal Units of Cargo. Transportation cost is also high when the volume of shipment is less than the capacity of the vehicle in use. Carrier costs are associated with the capacity of vehicles moved whether fully loaded or not. If vehicles travel empty, or if power units are under-utilized, costs for the carrier are nearly as much as with all space filled and power units working at rated capacity.

Optimal Vehicle Size. If less-than-carload or less-than-truckload shipping costs are high and size of shipment cannot be adjusted to the vehicle, it is important to match the vehicle capacity to the size of the load. When shipment size can be adjusted, unit cost economies normally occur with larger vehicles. Economies occur from savings in operator labor and from a higher ratio of payload to gross weight. Reducing vehicle weight will permit heavier payloads when weight restrictions on the roadway occur. For example, use of aluminum instead of steel in covered-hopper rail cars reduced car weight to approximately 63,000 pounds, permitting grain loads up to 200,000 pounds without exceeding a 263,000-pound weight restriction on a sizable portion of the nation's rail line. The economic incentive for larger vehicles is present in all modes of transportation.

Continuous Flow. Transport that maintains continuous movement can be undertaken at lower cost than when delays and speed variations occur. For railroads, delays occur when cars are stopped for grade sampling, when grain movement is stopped for storage or processing under transit provisions, when individual cars are classified and assembled into road trains, and when interconnecting railroads exchange freight and equipment. Delays occur when reduced speed or stopping is required in congested areas or at highway grade crossings.

A steel wheel on a steel rail produces relatively low amounts of friction but also provides less traction, hence, difficulty in creating speed. Because of relative traction conditions, trucks can overcome grades with less additional effort than locomotives. According to McElhinney, a truck requires only a little more than twice as much tractive force to go up a 2 percent grade than to run on a horizontal surface but a train requires five times as much.[1]

Expeditious loading and unloading, including access to terminals without delays and flow-through terminals that permit short turn-

[1]Paul T. McElhinney, *Transportation for Marketing and Business Students,* Littlefield, Adams & Co., Totowa, N. J., 1975.

around time, is important to all three major modes in grain transportation. Terminal delays reduce efficiency of rail freight car use and trucks and drivers in motor transportation. In barge transportation, delayed towboats and their crews are especially costly.

Direct Routing. Distance of travel is minimized when grain or grain products move as directly as possible from origin to destination. Out-of-line movement, permitted without extra charge by some carriers, can only increase cost to carriers. Differences in directness or minimum mileage movement exist among types of carriers in point-to-point movement. Movements between the same two points may result in a shorter distance for trucks than for rail or barge where circuity is normally involved. Point-to-point rail distances are frequently 10 to 15 percent greater than for trucks, and barge distances may be as much as 30 percent greater than rail.

Adaptation of Power Unit to Power Needs. Efficient use of the power source requires that the locomotive, towboat, or truck motor be adapted to the size of load. Maximum use of power is difficult when multiple containers are used in a single haul. If towboats are built to handle eight-barge tows, it is inefficient to move only two barges per tow. If railroad locomotives are built to produce the power to pull a 65-car train over normal grades, substantially fewer cars per train is inefficient. Many highway tractors generate more than sufficient power to carry loads up to the maximum permitted by highway load restrictions.

Many structure, conduct, and performance attributes as well as trends in transport services available to grain shippers are guided by the above characteristics of carrier costs. For example, the increasingly popular unit train in grain transport combines economies of larger-sized shipments, appropriate matching of power units and load, and continuous movement to achieve lower carrier costs than are possible with single-car movements. With increased intensity of competition among carriers for grain traffic in the decade of the 1970s, carrier costs became more important in determining rate systems than was true when railroads were the predominant carriers.

GRAIN TRANSPORTATION REQUIREMENTS

Grain is transported almost exclusively in bulk in the United States. Although semiperishable, grain does not require a highly controlled environment during transport. It does require protection from rain, and from contamination by insects or foreign materials while in transit.

Grain movements are seasonal. The volume of movement varies among years depending on market conditions and yields per acre in producing areas. Demand for services from an individual transport mode also varies in response to supply changes by competing modes.

Short-run availability of grain transport services is influenced by river navigation conditions, by variation in nongrain transport demands for rail freight cars and locomotives, and by changes in demand for truck transportation for nongrain uses.

Grain industry trends that have increased the demand for transportation in the decade of the 1970s include increases in (1) production of grain and soybeans, (2) the volume of production sold off farms, hence, entering the commercial marketing system, and (3) the amount of grain and soybeans sold for export (Table 4-1).

Grain increasingly moves from farms to country elevators at harvest time. Fifty to 60 percent of corn sold off farms in Iowa is marketed from October to December.[2] Eighty-five to 90 percent of the wheat marketed in Kansas is delivered to the local elevator in the harvest period. From local elevators, grain for domestic use is transported to processors, livestock feeders, millers, feed manufacturers, and elevators in other areas. Export grain may move directly from local assemblers to export elevators for loading on ocean vessels. Larger quantities of grain going ultimately for export move through inland terminals at locations such as Minneapolis, Omaha, Kansas City, Chicago, Enid, Hutchinson, Lewiston, and others, or through subterminals in producing areas where equipment and transportation arrangements for multiple carload or unit-train shipments have been established.

Grain for export moves from surplus producing areas to ports by those means of transportation that represent lowest cost to the shipper. Proximity of surplus producing areas and uniqueness of water transport channels provides a general guide to patterns of export flow. The Mississippi River system, the Great Lakes-St. Lawrence Seaway system and the Columbia-Snake River system are important inland waterway systems for movement of grain to ports. Exports of grain and soybeans by port areas in 1973 and 1978 are shown in Table 4-2.

The data in this table also indicate the distinct importance of Gulf of Mexico ports in exporting grain—historically handling about two-thirds of total U.S. grain exports. U.S. Department of Agriculture data separate port areas on the Gulf of Mexico as follows: (1) Mississippi River (New Orleans, Destrehan, Port Allen, Myrtle Grove, Ama and Reserve), (2) East Gulf (Mobile and Pascagoula), (3) North Texas Gulf (Beaumont, Port Arthur, Houston, and Galveston), and (4) South Texas Gulf (Corpus Christi and Brownsville, plus rail shipments to Mexico). These data indicate a considerable amount of port specialization by type of grain. Mississippi River and East Gulf ports export larger relative volumes of soybeans and corn, and North and South Texas Gulf ports greater relative volumes of wheat and grain sor-

[2]Phillip Baumel, John J. Miller, and Thomas P. Drinka, *An Economic Analysis of Upgrading Rail Branch Lines: A Study of 71 Lines in Iowa*, Federal Railroad Administration Report No. FRA-OPPD-763, March 1976.

Table 4-1 U.S. Wheat, Coarse Grains, Soybeans, and Rice Produced, Sold Off Farms, and Exported, 1970/71 to 1979/80 (million short tons)

Year	Wheat			Coarse Grains[a]			Soybeans			Rice		
	Output	Sold Off Farms	Exported	Output	Sold Off Farms	Exported	Output	Sold Off Farms	Exported[b]	Output	Sold Off Farms	Exported
1970/71	40.6	37.7	19.2	161.2	92.4	20.8	33.8	33.2	13.2	4.2	4.2	2.0
1971/72	48.5	45.3	17.9	209.1	121.9	27.0	35.3	34.6	12.7	4.3	4.3	1.6
1972/73	46.4	43.8	23.5	200.9	121.2	43.0	38.1	37.4	13.2	4.3	4.2	2.2
1973/74	51.3	49.2	41.3	205.7	129.6	44.5	47.0	46.3	14.6	4.6	4.6	1.8
1974/75	53.5	50.9	27.7	166.3	104.3	39.6	36.5	35.7	15.4	5.6	5.5	1.9
1975/76	63.7	60.8	34.1	203.9	130.8	55.4	46.4	45.8	13.8	6.4	6.4	2.4
1976/77	64.3	61.2	29.2	213.6	135.3	56.2	38.6	37.9	16.9	5.8	5.8	2.3
1977/78	61.1	57.6	26.3	224.7	140.8	61.8	52.9	52.1	17.9	5.0	5.0	2.4
1978/79	53.9	51.4	34.0	239.6	146.8	66.0	52.4	51.6	23.1	6.7	6.6	2.4
1979/80	64.3	61.7	39.4	257.9	161.1	78.9	63.5	62.7	24.5	6.8	6.8	2.6

[a]Coarse grains includes corn, oats, barley, rye, and grain sorghum.
[b]Whole soybeans only.

Source: U.S. Department of Agriculture, *Agricultural Statistics,* 1980, and various issues of *Agricultural Situation* and *Agricultural Outlook* reports.

Table 4-2 Selected Grains and Soybeans Inspected for Export, by Port Area, 1973 and 1978 (million short tons)

Port Area	Wheat		Corn		Sorghum		Soybeans		Total	
	1973	1978	1973	1978	1973	1978	1973	1978	1973	1978
Lakes	4.0	7.8	4.2	6.6	—	—	2.0	2.8	10.2	17.2
Atlantic	2.3	1.4	7.1	10.5	—	—	1.6	2.6	11.0	14.5
Gulf	24.6	18.7	24.1	34.4	5.6	4.8	10.8	17.7	65.1	75.6
Pacific	10.3	11.1	0.1	3.3	0.3	0.5	—	—	10.7	14.9
Total	41.3	39.0	35.4	54.7	5.9	5.3	14.4	23.1	97.0	122.1

Source: Agricultural Marketing Service, *Grain Market News*, USDA, 1973, 1978.

ghum. In 1977, 78 percent of corn and soybeans arriving at Gulf ports was by barge.

Patterns of inland movement of grain to ports not directly served by inland waterways is suggested by patterns of movement to Houston as identified by Fuller and Paggi for the period from June 1976 through May 1977.

Eighty-one percent of the grain and soybean inflow was rail-delivered; the remaining 19 percent was delivered by trucks. On the average, about 88 percent of the wheat receipts was transported via railroads. Whether wheat was shipped by an initial assembler (country elevator) or a secondary holder (inland terminal) appeared to influence selected mode. About 99 percent of the wheat shipped from secondary sources was transported via railroads, whereas initial assemblers shipped 58 percent by this mode. Approximately 45 percent of the grain sorghum and soybeans received at port were truck delivered. About 50 percent of these commodities originated within 300 miles of Houston, and 72 and 86 percent of the respective grain sorghum and soybean inflow from this area was hauled by trucks. Nebraska and Kansas were major grain sorghum suppliers, and nearly all their shipments were via railroads. Nebraska and Iowa supplied the port with 85 percent of its corn receipts, and nearly 100 percent were rail transported. Railroads were responsible for transporting about 98 percent of the port's corn inflow.[3]

Railroads were dominant in delivering of grain for export to Houston, in the above case. However, trucks are prominent in grain movement also, especially on shorter hauls of 300 miles or less and where flexibility in direction of movement and point of delivery are significant aspects of service. For example, trucks are important in delivery of grain to livestock feedlots and in delivery of processed feeds to users. Trucks also function prominently in long-haul movements to export ports and other destinations in combination with river barges.

TRANSPORTATION SERVICE TRENDS

Changing demands for transportation by grain shippers, changes in costs of providing service arising from real technology, changes in relative prices of inputs, and the behavioral characteristics of costs of providing services by carriers outlined earlier have produced distinct changes in the pattern of services offered by carriers in the past decade.

Expanding market movement of grain has expanded grain volume to be transported while dramatic export growth has sharply in-

[3]Stephen W. Fuller and Mechel S. Paggi, *Port of Houston: Intermodal Grain Transfer System and Market Area, 1976–1977*, Texas Agricultural Experiment Station B-1190, College Station, 1978.

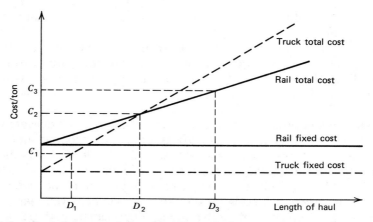

Figure 4-1. Cost-distance relationships for grain transportation by rail and truck.

creased the volume shipped relatively longer distances. Competitive conditions in grain transportation have forced greater emphasis on carrier cost patterns in establishing rate and service conditions.

Rail and barge transportation are generally lower cost than truck transportation on longer hauls. General cost relationships between rail and truck movement of grain as related to length of haul is illustrated in Figure 4-1. Costs of trucks reflect a low intercept value because of low fixed costs and low terminal costs but a relatively steep increase in costs as length of haul increases. Railroads represent a higher intercept cost and a lower cost progression as length of haul increases. This relationship suggests a cost minimizing use of trucks on short hauls (D_1) and railroads or barges on longer hauls (D_3), with cost equalizing at some intermediate point (D_2). The length of haul associated with D_2 varies significantly depending upon specific transport conditions. For large trucks the intersection point (D_2) frequently occurs between 250 and 300 miles. Increased energy costs tend to shorten the length of haul over which trucks are the lower cost mode.

Barges have a cost pattern over differing lengths of haul that is similar to railroads, although, in many cases, port (terminal) costs are higher than for rail, but line-haul costs are lower. Barge cost levels and cost configurations vary greatly among river segments, making it difficult to generalize about cost relationships between rail and barge in long-haul traffic. Similar adaptation of vehicles to distance hauled, as illustrated in Figure 4-1, applies to truck movement alone because of flexibility in size and design of trucks.[4]

Large-volume shipments to export destinations provide an oppor-

[4]Raymond G. Bressler and Richard A. King, *Markets, Prices and Interregional Trade*, John Wiley & Sons, Inc., New York, 1970, p. 115.

tunity for reducing costs of transportation through trainload shipments. Repetitions of trainload movements from the same origin to the same destination permits cost reduction through better equipment utilization. In grain transportation, the result has been the development of subterminals in producing areas, especially in corn, soybeans, and wheat shipping areas, and a shift in the pattern of local assembly of grain to larger shipping points.

Concurrent developments in costs and rate practices have reduced traffic on feeder rail lines, resulting in abandonment of rail service in many local communities. Investments in highways and improvements in trucks have caused shifts in grain and nongrain freight service in local communities to greater use of trucks. Rail service is no longer profitable on many local lines in rural communities.

Cost and competitive conditions have resulted in the following major service trends in grain transportation.

Increased use of barges has accompanied technological improvements in tow boats and navigation systems expanded waterway improvements, and increased movement of grain to export ports.

Railroads have responded to increased traffic potential in export movement by providing multiple-car and unit-train rates. End-to-end mergers of railroads to provide for longer hauls without interchange delays have helped to achieve a continuous flow and longer hauls by individual carriers.

Low earnings by railroads have discouraged such services as free transit and stopping for inspection of grain without charge to the shipper.

Railroad abandonment in rural communities has increased reliance on trucks for shorter distance movements to regional processors and to inland terminals and subterminals.

Cost, demand, and regulatory changes made transportation a volatile and dynamic area in the decade of the 1970s. Major changes in transport services are likely to continue in the 1980s.

Carrier Organization

Differing cost characteristics among transport modes are significant in determining organization and economic structure, and hence, pricing and service differences among modes. Organization and economic structure, in turn, help determine the institutionalized rules under which each type of transportation operates.

Railroads. Railroad costs include large elements of fixed costs associated with investment in tracks, terminals, and rolling stock. Investments in trackage and terminals characteristically involve excess capacity. The indivisible nature of such investment makes it rare that traffic will be matched with investment in a way that even approaches minimum average total cost as illustrated by the U-shaped, short-run average cost curve.

Railroad costs are also characterized by significant economies of scale over a substantial range of firm sizes as measured by size of investment or extent of the rail network controlled by a single firm. However, definitive studies of economies of size are not possible for railroads because different firms operate under very different conditions that cannot be totally accounted for in efforts to isolate a firm-size and unit-cost relationship. Studies designed to measure economies of scale have produced such different conclusions as (1) economies continue up to the point of incorporating all U.S. railroads in a single system, and (2) economies are limited to a maximum size of 10,000 employees.[5]

Class I railroads are identified as those railroads with $50 million or more annual operating income. In 1979, there were 41 Class I railroads in the United States carrying 98 percent of total railroad ton-miles of freight traffic.[6]

Railroads are multiple product firms producing transport services for various products, distances, directions, and at various times. Producing services involves substantial amounts of joint and common costs that can be either variable or fixed. Where costs are joint, common, or fixed in a multiple product firm, cost assignment to specific services is arbitrary, making it difficult to relate costs of service to rate patterns.

The organization and competitive structure for railroads involves only one firm in many local transportation markets. When commodity markets and production areas are brought into the competitive focus, railroad competitive structure may still be characterized as imperfectly competitive.

Motor-Carriers. In contrast to railroads, the trucking industry approaches pure competition. Few economies of scale for trucking firms have been identified, and the cost of entry for truckers is relatively low under uncontrolled entry conditions. A trucking firm's capacity can be expanded or contracted in relatively small, discrete units (a vehicle and a driver). Because private investment in highways is not required of grain truckers and there ordinarily is little or no investment in terminal facilities required, fixed costs are a small part of total costs.

Inland Water Carriers. Barge cost patterns are similar to those of trucks in many respects. Historically, barge operators have not been required to provide fixed investments for development or maintenance of waterways or for navigation improvements. Terminal facilities are provided by public investment through local or state governments or by shippers.

---

[5]Kent T. Healy, *The Effects of Scale on The Railroad Industry,* Committee on Transportation, Yale University, New Haven, Conn., 1961.
[6]Association of American Railroads, *Railroad Facts,* 1980.

Fixed costs for barge operators are costs associated with ownership of vehicles (barges and towboats). Although representing higher levels of investment than in the case of trucks, the capacity of barging equipment also can be adjusted to demand quite rapidly through investment and disinvestment in barges and towboats. Like trucking, the barge industry has a competitive structure that approaches pure competition.

Regulation

Railroads were the first major U.S. industry to be brought under federal government economic regulation. The Interstate Commerce Act of 1887 initiated rate, service, and entry control over railroad operations. The Act, and many subsequent amendments, specified rates and services patterned after common carrier obligations identified in British common law. However, these obligations were substantially modified, clarified, and further specified by statute, by Interstate Commerce Commission (ICC) rulings, and by court decision as applied to railroads, initially and later to other modes of transportation.

A common carrier must (1) serve the general public without restricting service to selected customers, (2) serve the public without undue discrimination or preferential service, (3) charge fair and reasonable rates, and (4) deliver goods entrusted to the carrier in the condition in which they are received. The carrier has the general responsibility of a bailee in the care of goods.

Motor carriers are not subject to interstate regulation when hauling whole grain or grain products. Section 203b of the Interstate Commerce Act exempts truck movement of unprocessed agricultural products from federal economic regulation. Historically, this has not exempted grain products (wheat flour, prepared feeds, feed mixes, etc.). Legislation in 1980 added livestock and poultry feed to the list of exempt commodities, however. Flour remains under regulation when transported interstate by truck.

A for-hire carrier of grain products may also obtain operating authority as contract carrier, which allows it to restrict their services to customers with whom they have signed specific contracts. In contrast, a common carrier must serve all customers who wish to purchase the services the carrier normally supplies.

Truck size, weight, operating authority, and tax requirements imposed by individual states on "nonresident" trucks provide regulatory impediments for interstate movement. Truckers may route themselves to bypass states where they consider regulatory restrictions to be onerous. Regulatory agencies in some states also prescribe economic regulation (rates, services, and entry) of intrastate movements of grains by truck.

Barge traffic has also been brought under the general regulatory surveillance of the ICC, however, barges may haul bulk commodities exempt from ICC economic regulation. Hence, economic regulation of barge transportation does not establish rate, service, or entry rules for the movement of grain or grain products on inland waterways. ICC regulatory provisions covering interstate movement of grains thus apply mainly to railroad transportation.

Rates. Railroad rates charged must be filed with the ICC. A rate increase must be on file 20 days before it becomes a legal and functional rate (10 days for a rate reduction), unless an exception is granted by the ICC. New rates are initiated by carriers and filed with the ICC. Shippers, other carriers, or public agencies may challenge the new rates only if they exceed 180 percent of railroad variable costs.

Grain rail rates may also be determined through contracts between railroads and individual shippers. Individual contracts were approved by the Staggers Rail Act of 1980. Contracting enables shippers to seek specific services and to identify the willingness of railroads to provide services at a negotiated price. Negotiated rates under contract conditions result in selective rate changes and have, in a short period, modified the grain rate structure in a manner uncharacteristic of changes under regulatory conditions before the Staggers Act was passed. Before October 1980, all new rate proposals were subject to challenge by competitors, shippers, or others, and when challenged, the defense of the rate proposal became very expensive for the railroad proposing the new rate. Under those conditions, rate systems maintained relatively stable geographic relationships unless major shocks caused the rate system to break down. Increased commercial freedom in rate making and contract authority have increased flexibility in both rail rates and rail services.

Through contracting with railroads, shippers seek (1) more reliable car supply, (2) faster, on-time delivery, (3) more frequent service, (4) improved transport equipment, (5) reduced rates, or (6) future service and rate guarantees.

Through contract with shippers, railroads seek (1) reduced operating costs through multiple-car, point-to-point handling, and greater productive use of rail cars, (2) traffic that they may not carry under common carrier rate and service conditions, (3) traffic patterns to fill in backhauls and seasonal gaps in traffic flows, (4) reduced investment in rail cars, and (5) future traffic guarantees for improved planning.

Historically, rail rate systems have been maintained and the level of rates increased for the entire system as inflation or market conditions warranted. Systemwide increases still occur in rail common carrier rates as a result of inflationary increases in costs. Percentage increases applied evenly to all points of origin result in absolute rate disadvantages for shippers with the higher rates in the initial structure.[7]

---

[7]For example, rail rates on grain from Goodland and from Concordia to Kansas City were increased between October 1976, and February 1979, by 19 percent. The absolute rate increase from Good-

Grain and most grain products are exempt from ICC economic regulation when moved by truck in interstate commerce as previously mentioned. Grain or grain products distributed by any grain firm in their own trucks are totally exempt from rate regulation. In addition, agricultural cooperatives may transport regulated commodities for use of its members even though not a party to the sale. Cooperatives may also transport regulated commodities for nonmembers as backhauls following exempt primary hauls, so long as the hauls do not exceed 50 percent of their annual primary tonnage.

Barge rates on grain and grain products are not regulated by the ICC. Before 1974, barge rates were regulated when grain barges were in tow containing three or more different commodities. Barge companies filed tariffs with the ICC and published single barge rates on grain. Since 1974, general publication of barge tariffs has ceased.

Entry and Exit.   Carriers subject to economic regulation may obtain operating authority as common carriers or as contract carriers. Common carrier authority only is issued to rail carriers.[8] Truckers or barge operators may obtain authority to operate as common carriers or as contract carriers. Contract carrier authority allows the carrier to limit services to shippers with whom they contract and allows the carrier to withdraw services as permitted by contracts. Common carriers must provide services for the general public and are not permitted to withdraw portions of an authorized service without approval by the authority-granting agency. Rail carriers are not permitted to withdraw service or abandon rail lines without approval of the ICC. Common carriers of other modes must have similar withdrawal authority.

Service.   Service regulation is concerned with service quality, amount of service made available, and the control of service differences that may be interpreted as discriminatory or unduly preferential to individual shippers. For grain shippers this includes total availability of freight cars for rail movement of grain, equitable distribution of available cars in times of shortage, and movement and delivery of loaded

---

land to Kansas City was 13 cents/cwt (7.8 cents/bu), and from Concordia to Kansas City the rate increase was 8 cents/cwt (4.8 cents/bu). Assuming the same elasticities of supply and demand at the two locations, the price difference for wheat between Goodland and Concordia might be expected to increase by 3 cents/bu. If wheat yields 35 bushels per acre in each community, the net return per acre from wheat has been reduced at Goodland relative to Concordia by $1.05 per acre. Discounted at 10 percent over 20 years, the 1979 value per acre of wheat land at Goodland was reduced relative to land of equal productivity at Concordia by $8.94 per acre by an equal percentage but unequal absolute increase in freight rates.

[8]Railroads, although common carriers, had limited authority to enter into contracts with shippers for services not offered to the general public following a November 1978 ruling by the Interstate Commerce Commission (Ex Parte 358-F). Contract authority was expanded and given legislative approval by the Staggers Act in October 1980.

cars with reasonable dispatch. Similar regulations apply to trucks operated as common carriers in regulated interstate movement of grain products.

Reasonable exercise of service obligations does not mean maintaining a rail car fleet in readiness to meet any possible surges in demand for freight cars. However, the ICC has at times established conditions encouraging investment by carriers in larger freight car fleets. The Association of American Railroads frequently issues car orders mandating the return of freight cars to lines serving areas in which the freight car supply is seriously below car requests for immediate shipment. The ICC has also used its authority to bring about a redistribution of car supply when regional shortages have developed.

Specific rules for equitable distribution of grain cars among individual shippers are difficult to identify. Shippers generally have not been successful in suits against carriers claiming damages from inequitable local distribution of freight cars. A matter of current concern is the availability for single-car shippers. Legislative and ICC rules limiting assignment of empty cars to unit-train shippers are designed to protect the smaller shipper in times of car shortages.

Carrier Obligation for Safety of Grain in Transit.   Carriers are responsible for safe delivery of goods entrusted to them for shipment. However, common carrier regulations exempt carrier responsibility if losses are due to acts of God, acts of a public enemy, acts of public authority, fault of the shipper, or losses due to the nature of or defects in the goods themselves.

Acts of God refer to natural disasters (tornadoes, flash floods, etc.) from which damage occurs even though reasonable diligence has been exercised on the part of the carrier to prevent loss. Acts of a public enemy generally refer to acts of war, and not to theft. Acts of a public authority refer to public seizure such as for the satisfaction of a lien.

Improper loading by the shipper that results in losses in transit will result in exception to liability on the part of the carrier. Loss in transit resulting from normal shrinkage or weight loss are not the responsibility of the carrier because the loss is due to the inherent nature of the goods. If grain of excessive moisture is shipped and spoilage occurs in transit, the carrier normally is not liable. If grain or grain products arrive at destination with insect infestation or insect damage, the carrier is not liable if infestation occurred before shipment. The carrier is liable if infestation occurred during transit.

Liability rules applying to railoads and highway carriers are modified in the case of water carriers, both domestic and international. Water carriers are exempt from liability when losses result from perils or dangers of navigable waters or fires aboard the vessel, unless negligence is shown. The water carrier is required to exercise due diligence to make the vessel "seaworthy" and to properly staff, equip, and supply the ship, and to provide protected space for cargo. The carrier is also required to "properly and carefully load, handle, stow, carry, keep, care for, and discharge the cargo."

GRAIN RATES AND TARIFFS

Grain and grain product freight tariffs are published by carriers and carrier associations with a major objective of recording the prices that are charged for the transportation of those products. Thousands of grain tariffs are in force in the United States with numerous alternative rates available between a given set of origins and destinations in many cases. Mistakes in assessing rates are often made because of the large number of alternatives in routing, shipping configuration, intermediate and enroute service available, and rate variations based on ultimate disposition of the grain. Expertise in use of freight tariffs requires study and understanding of methods and purposes of tariff construction and an understanding of rules and procedures guiding tariff publication and use. Tariffs are normally not difficult to use after tariff rules are learned. Staying current with tariff changes and application of tariff rules is tedious and may require substantial time and effort.

Rate Tariffs

Rate tariffs are more than price lists. Tariffs contain rules, obligations, and service limitations applied to specific movements. For common carriers, the ICC requires that rate tariff circulars contain the following divisions: (1) title page, (2) table of contents, (3) list of participating carriers, (4) alphabetical list of commodities covered, (5) alphabetical list of stations, (6) geographical list of stations, (7) explanation of symbols, reference marks and abbreviations, (8) list of exceptions, (9) rules and regulations, (10) statement of rates, and (11) routing provisions.

List of Participating Carriers.   Tariffs may be filed and published by a single carrier and encompass rates applying only to origins and destinations both of which are served by the carrier issuing the tariff. Tariffs that list rates and rules applying to more than one carrier or to intercarrier movements are published by a tariff publishing agent of the carriers involved, frequently in association with the carrier rate bureau. A multiple-carrier tariff is referred to as an "agency" tariff. Agency tariffs must list the carriers that have, through a letter of concurrence, authorized the publishing agency to act for them.

Alphabetical List of Commodities Covered.   Rate tariffs, whether class rate tariffs or commodity rate tariffs, must list commodities to which tariffs apply. Grains and grain products normally are transported under commodity rate tariffs that will list those grains and grain products to which the tariff specifically applies.

Lists of Stations. Points of origin and destination to which a tariff applies are listed both in alphabetical and geographical arrangements, the latter normally by states.

Explanation of Symbols. Freight tariffs are replete with abbreviations, reference marks, and symbols that aid in reducing the space required to print a tariff and to incorporate all of the detail that is required in a tariff. Some abbreviations have become generally recognized through common usage, including CL and LCL for carload or less-than-carload, or NOIBN for commodity class items "not otherwise indicated by name." Many abbreviations or symbols are not universally used and may be entirely foreign to new or occasional users of tariffs. Explanation of all abbreviations and symbols are therefore required to appear in each tariff.

Lists of Exceptions. Exceptions to governing tariffs may be inserted by carriers concerning routings, specific rates, or a specific combination movement that a carrier who otherwise concurs and participates in the tariff wishes to be exempt. Exceptions may also apply to classifications of types of grain or grain products where a previous tariff provides the basic classifications.

Rules and Regulations. The rules and regulations section of a freight tariff establishes loading and unloading conditions, conditions under which demurrage may be charged when cars are detained for loading or unloading, conditions and charges for stopping in transit, kinds of equipment (for example, refrigerated containers to be provided in transit), and other special conditions pertaining to carrier or shipper performance while the designated tariff is in use.

Statement of Rates. The statement of rates provides specific point-to-point rates or rate formulas and related numbers by which precise and unique rates can be determined for each movement.

Routing Provisions. Tariffs may require specific routing for the accompanying rate to apply, especially if the rate is attractive to the shipper. If that is the case, a shipper may make an attractive rate unavailable by selecting a route that does not apply. Shippers should therefore be aware of specific routing requirements. If the rate is the same over several routings and arrival time and location differences do not matter to the consignee, general efficiency of the carrier may be enhanced if alternative routings are permitted by the shipper with selection of final alternative by the carrier.

Tariffs, once they are published and approved by a regulatory authority, have the force of law and cannot be deviated from in assessment of rates, shipping conditions, rules, or routing without filing the change with the ICC and completion of the designated waiting period before implementation.

Grain Rates

The level and structure of transport rates influences the market area in which a given shipper may be competitive. The structure of transport rates (relationship of rates to one another) often is more significant to shippers than are changes in the level of rates. Shippers also consider rate stability to be important because it permits better planning of production, procurement, and sales. Marketing contracts among separated buyers and sellers can be completed on a firmly established price basis if transportation costs are established and are reasonably stable.

Carrier cost and regulatory conditions that mold rate systems vary among modes of transportation. By far the most complex system of rates for the three grain-carrying modes has been established by railroads.

Railroad Grain Rates.   Railroad grain rates were instrumental in developing public pressure for rate regulation prior to passage of the Interstate Commerce Act. Rates were reported to be highly discriminatory with adverse effects on those shippers without transport alternatives and, hence, they were without bargaining power. Rates were also highly unstable over time as rate wars developed among railroads.

As previously indicated a high level of fixed costs and a significant element of joint and common costs characterize the railroad industry. Excess capacity of tracks, terminals, and frequently freight cars is a "normal" condition for railroads. With these rate-making circumstances, demand characteristics of rail transportation become relevant price considerations. Harper lists several demand factors that are relevant for establishing the value of service ceiling on rates.[9] These include commodity demand factors (value of the commodity, economic conditions in the user industry, and rates on competing commodities), and route demand factors (competition with other carriers, production-point competition, and market competition).

The value of a commodity per unit of weight or volume has been an important criterion for establishing rail rates. Where value is high,

[9]Donald V. Harper, *Transportation in America, Users, Carriers, Government,* Prentice-Hall, Inc., Englewood Cliffs, N.J., 1978.

transport cost is a relatively small portion of the commodity's sale price. Increases in transport cost under those conditions has relatively little effect on quantity demanded, hence, demand for rail service is inelastic, and rates can be raised without significant loss of shipping volume.

Economic conditions in the user (shipper) industry may, in some circumstances, influence rate decisions by carriers and by the ICC. This is more likely to occur where economic conditions of shippers on a particular carrier's line have encountered market competition that will severely reduce volume shipped unless transport rate concessions are made. If shippers are experiencing heavy demand and a high level of prosperity, the reverse may be true.

Rates on competing commodities will influence rate actions by an individual carrier. Grains that substitute rather freely for one another generally have the same or similar rates in the railroad rate structure.

Competition with other carriers has become an increasingly important factor in the development of railroad rates. Motor carriers and inland water modes compete increasingly with railroads for grain traffic. Railroads have adjusted their rate structures in response to competition, even though with a pronounced lag. As river traffic increased, reductions in export rail rates on corn and soybeans from northern Corn Belt origins to Gulf ports has demonstrated that type of adjustment. Higher revenue to variable cost ratios, from origins more distant from water transportation and from locations where trucks offered little competition, have been demonstrated in analytical studies.[10]

Production-point competition exists when a commodity is produced in two or more areas and the producers compete in the same market. A rate increase affecting producers in one area will adversely affect their competitive position with other producers. Rail rates may be adjusted in a way that will permit production costs plus transportation costs to remain competitive with other production points.

Market competition occurs when two or more markets compete for the output of a single producing area. Each railroad serving the producing area must set rates in recognition of the possibility of loss of traffic to the competing market.

In addition to demand factors, rail rates also reflect such cost factors as (1) loading characteristics of the commodity, especially weight-density, (2) susceptibility to loss and damage, (3) volume of traffic, (4) regularity of shipments, (5) size of shipments, (6) type of equipment required, (7) length of haul, and (8) road operating conditions.

[10]Orlo Sorenson, Dale G. Anderson, and David C. Nelson, *Railroad Rate Discrimination: Applications to Great Plains Agriculture,* Great Plains Agricultural Council Publication No. 62, Lincoln, Neb., 1973.

Historically, grain rates over major areas were designed to move grain from farms through inland terminal markets located in or near surplus producing areas. Tariffs provided opportunities for intermediate stops through a system of gathering rates, also called flat rates, by which grain was delivered from local elevators to inland terminals. From inland terminals, inbound billing was used to qualify grain shipments for rates (proportional rates or transit balance rates) that were lower than for grain for which inbound billing was not available. Proportional and transit balance rates were designed to approximate through-rates for continuous shipment without intermediate stops. Inbound rates to inland terminals were normally higher on a ton-mile basis than outbound proportional or transit balance rates.

Grain rate systems in the past have contained a substantial amount of route and product equalizations. A 1951 publication describes product equalization as follows.[11]

As a general rule, the same rate applies on all grains, and the same rate applies to the products of grain as to the grain itself. . . . The more important products of grain are flour, millfeed (bran and shorts), corn meal, corn chop, and manufactured livestock and poultry feed.

Rate equalization over routes of unequal distance is designed to permit competitive equality for production areas, rail carriers, and intermediate processors over a broad area. For example, past rate patterns permitted wheat from Omaha or Kansas City to move through Chicago, Peoria, or St. Louis and subsequently to New York at the same rate regardless of origin, routing, or location of intermediate stops for processing or storage.

More recently, rate structures involving inland terminals (also called rate-break points) have been modified to accommodate new competitive dimensions provided by intensified bidding for grain transport by trucks and barges, and shifts in volume and direction of grain movement brought about by increased export volume.

Truck Grain Rates.   Trucking of grain is done largely by small trucking firms. Truck rates on whole grain are not regulated in interstate commerce. Interstate movements are negotiated between shipper and carrier. Truckers may also buy grain in one location and haul to another location for sale with trucking services compensated by the difference between purchase and sale prices. Truck rates for grain hauls respond to changes in demand and supply of trucking services although the amount of short-run rate variation has not been verified quantitatively.

---

[11]Walter Scott, John H. McCoy, Sterling Masters, and J. S. Chartrand, *Grain Freight Rates,* Kansas Agricultural Experiment Station Circular No. 280, Manhattan, 1951.

The truck is a versatile vehicle and may be shifted to hauling other commodities when short-run declines in grain demand occur. Some variation in rates undoubtedly occurs even with seasonal flexibility in the supply of trucks for grain hauls.

A greater proportion of trucking costs are variable than in the case of railroads. Equipment investment is much lower and occupationally more mobile than rails, hence, fixed investment can be modified quickly and, even in the short-run, fixed-cost levels provide a relatively small zone of discretionary pricing below full costs.

Trucking costs vary with size of truck, size of load, annual mileage, length of individual haul, and loaded miles relative to empty miles. However, under characteristic conditions, trucks are more competitive with railroads on short hauls (300 miles or less) than on longer hauls. Compared with other modes, trucks have relatively low terminal costs but relatively high line-haul costs.

Barge Grain Rates.   Barge grain rates also are unregulated and reflect negotiating conditions at any point in time. Barge rates may change abruptly depending on demand for barge movement of grain and backhaul conditions. Barge cost patterns indicate a high portion of total cost associated with terminal activity and relatively low line-haul costs, especially on river segments where the navigation channel permits larger-size flotillas and relatively deep draft.

SHIPPER-CARRIER RELATIONSHIPS

Dealing with for-hire carriers establishes a contractual relationship between the shipper and the carrier. Procedural relationships that are dictated by trade practices accompany contracts and the negotiation of contracts. Performance rules for shippers and carriers are also specified by law or by regulatory commissions.

Ordering Service

For domestic transportation modes, ordering service by a shipper can normally be done by telephone when shipments are planned. Lead time in ordering equipment is important. Telephone orders normally are followed and verified by an order memo to record the equipment order and avoid misunderstandings or miscommunications in the verbal order.

Barge operators frequently operate under annual or seasonal contracts with major grain shippers located at barge-loading points. Where contract arrangements exist, shippers may guarantee a minimum annual volume or a minimum percentage of total shipment to river port destinations. In return, the barge operator agrees to provide minimum quantities of equipment on a schedule fitting the shipping patterns of the grain elevator, or for rate concessions below existing single-barge rates.

Greater preshipment planning and earlier contracting are required for ocean shipping. Initial contact with carriers, usually through brokers to determine availability of service, is desirable. For grains, a shipping contract may be for a specified voyage (called a "voyage charter") or for a specified period of time (called a "time charter"). If ship arrangements can be worked out, the carrier will send the shipper a freight contract (called a "charter party"), which specifies the origin and destination of shipment, quantity to be shipped, loading, sailing, and port arrival dates, along with other detailed arrangements attendant to the specific contract. A written record of arrival for loading and sailing times is important. Delays, either by the shipper or carrier, can be costly. Demurrage claims for delayed ships incur financial liability at a rapid rate. Undue ship delays may also cause congestion at the shipper's port facilities resulting in subsequent damage claims against the carrier.

Loading

Grain loaded in bulk is a relatively simple operation, however, the shipper provides certain information concerning the shipment and exercises precautions with regard to rail cars so that faulty cars are not loaded.

Determining weight of grain loaded is important to the seller for merchandising purposes, and to establish claims if loss in transit occurs. Elevator load-out scales at local elevators do not provide supervised weights for the purpose of establishing loss claims but weights from a regularly inspected, automatic load-out scale normally will be accepted by carriers when losses occur. Supervised rail car or truck weights may be obtained at specific locations, ordinarily at central markets.

Obtaining samples for grading of grain may be done at loading time. Automatic spout samplers may be used for official grades if sampling is supervised by a federally licensed sampler. If sampling is not supervised, unofficial samples may be used to provide information to the shipper even though the grading information is not designated an official grade.

Demurrage

All modes of transport incorporate an allowance in their rates for loading time in which their vehicle is unproductive for road service. The additional time required for loading vehicles is a cost to the carrier for which charges are made to the shipper who has caused the delay. This charge is known as "demurrage."

Loading and unloading time allowed for rail cars without demurrage varies with the urgency of demand for cars to be refilled, but normally is 48 hours. The 48-hour period begins at 7:00 A.M. following "constructive placement" of the car. Constructive placement for grain shipment involves placing the cars in position for loading when they cannot be placed at the elevator's rail siding. Saturdays, Sundays, and holidays normally are not charged against loading time.

Routing of Shipments

Routing of grain shipments is important to the shipper under two conditions. If a specific carrier delivers only to certain points in the destination area, which may be less convenient to the consignee than delivery points of other carriers, it is important that the most favorable delivering carrier be selected. In truck, barge, or ocean transportation, the originating carrier normally is the destination carrier since the modes usually are not arranged into networks that exchange equipment and traffic.

A second situation involves differences in availability of enroute services, depending on the carrier. Availability of enroute inspection and weighing services may vary among routes. Opportunities for reconsignment of a shipment to an alternate destination or the availability of stops in transit may be different among routes. Route differences relating to the above services occur more commonly with railroads than with other modes of transport.

If consignee or service considerations do not affect routing of a shipment, open routing will permit the carrier more flexibility with a possible opportunity to improve efficiency.

Shipping Contracts

A contractual relationship exists between a shipper and a carrier. The terms of their contract are spelled out on the reverse side of the bill of lading in the case of common carriers. Contract barge or motor carriers specify shipper and carrier responsibilities in a long-term contract, using trip-ticket or load manifests to record individual shipments. Unregulated truckers frequently use trip tickets in lieu of formal contracts.

The Bill of Lading. Since 1919, a uniform bill of lading has been prescribed for common carriers regulated by the ICC. The bill of lading specifies the obligations of both carrier and shipper; it constitutes a receipt for goods assigned to a shipper and is a contract for carriage. Liability for goods in transit cannot be contracted away by the carrier except in special cases where "release rate" contracts may be approved by the ICC. Exceptions to common carrier liability exist in cases previously indicated. Although uniform among carriers within a mode, bills of lading for railroads differ slightly in specified liability of the carrier from that for water carriers, both domestic and ocean.

Uniform Order Bill of Lading. In truck, rail and barge transportation, there is a negotiable form of the bill of lading called the Uniform

Order Bill of Lading, making possible the transfer of title to goods after they have been shipped. The shipper may consign goods to himself or herself, holding title to the goods until they are consigned to someone else if sold while in transit. The order bill of lading allows the shipper to collect for the goods shipped before the consignee takes delivery. The order bill may be transferred through the banking system and may be used as collateral for a loan. The consignee must surrender the order bill to the carrier before taking delivery of grain.

Ocean Bill of Lading.   In the case of ocean shipping the bill of lading conditions are governed by rules established by leading maritime nations meeting at The Hague in 1921. Each convention participant passed national legislation to implement actions taken at The Hague. Both international law and the ocean bill of lading give substantial exemptions from liability. Ocean transport companies are essentially liable for their own negligence, which is substantially less than the bill of lading liability of domestic surface carriers. The Harter Act of 1893 requires that U.S. carriers "exercise due diligence to make the ships seaworthy, properly manned, and fit for cargo."[12]

Control of Shipments Enroute

Once a shipment has been surrendered to the carrier, routing has been determined, and the shipment has left the loading point, it is largely out of the shipper's control. Rail carrier tariffs frequently provide for some shipper control after release of the shipment. Shipments may be diverted or reconsigned after leaving the shipper's site. *Stoppage in transiter* (not to be confused with the transit privilege) is also available to the shipper if the rate engaged permits this service. This refers to the right of the shipper to stop a shipment before it can be delivered if the consignee is insolvent and cannot pay for the merchandise.

Tracing of shipments is often done when shipments are delayed or when precise timing of delivery is important to the consignee. Computerizing of rail car movements has simplified car tracing for the railroads.

Expedited (or special speeded-up) service is not possible when dealing with a common carrier. Faster delivery to a single customer would constitute discrimination and expose the carrier to reprimand by the regulatory authority.

Loss and Damage Claims

Shippers claims for enroute loss and damage to grain in transit are frequent. If destination weights indicate loss in transit, carriers are responsible for the loss in value of the grain if carrier responsibility can be documented. The shipper may be at fault if (1) losses occur at the

---

[12]Donald V. Harper, *Transportation in America, Users, Carriers, Government,* Prentice-Hall, Inc., Englewood Cliffs, N.J., 1978.

loading point in reelevating after weighing, (2) losses result from leaking spouts between scales and rail car, (3) the distributor is improperly set or leaking, or (4) dust collectors or auxiliary blowers remove weight after weighing for loading. If loss has occurred because cars have not been properly prepared for loading, the shipper is also responsible.

In 1975, the ICC established new rules for determining freight loss and damage. The rules (published as Section 1037 of the Code of Federal Regulations) include standards for settling claims concerning natural shrinkage, weight and weighing, car condition, and clear-record cars.

Natural Shrinkage.   In hearings preceding issuance of Ex Parte 263, carriers requested that the tolerance of ⅛ of 1 percent, which has generally been observed by the railroads in settling claims for loss and damages to shipments of grain, be changed to ¼ of 1 percent. The carriers' request for the higher tolerance was based on a study by the Southern Railway in which 77.4 percent of 864 hopper car movements of grain were reported to have destination weights differing from the origin weights of more than ⅛ of 1 percent and less than 1 percent; 16.6 percent reported differences of ⅛ of 1 percent or less; and 2.4 percent reported discrepancies of more than 1 percent.

Weights and Weighing.   In considering the question of the probative value of weights to be used in settling claims the ICC concluded in the 1975 hearings that the use of estimated weights should be rejected. The use of unsupervised, as well as supervised weights was accepted, provided that the former are properly documented. Consequently, the use of weights that are not based on scale weights (such as estimates) will not be allowed in claims cases because of their demonstrated unreliability.

Freight Charge Claims

Freight shipments by common carrier are entitled to the lowest applicable rate. Because many tariffs specifying different shipping conditions and various routings exist for rail shipments of grain, errors can be made in the selection of the legally applicable rate. When overcharges occur, shippers may file claims with the carriers for return of the overcharge. Auditing of freight bills either internally or by an external auditor is common practice. Interest may be claimed on the amount of the overcharge if held for over 30 days.

Summary

Transportation adds place utility to commodities. It is involved in moving goods from a location of less intensive wants to another where greater want satisfaction can be obtained from those goods.

The transportation network in the United States includes five major modes or types of transport: railway, highway, inland waterway, pipeline, and airway. Grain and grain products are transported primarily by rail, truck, and barge.

The demand for transportation increased substantially during the 1970s because of larger harvests of grain and soybeans, larger volumes of farm output being marketed off farms, and larger movements of grain and soybeans into the export market.

Rail and barge transportation costs are generally lower than trucking costs on longer hauls. Large trucks can compete favorably with railroads on hauls up to 250 to 300 miles. Increased energy costs shorten the length of haul over which trucks are the lower cost mode.

While the government has been interested in deregulating transportation, airlines have made the greatest progress in that effort. Most transportation regulations have changed little in recent years. Grain and grain products, however, are exempt from ICC regulations when moved by truck in interstate commerce. Grain or grain products distributed by any producer or grain firm in their own trucks are totally exempt from rate regulation.

Grain rail tariffs have changed dramatically with the increased export demand for grain. The railroads have offered low unit-car rates (from a specific point of origin to a specific destination point) without service frills. These rates have increased rail car utilization and reduced the cost of providing rail service. The unit-car rates have forced changes in the structure of the elevator and transportation system from farm to elevator. Trucks are hauling grain longer distances to larger elevators. This change in structure has increased the efficiency of marketing grain, but has reduced price competition for the producers' grain.

Selected References

Association of American Railroads, *Railroad Facts*, 1980.

Baumel, C. Phillip, John J. Miller, and Thomas P. Drinka, *An Economic Analysis of Upgrading Rail Branch Lines: A Study of 71 Lines in Iowa*, Federal Railroad Administration Report No. FRA-OPPD-763, March 1976.

Bressler, Raymond G., Jr. and Richard A. King, *Markets, Prices and Interregional Trade*, John Wiley & Sons, Inc., New York, 1970.

Fuller, Stephen W. and Mechel S. Paggi, *Port of Houston: Intermodal Grain Transfer System and Market Area, 1976–1977*, Texas Agricultural Experiment Station B-1190, College Station, 1978.

Harper, Donald V., *Transportation in America, Users, Carriers, Government*, Prentice-Hall, Inc., Englewood Cliffs, N.J., 1978.

Healy, Kent T., *The Effects of Scale on the Railroad Industry*, Committee on Transportation, Yale University, New Haven, Conn., 1961.

McElhinney, Paul T., *Transportation for Marketing and Business Students,* Littlefield, Adams & Co., Totowa, N. J., 1975.

Scott, Walter, John H. McCoy, Sterling Masters, and J. S. Chartrand, *Grain Freight Rates,* Kansas Agricultural Experiment Station Circular No. 280, Manhattan, 1951.

Sorenson, Orlo, Dale G. Anderson, and David C. Nelson, *Railroad Rate Discrimination: Applications to Great Plains Agriculture,* Great Plains Agricultural Council Publication No. 62, Lincoln, Neb., 1973.

GRAIN GRADES AND STANDARDS

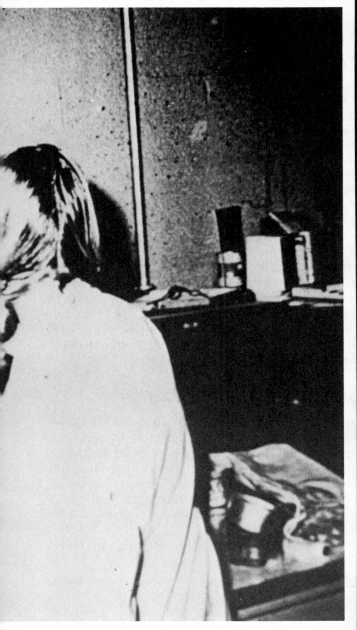

GRAIN GRADES AND STANDARDS*

CHAPTER 5

One of the requirements for a perfectly competitive market is a homogeneous product to facilitate price comparisons by buyers. The grain market meets this requirement by providing buyers with a standardized product where the products of different firms are interchangeable in the preference pattern of consumers. This interchangeability need not be on a one-for-one basis. If the characteristics of different products are such that their relative value in use can be established on a fixed, known ratio, then the homogeneity criterion can be met for purposes of competition among buyers and sellers. Uniformity of terminology and measurement of important characteristics are essential for establishing relative values between the various forms of the product.

In the case of grain grades and standards, this uniformity or standardization serves three basic purposes: (1) it permits buying and selling of the product by description rather than by inspection of each lot offered for sale; (2) it permits commingling of grain from many sources into a few categories or grades having uniform characteristics thereby reducing the need for segregated storage; and (3) it provides a method for buyers to estimate the value of a particular lot and to communicate this value back through a complex marketing system to handlers and producers. Grading and standardization is, therefore, one of the primary functions of a market system, and is essential for efficient operation of the market for grains.

HISTORY OF GRADES AND STANDARDS

The first grades and standards were established in 1856 for wheat by the Chicago Board of Trade. This was a simple designation of white, red, and spring prime quality wheat. In 1857, the Chicago Board of Trade appointed grain inspectors, and the wheat grades were changed to club spring, No. 1 spring, and No. 2 spring. This was the first use of numerals in grading. Grades were also assigned to corn, oats, and barley in that year. In 1858, official grain inspectors were appointed by the Board of Trade in Chicago and Milwaukee.

Exchanges in other cities quickly followed Chicago's lead in devel-

*Lowell D. Hill, L. J. Norton Professor of Marketing, Department of Agricultural Economics, University of Illinois, Urbana.

oping grain standards and establishing inspection points. Between 1858 and 1865 grades were adopted and inspectors were appointed in Detroit, St. Louis, Cleveland, and Toledo. The New Orleans Board of Trade did not adopt grain grading and inspection until 1881. Despite annual revisions in grades and inspection procedures, frequent complaints of unfair and inaccurate grading were voiced in Chicago as well as in other markets where grain was graded.

In an attempt to provide a more uniform system, individual states developed grading and inspection regulations on a statewide basis. Illinois was the first to provide inspection under the control of the Railroad and Warehouses Commission in 1871. Minnesota followed suit in 1885, as did several other states soon after. This system failed to solve the problems, however, because each state adopted its own grades and terminology. These varied from state to state and year to year, creating confusion and dissatisfaction among producers.

Despite many attempts by state agencies and grain trade organizations to improve the system, the inequities became increasingly more evident to producers and the grain trade. Frequent attempts to institute federal regulations during the late 1800s met with considerable resistance, and it was not until 1917 that official grain grading and inspection under federal control was established.

The Grain Standards Act was a part of the appropriations bill for the U.S. Department of Agriculture for the fiscal year ending June 30, 1917. The Act prohibited both interstate and foreign shipments unless inspected and graded according to appropriate U.S. grain standards. The Secretary of Agriculture was authorized to issue a license for inspecting and grading grain to anyone who was competent. Anyone not holding a federal license was forbidden to issue a U.S. grade certificate. The regulation provided for licensed inspectors wherever the need arose, and for an appeal system to be handled by federal employees. Federal employees were not permitted to make original inspections, but were only allowed to handle appeals following an original grade by a licensed inspector employed by state agencies, boards of trade, or private entrepreneurs.

Numerous changes were made in the grade standards between 1917 and 1976. Most of the changes involved only nomenclature or small numerical changes such as raising the allowance for heat-damaged kernels or raising or lowering the limits for test weight. Several more significant changes were made in inspection procedures.

The Grain Standards Act was amended five times between 1917 and 1975. The first was in 1940 when soybeans were added. A second amendment was passed in 1956 to protect the integrity of grade certificates. This made samplers and shippers as well as inspectors liable for complicity in the issuance of a false or incorrect grade certificate with respect to grain shipped in interstate and foreign commerce. A third amendment was made in 1968 dropping the mandatory inspection for interstate shipment and making other minor changes. This amendment permitted interstate shipments between firms on the basis of their own evaluation of quality and eliminated the necessity of placing rail cars out of position in inspection yards until an official inspection could be made. In 1970, the fourth amendment simply added the prefix "U.S." to the numerical designation, and a fifth amendment was made in 1974 changing the name to United States Standards.

With the uncovering of numerous abuses of the grain standards in 1975, an in-depth investigation of the grain standards and inspection procedures was conducted by the General Accounting Office as well as by agencies of the USDA. Several indictments were made against grain firms and inspection agencies. The result was a major revision of the Grain Standards Act, eventually passed into law as the Grain Standards Act of 1976. Among the more important changes that were introduced were the following two. (1) Inspection agencies at all of the major export points in the United States were to be operated by the Federal Grain Inspection Service, a new agency established within the USDA. This inspection service had the option of authorizing state agencies to perform the inspections where they felt this was in the best interest of the industry. However, grading at many of the ports was immediately taken over by federal inspectors, and the private agencies and the agencies operated by boards of trade were eliminated from grading export grain in these ports. (2) Official weights were placed under the jurisdiction of the inspection division.

The primary responsibility of the USDA in grain grading has been to reflect the needs, as expressed by the industry, in providing uniform measures of grain quality. In addition, they have the responsibility of supervising licensed inspectors to verify the accuracy and equity of treatment of buyers and sellers. Following the 1976 Grain Standards Act, the USDA was also charged with responsibility for developing the research and information to evaluate the present grades and standards in order to determine whether changes were needed to maintain equity and our competitive position in world markets.

INSPECTION PROCEDURES

Three types of grading certificates are issued by the Federal Grain Inspection Service or their licensed representatives. One of the three is the "white certificate," issued when the sampling and grading have been performed by licensed employees of an official inspection agency. The white certificate attests to the accuracy both of the sample and of the grading, thereby indicating that the results of the sample are representative of the lot from which it was taken. This white certificate is required for all grain sold for export, and for any sale which designates an official U.S. grade.

A "yellow certificate" may be issued if the elevator is equipped with a diverter-type mechanical sampler, operated by an officially licensed operator. This operator indicates the accuracy of both the sampling and grading procedure, and the grain must be graded by an official agency. It cannot be used for grain exports.

The third is the "pink certificate," often referred to as a submitted sample. This certificate attests only to the accuracy of the grading. Since the individual buyer or seller may submit anything in the sample, the official inspection agency cannot guarantee the sampling method, or that it represents the lot from which it was taken. Therefore, the pink certificate attests only to the quality and grade of the grain in the sample.

Anyone who questions the accuracy or representativeness of the sample may request an appeal inspection by the regional office of the Federal Grain Inspection Service. The appeal may take either of two forms. The regional office may be requested to resample the grain, assuming the car or barge is still intact, and issue a certificate indicating that it was an appeal certificate on that particular lot of grain. The second alternative is for the regional office to grade the file sample. Inspection agencies are required to maintain a file sample on every certificate issued for a specified period of time—30 to 90 days depending on the type of inspection. This file sample is obtained by dividing the original sample, using one-half for grading and preserving the other half. The inspection agency issues a new certificate that will show both the original grade and the appeal grade. In any difference in grade factor between the original inspection and the appeal inspection, the results of the appeal supersede the results of the original inspection. As a result of random sampling variation, identical results from each half of the sample are unlikely. Grade changes during an appeal may be the result of three causes: (1) error of interpretation by inspectors, especially on subjective grade factors, (2) error of measurement by mechanical equipment, for example, improperly calibrated moisture meters, and (3) random variation. Grain that is blended close to the grade limit has a high probability of showing a different grade when the file sample is examined.

This problem can be illustrated by using the factor of heat damage in corn, where the No. 1 grade limit is 0.1 percent, the No. 2 grade limit is 0.2 percent and No. 3 limit is 0.5 percent. If a 1000-gram sample has exactly 0.2 percent heat damaged kernels the probability that a 250-gram subsample will grade No. 1 is .14, No. 2 is .44, and No. 3 is .42.[1]

The rates charged for inspection by private agencies are determined by the individual inspection agencies. Although the Federal

[1]See T. E. Elam and Lowell D. Hill, "Potential Role of Sampling Variation in the Measurement of Corn Grading Factors," *Illinois Agricultural Economics,* Vol. 17, No. 1, January 1977, pp. 14–18, for a more detailed treatment of this problem.

Grain Inspection Service supervises the rates being charged and has regulations concerning discriminatory practices, they do not establish the rates, and rates may differ among inspection agencies. Each inspection agency is allowed a particular region within a state or access states over which it has sole jurisdiction. This prevents inspection agencies from competing on price; more importantly, it prevents them from competing on the quality of the grain designated on the certificate. Rates for inspection services performed by the Federal Grain Inspection Service are established at the national level for all inspection points.

DESCRIPTION OF THE STANDARDS FOR GRAIN

Grades and standards for all grains are based on numerical values for a set of factors selected to reflect quality of each type of grain. The numerical grade is determined (using the lowest factor approach) by the lowest quality of any of the factors. In the case of corn there are five factors: moisture content, test weight, broken corn and foreign material (BCFM), heat-damaged kernels, and total damaged kernels (Table 5-1). For example, if a sample of corn has a test weight of 58 pounds per bushel, BCFM of 1 percent, no heat damage, total damage of 2 percent but moisture of 15 percent, it would be graded No. 2, even though the sample was equal to No. 1 corn on all factors but moisture. If this sample contained 26 percent moisture, it would be U.S. sample grade, even though it was equal to No. 1 on all other factors.

Moisture Content

The standard for determining moisture content of grain is the 72-hour, 103¼°C. air oven method, in which all moisture is evaporated

Table 5-1   U.S. Grades and Grade Requirements for Corn

U.S. Grade	Minimum Test Weight (lb/bu)	Maximum Limits (Percent)			
		Moisture	BCFM[a]	Total	Heat-Damaged Kernels
No. 1	56.0	14.0	2.0	3.0	0.1
No. 2	54.0	15.5	3.0	5.0	0.2
No. 3	52.0	17.5	4.0	7.0	0.5
No. 4	49.0	20.0	5.0	10.0	1.0
No. 5	46.0	23.0	7.0	15.0	3.0
Sample[b]					

[a]Broken corn and foreign material.
[b]U.S. Sample grade shall be corn that does not meet the requirements for any of the grades from U.S. No. 1 to U.S. No. 5, inclusive; or that contains stones; or that is musty or sour, or heating; or that has any commercially objectionable foreign odor; or that is otherwise of distinctly low quality.

from the grain sample, and the percent moisture is calculated by determining the change in weight. Because of the time required to determine moisture in this manner, the USDA approved the Motomco electronic meter as an acceptable alternative. Because the meter reading is a function of the electrical properties of the grain, it can be influenced by many factors other than moisture. Repeatability of readings, even on the same sample of grain, is often a problem for all electronic meters. The higher the moisture content the greater the variability.

There are several brands of moisture meters in commercial use in the United States. Since inspections of most of these meters are conducted by individual states, there is a lack of uniformity in methods and comparability among meter readings. Although most states require that operating meters be calibrated against a master meter of the same brand, few require that all meters be checked against the air oven standard. As a result, different brands of meters often fail to give comparable readings on the same sample. Following action taken by Iowa an Illinois in 1980 (through the efforts of the National Task Force on Grain Moisture Measurement Assurance subcommittee of the National Conference on Weights and Measures), a move is underway to require recalibration of all meters including the official USDA charts for the Motomco, in which correspondence with the air oven method is required at each moisture level, within prescribed tolerances.

Test Weight

Test weight is a measure of grain density and is determined by weighing the quantity of grain required to fill a one-quart bucket and converting this to bushel equivalent. Conceptually, a 60-pound test weight means that a Winchester bushel containing 1.25 cubic feet by volume will hold 60 pounds when filled with that grain. Test weight does not affect the quantity of grain purchased or sold, because a "legal weight" has been established for all grains. For example, the legal weight for corn is 56 pounds, and a legal bushel will always be 56 pounds regardless of its test weight. The bushels of corn contained in a truck are determined by dividing the weight of the grain by 56. If it weighs 56,000 pounds, the buyer must pay for 1000 bushels regardless of test weight. Light test weight will simply require a larger truck to hold the 1000 bushels.

Broken Corn and Foreign Material

Broken corn and foreign material (BCFM) is defined in the standards as kernels and pieces of kernels of corn and all matter other than corn that will pass readily through a 12/64-inch sieve, and all matter other than corn that remains in the sieved sample. The official determination of BCFM is made by putting a 1000-gram sample through a Carter dockage machine. This equipment contains a 12/64-inch round-hole screen. It operates with a controlled standardized shaking motion and air flow to separate BCFM from whole corn by means of particle size, and visual inspection for noncorn in the material passing over the screen. Where a Carter dockage machine is not available, BCFM is determined by using round pans with 12/64 inch screens and shaking by hand.

Total Damaged Kernels

The grade factor of total damaged kernels (DKT) is defined as kernels and pieces of kernels of corn that are heat damaged, sprouted, frosted, badly ground damaged, badly weather damaged, moldy, diseased or otherwise materially damaged.

Heat-damaged Kernels

Heat-damaged kernels are kernels and pieces of kernels of corn that have been materially discolored and damaged by heat. In practice this classification is often subdivided into (1) damage caused by the heat of fermentation in corn where bacterial action is present, and (2) damage caused during artificial drying, where kernel temperature becomes sufficiently high to cause discoloration or charring. Heat damage is determined from a 250-gram sample by separating heat-damaged kernels by visual inspection. Percent of damage is calculated as the ratio between the weight of damaged kernels and the weight of the total sample. Heat damage is considered a subset of total damage and is included in determining the percent of DKT. The DKT limit for No. 2 corn is 5.0 percent, which can include no more than 0.2 percent of heat damage.

Soybean grades are similar to corn except for slight differences in values and the addition of two factors—splits and color (Table 5-2). Splits are defined as pieces of soybeans that are not damaged. Foreign material in soybeans is identified by an 8/64-inch screen rather than the 12/64 inch used for corn, and is obtained by using hand sieves rather than the Carter dockage machine.

Grades for wheat are more complex because of the many classes and subclasses. The other factors are similar to those of corn except for differences in factor limits (Table 5-3). Moisture is not a grade-determining factor for wheat, but it is shown on the certificate in order to calculate volume.

DISCOUNTS AND QUALITY PRICING

Discounting grain of varying quality is a method for equating value and price. Each of the grade factors, while they may determine the numerical grade, are also used as a basis for determining the final price for the grain. For example, corn with excessive moisture is generally discounted at so many cents per bushel per percentage point or fraction thereof above the No. 2 maximum moisture limit. The dis-

Table 5-2 U.S. Grades and Grade Requirements for Soybeans

U.S. Grade	Minimum Test Weight (lb/bu)	Maximum Limits (Percent)					
		Moisture	Splits	Damaged Kernels		Foreign Material	Other,[a] in Yellow or Green Soybeans
				Total	Heat Damaged		
No. 1	56.0	13.0	10.0	2.0	0.2	1.0	1.0
No. 2	54.0	14.0	20.0	3.0	0.5	2.0	2.0
No. 3[b]	52.0	16.0	30.0	5.0	1.0	3.0	5.0
No. 4[c]	49.0	18.0	40.0	8.0	3.0	5.0	10.0
Sample[d]							

[a] Brown, black, and/or bicolored soybeans.

[b] Soybeans that are purple mottled or stained shall be graded not higher than U.S. No. 3.

[c] Soybeans that are materially weathered shall be graded not higher than U.S. No. 4.

[d] U.S. Sample grade shall be soybeans that do not meet the requirement for any of the grades from U.S. No. 1 to U.S. No. 4, inclusive, or that are musty, or sour, or heating; or that have any commercially objectionable foreign odor, or that contain stones, or that are otherwise of distinctly low quality.

Table 5-3 U.S. Grades and Grade Requirements for Wheat

U.S. Grade	Minimum Test Weight (lb/bu)		Maximum Limits (Percent)						
			Defects					Wheat of Other Classes[a]	
	Hard Red Spring Wheat or White Club Wheat	All Other Classes and Subclasses	Heat-Damaged Kernels	Damaged Kernels (Total)	Foreign Materials	Shrunken and Broken Kernels	Defects (Total)	Contrasting Classes	Wheat of Other Classes (Total)
No. 1	58.0	60.0	0.1	2.0	0.5	3.0	3.0	1.0	3.0
No. 2	57.0	58.0	0.2	4.0	1.0	5.0	5.0	2.0	5.0
No. 3	55.0	56.0	0.5	7.0	2.0	8.0	8.0	3.0	10.0
No. 4	53.0	54.0	1.0	10.0	3.0	12.0	12.0	10.0	10.0
No. 5	50.0	51.0	3.0	15.0	5.0	20.0	20.0	10.0	10.0
Sample[b]									

[a]Red durum wheat of any grade may contain not more than 10.0 percent of wheat of other classes.

[b]U.S. Sample grade shall be wheat that does not meet the requirements for any of the grades from U.S. No. 1 to U.S. No. 5, inclusive; or that contains more than two crotalaria seeds (Crotalaria spp.) in 1000 grams of grain, or contains castor beans (Ricinus communis), stones, broken glass, animal filth, an unknown foreign substance(s), or a commonly recognized harmful or toxic substance(s); or that is musty, or sour, or heating; or that has any commercially objectionable foreign odor except of smut or garlic; or that contains a quantity of smut so great that any one or more of the grade requirements cannot be applied accurately; or that is otherwise of distinctly low quality.

count on all grade factors is determined primarily by the market, which presumably reflects differences in value due to quality differences. Many of the discounts appear to be related to tradition, and remain relatively constant over many years and geographical regions despite changes in relative value.

One of the more important discount factors is that of moisture. The moisture discounts serve as the basis for price adjustments that (1) compensate for the different proportion of water and dry matter in corn, (2) covers the cost of conditioning high moisture corn so that it may be safely stored and merchandised, and (3) adjusts the quantity of drying capacity to the demand for drying. In addition, a fourth item sometimes included is that of the risk involved in handling high-moisture corn.

Discounts based on the percentage points of moisture above a base level confuse the three purposes. Because the value of grain varies with the moisture content, farmers and elevator managers have found it difficult to accurately evaluate their alternatives in terms of drying and storage and to estimate the real value of the grain that they are trading.

Since excess moisture in corn neither adds to nor detracts from the value of the dry matter content, all corn should be purchased on the basis of its No. 2 weight using existing shrink tables, with a drying charge levied against the seller to cover the cost of conditioning the corn (or other grain) to its base moisture. In order to use this procedure for calculating price and value of corn, it is important to understand the principles for calculating shrink.

The shrink or loss of weight that occurs in drying high-moisture grain is the same regardless of the grain being considered. Therefore, it is possible to develop tables that show the shrink, or conversely, that show the bushels remaining when a certain quantity of grain is dried (Table 5-4). These are excerpted from much more complete tables generally referred to as the "Minary Charts." Table values, as well as Minary Charts, can be calculated from a simple mathematical relationship that is independent of the condition of the grain, the moisture level from which it started, and the kind of grain being considered.

Let's consider the calculation of shrink when drying corn, to illustrate the procedures and establish the basic formula. One hundred pounds of 25 percent moisture corn contains 75 pounds of dry matter and 25 pounds of water (Figure 5-1). During drying, water is evaporated, which reduces the amount of water and therefore the total weight of the original quantity of corn. Removing 10 pounds of water does not result in 15 percent moisture corn, however, but in 16 ⅔ percent moisture corn (15 pounds of water in 90 pounds of total weight remaining is 16 ⅔ percent moisture). Because the total weight is changed during drying, 100 pounds of 25 percent moisture corn must have 11.76 pounds of water removed to become 15 percent moisture corn. (This result is easily verified by dividing 13.24 pounds of water

Table 5-4 Bushels of Corn Remaining When 1000
Bushels of Corn Are Dried to Selected Moisture Levels[a]

Beginning Moisture (Percent)	Ending Moisture Levels (Percent)							
	13.0	14.0	15.5	16.0	17.0	18.0	19.0	20.0
13.0	1000							
13.5	989.3							
14.0	983.5	1000						
14.5	977.8	989.2						
15.0	972.0	983.4						
15.5	966.3	977.6	1000					
16.0	960.5	971.7	989.1	1000				
16.5	954.8	965.9	983.2	989.0				
17.0	949.0	960.1	977.2	983.1	1000			
17.5	944.3	954.3	971.3	977.1	989.0			
18.0	937.5	948.5	965.4	971.2	983.0	1000		
18.5	931.8	942.7	959.5	965.2	976.9	988.9		
19.0	926.0	936.9	953.6	959.3	970.9	982.8	1000	
19.5	920.3	931.0	947.7	953.3	964.9	976.7	988.8	
20.0	914.5	925.2	941.7	947.4	958.9	970.6	982.6	1000
20.5	908.8	919.4	935.8	941.4	952.8	964.5	976.5	988.7
21.0	903.0	913.6	929.9	935.5	946.8	958.4	970.3	982.5
21.5	897.3	907.8	924.0	929.5	940.8	952.3	964.1	976.2
22.0	891.6	902.0	918.1	923.6	934.8	946.2	958.0	970.0
22.5	885.8	896.2	912.2	917.6	928.7	940.1	951.8	963.7
23.0	880.1	890.3	906.2	911.7	922.7	934.0	945.6	957.5
23.5	874.3	884.5	900.3	905.7	916.7	927.9	939.4	951.2
24.0	868.6	878.7	894.4	899.8	910.7	921.8	933.3	945.0
24.5	862.8	872.9	888.5	893.8	904.6	915.7	927.1	938.7
25.0	857.1	867.1	882.6	887.9	898.6	909.6	920.9	932.5
25.5	851.3	861.3	876.7	881.9	892.6	903.5	914.7	926.2
26.0	845.6	855.5	870.7	875.9	886.6	897.4	908.6	920.0
26.5	839.8	849.7	864.8	870.0	880.5	891.3	902.4	913.7
27.0	834.1	843.8	858.9	864.0	874.5	885.2	896.2	907.5
27.5	828.3	838.0	853.0	858.1	868.5	879.1	890.1	901.2
28.0	822.6	832.2	847.1	852.1	862.5	873.0	883.9	895.0
28.5	816.8	826.4	841.2	846.2	856.4	866.9	877.7	888.7
29.0	811.1	820.6	835.2	840.2	850.4	860.8	871.5	882.5
29.5	805.3	814.8	829.3	834.3	844.4	854.8	865.4	876.2
30.0	799.6	809.0	823.4	828.3	838.4	848.7	859.2	870.0

[a]Invisible shrink calculated at 0.5 percent.

remaining by 88.24 pounds of total weight remaining and multiplying by 100 to get 15 percent.)

The formula for calculating shrink, remaining bushels, or moisture content, is based on a simple relationship.

$$DM_w = DM_d \qquad (1)$$

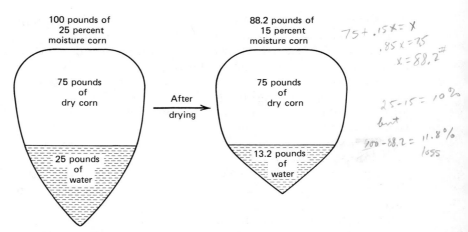

Figure 5-1. Water loss during drying.

where *DM* stands for dry matter in the corn and the subscripts w and d stand for wet grain before drying, and dry grain after drying. This relationship states that drying grain removes only water and does not affect the quantity of dry matter (an assumption that will be relaxed later to provide a more general formula). Since measurements are generally made on the percent of moisture, the relationship is

$$(100 - \%M_w)Q_w = DM_w \tag{2}$$

where $\%M_w$ is the moisture percent of the wet corn, $\%M_d$ is the moisture percent of the dried corn, and Q_w the quantity (weight or bushels) of wet corn. Substituting into formula (1) gives

$$(100 - \%M_w)Q_w = (100 - \%M_d)Q_d \tag{3}$$

To solve for the bushels remaining after drying (Q_d) the variables can be transposed to give

$$\frac{100 - \%M_w}{100 - \%M_d} Q_w = Q_d \tag{4}$$

In the previous example the Q_d was calculated by (4)

$$\frac{100 - 25}{100 - 15} (100 \text{ pounds}) = Q_d$$

$$\frac{75}{85} (100 \text{ pounds}) = 88.2 \text{ pounds}$$

The process of commercial drying often results in some loss of weight beyond the removal of water. This loss may be in the form of "bees wings" blown into the air or small particles lost in handling. The loss is usually smaller than the sampling variance for moisture and cannot be readily verified by experimental methods. It also varies with management practices of the elevator. Consequently, a rule of thumb has been adopted that designates this "invisible" loss as equal to ½ of 1 percent of the wet weight. This factor is included in the Minary Charts and can be incorporated into formula (4) by subtracting $(0.005Q_w)$ from the remaining bushels.

As a shortened procedure for calculating shrink many elevators have adopted what is called a "shrink factor." This procedure consists of taking a rule-of-thumb value, such as 1.25 percent, and multiplying that percentage times the percentage points of moisture removed from each bushel. This would be calculated as follows. Corn that is to be dried from 25.5 percent moisture to 15.5 percent moisture would require the removal of 10 percentage points of moisture. The shrink factor of 1.25 would mean multiplying 0.0125 times 10 percentage points, times the bushels of corn delivered. The resulting value would be the shrink and would be subtracted from the delivered bushels in order to obtain the net bushels on which the elevator would base its payment. As the beginning and ending moistures change, however, the proper relationship of the shrink factor also changes. Thus, a constant factor for all moisture levels cannot be used as an accurate substitute for the Minary Charts or the formula. The factor is approximately equal to 1.183, if the grain is dried to 15.5 percent moisture. Table 5-5 compares of two different shrink factors, the dry matter basis calculated on the formula, and the Minary Charts, which include

Table 5-5   Bushels of 15.5 Percent Moisture Corn Remaining from 1000 Bushels of Corn at Various Beginning Moisture Levels, with Shrink Computed by Use of Four Different Adjustment Factors

Adjustment Factor	Beginning Moisture (Percent)							
	16	*18*	*20*	*22*	*24*	*26*	*28*	*30*
Dry matter basis[a]	994	970	947	923	899	876	852	828
Minary Chart	989	965	942	918	894	871	847	823
Factor of 1.2[b]	994	970	946	922	898	874	850	826
Factor of 1.25[c]	994	969	944	919	894	869	844	819

[a]These values were obtained by dividing the percentage of dry matter in the corn at the beginning moisture level by the percentage of dry matter remaining at 15.5 percent moisture and multiplying this ratio by 1000 bushels. No invisible shrink was included in the computation.
[b]These values were calculated by multiplying $0.012 \times$ points of moisture removed $\times$ 1000 bushels and subtracting from 1000 bushels. The factor $1.2 \times$ moisture removed gives the shrink per 1000 bushels.
[c]These values were calculated by multiplying $0.0125 \times$ points of moisture removed $\times$ 1000 bushels and subtracting from 1000 bushels.

the formula plus 0.5 percent invisible shrink. Shrink factors above 1.25 are sometimes used as an indirect way of covering other costs, such as handling losses or creation of excess foreign material during drying. The use of shrink factors to conceal other charges is generally undesirable from the standpoint of pricing efficiency in a competitive market and does not permit price to serve the function of communicating differences in value to producers.

Farmers who wish to determine the profitability of owning their own dryer must take into consideration the shrink and the moisture discount that apply to the particular moisture level and market in which they are selling. Since many elevators are still using a discount schedule, a simple exercise will serve to illustrate the procedures for calculating returns to owning a dryer.

Table 5-6 compares the returns from selling 1000 bushels as wet corn, at a price reduced by the moisture discount, with returns from selling the bushels remaining after the grain has been dried. Alternative beginning moisture levels and base prices are shown in the table.

For purposes of illustration, assume a beginning moisture level of 25.5 percent, a base price of $2.00, and a discount of 4 cents per bushel per point. Total returns are $1600 for the 1000 bushels sold as wet corn. If this 1000 bushels were dried to 15.5 percent moisture, shrink tables (such as Table 5-4) show that there would be 876.66 bushels left after drying. This dry corn can be sold (at no discount) at the base price of $2.00 per bushel.

Total receipts when sold at 15.5 percent moisture would be $1753.32. The difference between the value of the corn if sold dry and the value sold wet ($1753.32 − $1600) = $153.32, the return to drying. If this return is greater than the farmer's cost of drying, then it is profitable to dry the corn before delivery. If drying costs are greater than returns to drying, the farmer should sell the corn at the higher moisture level and accept the price discount.

For a fixed discount scale, returns to drying decrease as the base price of corn increases, and as the beginning moisture level decreases. For example, when the base price of corn is $3.00 per bushel the farmer receives $1.50 more by selling 18.5 percent moisture corn, than if the corn is dried to 15.5 percent moisture.

An elevator cannot pay more for wet corn than for dry corn. The solution is to change the moisture discount or go to a shrink plus drying charge. Table 5-7 shows the effect of changing prices, discounts, and moisture levels. For example, at a price of $3.00 per bushel, and 4 cents per point discount, returns from drying 30 percent corn to 15.5 percent are 5 cents per bushel (Table 5-6). Since this represents a removal of 14.5 percentage points (30.0 − 15.5), Table 5-7 shows returns per bushel per point are 0.345 cents (5.0¢ ÷ 14.5 percent). Returns per point drop from 0.345 cents at 30 percent to 0.111 cents at 20 percent moisture. Raising the discount from 4 cents per point to 5

Table 5-6 Moisture Discounts, Shrink and Returns from 1000 Bushels of Corn at Various Prices of No. 2 Corn, and 4 Cents Discount per Point[a]

Moisture Level (percent)	Market Discount (cents/bu)	Total Receipts When Sold as Wet Corn	Bushels of 15.5% Corn After Drying[b]	Total Receipts When Sold as 15.5% Corn	Returns from Drying	
					Total	Cents per Bushel
			Number 2 Corn Priced at $2.00/Bu			
30	58	$1420	823.40	$1646.80	$226.80	22.7
28	50	1500	847.07	1694.14	194.14	19.4
25.5	40	1600	876.66	1753.32	153.32	15.3
22.5	28	1720	912.16	1824.32	104.32	10.4
20	18	1820	941.75	1883.50	63.50	6.4
18.5	12	1880	959.50	1919.00	39.00	3.9
			Number 2 Corn Priced at $2.50/Bu			
30	58	$1920	823.40	$2058.50	$138.50	13.9
28	50	2000	847.07	2117.68	117.68	11.8
25.5	40	2100	876.66	2191.65	91.65	9.2
22.5	28	2220	912.16	2280.40	60.40	6.0
20	18	2320	941.75	2354.38	34.38	3.4
18.5	12	2380	959.50	2398.75	18.75	1.9
			Number 2 Corn Priced at $3.00/Bu			
30	58	$2420	823.40	$2470.20	$50.20	5.0
28	50	2500	847.07	2541.21	41.21	4.1
25.5	40	2600	876.66	2629.98	29.98	3.0
22.5	28	2720	912.16	2736.48	16.48	1.6
20	18	2820	941.75	2825.25	5.25	0.5
18.5	12	2880	959.50	2878.50	-1.50	-0.2

[a]Market discount is computed on the basis of 4 cents for each percent of moisture above 15.5 percent.
[b]The weight loss through drying includes 0.5 percent invisible shrink.

Table 5-7 Returns from Drying Corn
at Various Prices and Moisture Levels,
in Cents per Bushel per Point[a]

Moisture Level (percent)	Price per Bushel of Corn		
	$2.00	$2.50	$3.00
	Cents/Bu with 4 Cents/Point Discount		
30	1.566	0.959	0.345
28	1.552	0.944	0.328
25.5	1.530	0.920	0.300
22.5	1.486	0.857	0.229
20	1.422	0.756	0.111
18.5	1.300	0.633	−0.067
	Cents/Bu with 5 Cents/Point Discount		
30	2.566	1.959	1.345
28	2.552	1.994	1.328
25.5	2.530	1.920	1.300
22.5	2.486	1.857	1.229
20	2.422	1.756	1.111
18.5	2.300	1.633	0.967

[a]Computed from the same data as Table 5-6.
Cents per bushel per point are obtained by dividing cents per bushel, returns from drying
(Table 5-6) by the points of moisture above 15.5
percent.

cents per point increases returns to drying from 0.3 cents to 1.3 cents
at 25.5 percent moisture.

With frequent changes in price and moisture it becomes extremely
difficult to adjust the discount system rapidly enough to maintain constant returns to drying. A variable moisture discount is not a satisfactory method for adjusting value for excess moisture. An alternative is for
the elevator to reduce the weight of grain purchased to a 15.5 percent
basis ("pencil shrink") and then charge the farmer for the cost of
drying. The drying charge becomes explicit and can respond to the
forces of supply and demand. Under this method both farmers and
elevators can better assess the relative cost of their alternatives.

Due to the variability of moisture readings (even on the same
sample), and the difficulty of drying corn within ½ percent of a predetermined level, many elevators shrink corn to 15 percent to provide
a margin of safety and to allow for additional invisible shrink through
foreign material losses. If the 1000 bushels of 25.5 percent moisture
corn were shrunk to 15 percent (instead of 15.5), the producer would

receive $871.41, and would pay $105 in drying costs—leaving a net payment of $766.41. If the corn is to be stored without aeration, a reduction of 13 percent (to 12.5 percent) may be desirable, increasing both shrink and drying costs. With corn prices at $3.00 per bushel, drying corn to 13 percent and selling it at the 15.5 percent base price results in a loss to the farmer of 8.6 cents per bushel. This loss of water, which could have been sold at the price of corn plus the fuel required to dry the corn from 15.5 to 13.0, makes overdrying a very costly practice.

EVALUATING THE ADEQUACY OF GRAIN STANDARDS

The change in harvesting methods and in varieties and research on the relationship between quality and value in end use have raised several questions about the ability of the present standards to meet the three purposes of standardization. The following six issues on the corn standards illustrate the shortcomings for all grains.

1. The FM or BCFM factors in most grains classify broken pieces of grain, dirt, weed seeds, and other grains as having equal value. We need a method for separating these materials. Changing screen size does not solve the problem but only changes the size of dirt, weeds, or grain that will still be lumped together as FM.

2. The lowest factor approach to numerical grades places grain of widely different characteristics in the same grade even though they differ on all but one factor (e.g., moisture). For instance, corn that is No. 1 on all factors except moisture, but No. 5 on moisture, would grade the same as corn that is No. 5 on all factors including mold. This procedure provides the incentive for blending every rail car or every vessel to the minimum quality on all factors.

3. The range of values between grades—especially in the case of heat damage—is too small to distinguish with our present sample size and sampling procedures. The probability of obtaining a correct grade for No. 2 corn on the basis of heat damage is less than one-half. Factor limits should be established that are consistent with statistical properties and sampling methods.

4. The base level of 15.5 percent moisture for No. 2 corn is not a safe level for long-term storage, but if corn is dried below that level the farmer takes the weight loss when it is sold. The elevator then has a strong incentive to blend wet corn with dry corn to make 15.5 percent moisture. An alternative system is needed to remove the incentive for blending, and to assure that the farmer is paid on the basis of the corn and not the water.

5. The present set of grades excludes economic factors of importance while including others of very limited economic importance to end users. The best example is test weight. Research at several universities has shown almost no relationship between test weight and feeding value,[2] nor has research shown any relationship

2Lowell D. Hill and A. H. Jensen, "The Role of Grades and Standards in Identifying Nutritive Values of Grains," *Feed Composition, Animal Nutrient Requirements and Computerization of Diets*, Fonnesbeck, Harris, and Kearl, eds., Utah Agricultural Experiment Station, Utah State University, Logan, 1977.

between test weight and processing value, yet we continue to downgrade and discount light test weight corn.

6. If broken corn is an important factor on which to grade (and discount) corn, then the price differential must be carried back to the point of breakage. This means primarily that brittleness must be included as a grade factor at the farm in order to provide the economic incentive to dry at lower temperatures, harvest at lower moisture levels, design and adjust equipment to minimize stress cracks, and to plant varieties that are less likely to break during handling.

QUALITY MEASUREMENT IN OTHER COUNTRIES

In order to facilitate exchange in a modern, industrialized society, organizations in various countries have developed rules and procedures by which the quality of goods is determined in open trade. These rules can be simple or complex, ranging from visual inspection of the commodities at a neighborhood fruit stand, and subsequent acceptance or refusal to purchase the goods, to very technical contracts and standards specifying the processing characteristics of a material whose terms are worked out only through extensive negotiation.

Both buyer and seller of any lot of grain are interested in determining the value of the lot as a basis for establishing a price. The greater the distance between buyer and seller, and the more complex the marketing system, the more that buyer and seller must rely on grading standards and standardized terminology for a description of the characteristics of the grain.

Quality has been contractually specified in many different ways in the history of grain trading.[3] At present, there are two methods in general use that account for the majority of the contracts in world markets. Most grain sold by U.S. exporters is sold on the basis of certificate final with respect to quality. The certificate is issued under federal inspection at the point of loading, using a numerical standard based on quantitative measurement. Most grain, other than U.S.-origin grain, is exported under a "fair average quality" (FAQ) contract where quality is guaranteed to be at least equal to the average of all such grain shipped during a specified period. One important variation of the certificate final system is found in the operations of the Canadian Marketing Board. The board regulates the sale of all export grain, paying particular attention to the quality of their grain entering the world market. Often the board will sell a higher quality grain than the contract specifies, because blending of low quality grain with high quality grain is prohibited. This system operates on a certificate final basis much the same as the U.S. system, but with tighter restrictions to

---

[3]A good description of several of these contracts is provided by G. H. Morsink, "Comparative Quality of U.S. Corn for Feed, Food, and Oil in the Netherlands," in *Corn Quality in World Markets*, Lowell D. Hill, (ed.), The Interstate Printers and Publishers, Inc., Danville, Ill., 1975.

insure quality and some variability in the factor limits from one crop year to the next. In contrast to the certificate final system, the FAQ contract calls for quality to be determined at the port of import rather than at the point of export.

Collecting the FAQ Sample

The standard for FAQ is made up of the average quality of grain delivered from a particular origin during each week. The FAQ for French maize is different from Argentine maize, and the FAQ sample for one origin may be different from one month to the next. In addition, the regions of a country may have a different FAQ standard if there are differences in the quality produced in the different regions.[4]

In order to determine the FAQ standard for any particular origin or month, those vessels containing grain sold on a contract that specifies FAQ at destination are sampled in accordance with rules specified in the contract. The samples are taken by a superintendent's company—much like American grain inspectors under the U.S. grain grading system. The superintendent's company has a jurisdictional area that they cover much the same as private grain inspectors cover a territory in the states.

The samples are drawn by mutual agreement of buyer and seller at regular intervals in the hold of the ship. Both buyer and seller agree on the areas of the ship from which the samples are drawn. The number of samples to be drawn, their size, and the sampling intervals are specified in the contract. When a ship is unloaded and all samples are taken, the buyer and seller jointly select or agree on a sample that they consider to be representative of the quality in that ship, or of the lot that was purchased. The sample is then sealed and sent to the analysis center in London for use in establishing the FAQ standard for that month. The organization responsible for the FAQ standard in London is the Grain and Feed Trade Association (GAFTA). FAQ systems are used in several countries in the world, but all are similar to that of the GAFTA contracts.

Determining the FAQ Standard

The sample to be used for establishing the FAQ standards is obtained from several ports and from all vessels delivered under an FAQ contract during the contract month. When these samples are received at the GAFTA office, a committee of the trade association meets to inspect the samples that have been submitted for use in arbitration and for use in preparing the FAQ standard sample for that month. The committee inspects the samples and determines which samples appear

---

[4]Steve C. Bermingham and Lowell D. Hill, *A Fair Average Quality for Grain Exports,* Department of Agricultural Economics, Agricultural Experiment Station, AE-4459, University of Illinois, Urbana, July 1978.

to be representative. Exceptionally good quality or exceptionally poor quality samples (in terms of visual appearance) are usually excluded by the committee in constructing the FAQ standard for that month. There may be times, however, when the committee will leave all the samples in the standard, taking the view that the good and the bad balance each other in the composite average. Those samples in the middle range of quality are combined to form the FAQ standard sample for that month. The samples are weighted to represent the tonnages involved in the shipment. For example, a sample taken from a 50,000-ton ship would have more of its contents included in the FAQ standard than would a 25,000-ton cargo. This standard is the official guide against which individual shipments are compared, and is used by an arbitration committee involved in any dispute between two parties of a contract.

Arbitration and Appeals

When two parties of a contract have a dispute about the fulfillment of the obligations of the contract, mechanisms for settlement of the dispute are set forth in the rules of the trade association. The sample that is submitted by the buyer, as representative of the quality received, is sent to the trade association for comparison. The submitted sample is placed next to the FAQ standard sample with the identity of the samples concealed. The party that is claiming inferior quality must then determine which sample is inferior. If the FAQ standard is inferior, the argument is virtually halted there, even though the rules state that the decision may be appealed. If the party is successful in identifying their sample of grain as inferior to the FAQ sample, arbitration may then proceed.

When the need arises for an appeal against an award of arbitration, members of the assocation's committee of appeal elect from among their number (usually about 75) a panel of 5 to serve as a board of appeal. To maintain balance and equity, the committee of appeal consists of buyers, sellers, and other members of the trade. The members of the committee have in their minds a very clear framework for what the quality of a particular origin "should" be. The contract is then analyzed for the intent and the allowances for the particular characteristics. The contract usually reads "about fair average quality of the season's shipments." The word "about" is generally interpreted to mean that the value of the disputed sample is within ½ of 1 percent of the contract price. If the submitted sample is determined to be within the allowance, no award is given and the dispute is essentially abandoned, although the decision of the arbitrators may be appealed. If the arbitrators or the board of appeal decide that the submitted sample is of lower quality than the standard, monetary allowance would usually be made in the arbitration award.

In some cases, the parties of a contract may settle their disputes between themselves. For example, if a seller wishes to keep the business of an important buyer, concessions on the quality may be made when it is obvious that the delivered quality of grain in the lot is below the FAQ standard. Therefore, the contract specifying FAQ at destination has a considerable amount of flexibility and allows for judicious settlement of claims.

Establishing Quality Under the Certificate Final System

In most shipments from U.S. ports, the contract between buyer and seller reads "certificate final with respect to quality." The certificate will carry the results of the official inspection and grading, performed by the Federal Grain Inspection Service. The information on the certificate includes the numerical grade for the entire vessel (or for sublots within the vessel) as well as information on any factor that exceeds the limits of that grade.

The samples are taken from the grain stream by a mechanical sampler as the vessel is being loaded. The sampler must be located after the last elevation before the grain reaches the vessel. Since the contract specifies "certificate final," the responsibility of the exporter, insofar as quality is concerned, ends at the point where the grain is sampled. Changes in quality (especially increased breakage and BCFM) during loading and unloading of the vessel are not taken into account in determining the grade. Any complaints or claims of the buyer on the quality of grain received at destination must be based on the accuracy of the original certificate, not on changes in quality after loading. Once the grain is loaded, resampling or inspection is virtually impossible, and the file samples saved from the original inspection become the basis for evaluating the accuracy of the original grade. Buyers, therefore, have little practical recourse on certificate final purchases, except the interest of the exporter in maintaining a reputation and customer goodwill.

Advantages and Disadvantages of the Two Systems

For the seller, an FAQ contract would decrease many of the difficulties that accompany a poor quality crop. The exporter agrees to deliver the average quality for the period. If overall quality is low, there is no obligation to raise the quality by blending, cleaning, or drying, because the standard of comparison will be equally low. The seller does not have to accept quality discounts because of a poor quality crop. Given the U.S. system of private firms exporting grain, some problems could arise, however, if individual firms or certain ports in the United States delivered exceptionally good quality grain, thereby raising the standard for the month against competing firms or origin ports. Under FAQ, quality is determined at destination rather than origin, and thus the contract increases the risk and responsibility of the exporter for maintaining quality during loading and transport. But since the FAQ standard would be determined on grain subjected to the same loading and transport conditions, the increased risk is probably not significant.

For the buyer, FAQ provides a quality assurance at destination and places the responsibility on the seller to deliver grain meeting the standard. The disadvantage to the buyer is that the standard against which the quality of each vessel is measured may vary from month to month and across crop years, while numerical standards remain quantitatively the same. Under numerical standards, a buyer knows what the quality of the grain is at the time of inspection without seeing the sample. The standards do not change over time or among origins, and price adjustments can be negotiated on each quality factor, giving the buyer an opportunity to weigh price against value.

Numerical standards for origin grades may be the basis for misunderstanding and dispute. Knowing the numerical standard and the quality represented by a certain grade, the buyer may expect higher quality than is received as a result of quality deterioration during handling and transport subsequent to the issuance of the grade certificate. Over a period of time, buyers should be able to estimate the expected loss of quality and adjust their expectations and price decisions accordingly, but they still may be dissatisfied. On the FAQ system, both the standard and the quality are determined at the point of import, close to the final destination, and often under direct supervision of the buyer. Expectations and reality are, therefore, much more readily reconciled.

An FAQ grading system simplifies the grading procedures for grain, protects producers from quality problems generated by circumstances beyond their control, such as weather, and provides a mechanism for the orderly settlement of disputes that a certificate final procedure does not. The FAQ system does, however, introduce a possible element of variability in quality that is a disadvantage to the buyer. From the point of view of the seller, FAQ implies a delivered quality rather than origin quality—an increased risk that sellers resist without monetary compensation in the form of price premiums.

Summary

The ultimate goal of grades and standards for grain is to improve the efficiency with which buyers communicate their preferences to sellers. Grades do not establish value but merely standardize the terminology with which the market communicates value information between buyers and sellers. Any change in standards must increase the value of the information by at least the increased cost of implementing the change. In general this requires that inspection and grading procedures be rapid and inexpensive, yielding estimates of quality that are efficient (i.e., of minimum variance) and unbiased.

In the short run, standards have little effect on quality, or total value of the crop, but only describe the quality in terms accepted by the industry. In the longer run, the fact that the trade generally prices grain on the basis of established grade factors provides an incentive for changing production and marketing practices to alter the quality characteristics of the crop. For example, discounts for test weight reward those farmers who grow higher test weight grain and stimulate breeders to select for that characteristic.

Selected References

Agricultural Marketing Service, Grain Division, *Comparisons of Various Moisture Meters With the Oven Method in Determining Moisture Content of Grain,* AMS-511, U.S. Department of Agriculture, Washington, D.C., August 1963.

Agricultural Marketing Service, Grain Division, *Historical Review of Changes in the Grain Standards of the United States,* AMS-513, U.S. Department of Agriculture, Washington, D.C., 1963.

Agricultural Research Service, *Damage to Corn From Pneumatic Conveying,* ARS-NC-5, U.S. Department of Agriculture, Washington, D.C., January 1973.

Agricultural Research Service, *Grain Breakage Caused by Commercial Handling Methods,* Marketing Research Report No. 968, U.S. Department of Agriculture, Washington, D.C., June 1973.

Agricultural Research Service, *Breakage Tester Predicts Handling Damage in Corn,* ARS-NC-49, U.S. Department of Agriculture, Washington, D.C., September 1976.

Bermingham, Steve C. and Lowell D. Hill, *A Fair Average Quality for Grain Exports,* Department of Agricultural Economics, Agricultural Experiment Station AE-4459, University of Illinois, Urbana, July 1978.

Dorfman, Robert and Peter O. Steiner, "Optimal Advertising and Optimal Quality," *American Economic Review,* Vol. 44, No. 5, December 1954.

Elam, T. E. and Lowell D. Hill, "Potential Role of Sampling Variation in the Measurement of Corn Grading Factors," *Illinois Agricultural Economics,* Vol. 17, No. 1, January 1977.

Farris, Paul L., "Uniform Grades and Standards, Product Differentiation and Product Development," *Journal of Farm Economics,* Vol. XLII, No. 4, November 1960.

Freeman, Jere E., "Quality Factors Affecting Value of Corn for Wet Milling," *Transactions of the American Society of Agricultural Engineers,* Vol. 16, No. 4, 1973.

Grain Standards Committee, *Farmers' Stake in the Grain Standards,* Great Plains Wheat, Inc.

Hill, Lowell D., ("Federal Grades and Standards as Measures of Corn Quality"), *Proceedings of Grain Conditioning Conference,* University of Illinois, Urbana, 1974.

Hill, Lowell, D. ("Corn Quality in World Markets"), *Proceedings of the Grain Dealers' Conference,* University of Illinois, Urbana, 1975.

Hill, Lowell D., Marvin R. Paulson, and Bruce L. Brooks, *Grain Quality Losses Between Origin and Destination of Export Grain—A Case Study,* Department of Agricultural Economics, Agricultural Experiment Station, AE-4399, University of Illinois, Urbana, 1976.

Hill, Lowell D., Marvin R. Paulson, and Daniel Hiller, *Corn Breakage as Affected by Handling During Shipment,* Department of Agricultural Economics, Agricultural Experiment Station, AE-4403, University of Illinois, Urbana, 1976.

Hill, Lowell D., Steve C. Bermingham, and Randall Semper, *Sampling and Measurement Problems in Grain Grading,* Department of Agricultural Economics, Agricultural Experiment Station, AE-4407, University of Illinois, Urbana, 1976.

Hill, Lowell D. and A. H. Jensen, "The Role of Grades and Standards in Identifying Nutritive Value in Grains," *Feed Composition, Animal Nutrient Requirements and Computerization of Diets,* Fonnesbeck, Harris, and Kearle (eds.), Utah Agricultural Experiment Station, Utah State University, Logan, 1977.

Hill, Lowell D., ("Changes in Grain Quality During Transport"), *Proceedings—1977 Corn Quality Conference,* Department of Agricultural Economics, Agricultural Experiment Station, AE-4454, University of Illinois, Urbana, 1978.

Hoffman, Kathryn J. and Lowell D. Hill, "Historical Review of the U.S. Grades and Standards for Grain," *Illinois Agricultural Economics,* Vol. 16, No. 1, January 1976.

Ladd, George W. and Verophol Suvannunt, "A Model of Consumer Good Characteristics," *American Journal of Agricultural Economics,* Vol. 58, No. 1, February 1976.

Ladd, George W. and Marvin B. Martin, "Prices and Demands for Input Characteristics," *American Journal of Agricultural Economics,* Vol. 58, No. 1, February 1976.

Ladd, George W. and Dale R. Miller, "Relation of Corn Grades to Feed Quality," *Staff Paper Series,* No. 87, Department of Economics, Iowa State University, Ames, October 1978.

Mehren, George W., "The Function of Grades in an Affluent Society," *Journal of Farm Economics,* Vol. 42, No. 5, December 1961.

Mittleider, John F. and Donald E. Anderson, *An Analysis of the Relationships Among Specific Quality Characteristics for Hard Red Spring and Durum Wheat,* Department of Agricultural Economics, North Dakota Agricultural Experiment Station, Bulletin No. 122, North Dakota State University, Fargo, August 1977.

Peplinski, A. J., O. L. Brekke, E. L. Griffin, G. Hall, and Lowell D. Hill, "Corn Quality as Influenced by Harvest and Drying Conditions," *Cereal Foods World,* Vol. 20, No. 3, March 1975.

Petry, Timothy A. and Donald E. Anderson, *Comparative Analysis of United States and Canadian Wheat Grades,* Department of Agricultural Economics, North Dakota Agricultural Experiment Station, Bulletin No. 99, North Dakota State University, Fargo, November 1974.

Pettus, David M., "Revised Grain Standards Act: A Modern Law for Modern Times," *Agricultural Marketing,* October 1968.

Rosen, Sherwin, "Hedonic Prices and Implicit Markets: Product Differentiation in Pure Competition," *Journal of Political Economy,* Vol. 82, No. 1, January 1974.

White, G. M. and I. J. Ross, "Discoloration and Stress-Cracking in White Corn as Affected by Drying Temperature and Cooling Rate," *1970 Winter Meeting, American Society of Agricultural Engineers,* December 1970.

Zusman, Pinhas, "A Theoretical Basis for Determination of Grading and Sorting Schemes," *Journal of Farm Economics,* Vol. 49, No. 1, Part 1, February 1967.

PRICING GRAINS

PRICING GRAINS*

**CHAPTER
6**

Paralleling the physical system for marketing grains is the pricing system, which provides for the interchange of bids and offers and agreements to buy and sell among traders throughout the country and the world. The pricing system has two major functions to perform: coordinating production and utilization decisions of farmers, merchants, processors and consumers and helping to determine the distribution of income among these different groups.

The prices of grains, relative to each other and to other commodities, determine how much land, labor, machinery, and other inputs will be used in growing, storing, processing and distributing grain and grain products. Price differences over time help determine in each period how much grain is consumed and how much is stored for future use. Price differences between locations provide incentives to transport grain to where the need is greatest, and price differences between grades provide incentives to produce the kinds of grains that are in greatest demand.

For the grain farmer, the price and quantity of grain produced determines how much income is available for family living. For the consumer, grain prices are a determinant of the cost of food, affecting prices not only of cereal products but also products derived from livestock. And, for the businesspeople engaged in assembling, storing, feeding, processing, and distributing grains and grain products, a few cents difference in price per bushel can be the difference between a profit and a loss.

THE PRICE DISCOVERY PROCESS

The process by which the price is found which equalizes quantities supplied by sellers with quantities demanded by buyers is called "price discovery." For grains, price discovery occurs through the many and varied contacts between buyers (or potential buyers) and sellers (or potential sellers). These contacts are dispersed geographically, except for the futures markets and a few spot markets where traders or their representatives gather on trading floors. Except in futures trading, most contacts are between one potential buyer and one potential seller

*Richard G. Heifner, Staff Economist, Agricultural Marketing Service, USDA, Washington, D.C. Information in this chapter represents the views of the author and not necessarily the views of the U.S. Department of Agriculture.

at a time, such as a farmer talking to a country elevator manager, or an elevator manager talking to a processor-buyer by phone. Most buyers and sellers have contacts with more than one opposite party, and the overlapping contacts tie the entire market together.

For each individual trader the price discovery process involves a search for the opposite party who offers the best available terms. The search typically begins with a review of market reports, and then enters a period of negotiation where bids and offers are exchanged with one or more opposite parties. The search culminates when an oral or written contract or sales agreement is reached.

A contract is an agreement between two parties providing for an exchange of a commodity for money or for another commodity. The agreement must specify not only the price, or a formula for determining the price, but also the quantity, quality, time, and place of delivery, as well as time and method of payment and provisions for guaranteeing performance. In negotiating contracts some of the terms of trade other than price are frequently implicit, being set by custom or rule. In futures trading, the contracts traded are so highly standardized that only price and quantity need be specified during the negotiation process.

Not only futures contracts but most cash contracts are forward contracts in that they specify delivery at a later date. Some contracts call for "spot delivery," which is interpreted as delivery within a few days.

This chapter discusses the price discovery process as it occurs at the farmer-first handler level, and at the merchant-processor level. Then, the factors determining price and the implications for price forecasting will be examined. Next, alternative pricing strategies that farmers and country elevators can employ will be considered. The last section briefly explores ways that the grain pricing system might be improved.

TRANSACTIONS BETWEEN FARMERS AND FIRST HANDLERS

Virtually all of the soybeans, over 95 percent of the wheat, and nearly two-thirds of the corn produced in the United States are sold for use off the farms where they are grown. Since sales of these three crops account for almost one-fourth of U.S. gross farm income, the farm price is a key factor in determining income, not only to the farmers directly involved but to agriculture as a whole.

The farmers who sell grains vary greatly in size and type of farming operation, ranging from part-time operators who may sell only a few hundred bushels of grain per year to large operators who sell hundreds of thousands of bushels annually. The time and effort each can advantageously devote to pricing grain depends on the amount of grain to be sold. Small farmers typically look to only one or a few buyers as outlets, while large producers may deal with a number of buyers including some at distant locations.

The firms that buy grain from farmers include country elevators, subterminal and terminal elevators, processors, and feeders. Any such firm who buys directly from farmers is called a first handler. First handlers typically maintain daily contact with other buyers and sellers by telephone. Many buy and sell grain almost every day, particularly during the harvest season.

The Bid Pricing System

Under normal conditions most first handlers determine and post spot bid prices each day for the types and grades of grain that they want to buy. Elevator operators determine their bid prices by subtracting operating margins and transportation costs from prices bid by the firms they sell to. Processors and feeders base their bid prices on current market quotations, adjusting their bids up and down to obtain the desired flow of grain into their plants. During periods of active price movements, first handler bid prices may be changed several times within the day. When prices are highly volatile the bid price may not be posted at all; instead, it is quoted in response to the farmer's call, after checking the latest futures quotation. If the farmer has a large amount to sell, the buyer may call more than one outlet to confirm the price. Bid prices apply to a standard grade and quantity, such as No. 2 yellow corn, 15 percent moisture or lower. The elevator maintains a discount and premium schedule that is applied when grades or quality differ from the standard.

Posted bid prices apply to any farmer's grain that is brought into the elevator and meets the grade requirements. Farmers usually sell at the posted price. Large farmers may occasionally be able to negotiate price or other terms that are more favorable than the elevator's posted bid.

How Sales Are Made

Nearly half of the wheat and soybeans and about a quarter of the corn in the United States are delivered directly from the combine to the elevator, while the remainder goes into on-farm storage. Grain brought to the elevator during harvest is weighed, graded, and sold or entered into storage in the farmer's account. Delivery of grain directly from the combine to the local elevator at harvest eliminates an extra handling. If the grain has not already been contracted, the farmer typically is allowed a few days to indicate whether the grain should be sold immediately or placed in commercial storage. Once storage is initiated the farmer can sell to the elevator on any date thereafter, with storage charges being deducted from the returns on the grain. For grain delivered out of farm storage, price normally is set before delivery, subject to grade and moisture determinations.

Various arrangements have developed to allow the time of sale to differ from the time of physical delivery. The range of dates when sales can be made is illustrated in Figure 6-1. In choosing the date of sale the farmer must consider price risk and make judgments as to possible price fluctuations.

Forward Pricing

Forward pricing involves an agreement between the seller and buyer that sets price and other terms of sale and provides for ownership transfer at a later date. Crop producers find forward pricing useful as a means to fix the price on expected output before harvest. By pricing forward they protect themselves from loss due to price declines but surrender the potential for speculative gain due to price increases. Farmers can price their crops before harvest by selling futures contracts or by entering cash forward contracts with first handlers. The amount of a crop that can be advantageously priced before harvest is limited by yield uncertainty.

Pricing After Harvest

Grain prices typically rise after harvest reflecting the costs of storing grains from harvest time to the time of utilization. Therefore, the farmer whose cost of storing grain is less than this expected seasonal price rise can often profit by holding the crop for sale sometime after harvest. This, of course, postpones receipt of payment and entails continued exposure to price risks. Since most of the seasonal price increase occurs during the first four to six months after harvest, carry-

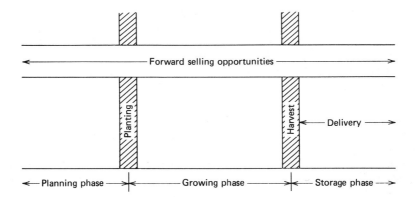

Figure 6-1. Forward selling opportunities during the planning, growing, and storage phases of annual crop production.

ing stocks longer than this is quite speculative, much like buying and holding a futures contract.

Delayed Pricing

In recent years, a different method for farmers to postpone pricing beyond harvest has come into use. In this method, called delayed pricing, the title to the grain is transferred from the farmer to the elevator without setting the price. The elevator sells and ships the grain to the next buyer, usually covering this short sale with a long hedge in the futures market. At a later date, chosen by the farmer, the farmer's price is set based on the elevator's then current bid; the farmer pays intervening storage costs, the elevator lifts its hedge, and final settlement is made.

Delayed pricing allows the elevator to free its bin space to handle other farmers' grains while letting the farmer postpone pricing until a future date. With this arrangement the farmer loses title to the grain before receiving final payment. Under this arrangement there is a greater chance of loss if the elevator should fail.

TRANSACTIONS AMONG GRAIN MERCHANTS AND PROCESSORS

Participants in the grain trade beyond the farmer-first handler level include subterminal elevators, terminal elevators, processors, feeders, exporters, and foreign buyers. Transactions among these traders involve much larger quantities than do purchases from farmers. A common unit of trade is the hopper carload (about 3500 to 4000 bushels), but trainload (up to 500,000 bushels) and shipload-size transactions are common for grain destined for export.

The commercial grain market is primarily a telephone market. The great bulk of transactions are negotiated by telephone between a buyer and a seller, both operating from their own offices. Agreements made by telephone are followed by written confirmation. A remarkable feature of this market is that verbal agreements, involving hundreds of thousands or millions of dollars are used with a minimum of misunderstanding and disputes.

The Bid Pricing System

Price discovery occurs through several different kinds of trading processes. Grain futures are traded on open markets where buyers and sellers are equally likely to initiate transactions and any number of traders may be involved. In contrast, most cash grain transactions are negotiated privately between individual buyers and sellers by telephone. In the cash grain market the search for a mutually satisfactory price most often starts with the buyer's bid, which is normally based on the latest futures price with adjustments for differences in grade, location, and time of delivery.

After the close of futures trading each day (about 1:15 P.M., CST), each of the major processors, exporters, and other merchants decides on a set of prices it will use to bid for grain until the futures market opens the next day. These bid prices are telephoned to the country elevators and other firms from which the merchants and processors regularly buy. The bid prices normally hold until futures trading opens again the next morning. Once the futures market opens, the bid prices may be adjusted to reflect changes in that day's futures price. To make these adjustments automatically during periods of fluctuating futures prices, bids are commonly made in terms of the "basis."

Basis Pricing

The basis is the difference between a specific cash price and the price for a specific futures contract, normally the "nearby contract," the contract that is nearest to maturity. To give an example for basis pricing, let's assume an Illinois corn processor might bid "15 under" for 30-day corn. This means the firm is willing to pay 15 cents below the maturing future for corn deliveries to its plant during the next 30 days.

The potential seller can convert a basis bid to a cash price by simply subtracting the basis from the closing futures price. More likely, sellers will simply compare the "15 under" bid with similar basis bids for other merchants, and thereby make their decisions about selling and about their own bids to farmers.

The advantage in quoting price in terms of the basis is that adjustments for changes in the general price level for the grain, as indicated by the futures price, are made automatically. For example, if a buyer bids "15 under" one afternoon, and the futures price opens up 10 cents the next morning, potential sellers know without being called that the bid is following the futures up. Thus, quoting price in terms of the basis provides an efficient means to exchange bids and offers. The practice is so common that traders use the term "flat price" to indicate when the full price is being quoted rather than the basis.

Often, sales agreements specify price in terms of the basis. In the grain trade, this practice is commonly called "booking the basis." Either the buyer or seller (by mutual agreement) is allowed a specified period of time to choose a date when the cash price for the transaction is determined by applying the agreed-on basis to the then-current futures quotation. Booking the basis sets the delivery terms and fixes price relative to a specific futures price, but it leaves both buyer and seller exposed to price level risk. Hence, the practice is frequently accompanied by hedging in the futures by one or both parties. Such a sales agreement is usually fulfilled by an exchange of futures, at the agreed-on futures price plus or minus the agreed—on basis. The futures exchanges have special rules to facilitate this type of trade, which is called an "ex-pit transaction."

Time of Delivery

Commercial grain sales agreements may call for "spot" delivery or "forward" delivery. Spot delivery normally means delivery within a few days. The bulk of the commercial cash grain trade involves contracts for forward delivery. More than two-thirds of the corn, wheat, and soybeans traded are priced for delivery more than 10 days in the future. Examples of common terms with regard to time of delivery are: "10 days," "30 days," "January," and "first half of March." By buying for forward delivery, processors and exporters are able to schedule uniform flows of products into their plants. Forward selling also enables country elevators to fix price before they ship their grain and schedule their loading-out activities ahead of time.

Floor Trading on Organized Exchanges

A notable exception to the dominant practice of trading by telephone for forward delivery is the floor trading in spot or cash grain at Minneapolis and Kansas City. In these markets the grain bought and sold is in railroad cars, on a designated siding in the city, ready for delivery within a few days. In both exchanges, cash grain trading shares the trading floor with futures trading. Samples of the grains available for sale are displayed in pans on the seller's or broker's table on the trading floor. Potential buyers or their representatives circulate among the tables and negotiate with sellers on an individual basis. Transaction prices are posted around the trading floor.

Floor trading in spot grains reached its heyday in the era when country grain buyers commonly shipped grain on consignment to a grain broker at the terminal markets. The broker then took charge of the grain as it arrived on track in the terminal city and offered it for sale on the floor of the grain exchange. The consignment method of selling grain has largely been replaced by "to arrive" cash contracts between country elevators and terminal merchants in corn, soybeans, and most classes of wheat. However, consignment sales by country elevators continue to be important for malting barley and durum wheat at the Minneapolis Grain Exchange. These are grains where the grade standards only partially reflect the quality factors important to buyers. Hence, buyers wish to see a sample before offering a price. Only a few grain brokers still operate on the major markets.

Pricing Export Grain

Grain pricing in the export market has much in common with domestic grain pricing. Overseas prices and domestic prices are closely related on a day-to-day basis. For many export sales, the price negotiation process is essentially the same as for domestic trades. Transactions are negotiated by telephone by traders operating from their offices and dealing with opposite parties they know and trust. But, because of the size and complexity of the transactions, direct personal contact between buyers and sellers or their representatives plays a larger role in the export trade. And some foreign buyers buy by calling for tenders or offers from all potential sellers at once, rather than by negotiating individually with sellers.

The export trade differs from the domestic grain trade in that most transactions are in shipload quantities or larger. Several different types of sales arrangements are used. The most common is an "f.o.b." sale—f.o.b. signifying free on board ship at point of origin. Other types of sales arrangements where the buyer pays for transportation include "f.s.t." meaning free on board, stowed, and trimmed and "f.a.s." meaning free alongside the ocean vessel designated to carry the commodity. When the seller pays for transportation the sale can be "c. and f." meaning the seller pays cost and freight or "c.i.f." meaning the seller pays cost, insurance, and freight. Some sales agreements call for the seller to deliver to an interior destination in the receiving country.

An export sales contract must contain the same basic provisions as a domestic contract, but much more detail is required. The contract must spell out what currency is to be used for payment. It must prescribe shipping arrangements in detail, and explain what constitutes default and what recourse is available for the party defaulted against. Because of their complexity export contracts commonly are written on standard forms developed by trade associations.

The need to charter ocean shipping and arrange for changing foreign currencies to U.S. dollars causes the export trade to differ from the domestic grain business. Because of the advantages of having representatives in grain importing countries, and the special skills needed in managing ship chartering and foreign exchange transactions, the bulk of the export sales are handled by a few major firms who specialize in the export business.

PRICE DETERMINATION AND PRICE FORECASTING

What determines the price of grain? A quick answer is that price is determined by the interaction of supply and demand. A price increase, if correctly anticipated, will increase the amounts farmers are willing to grow and sell while reducing the amounts of grain products that consumers want to buy. Thus, for example, when carry-over from the previous year is low and anticipated exports high, there is some relatively high price that will just equalize the amount domestic and foreign consumers are willing to buy with the amount produced. Similarly, in a year when yields are high, the extra supply will only be used at lower than normal prices.

In the United States, as in most of the world, grain prices are determined jointly by government programs and market forces. Through its price support programs the federal government effectively sets lower bounds for grain prices, enforcing such bounds by taking grains into storage whenever price falls to the support level. The government also limits price movements on the upper side by releasing stocks into the market. And on occasions, the government has intervened in the export market for grains and oilseeds through subsidies and embargoes.

Much of the time during recent decades, prices have rested on support levels, but on numerous occasions, and particularly between 1972 and 1977, market demand has lifted prices substantially above the level of support. When prices are above the support level, and below the level where government stocks would be released, they respond relatively freely to market forces. Even when prices are resting on supports, the price differences associated with grade, location, and time within the year are primarily determined in the market place.

Daily price determination in the marketplace is the result of simultaneous actions of buyers and sellers at many locations. Price must be agreed on at each change in ownership as grain passes from the farmer through the processing and distribution sector to final consumption.

Futures trading brings out the time dimension in grain pricing and provides central open market places where the full range of price making influences may come to bear. Since futures contracts call for delivery at elevators in the major cities—Chicago, Minneapolis, Kansas City, Toledo, and St. Louis—grains at the terminal elevator-processor stage of the marketing process are priced by the futures markets. Futures contracts provide for deliveries at only a few locations and for only a limited range of quality specifications. Since futures contracts are highly standardized, and contracts that price different classes of the commodity available only for wheat, the spatial and quality dimensions in grain pricing are largely provided by the cash market. Thus, it is futile to search for a single point where the price of grain is determined. Instead, price determination is best viewed as a dispersed, multidimensional process, with the futures markets serving as focal points where many of the price making forces come to bear.

To market grain successfully the farmer or elevator manager must not only be familiar with trading arrangements, as just described, but also acquire up-to-date information about price levels for alternative outlets. Information about current prices is obtained from buyers and from other market information sources as described in Chapter 8. Beyond this, however, the farmer or grain merchant will more likely be successful if they have the knowledge of the factors that determine price and some ability to predict futures prices.

The concept of supply and demand are useful for price forecasting because factors effecting changes or shifts in supply or demand relationships can be identified. For example, suppose a drought occurs during the growing season. Because yields are lowered and planted acreage cannot be changed, supply will be less. This reduced supply will command a higher price in the market. Alternatively, suppose that a large unanticipated export sale occurs after the crop is harvested. This is an unanticipated shift in demand. It, too, would result in a price increase as domestic and foreign buyers compete for the remaining quantity.

Seasonality in Grain Prices

The concepts of supply and demand help to explain some of the standard recurring relationships among grain prices. These include seasonal patterns in prices, price differences between locations, and price differences due to grade and quality differences.

Grain prices tend to be lowest at harvest and then gradually increase to a peak sometime prior to the next harvest. This seasonal price increase provides a return to those who store grain for use later in the year. Without such seasonality in price, individuals and firms would have no motivation to supply the needed storage services.

The monthly prices received by farmers for corn during four marketing years in the late 1970s are graphed in Figure 6-2. The figure illustrates a tendency for price to reach a seasonal low in November and increase thereafter, but it also shows that the seasonal pattern is frequently obscured by other factors reflecting shifts in supply and demand. Consequently, to obtain a better picture of the underlying seasonal pattern we must normally average together a series of years so that the more or less random shifts in supply and demand tend to cancel each other out. Figure 6-3 presents an index of the

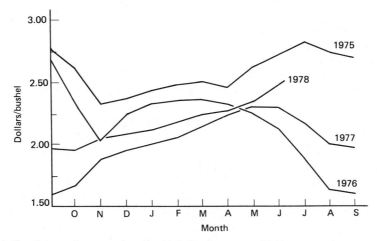

Figure 6-2. Corn, prices received by U.S. farmers, monthly, marketing years 1975/1976 to 1977/1978. *Source:* U.S. Department of Agriculture, *Agricultural Prices,* 1975 to 1978.

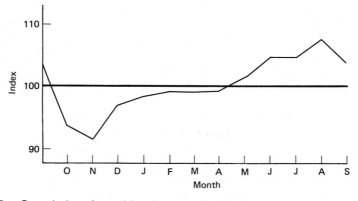

Figure 6-3. Corn, index of monthly prices received by farmers in the United States, based on data for marketing years 1968 to 1977. (Index constructed by averaging the ratios of monthly prices to the unweighted average price for each marketing year.)

seasonal price pattern for corn based on data for marketing years 1968 to 1977.

An important characteristic of the seasonal price pattern for corn is that price tends to rise rather rapidly and consistently during the first month or two after harvest, but with much less consistency during the rest of the storage year. For wheat and other grains the pattern is similar but generally less pronounced. This tapering off of the seasonal price rise is explainable in terms of the supply and demand for bin space. Owners of bin space are able to capture the largest return on storage immediately after harvest when the bins are full. As stocks are worked down, some bin space owners continue to hold stocks or make space available at lower expected rates of return rather than letting the space stand idle. Thus, the montly returns from carrying stocks are normally highest immediately after harvest and decline thereafter.

Price Differences Over Space

The theory of supply and demand also helps explain why grain prices are different at different locations. Prices in the United States tend to be lowest in the major producing areas where excess supply is greatest, and highest at major processing and utilization centers and at ports. These price differences are needed to pay haulers for moving grain from the production areas to the points of utilization and export. The basic differences tend to persist from month to month, but may change due to local shifts in demand and supply. For example, a North Dakota country elevator may sometimes ship wheat to Portland, and sometimes to Minneapolis, as relative prices shift between the two terminals.

State average prices received by farmers for corn in 1976 are shown in Figure 6-4. The lowest prices tend to be in the Corn Belt states with higher prices in areas of deficit corn production in the East, the West and the South. The possibilities for shipping from point to point prevent price differences between any two states from exceeding transportation costs. But price differences between states or regions may be less than transportation costs when there is little or no direct movement from one to the other. Instead, relative prices at two different points may be determined by the costs of shipping from each to a third destination. For example, the fact that Iowa and Indiana had the same average price in 1976 may reflect the roughly equal costs of moving grain from the two areas to the Gulf for export.

Price Differences Due to Quality

In general, higher quality grains command higher prices. But just as spatial price differences change due to changes in supply and demand at different locations, so do quality differentials. To illustrate, Table 6-1 shows the differences in price paid during late September in four different years for No. 1 Dark Northern Spring wheat of different protein levels. Due to the shortage of high protein wheat, protein premiums were high in 1976. For the 1977 crop they were about normal. In contrast, the relative abundance of high protein wheat in 1978 resulted in relatively low premiums for wheat with 14 percent

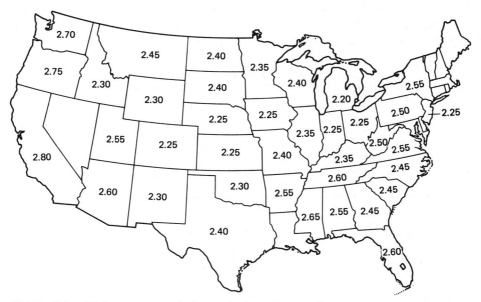

Figure 6-4. State average prices received by farmers for corn, 1976 crop. (*Source:* U.S. Department of Agriculture, *Agricultural Prices, Annual Summary,* 1976.)

Table 6-1 Price Premiums for High Protein Wheats Relative to Ordinary Protein No. 1 Dark Northern Spring Wheat at Minneapolis, End of September, 1976 to 1979 (cents per bushel)

Protein Percent	Date			
	9/30/76	*9/29/77*	*9/28/78*	*9/27/79*
13	30	12	18	7
14	45	22	20	12
15	58	44	20	38

Source: U.S. Department of Agriculture, *Grain Market News.*

protein or more. In 1979, premiums were small except for the highest protein level.

The supply of and demand for each of the different classes of wheat also influence price differences between these classes. The hard wheats often command a premium over the soft wheats because of their baking qualities and higher protein levels. But soft wheats are required for certain cakes and pastry products. Table 6-2 shows that premiums did indeed exist for hard wheat at Kansas City and Minneapolis compared to soft wheat at Chicago for the 1976 and 1977 crops. In September 1978, however, with a relative shortage of soft wheat compared to hard wheat, the hard wheats at Minneapolis and Kansas City sold for less than soft wheat at Chicago. This price advantage for soft wheat persisted for the 1979 crop.

Patterns in Price Movements

Many of the demand and supply shifts for grains, particularly those associated with weather, appear to be random and unpredictable. In-

Table 6-2 Price Differences for Hard Wheats at Kansas City and Minneapolis, Relative to No. 2 Soft Red Winter Wheat at Chicago, End of September, 1976 to 1979 (cents per bushel)

Wheat, Grade, and Market	Date			
	9/30/76	*9/29/77*	*9/28/78*	*9/27/79*
No. 1 Hard Winter, ordinary protein, Kansas City	27	13	−41	−3
No. 1 Dark Northern Spring, ordinary protein, Minneapolis	34	9	−21	−14

Source: U.S. Department of Agriculture, *Grain Market News.*

deed, one theory about the behavior of prices suggests that if the futures price reflects all currently available information about future demand and supply, as it should in an efficient market, changes in the futures price will be random. In contrast, many traders believe that short-term futures price movements tend to follow certain patterns. Attempts to detect and predict such patterns using price charts or computers are called "technical analysis." This contrasts with "fundamental analysis," which attempts to explain and predict price movements using the principles of supply and demand. Various types of technical analysis are extensively used by commodity futures speculators, as well as stock traders, but the validity of these methods is widely disputed.

PRICING STRATEGIES FOR FARMERS

Let us now consider some of the strategies that a farmer might follow in pricing grains. Grain pricing decisions do not begin at harvest. Instead, decisions about pricing begin at the time production decisions are made. In other words, a farmer needs to form initial marketing plans at the same time production plans are made. This calls for assembling information about prospective prices and costs during the production planning stage so that alternative cropping and marketing strategies can be evaluated together.

Unlike decisions about crop acreage and fertilizer levels, decisions about when and where to market can be modified after planting time, as new information about supply and demand becomes available. For example, a farmer who has a good crop developing and expects an abundant harvest may forward contract more of the crop during the growing season than would be contracted otherwise. Thus, a crop producer's marketing strategy involves an initial plan and a series of revisions based on later developments.

In marketing grain, a farmer makes decisions about when to sell and whom to sell to. The following discussion will focus primarily on the first type of decision—the timing of sales.

Because grains are storable and active forward markets exist, farmers can price their grains at many different times, as was shown in Figure 6-1. Obviously, the farmer would like to sell when the net return is highest, but there is no infallible rule that guarantees this result. However, there are some principles that provide guidance. They involve taking advantage of seasonal price patterns, using government support programs, tax management, and risk management.

Taking Advantage of Seasonal Price Patterns

As discussed previously, grain prices tend to follow seasonal patterns that farmers need to consider in timing sales. This does not mean that sales should be made only during that part of the year, say six months after harvest, when prices are usually highest. Instead, farmers need to consider their own grain storage costs, relative to the expected price increase, and continue to hold grain only so long as expected price appreciation exceeds their storage costs.

The costs of storage differ among farmers, and between farmers and elevators. They include interest, insurance and taxes on the grain, charges for bin space, and quality losses (if any). Interest on the money invested in the grain normally is the largest single item. In estimating the cost of bin space it is essential to distinguish between short-term decisions (storing for an extra month, say) and long-term decisions (building new bins). For short-term storage decisions only the marginal or out-of-pocket costs for bin space need be considered. Bin space costs may be virtually zero if existing bin space would otherwise remain unused. Quality losses should be negligible if grain is stored at proper moisture content and insect infestation is prevented.

A first and obvious principle is to fill storage bins at harvest to capitalize on the rapid price rise that normally occurs the first month or two after harvest. Farmers storing in their own bins often can profitably hold grains later into the year than those renting storage space, since their marginal cost per month for bin space is virtually zero.

Comparison of futures prices with current cash prices shows what the market says about prospective returns from storage. If the futures price exceeds the local cash price by more than storage costs and the expected basis, storage is indicated. If the cash-future spread is narrow or inverted, that is, if the price for near term delivery exceeds the price for distant delivery, storage is not advisable unless the local basis is temporarily out of line due to transportation bottlenecks or other causes.

Using Government Programs

Government support programs provide the farmer with a type of price guarantee that is not available in the marketplace. Through judicious use of the support program a farmer can be assured of obtaining at least the support price applicable to the stored crop, while holding open the possibility of doing better if the market price should rise above the support level. This advantage must be weighed against other advantages and disadvantages of participating in the support program. Compliance with acreage limitations normally is the most burdensome requirement. Eligibility for direct payments and payments for storage can be advantageous. Farmers should also note that supports provide some price protection. Even for farmers not participating in the government program, supports help keep the market from falling below a specified level.

Tax Considerations in Selling Grains

Farmers who pay income taxes on a cash basis can transfer tax liability from one tax year to the next by postponing crop sales to the next tax year, and by purchasing inputs in the current year. The taxes must, of course, be paid eventually, but in the meantime the farmer has what amounts to an interest-free loan from the government equal to the amount of taxes postponed. For example, a farmer in the 28 percent federal income tax bracket, with 10,000 bushels of wheat worth $3.00 per bushel, might postpone 10,000 × $3.00 = $30,000 in taxable income and $8400 in tax liabilities from one year to the next. This amounts to an interest-free loan, which at a 10 percent interest rate, would be worth $840 a year or 2.8 percent of the value of the wheat involved. This demonstrates that tax considerations are important in determining when to sell. Of course, to the extent that a large number of farmers, all using the same tax year, follow this practice, prices may be affected and the advantages for each reduced.

Some states assess property taxes on stored grain. This can provide a motive for farmers and others to sell grains ahead of the assessment date. This practice can result in price distortions if followed by enough sellers.

Risk Management

By its very nature farming is a risky activity. Before establishing a pricing strategy, farmers need to consider the amount of risk they are willing to accept or, equivalently, how much they are willing to pay for safety of return. Most farmers, like other businesspeople, are in business to make money, not to avoid risk, but most require some security and are unwilling to take unlimited risk for a small expected profit. Hence, for most farmers the best course does not involve completely disregarding risk, nor does it involve minimizing risk, but rather finding the combination of risk and expected return that is most satisfactory.

Second, farmers need to appraise objectively their ability to forecast price changes. If they could accurately predict price changes they could maximize profit by selling only when price is at or near its peak. Farmers are the first to know about local crop conditions that affect prices. But predicting price changes on a national or world market requires much broader information. If farmers were especially good at making such predictions they could probably make more money by engaging in pure speculation, instead of farming. Typical farmers or businesspeople are probably wise to follow a middle course, somewhere between pure speculation, where they are relying entirely on their own ability to forecast price movements, and pure risk avoidance.

Farmers can reduce their risks in crop production by buying crop insurance and by selling forward, using either cash forward contracts or futures contracts. Crop insurance reduces their average return by the cost of the insurance. In contrast, there is little clear evidence that forward selling either reduces or increases average return over a period of years. Its main effect is to give producers a known price over the growing season, rather than an unknown price.

When yields are uncertain, as they are in most situations, forward selling does not fix producer returns. A poor crop may not only mean that they have little to sell but also requires them to buy back their forward contracts at a high price. Consequently, selling the entire expected crop at planting time generally cannot be recommended even for the producer who is very averse to risk. The amount that can most advantageously be sold forward depends on the elasticity of demand and how closely local yields are correlated with U.S. yields. Some research has suggested that overall risk is minimized by selling about one-half to two-thirds of the crop at planting.

Another strategy that has sometimes been suggested to farmers is to spread sales over the year, perhaps pricing a third of the crop at planting, another third at harvest, and the remainder, at three to five months after harvest. This strategy helps insure that farmers get an average price near the average market price for the year. It may reduce their regret from having sold at a price less than their neighbors received, but spreading sales over time is only partly effective in reducing price uncertainty. Indeed, once yield is assured, risk can be minimized by selling the entire crop at the then existing forward price.

PRICING STRATEGIES FOR COUNTRY ELEVATORS

In the country elevator business, returns depend on relatively narrow margins between prices received for grains and prices paid to farmers, plus fees charged for storage, drying, and other services rendered by the elevator and profits from sideline activities such as selling feed and farm supplies. Three types of pricing strategies, ordered from the most passive to the most aggressive, are described here. First is ordinary margin pricing, where the elevator's bid price is set each day, simply by subtracting a predetermined margin and appropriate transportation costs from the bids it receives, and grains purchased from farmers are immediately sold to second handlers. Second is the use of hedging to give the firm flexibility in carrying inventories in its own account, while keeping low its exposure to price risks. Third is pure speculation, carrying unhedged cash grain inventories or speculative positions in grain futures.

Margin Pricing with Minimal Net Positions

The basic pricing decisions made by all elevators are decisions about margins, fees charged for storage, and for other services. These margins are small relative to the price of the grain, normally only a few cents per bushel. By reducing margins and fees the elevator can usually attract more business, but the profit per unit will decline. Increasing margins and fees produces the opposite effect. For the profit-seeking elevator, the basic pricing task is to adjust margins and fees to obtain the desired or maximum attainable level of total return over cost.

In conducting their business, elevators take title to large quantities of grain that often fluctuate markedly in value. A small percentage drop in the price of grain in inventory can easily wipe out the firm's margin and result in serious loss. One way that the country elevator can minimize its exposure to such price risks on grain inventories is to sell the grain as soon as it is bought from farmers. Many country elevators follow this practice, selling on the cash market each day approximately the same amount of grain that they buy, so that their net position remains small. Sometimes the grain is shipped as soon as it is sold; other times it is held until called for by the buyer. The advantages of this type of inventory management is that it is simple and relatively safe. Once the decision about the handling margin is made, the elevator manager need only subtract the margin and appropriate transportation costs from the bids received from buyers to determine the bid price. This is the type of strategy that can be conveniently spelled out by a board of directors and implemented by a manager who has limited time and ability for analyzing the prices. A disadvantage of this approach is that use of the elevator's storage facilities is largely left up to other decision makers, farmers, and second level buyers. The elevator may find itself simply running grain through the plant and loading it out at a buyer's request, with limited opportunities to earn storage and merchandising returns.

Hedging Owned Inventories

Elevator managers who wish to take a more active role in controlling their grain inventories, and in seeking storage merchandising returns, find the futures market a useful tool. They may, for example, want to accumulate inventories so they can offer potential buyers multicar shipments. Or a large spread between a distant futures price and the cash price offered by buyers may suggest that storage for the elevator's own account would be profitable. Hedging in the futures market enables elevators to take advantage of such opportunities by accumulating and controlling their own inventories without undue exposure to price risk.

Effective hedging requires knowledge of futures trading practices and understanding of basis relationships. Even with hedging, firms remain exposed to basis risk. Like any other hedgers, country elevators must be able to predict the basis that will prevail when the hedges mature. Fortunately, the basis typically is much more stable and predictable that the price level itself. But unforeseen events, such as transportation bottlenecks and strikes, occasionally disrupt normal basis relationships, imposing losses on hedgers as well as others.

Hedgers must be prepared to meet margin calls when the price moves against their futures position. They should have an understanding with their banker wherein the banker stands ready to finance such margin calls. It is in the banker's interest for their borrowers to hedge.

When the borrowers have a margin call on a bona fide hedge, the banker who understands futures trading will realize that the value of collateral has increased so that financing the margin call is sound business. Of course, the banker must be assured that the elevator does indeed have a valid hedge so that losses in the futures are balanced by equal gains in the value of the firm's cash position.

Speculation

Like farmers and other grain merchants, country elevators have opportunities for pure speculation, either by carrying unhedged inventories or speculative futures positions. Because they are talking to knowledgeable people in the grain business, and buying and selling grain daily, elevator managers may have some unique information about price prospects. But they also compete with other speculators who may have better access to information about prospective prices elsewhere throughout the country and the world. There have been many elevator managers who started futures trading as pure hedgers and later became speculators, sometimes inadvertently, sometimes successfully, and sometimes to their subsequent regret.

CAN THE GRAIN PRICING SYSTEM BE IMPROVED?

In coordinating production and consumption throughout the grain industry, and in determining the income of grain growers and the prices to consumers for foods derived from grains, the grain pricing system has a tremendous job to perform. Most indications are that the pricing system is performing well, but it is nonetheless appropriate to ask if it could be made to work better. This question cannot be fully answered here, but some potential problems and possible solutions can be identified.

What distinguishes good performance from bad performance in a pricing system? If the system is working properly, each participant in the market—farmer, merchant, processor, or consumer—will receive or pay full value, but not more, for the grain or grain products sold or purchased. It would be impossible for any seller or buyer to obtain a more favorable price by switching to a different outlet or a different source of supply, once all the costs are taken into account. The market system tends to assure that this condition holds, since each participant has a motive to search diligently for the most favorable price and source of supply or outlet.

But there are at least two important phenomena that can impede the effective functioning of the market and prevent traders from finding the best prices. One is the tendency for decision makers to err because of faulty expectations or lack of information. Such decision errors can lead to a waste or resources and undue price fluctuations.

Second is the tendency toward monopoly or monopsonylike behavior, when the numbers of firms on one side of the market is small enough that, by individual or group effort, they can change price in their favor.

One place to look for pricing problems is where sources of supply or outlets are limited in number. For example, many farmers sell to only one elevator. If that elevator has no close competitors it may, on the average, take a wider margin than necessary to cover cost and normal profit. Similarly, if the subterminal, terminal elevator or processor has no close competitors it, too, might take larger margins and profits than otherwise, Thus, whenever the number of buyers or sellers for a particular type of grain in a particular area is small, temptations to price noncompetitively arise. But countering this temptation is the threat of other firms entering the area should profits become too lucrative.

Another place to look for pricing failure is when prices exhibit exceptionally large fluctuations. The prices of wheat, corn, and soybeans change almost every day, and often markedly within a day. These changes reflect new information arising each day about supply and demand. Observing the changing price provides an efficient way for grain buyers and sellers to acquire information about these changes in supply and demand. But prices may sometimes fluctuate more violently than warranted by market conditions. When daily or weekly price changes are very large, as they were during the 1972 to 1975 period, manipulation is frequently alleged. But there is no proof that manipulation is a major factor contributing to price volatility. Irrational behavior by traders may be a different matter. There is at least reason to suspect that the bulk of traders occasionally overreact or underreact to major news events, such as large sales to Russia or China. If there is an over- or underreaction, prices should eventually return to economically justified levels. In practice, even retrospectively, it is difficult to identify periods when the market overreacts to new developments. Many of the large fluctuations observed in the early 1970s may have been justified when viewed in terms of the information then available. There are no easy answers as to where and when the pricing system is defective.

ALTERNATIVE PRICING SYSTEMS

The grain pricing system now in existence has evolved in a piece-meal fashion over many years. Could a better system be designed and put into effect?

Improved grain pricing may begin with refining or fine tuning the existing system. With continual changes in communication technology, methods of measuring quality, and new product uses, there is an ongoing need to modify the information system and the grading system for grains. There also are opportunities to improve futures contracts from time to time. (These possibilities are discussed in Chapter 7.)

Another possibility for improving grain pricing would be to develop a system using computer and computer terminals in merchant's and processor's offices to trade grains. Modern computers and electronic communication devices seem well suited for processing the large volumes of information that serve as the lifeblood of modern markets. Indeed, electronic devices are already widely used for disseminating grain price information. But use of computers could be carried a step further, so that trades are actually executed and confirmed electronically. Each trader would be able to quickly scan all the existing bids and offers for the types of grain and locations of interest, and then enter bids and offers for wide exposure to other traders. The computer would determine when a bid and offer matched, notify each party instantaneously that a trade had been completed, and produce written copies of the sales documents. Potential advantages of electronic trading would be increased and more timely information for each trader, about other trader's bids, offers, and completed transactions, and reduced time required in telephoning other traders one at a time. A possible disadvantage of electronic trading would be reduced personal voice contact with other traders that facilitates sharing of nonstandard kinds of information such as local crop prospects and how the harvest is progressing.

In contrast to electronic trading and other schemes for making a dispersed pricing system operate more effectively, a movement could be made toward a system where more pricing decisions were centralized. This might involve installing a marketing board, a government or quasi-government agency, with exclusive marketing privileges and powers to set prices and control quantities marketed, such as the Canadian Wheat Board. The degree to which prices and quantities are controlled can vary greatly depending on how the marketing board is organized and operated. At one extreme, daily or weekly prices by location and grade might be set well ahead of time by the board, virtually eliminating the existing market system for establishing price. Price uncertainty would be reduced or eliminated so long as the board maintained control. But the problem of determining price for each possible combination of location, time, and grade would be enormous, and many mistakes could be made. It would be much more feasible to control price only for a limited number of locations, time, and grade combinations and leave the others to be determined in the market. An advantage of the marketing board approach would be reduced price uncertainty for producers, merchants, and processors. Other possible gains might arise through concerted action in pricing grains on the world market. A major disadvantage would be the inefficiencies that would be engendered in attempting to set prices administratively. Canada and Australia have used marketing boards for grains with mixed success.

Summary

The grain pricing system performs important functions in coordinating the decisions of grain farmers, merchants, processors, and consumers and in determining the allocation of income or buying power among these groups. Price is determined by the interaction of demand and supply, both in the short run and the long run. The process by which these different groups contact each other, exchange bids and offers, and reach exchange agreements specifying price and other terms of trade is called price discovery. The price discovery process for grains is keyed heavily to futures trading and involves a system of bids for cash grains that are communicated each day from buyers to sellers via telephone.

Grain prices are often quoted in terms of the basis, the difference between the cash price, and a specific futures price. To make effective pricing decisions, farmers and country elevators need to understand the basic factors affecting price differences over time, space, and quality. In addition, knowledge of and ability to use futures markets can be valuable. Indications are that the grain pricing system functions well. Imperfect competition and erratic behavior by traders sometimes result in pricing aberrations, but they tend to be short lived.

Selected References

Heid, Walter G., Jr., *U.S. Wheat Industry.* Economics, Statistics, and Cooperatives Service, USDA, Agricultural Economics. Report No. 432, Washington, D.C., August 1979.

Heifner, Richard G. et al., *The U.S. Cash Grain Trade in 1974: Participants, Transactions and Information Sources,* USDA, Agricultural Economics Report No. 386, Washington, D.C., September 1977.

Helmuth, John W., *Grain Pricing,* Commodity Futures Trading Commission, Economics Bulletin, No. 1, Washington, D.C., September 1977.

Paul, Allen B., Richard G. Heifner, and John W. Helmuth, *Farmers' Use of Forward Contracts and Futures Markets,* Economics, Statistics, and Cooperatives Service, USDA, Agricultural Economics, Report No. 320, Washington, D.C., March 1976.

Sogn, A. B. and R. U. Rudel, eds., *Marketing Alternatives for Producers of Wheat,* South Dakota State University, Brookings, 1973.

Tomek, William G. and Kenneth L. Robinson, *Agricultural Product Prices,* 2nd ed., Cornell University Press, Ithaca, New York, 1981.

Turner, Mike et al., *Who Will Market Your Grain? Producer Alternatives,* Extension Service D-1057, Texas A&M University, College Station, March 1978.

FUTURES: MARKETS, PRICES, AND HEDGING

FUTURES: MARKETS, PRICES, AND HEDGING*

CHAPTER
7

ORGANIZED COMMODITY MARKETS

Organized commodity markets, such as the Chicago Board of Trade, the Kansas City Board of Trade, and the Minneapolis Grain Exchange, have played an important role in the development of an efficient grain marketing system in the United States. These markets were organized in the latter half of the nineteenth century. They brought together buyers and sellers for grain trading in a central marketplace, facilitating open and competitive trading in grain. Market information and price discovery mechanisms were thereby improved, which increased competition and broadened the market for the famrers' grain.

There have been changes over the years in the manner in which grain is marketed on these exchanges, but the principal methods have remained the same. The essential element is that both cash and futures trading on these markets amount to a public auction. Sellers of grain want as many bids as they can get because this increases their chances of obtaining the best possible price. Buyers, too, want to choose from as many offers as possible. Both buyers and sellers are interested in knowing what others are paying for grain of a particular quality for delivery at a specific time. Grain exchanges provide buyers and sellers with such price information and opportunities for trading in a competitive marketplace.

Futures trading through which futures prices for grain are derived takes place *only* on organized grain exchanges. By providing centralized futures trading under rules and regulations, organized commodity markets have helped make grain marketing a highly competitive business. These markets serve as clearinghouses of grain supply and demand information for efficient price discovery.

Evolution of Futures Trading in Grain

There is a widespread belief that futures markets are primarily speculative. However, a history of their development reveals that they developed out of an economic need for hedging. A study of the history of

*Reynold P. Dahl, Professor, Department of Agricultural and Applied Economics, University of Minnesota, St. Paul.

corn marketing in the 1850s indicates how futures trading developed out of that need.[1]

The opening of the Illinois-Michigan Canal, connecting the Illinois River with Lake Michigan, made possible shipment of corn by water from central Illinois to Chicago. This reduced transportation costs and facilitated the movement of corn into Chicago. Previously, transportation costs were very expensive. There were no railroads going into Chicago and most grain movements into the city were by horse and wagon. In 1884, the value of wheat in Chicago was about equal to the cost of hauling it 60 miles by horse and wagon. Corn prices were lower than those for wheat, so corn could be profitably hauled for even shorter distances than wheat.

After the Canal opened in 1848, the amount of corn shipped to Chicago increased rapidly. Dealers invested in corncribs, which were constructed along the Illinois River. They purchased corn from farmers who hauled their corn to the river dealers by sleigh or wagon over the frozen roads in the winter. The dealers would hold the corn in cribs to permit drying, after which it would be shelled and shipped in the spring or early summer.

Financing their accumulation of corn stocks strained the financial resources of these early dealers and limited their operations. Also, they assumed heavy price risks on the corn because they did not know what price they could sell the corn for the following spring in Chicago. Hence, they developed the practice of going to Chicago and finding a merchant who would buy corn for May delivery. In other words, they entered into time contracts, or "to arrive" contracts, with Chicago merchants. These contracts served two important economic needs. First, they enabled dealers to obtain financing from commission men who were then willing to advance them money for corn purchases. Second, they enabled dealers to shift price risks to someone else.

The first such contract was recorded on March 13, 1851, calling for delivery of 3000 bushels of corn in June, at a price one cent lower than the quotation for corn that day. The use of these time contracts increased rapidly during the 1850s. These early time contracts were very informal, either verbal or simply evidenced by a memorandum. Only the quantity, price, and time of delivery were specified, although some had a proportion of the price paid in cash.

Merchants in Chicago began to trade these contracts, and speculators often bought them hoping to profit from correctly anticipating a price rise. As trading in the contracts increased, they were gradually standardized in written form with respect to number of bushels, delivery in specified calendar months, and the terms of payment.

The Chicago Board of Trade, which had been organized in 1848,

[1]Harold S. Irwin, *Evolution of Futures Trading,* Mimir Publishers, Inc., Madison, Wis., 1954, pp. 69–83.

established rules governing the trading of these time contracts in 1865. The transition to full-blown futures trading in corn took place sometime between 1870 and 1875 with the development of the standardized futures contract and the clearing of those contracts through a clearinghouse.

The clearinghouse took the role of intermediary between buyer and seller. After a futures trade was consummated, the buyer was deemed to have bought from the clearinghouse and the seller was deemed to have sold to the clearinghouse. The clearinghouse calculated each day the gain and loss resulting for all outstanding contracts because of the price change that day. It then collected funds from the losing futures contacts and paid these funds to the futures having gains. Clearinghouse operations made two important contributions that made a fully developed futures market possible. First, it reduced the risk of default on a futures contract to one day's market price change. Second, the clearinghouse made it easier for a trader to be released from obligations assumed under the original contract. Traders did not need to search out one another, instead, they merely needed to make an equal but opposite futures transaction.[2]

If a trader had originally bought a futures contract, the obligation could be satisfied simply by selling a futures contract of the same month. Similarly, if a futures contract had been sold originally, the trader only needed to buy one of the same month. The clearinghouse could offset these two transactions, freeing the traders from their original obligation to either take or make delivery.

Trading in futures contracts and clearing through a clearinghouse, with its ability to offset one futures transaction with another, resulted in two economic effects. First, it opened futures trading to people without physical commodity handling facilities. Thus, speculation in futures was facilitated. Second, it facilitated hedging by grain warehousemen and processors. *Grain merchants were able to transfer unwanted price risks to speculators without actual change in the ownership of grain.*

In summary, the evolution of futures trading in grain clearly shows that futures trading developed out of an economic need for hedging. The early corn dealers in Illinois needed to shift price risks and finance their inventories. The early time contracts that grew out of these needs ultimately evolved in fully developed futures trading, which made hedging more efficient. Our grain futures markets continue to serve this important economic need today.

Futures Markets and Commodities Traded

One of the most significant developments in the U.S. economy during the past decade has been the sizable increase in futures trading. The

[2]Robert H. Diercks, "Why Grain Exchanges," speech before the Minneapolis Farm Forum, Minneapolis, Minnesota, March 1, 1977.

total number of futures contracts traded on U.S. futures markets rose from 13.6 million in 1970 to 92.1 million in 1980, an increase of 577 percent. The Chicago Board of Trade and the Chicago Mercantile Exchange traded the largest number of futures contracts in both 1970 and 1980, but some of the smaller exchanges have also shown rapid growth.

Most of the increase occurred in two contract groups: agricultural commodities and financial instruments (e.g., GNMA mortgages, U.S. Treasury bills, and U.S. Treasury bonds).

Futures trading in the United States had its origin in the marketing of grain, and it is in grain marketing where futures trading has achieved its highest development. Grain, soybeans, and soybean products accounted for 39.5 million or 43 percent of the 92.1 million futures contracts traded in 1980. The volume of futures trading in grain nearly doubled during the three years 1978 through 1980, while the volume in soybeans and products rose 30 percent during the same period (Table 7-1).

Futures trading in grains, soybeans, and products is conducted on four futures markets: the Chicago Board of Trade, the Kansas City Board of Trade, the Minneapolis Grain Exchange, and the Mid-America Commodity Exchange. The Chicago Board of Trade, our nation's largest futures market, traded nearly 36 million futures contracts, or over 90 percent of the total volume of trading on the four markets in 1980 (Table 7-2). Corn and soybeans had the largest 1980 trade volume, with nearly 12 million contracts traded in each on the Chicago Board of Trade. Wheat ranked third, with 5.4 million contracts traded on the Chicago Board of Trade. Wheat is the only grain traded on all

Table 7-1 Total Futures Contracts Traded, by Commodity Group, 1978, 1980

Commodity Group	1978	1980
Grain	10,402,343	20,349,023
Soybeans and products	14,874,579	19,207,489
Precious metals	13,979,290	13,171,816
Financial instruments	2,325,020	12,469,878
Livestock and products, and poultry	9,686,499	11,639,579
Imported agricultural commodities	1,425,339	4,886,416
Foreign currency	1.560,749	4,222,820
Other agricultural commodities[a]	1,967,495	3,052,307
Nonprecious metals	1,409,365	1,448,108
Lumber products	831,346	1,010,424
Petroleum products	147	238,309
Total	58,462,171	92,096,109

[a]Cotton, orange juice, potatoes, and eggs.

Source: Commodity Futures Trading Commission.

Table 7-2 Futures Contracts Traded on U.S. Grain
Futures Markets, by Commodity, Selected Years

Exchange and Commodity	Contract Unit	*Thousand Contracts*			
		1963	1973	1978	1980
Chicago Board of Trade					
Wheat	5,000 bu	824	1,567	2,556	5,428
Corn	5,000 bu	823	4,075	6,127	11,947
Oats	5,000 bu	140	183	216	321
Rye	5,000 bu	128	0	0	0
Soybeans	5,000 bu	2,846	2,743	8,477	11,768
Soybean oil	60,000 lb	636	1,763	2,909	3,168
Soybean meal	100 tons	263	660	2,493	3,219
Total		5,660	10,991	22,778	35,851
Kansas City Board of Trade					
Wheat	5,000 bu	112	346	756	1,298
Grain sorghum	280,000 lb	a	a	0	a
Total		112	346	756	1,298
Minneapolis Grain Exchange					
Spring wheat	5,000 bu	41	172	284	334
Durum	5,000 bu	0	a	0	0
Sunflower seeds	100,000 lb	0	0	0	27
Total		41	172	284	361
Mid-American Commodity Exchange					
Wheat	1,000 bu	7	75	206	551
Corn	1,000 bu	2	103	256	441
Oats	1,000 bu	a	9	1	2
Soybeans	1,000 bu	29	56	995	1,053
Total		38	243	1,458	2,047
Total all markets		5,851	11,752	25,276	39,557

[a]Less than 1000 contracts.

Source: Futures Industry Association.

four futures markets. The Kansas City Board of Trade, now with a larger share of the total futures trading in wheat, has experienced an impressive growth rate in the trading of its hard red winter wheat futures contract. The Minneapolis Grain Exchange has also had a substantial growth in trading of its hard red spring wheat futures contract, but the trading volume in this market is still small relative to Chicago and Kansas City.

Soybean meal and soybean oil also had record trade volumes on the Chicago Board of Trade in 1980, with 3.2 million contracts traded in each of these soybean products. Oats ranked in last place, with 312 thousand contracts traded. There was also a small volume of trade in a new commodity—sunflower seeds—on the Minneapolis Grain Exchange.

All four of the futures markets on which grains are traded have shared in the increased volume of trading. But the Chicago Board of Trade has benefited the most since it has such a large share of the total. The Mid-American Commodity Exchange has shown the largest percentage growth in futures trading since 1963, primarily because its smaller contracts appeal to small speculators and hedgers.

Reasons for the Increased Volume of Futures Trading in Grain

There are two principal reasons for the increased volume of futures trading in grain, soybeans, and soybean products since 1963. First, in the mid-1960s a significant change was made in U.S. government programs to support incomes of grain producers. Direct income payments from the government were substituted for price support loans at levels above "free" market prices as the principal vehicle for supporting farm income. Second, world grain trade increased dramatically during the decade of the 1970s.

From World War II until 1963, the incomes of wheat and feed grain producers were supported primarily through the price support mechanism, which assured them minimum prices through loans considerably above free market prices. Farmers who restricted acreage were eligible for loans. The CCC accumulated sizable surplus stocks through such price support operations. It was frequently said that the government was the market during this period—a fairly accurate description. Market prices could only fluctuate within a narrow range around the loan rate. The price support loan set a floor, and market prices could not decline appreciably below that amount. Also, prices could not rise considerably higher than the support price. The CCC held large stocks, and was authorized to sell when the price reached 105 percent of the loan rate plus carrying cost. The early, low level of trading on our grain futures markets reflected the reduced hedging needs associated with the lessened price variability, the low level of "free" stocks, and heavy stock carrying by the CCC.

This situation began to change after 1963, when a significant shift took place in the method of supporting the incomes of grain farmers. Direct income payments were substituted for high price supports. These payments were not received through the market, but rather as direct income payments from the government. Acreage diversion payments were also initiated. Participating grain farmers had to divert acreage to soil conserving usage as a requirement for income payments. Price support loan rates were lowered to levels closer to free markets prices, so that markets could again assume a greater role in price determination. This new program was successful in reducing the level of government-owned grain stocks in the following years. Significantly, the level of free stocks also rose as private firms were again willing to carry stocks. The level of business on our nation's futures markets began to climb. This reflected the increased hedging prompted by more private stock carrying and the greater price uncertainty in the new farm programs. As shown in Table 7-2, the volume of futures trading in grain, soybean products doubled between 1963 and 1973.

Rapidly expanding world markets for U.S. grain acted as a further stimulus to increased futures trading during the decade of the 1970s. Total U.S. grain exports increased from 1.7 billion bushels in the 1970/71 marketing year (July 1970 through June 1971) to 4.9 billion bushels in 1979/80. Grain production shortfalls, notably in the Soviet Union, but in other countries as well, together with rising incomes in many countries increased the demand for American grain. Changes in world grain production, together with reduced levels of world grain stocks, have also resulted in wide swings in grain prices. Increased grain exports and greater price variability have increased hedging needs of the U.S. and world grain trade. Volatile grain markets have also attracted an increased volume of speculative trade in futures. Worldwide inflation, which emerged as a major economic problem during the decade, has also stimulated speculation in commodity futures.

Types of Trading—Cash and Futures

Two types of trading take place on organized grain exchanges. First, cash or spot trading involves the sale and receipt of grain for immediate delivery, or forward delivery at some specified time and place. Second, futures trading is done through the use of standardized futures contracts. Futures prices, as derived from trading of futures contracts, are central to the entire grain pricing and marketing mechanism.

Cash grain may be traded for immediate delivery or for delivery within some specified time period, for example, within 30 days. The latter type of transaction is referred to as "to arrive" sales. In reality, they are forward cash contracts. A to arrive sale is a contract under which a buyer agrees to accept from a seller a certain quantity of grain to be shipped to an agreed—on destination within a specified time period at an agreed—on price for a base grade. The contract usually specifies price adjustments for such quality factors as moisture, test weight, and protein. Sometimes a maximum moisture, minimum protein, or other limits that the buyer will accept are also specified within the contract.

Differences Between Futures Contracts and Forward Cash Contracts

Forward cash contracts, or to arrive contracts, are common in grain marketing. For example, some farmers sell grain to their country elevator in midsummer for delivery at harvest. The price is fixed at the time the contract is made. This is a contract for later performance. Country elevators also sell a high proportion of the grain purchased from farmers to terminal merchants on to arrive or forward cash contracts. Finally, terminal grain merchants often sell grain to processors and other users on forward cash contracts. Nearly all transactions between grain exporters and import buyers are on forward cash contracts.

Futures contracts differ from forward cash contracts, or to arrive contracts, in several respects. First, only a small percentage—one or two percent—of futures contracts are settled by the actual delivery of grain, while cash forward contracts are almost always settled by delivery. Most futures contracts are satisfied by offsetting purchases or sales of futures before trading in the particular contract month expires. Hence, futures contracts are not used for merchandising, that is, the actual purchase or sale of grain. The purpose of future contracts is pricing. Futures contracts facilitate the trading of grain on forward cash contracts by making it possible for grain merchants to hedge price risks associated with forward cash contracts. Futures contracts often serve as temporary substitutes for intended later transactions in cash markets. In other words, they are used for hedging.

Second, as stated before, futures contracts are traded only on organized grain exchanges or boards of trade under the rules and regulations of these markets. Furthermore, these markets must be designated and approved as a contract market for various grains by the Commodity Futures Trading Commission, an agency of the U.S. government, which regulates futures trading. Forward cash contracts, on the other hand, are made in many decentralized markets or wherever a buyer and seller might agree to such a contract. They are not regulated by an organized exchange or by the federal government.

Third, futures contracts are highly standardized as to terms such as quality, deliverable grades, time of delivery, and place of delivery. Forward cash contracts are not standardized, and their terms vary considerably.

CHARACTERISTICS OF FUTURES TRADING

The Futures Contract

Standardized contracts calling for the delivery of grain in some designated future month are traded in the futures market. Prices of futures contracts are determined by auction in a trading pit; the trading is conducted only at designated times, and takes place under rules and regulations of the exchange. All terms of futures contracts, except the price, are standardized by the exchange. A futures contract calls for delivery of a specified quantity and quality of grain, at a specified place or places, in some designated month in the future. These contracts are binding, and their integrity is preserved under the rules and regulations of the exchange.

Example of a Futures Contract

Futures contracts and associated trading terminology are more readily understood through use of the following illustration.

June 25, 1981

Trader A

Buys 5000 bushels of December corn at $3.48

Trader B

Sells 5000 bushels of December corn at $3.48

Trader A has entered into a contract to take delivery of 5000 bushels of corn in December and will pay $3.48 per bushel. Trader B has entered into a contract to deliver 5000 bushels of corn in December and will receive $3.48 per bushel. After the trade, each must deposit about $1500 as margin money with the commission merchant, through whom the trade is made to guarantee contract performance. Also, after the trade, Trader A is deemed to have bought from the clearinghouse and Trader B is deemed to have sold to the clearinghouse. This eliminates the necessity for each trader having to settle the contract by trading with each other either before or during the delivery month. The clearinghouse guarantees the performance on all futures contracts.

Assuming that neither of the above traders had a market position before the above trade was made, Trader A is a *new buyer* and is now "long"; Trader B is a *new seller* and is now "short."

If both traders leave their contracts open until the delivery month, the seller (Trader B) may delivery at any time during December up until the last few days, and it is up to the buyer (Trader A) to accept delivery and pay for the corn. If the seller decides to deliver on the contract, a warehouse receipt is delivered representing 5000 bushels of U.S. No. 2 yellow corn stored in a public terminal elevator, in Chicago, Toledo, Portage (Ind.), or St. Louis, that has been declared regular by the Chicago Board of Trade. Alternate grades are also deliverable at price differentials stipulated in the contract. If the seller chooses to make delivery in either Toledo or St. Louis, a discount under the Chicago contract price is applicable.

If the seller delivers on the contract, a warehouse receipt must be presented to the clearinghouse, which in turn delivers it to the oldest long in the market. This may or may not be Trader B with whom the original contract was made.

Very few futures contracts are settled by delivery. They are usually settled by offsetting purchases or sales of futures contracts sometime before the delivery month, illustrated as follows.

July 23, 1981

Trader A

Sells 5000 bushels of December corn at $3.53

Trader B

Buys 5000 bushels of December corn at $3.53

Trader A gains 5 cents/bu and $250 on the contract
Trader B loses 5 cents/bu and $250 on the contract

In trade terminology, Trader A is "long liquidating," and Trader B is "short covering." Each of these traders has satisfied the obligation regarding delivery after offsetting trades are made. Traders A and B need not make offsetting trades by dealing with each other. Each may make an offsetting trade at any time after the original contract was made by dealing with another trader. This is possible since the clearinghouse serves as an intermediary in all futures contracts. The clearinghouse also marks all contracts as to the settlement price (the closing price) each day. In the preceding illustration, Trader A would have collected a net of 5 cents per bushel, or $250, from the clearinghouse, and Trader B would have paid a net of 5 cents per bushel, or $250 to the clearinghouse from June 25 to July 23.

While very few futures contracts are settled by actual delivery, the privilege of making or taking delivery is important because it is the delivery mechanism that assures the convergence of the cash and futures prices in the delivery month. It is significant that futures contracts are not often used for the actual purchase or sale of grain. Instead, they facilitate hedging by serving as temporary substitutes for intended later transactions in cash grain.

RELATIONSHIP OF FUTURES PRICES FOR DIFFERENT DELIVERY MONTHS

Futures contracts are traded for specific delivery months. The delivery months for wheat, corn, and oats are March, May, July, September, and December. The delivery months for soybeans are January, March, May, July, August, September, and November. Grain production is highly seasonal, and the delivery months are related to the harvest, marketing, and consumption of grain throughout the year. The wheat harvest begins in late May or early June, so the wheat marketing year is June 1 to May 31. The first future delivery month in the wheat marketing year is July, which is called the "new crop" future. Successive delivery months are September, December, March, and May, the "old crop" future.

Corn is harvested later in the year than wheat, so the corn marketing year is October 1 to September 30. The first future delivery month in the corn marketing year is December, which is "new crop." Successive delivery months are March, May, July, and September, the "old crop" future for corn. (Occasionally, however, the September corn futures is partially new crop since corn harvested in southern states may be available for delivery on September futures.)

The prices of futures in different delivery months are usually different. Sometimes each successive future in the marketing year is priced higher than the previous delivery month. This is called a "carrying charge market."

Carrying Charges

The following illustration shows a carrying charge market for corn.

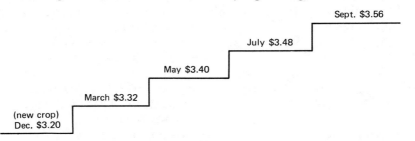

Each future in the corn marketing year, beginning with December (the new crop future), is priced lower than the following future. A carrying charge market usually occurs in a year when there is a large corn crop. Such a market provides an incentive for grain merchants to store corn for consumption later in the crop year. Corn can be purchased for December delivery for $3.20 and simultaneously sold for September delivery for $3.56. Hence, the market will return 36 cents per bushel for storing corn from December to September.

Distant futures cannot exceed the price of near futures by more than full carrying charges because of the possibilities of arbitrage between futures. Assume, for example, that on March 1, the March future is $3.32 and the May future is $3.42. Traders would then buy March, and simultaneously sell May. They would take delivery on the March future, hold the warehouse receipts for two months, pay the 8 cents per bushel cost of storage, deliver the warehouse receipt on the May future on May 1, and make a profit of 2 cents per bushel. Such arbitrage would force prices back to the minimum 8 cent differential or less.

Price differentials between future delivery months rarely reflect full carrying charges, even in years of very large corn crops. The reason is that grain merchants who own elevators are willing to store grain for their own account at less than the commercial storage rate. Storage costs to an elevator owner include variable costs of operating the elevator, interest on capital invested in the grain, insurance, and shrinkage. There is also a convenience yield to the owner of grain stocks because the possession of such stocks may afford the grain merchant opportunities to merchandise those stocks at a profit at some time during the storage period. This convenience yield may be high enough to make the actual out-of-pocket costs of grain storage to a grain merchant quite low. Hence, competition between grain merchants to store grain forces futures markets to reflect less than full carrying charges even when grain crops are large and there is an abundance of grain to store.

Inverse Carrying Charges

Sometimes distant futures sell for lower prices than near futures. This is known as an "inverted market" or a market with inverse carrying charges as illustrated.

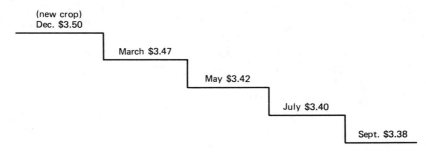

Inverse carrying charges usually occur in years when grain supplies are short relative to the demand. Grain futures prices were inverted in 1973/74 when the export demand for grain was very strong relative to supplies available. In such periods, buyers of grain are willing to pay higher prices for grain for current delivery than for forward delivery. The market provides an incentive for owners of grain to sell for current delivery, rather than store for future delivery.

There is no automatic or theoretical limit on the possible premiums that near futures may go to distant futures. The amount of the premium depends entirely on how much buyers are willing to pay for grain for immediate delivery. Lack of transportation equipment, such as railroad cars to ship grain, can also induce inverse carrying charges.

Price Relationships Between Old and New Crop Futures

The preceding explanations of carrying charge and inverted markets consider only the relationship between futures prices within a given marketing year. Sometimes the futures price of the last delivery month in the old crop year differs markedly from the futures price of the first delivery month in the new crop year. For example, in a year when the supply of corn is very tight relative to the demand, old crop corn futures (September) usually sell at a substantial premium to new crop futures (December) as shown.

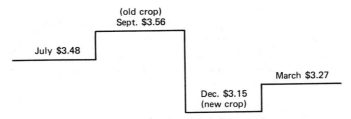

The sharply lower price for the December future provides an incentive for merchants and others who own corn to sell in the old crop year rather than carry it into the new crop year. The earlier explanation of the large discount of December under September was that the December future reflects the expectation of a large corn harvest between Setpember and December, depressing the price of the December future but will not affect the price of the September future. Research showed this explanation to be mistaken.[3] It is only the supply of corn already in existence that explains the new crop discount. It is the short supply of old crop corn that results in the premium of September future to the December future, not the expectations of a large harvest after September.

The size of the premium of old crop futures over new crop futures can be very large in some years. In years of short soybean supplies, for example, it has not been uncommon for July (old crop) soybeans to sell at a premium of several dollars over November (new crop) soybeans in June.

On the other hand, in years of large crops when a sizable carryover is in prospect, new crop futures usually sell at a premium over the old crop. In 1978, for example, the United States harvested a record corn crop of 6.9 billion bushels. The following futures were reported on January 22, 1979.

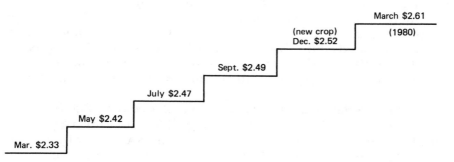

The supply of corn in the 1978/79 marketing year was expected to exceed the disappearance, so the carry-over at the end of the crop year increased substantially. This caused the discount of the September futures (old crop) relative to the December (new crop) futures. Hence, warehousemen had an incentive to carry old crop corn into the 1979/80 marketing year.

The relationship among futures prices of the various delivery months is a highly useful guide to inventory policies of grain merchants and processors. The above analysis considers only futures prices. But we must also consider the relationship of cash and futures prices to understand hedging.

[3]Holbrook Working, "The Theory of Price of Storage," *American Economic Review*, Vol. 39, No. 5, December 1949, pp. 1254–1262.

CASH AND FUTURES PRICE RELATIONSHIPS—THE BASIS

The cash or spot price is the price of grain for immediate delivery, or forward delivery at some specified place. Much cash grain is traded at so many cents over or under a given futures contract price, usually the future in the nearest delivery month, rather than as a flat price. For example, if cash corn prices on April 10 are quoted at "15 cents over," cash corn is selling at 15 cents above the price of the May corn future, or cash corn is at a 15-cent premium over the May future. If cash corn is quoted at "12 cents under," it is selling at 12 cents below the price of the May corn future, or cash corn is at a 12-cent discount under the May future. The basis, at a premium or discount, together with the flat prices is illustrated as follows.

	Flat Price	*Basis*
Corn price	$3.65	
May future price	$3.50	15¢ over
Cash corn price	$3.38	12¢ under

Cash grain that is quoted and traded at so much over or under the futures price is called "basis trading." The cash basis, commonly known as the basis, is simply the cash price in cents per bushel above or below the futures price, usually in the nearest delivery month. Thus, the futures price in basis trading is the reference price from which cash grain prices are quoted at so many cents over or under.

To a grain merchant, 15 cents over is much more meaningful than the flat price of $3.65, or 12 cents under is more significant than the flat price of $3.38 in the illustration. The reason is that most grain merchants practice hedging, taking positions in both cash and futures markets that are equal or opposite each other. A merchant who is long cash grain, will usually be short futures; the merchant who is short cash grain, usually will be long futures. At any particular time the basis will give a guide to inventory and hedging policy. When cash grain is at a sizable discount to futures prices, a merchant will strive to be long cash grain and short futures. On the other hand, when a merchant has to pay larger than normal premiums for cash grain, an attempt will be made to be short cash grain and long futures.

How the Basis Changes Over Time

Changes in the basis over time are more predictable than changes in the flat price of cash grain. The change in the basis over time can be forecast because the cash and futures prices must be nearly equal in the delivery month at the delivery point. In other words, the cash and futures prices converge as the delivery month approaches.

At the Delivery Point.   The convergence process and the behavior of the basis over time at the delivery point is shown graphically in Figure 7-1.

When cash grain is at a discount to the futures prices, such as in the lower part of the figure, there is a positive price of storage. This is the time to store cash grain and hedge it through the sale of futures. As the delivery month approaches, cash prices strengthen relative to futures prices—the basis strengthens. The gross return earned on the storage is equal to the amount by which the basis strengthens. This strengthening in the basis usually does not occur evenly, but the trend will be for the basis to strengthen as the delivery month approaches. If, for example, a merchant purchases cash grain at 25 cents under the May future on October 1, and hedges by selling May futures, a gross return of 25 cents will be earned if the cash grain is sold and the hedge lifted in May when the delivery market basis is zero.

When grain supplies are short relative to demand, the price of grain for current delivery often is at a premium over the price for future delivery. This is illustrated in the upper part of Figure 7-1. If cash prices are at a premium to futures prices, the market reflects a negative price of storage. The reason is that if a merchant purchases cash grain at 25 cents over the May future on October 1 and hedges by selling May futures, a 25 cent loss will occur if storage continues until May 1, when the hedge is lifted and the cash grain is sold. In a premium market, consequently, merchants have an incentive to keep their grain inventories at a minimum. In fact, they try to sell grain for forward delivery at high current prices, and purchase futures as

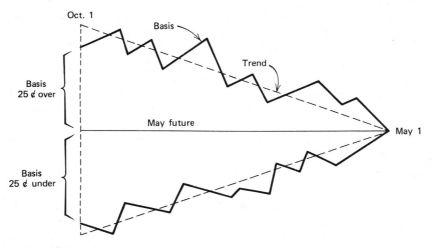

Figure 7-1.   Behavior of the May basis over time in a discount and premium market at a delivery market.

temporary substitutes for the cash grain until it is purchased for delivery.

At Local Points.   The basis at local country points moves in a similar manner over time as the basis at the delivery point. However, the basis at a local point reflects the cash price of grain at a specified location in the country. If grain normally moves from that location to the delivery point, the basis will usually be lower at the country point by the cost of transportation to the delivery point. For example, if on October 10 the basis for corn in Chicago is 15 cents under the December future, the basis for corn in a country point in western Illinois may be 21 cents under. The 6 cent difference reflects the transportation cost to Chicago. Cash corn prices in Chicago would be higher than in western Illinois, reflecting the cost of shipping corn to Chicago.

On the other hand, if grain does not normally move from the local point to Chicago, the basis at that location will reflect transportation costs from Chicago. Hence, the basis at such a point will be higher than at Chicago.

The basis at local country points is not only affected by the cost and availability of transportation; other factors affecting the local basis are the supply and demand for corn at a local point. A small local supply of corn, for example, will strengthen the local basis relative to Chicago. On the other hand, a large corn supply at the country point will weaken the country basis relative to Chicago.

Figure 7-2 illustrates the movement in the basis over time at the delivery point (Chicago), for corn futures, and the basis at some country point where cash prices are typically lower than at Chicago because of transportation costs. The difference in the basis between the two

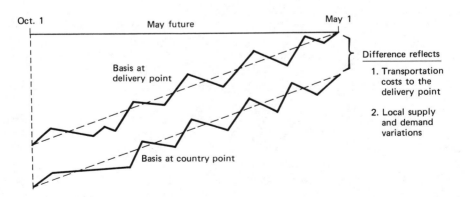

Figure 7-2. Behavior of the May basis over time at the delivery point and at a country point.

points reflects transportation costs and variations in the supply and demand for cash corn at the local point and at the delivery point. However, the basis tends to narrow as the delivery month approaches at the country point as well as at the delivery point.

HEDGING

Hedging is an important marketing tool for grain merchants, processors, and producers. Hedging is best described as "the purchase or sale of a futures contract on an organized commodity market as a temporary substitute for an intended later transaction in the cash market." There are many different types of hedging, but the common element in all of them is that futures contracts serve as temporary substitutes for intended later cash transactions.

Hedging often is oversimplified in principles of marketing textbooks, and even in more advanced economics books, because it is usually illustrated with an example of pure risk avoidance hedging. Our discussion of hedging will begin with an illustration of pure risk avoidance hedging as a convenient departure point from which to discuss other types of hedging that are more important and have more significant economic effects.

Pure Risk Avoidance Hedging

Grain merchandising operations of a country elevator are often used to explain this type of hedging. Assume that on October 15 a country elevator purchases corn from farmers at $3.30 per bushel. It will take time for the elevator to accumulate a sufficient quantity of corn for efficient transportation and sale. During the time the elevator holds the corn, it must assume the risk of a price decline. Consequently, to avoid this price risk, it hedges by selling an equivalent amount of December corn futures at $3.38. The price of cash corn then declines to $3.25 per bushel on November 15 when the cash corn is sold, resulting in a 5 cent loss, but this loss is offset by an equal 5 cent gain on the future. Cash and futures prices move together, so the future is purchased at 5 cents less when the hedge is lifted on November 15 than the price at which it was sold on October 15 when the hedge was placed (Table 7-3).

The effectiveness of pure risk avoidance hedging is usually illustrated, as in the example, by a parallel movement in cash and futures prices. In other words, the basis is the same when the hedge is lifted as it was when the hedge was placed. It is true that price risks can be avoided through hedging and, over short time intervals, hedgers may assume that the basis will not change. Over longer periods of time, however, the hedger can anticipate a change in the basis and profit from it. Hedgers can forecast this change in the basis because of the convergence principle—the tendency of cash and futures prices to

Table 7-3 Pure Risk Avoidance Hedging

	Cash Grain		Futures Transactions		Basis
Oct. 15	Buy cash corn	$3.30	Sell December corn	$3.38	8¢ under
Nov. 15	Sell cash corn	$3.25	Buy December corn	$3.33	8¢ under
	Loss	5¢	Gain	5¢	

converge as the delivery month approaches. Hence, hedgers often strive to make profits through hedging by correctly forecasting the change in the basis. This is what grain warehousemen attempt to do; they attempt to earn carrying charges on grain in storage through hedging. The effectiveness of hedging by grain warehousemen depends on the inequality in the movement of cash and futures prices over time—a change in the basis.

Storage Hedging

The key to successful storage hedging is understanding how the basis behaves over the marketing year. This is shown by the July basis for corn. Table 7-4 shows weekly cash corn prices and July corn future prices, from October 2, 1980 to June 25, 1981, at Stewartville, Minnesota. The July basis is calculated by subtracting the July future price from the cash price. Figure 7-3 shows the 1980/81 July basis for corn at Stewartville (plotted from Table 7-4). In its construction, the July future price each week is taken to be zero; the basis is plotted on the proper number of cents below the zero mark.

Figure 7-3 shows clearly that the July basis is the lowest in the fall shortly after harvest, in November and December. It then strengthens, and reaches its highest level in May and June and weakens again. On December 4, 1980, the July basis was the lowest at $1.08 under, and it was the highest on June 4, 1981, at 40 cents under; the basis strengthened 68 cents during this period.

How does the seasonal pattern in the 1980/81 July corn basis just described compare with previous marketing years? Figure 7-4 shows the July basis patterns for the three marketing years, 1977/78, 1978/79, and 1979/80. The individual years reflect a similar seasonal pattern of weakness in the fall and strength in late spring; that is, the basis strengthened substantially in each marketing year. The reason for this typical basis behavior is that corn supplies are usually large in the fall so elevator and transportation facilities are often pressed to their limits. Hence, the market offers incentives to farmers and marketing firms to store corn to relieve the glutted market. The basis is then low, reflecting favorable returns to storage. Later in the marketing year, as supplies diminish, the basis strengthens and encourages corn to be brought out of storage and into marketing channels. However, there is variability in the July basis pattern from year to year as market funda-

Table 7-4 Weekly Cash Corn Prices, Stewartville,
Minnesota, Chicago July Futures Prices, and the Basis,
October 2, 1980, to June 25, 1981

Date	Stewartville Cash Price	Chicago July Futures Price	July Basis
10/2/80	$2.67	$3.62	$−0.95
10/9/80	2.85	3.65	−0.80
10/16/80	2.81	3.71	−0.90
10/23/80	2.88	3.84	−0.96
10/30/80	2.95	3.85	−0.90
11/6/80	2.89	3.91	−1.02
11/13/80	2.96	3.94	−0.98
11/20/80	3.11	4.11	−1.00
11/26/80	3.09	4.11	−1.02
12/4/80	2.90	3.98	−1.08
12/10/80	2.80	3.74	−0.94
12/18/80	2.95	3.82	−0.87
12/24/80	2.99	3.82	−0.83
12/31/80	3.00	3.84	−0.84
1/8/81	2.99	3.84	−0.95
1/15/81	3.03	3.82	−0.79
1/22/81	2.98	3.83	−0.85
1/29/81	2.89	3.72	−0.83
2/5/81	2.98	3.81	−0.83
2/12/81	2.95	3.79	−0.84
2/19/81	3.00	3.85	−0.85
2/26/81	2.97	3.76	−0.79
3/5/81	2.90	3.61	−0.71
3/12/81	2.94	3.66	−0.72
3/19/81	3.02	3.72	−0.70
3/26/81	3.05	3.71	−0.66
4/2/81	3.04	3.73	−0.69
4/9/81	3.12	3.82	−0.70
4/15/81	3.12	3.74	−0.62
4/22/81	3.17	3.77	−0.60
4/29/81	3.15	3.66	−0.51
5/7/81	3.10	3.65	−0.55
5/14/81	3.10	3.55	−0.45
5/21/81	3.04	3.47	−0.43
5/28/81	3.06	3.48	−0.42
6/4/81	3.00	3.40	−0.40
6/11/81	2.98	3.45	−0.47
6/18/81	2.94	3.43	−0.49
6/25/81	2.93	3.38	−0.45

mentals change. A brief look at the changing corn market supply and
demand in the marketing years 1977/78 through 1980/81 is
illustrative.

The 1977/78 July basis was weakest in October. It then strength-

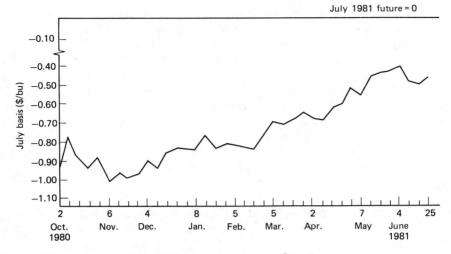

Figure 7-3. July corn basis, Stewartville, Minn., Oct. 2, 1980 to June 25, 1981.

ened and remained relatively constant until May. Seventeen percent of the 1977 Minnesota corn harvest was sold in October, versus 11 and 12 percent for 1978 and 1979, respectively. A dry fall in 1977 permitted more than a third of the Minnesota corn crop to be harvested by the end of the first week in October. This meant a larger than normal corn supply was marketed in October.

The 1978 Minnesota corn harvest was larger than in 1977, but corn

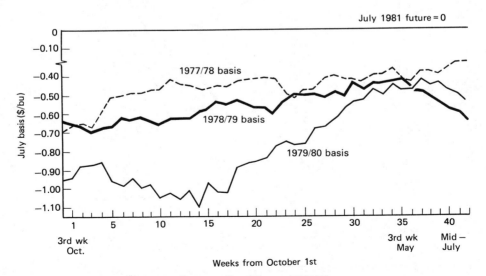

Figure 7-4. July corn basis, Stewartville, Minn., 1977/78, 1978/79, and 1979/80.

was marketed more evenly over the 1978/79 marketing year. The July basis reflects a more stable strengthening pattern in 1978/79.

The July basis in 1979/80 was exceptionally weak in the early part of the marketing year—fall and early winter. This was due to several factors. First, a late summer strike by Duluth grain handlers created barge traffic problems on the Mississippi River, because grain normally shipped on the Great Lakes was forced to seek alternative market outlets. Second, the U.S. embargo on grain sales to Russia (in January 1980) plugged marketing channels, particularly in the Gulf, which weakened the basis. Finally, record high interest rates raised the cost of carrying grain stocks, and depressed cash prices relative to futures prices.

Seasonal Index of the July Basis. Figure 7-5 shows the monthly seasonal index of the July corn basis at Stewartville for the nine marketing years, 1971/72 through 1979/80. The seasonal pattern is very strong. This index removes the short-term variations and long-term trends in the July basis. It shows only the regular movement in the July basis over the marketing year. The seasonal low in the July basis occurs in October when the index is 140 percent of the seasonal average. The

Figure 7-5. Seasonal index of the July corn basis, Stewartville, Minn., 1971/72 through 1979/80.

July basis strengthens through the marketing year, until May, when it is 60 percent of the seasonal average. It then weakens into the July delivery month. The zone of irregularity around the seasonal index is shown in the figure by one standard deviation above and below the seasonal index line. This zone includes two-thirds of July bases over the marketing year. Storage hedging, as well as other types of hedging, usually involve forecasting the basis movement over time. The seasonal index clearly shows the typical behavior of the July basis and its variability over the marketing year. While such information is useful to the hedger, one must also analyze market supply and demand fundamentals and their possible effects on the basis in any given marketing year.

Examples of Storage Hedging.   Examples using actual prices from the 1980/81 and 1979/80 marketing years are helpful in understanding storage hedging. The harvest time basis was very weak in both marketing years (Figures 7-3 and 7-4), for reasons previously discussed. Suppose a farmer near Stewartville harvested corn the first week of November 1980. The Stewartville elevator was bidding $2.89 per bushel on November 6, 1980, the July future was selling for $3.91, and the basis was $1.02 under (Table 7-4). The farmer recognized from past experience that this was a weak basis, and that the July basis would likely narrow substantially by May 31, 1981. Assume that the farmer stored corn, hedged it through the sale of July futures on November 6, 1980, then sold the corn locally and lifted the hedge on May 14, 1981. The results would have been as follows.

Date	Cash	Futures	Basis
Nov. 6, 1980	Store 5000 bu corn (local cash price is $2.89)	Sell July futures @ $3.91	$-1.02
May 14, 1981	Sell 5000 bu @ $3.10	Buy July futures @ $3.55	-0.45 $+0.57

The farmer's return to storage from November 6, 1980 to May 14, 1981 was 57 cents per bushel, or the amount that the basis narrowed. Another way of looking at the results is through the net price received. If corn had been sold at the Stewartville elevator on November 6, the price would have been $2.89 per bushel. By storing and hedging, the farmer received $3.10 plus 36 cents gained on the future, or $3.46 per bushel. This is 57 cents more, which equals the change in the basis. Had the farmer stored corn without hedging, the price received would be $3.10 per bushel or 21 cents more than a November 6, 1980, sale.

What would have been the results of a storage hedge placed in the fall of 1979? This was also when the harvest time basis was very weak. Assume that the hedge was placed the first week in November 1979, and lifted the second week of May 1980. The results are shown as follows.

Date	Cash	Futures	Basis
Nov. 8, 1979	Store 5000 bu corn (local cash price is $1.97)	Sell July futures @ $2.96	$−0.99
May 15, 1980	Sell 5000 bu @ $2.31	Buy July futures @ $2.82	−0.51
			$+0.48

The net price received for the corn through the storage hedge was $2.45 per bushel ($2.31 plus 14 cents gain on future). For storing without hedging that year, the farmer would have received $2.31, or 38 cents more than if sold on November 8, 1979. So storage hedging yielded a good gross return to corn storage in both the 1980/81 and 1979/80 marketing years. While the results may not compare as favorably with other marketing alternatives every year, storage hedging usually yields consistent returns to corn storage. Opportunities for storage hedging often appear in years of abundant corn supplies when the basis is usually very weak after harvest.

The above examples show only the gross return to storage hedging. To calculate the net returns, the farmer would have to subtract the variable costs of farm corn storage, which include the interest cost on capital invested in the corn, the cost of taxes and insurance on stored grain, and any physical loss of corn due to handling and shrinkage while in storage. These are the only costs that enter into short-run decisions on corn storage, if the farmer already has corn storage facilities on the farm. Many farmers have their own farm storage, which has expanded substantially in the past decade.

Storage Hedges Can Be Lifted Sooner Than Planned.   In the above storage hedging examples, hedges were placed in the fall when the July basis is usually the lowest, and lifted in early May when the July basis is usually the strongest. A grain merchant or farmer may place a storage hedge in the fall, anticipating lifting it in early May. However, if the basis strengthens unexpectedly before May, it probably would be a wise decision to lift the hedge and sell the grain sooner than anticipated. An important advantage of storing cash grain and pricing it through the sale of futures when the basis is weak is the opportunity to sell the cash grain when cash prices strengthen relative to futures. Sometimes this can occur, at unexpected times, when there is an increase in the demand for cash grain for spot delivery.

The Best Delivery Month in Which to Hedge.   A grain merchant or producer who had decided to place a storage hedge will hedge in the future delivery month that has the highest price relative to the others after considering the storage costs of carrying the grain.

On October 2, 1980, for example, these were the corn prices:

Stewartville cash price	$2.67
December corn future	3.43
March corn future	3.55
May corn future	3.61
July corn future	3.62

December is the near future on this date, so the near basis is 76 cents under. The carrying charge between December and July is 19 cents. The July basis is the sum of the two, or 95 cents under.

A storage hedger placing a hedge on October 2, 1980, and feeling that the carrying charge of 19 cents between December and July is as wide as it will get, will hedge directly in the July future. But if the hedger feels that this carrying charge will widen, the first hedge will be in the December future and, before it expires, the hedge will be moved forward to the March, May, or July future. Which of the latter three futures is selected depends on one's judgment of the carrying charge. The hedge is moved forward by buying back the December future and selling the March, May, or July future.

It should be emphasized that it is useful to think of the basis relative to the near future plus a carrying charge between the near and distant futures. In the grain trade, the basis is usually quoted relative to the near future.

Hedging Forward Cash Sales of Grain and Processed Products

Access to futures markets for hedging enables grain merchants to make forward cash sales at a fixed price even though they do not own the grain at the time the sale is made. Forward cash contracts are used extensively in the merchandising of grain and grain products such as flour, feed, soybean meal, and soybean oil. Merchants and processors can fix the price at the time the forward cash sale is made by using futures prices as a guide, with adjustments for their operating costs. After making such forward cash sales, they purchase futures contracts, which serve as temporary substitutes for the cash grain until it is purchased for delivery or processing. This is called "long hedging" because the merchant is *short cash grain or products* and *long futures.*

Long hedging is usually most effective in inverted markets when cash prices are at a premium over near futures, and near futures are higher priced than distant futures. Such price relationships often occur in years when supplies are short relative to demand. Negative prices of storage prevail, so merchandisers and processors have little incentive to carry inventories. In fact, since the market is paying higher prices for current delivery than for future delivery, they keep their inventories at minimum levels. They also look for opportunities to make forward cash sales of grain they do not own at high current prices and hedge those sales through the purchase of futures—in other words, engaging in long hedging. As the cash and futures prices converge as the delivery month approaches, the spot premium usually declines, yielding a profit on the hedge.

Long Hedging Grain Merchants.   This can be illustrated with an example of country elevator grain merchandising operations. Assume that on February 10 a country elevator has an opportunity to sell corn to a local feeder for delivery in early May at 5 cents over May corn futures, which are currently priced at $3.45. The merchant does not own the corn now, but past experience suggests that corn can be purchased from farmers in late April at 12 cents under May corn futures. This is an attractive opportunity because selling corn at 5 cents over and purchasing it at 12 cents under will result in a gross return of 17 cents per bushel (Table 7-5).

After making the sale, May corn futures are immediately purchased and they serve as a temporary substitute for the cash corn until it is purchased. On April 25, corn is bought for delivery to the feeder at $3.48 and the hedge is lifted by selling May futures at $3.60. The basis is 12 cents under, as expected, so a perfect hedge resulted in the 17-cent net return as shown in this example.

It should be emphasized that the success of this forward sale depends on the accuracy with which the merchant can forecast the actual buying basis—the basis that will prevail when corn is purchased. This forecast must be made at the time of the forward cash sale. The grain merchant uses knowledge of historical relationships in the basis, and personal judgment of market factors, to estimate the basis at the time corn is purchased. As discussed earlier, the merchant can forecast the basis in the delivery month because the cash and futures prices converge as the delivery month approaches. If the merchant, as in this case, is located at a point other than the delivery point, the basis in the delivery month will reflect transportation costs to the delivery point, depending on the location, as well as local supply and demand conditions.

Table 7-5   Long Hedge of a Forward Cash Sale of Corn

Cash			*Futures*		*Basis*
Feb 10					
Sell corn for delivery in early May	$3.50		Buy May futures	$3.45	5¢ over
Apr 25					
Purchase corn from farmers		$3.48	Sell May futures	$3.60	12¢ under
	Gain	$0.02	Gain	$0.15	17¢ net gain

It is also common practice for terminal grain merchants to make forward cash sales of grain they do not own and hedge these sales through the purchase of futures. An example of such hedging by terminal merchants would be very similar to the long hedging example practiced by a country elevator.

Furthermore, nearly all of the sales of grain by exporters are made on forward cash contracts calling for delivery up to one year in advance. The exporter can quote forward prices for grain not owned because the futures market can be utilized for pricing and hedging as discussed before.

Long Hedging by Grain Processors. Grain processors such as flour millers, feed manufacturers, and soybean crushers also make extensive use of futures to hedge the forward sale of processed products before they own the raw material and the processing takes place. For example, in January 1977, Central Soya sold soybean meal and oil products for delivery in October, November, and December 1977.[4] They were able to make such forward sales because of their access to the futures market, even though the 1977 soybean crop would not be planted until May or June. November soybean futures were purchased when the product sales were made, and these futures served as a temporary substitute for the cash soybeans that they intended to purchase in the fall. When the cash soybeans are purchased, the soybean futures are then sold to lift the hedge. The soybeans are then processed and the products—meal and oil—are delivered to the buyers. A hedge of this nature is a means of protecting against the price risk instead of charging larger margins to compensate for the unknown degree of risk.

Flour millers also frequently practice long hedging when they hedge the forward sales of flour. It is common practice for bakers to buy flour from millers on forward cash contracts. Even though there is no organized futures market in flour, millers are able to quote prices on flour for forward delivery because they can hedge those sales through the purchase of wheat futures. The wheat futures serve as temporary substitutes for the cash wheat for milling until it can be purchased. As the miller purchases the cash wheat and mills it into flour, the wheat futures are sold.

This hedging practice has been called operational hedging by Professor Working because it facilitates the operations of a grain merchandising or processing business. Flour millers typically do not store large quantities of wheat. They can, nevertheless, make large forward sales of flour because of their access to the futures market for hedging. Millers can purchase large quantities of futures immediately after forward flour sales are made. Later, the miller can purchase the cash

[4]Robert B. Parrott, "A Professional's View of Trading," *Views From the Trade, Readings on Futures Markets,* Vol. III, A. E. Peck, ed., Chicago Board of Trade, Chicago, Ill., 1978, pp. 197–198.

wheat of the desired classes, grades, and protein needed to mill the flour. Such purchases can usually be made more advantageously over a period of time.[5] As the cash wheat is purchased for milling, the wheat futures are sold, lifting the hedge.

Hedging Processing Margins

Soybean crushers have access to futures markets for both their raw material (soybeans) and finished products (soybean meal and soybean oil). This allows considerable flexibility in hedging operations. In fact, some of the more sophisticated and complicated uses of futures markets are found in the hedging operations of soybean processors.

When soybeans are processed, meal and oil are obtained simultaneously. The difference between the value of the meal and oil obtained from a bushel of soybeans and the value of the soybeans is often called the "crushing margin"—a rough measure of the profitability of crushing soybeans.

Soybean crushers frequently utilize soybean, soybean meal, and soybean oil futures to establish or lock in their crushing margin. This is commonly known as "putting on the crush." It is accomplished by buying soybean futures and selling equivalent amounts of soybean meal and soybean oil futures.

Assume that on August 15, 1978, the following futures prices are quoted for soybeans, soybean oil, and soybean meal.

January 1979 soybeans	$7.37 per bushel
January 1979 soybean oil	$0.27 per pound
January 1979 soybean meal	$197.00 per ton

These prices reflect a "board" crushing margin per bushel in January futures as follows.

11 pounds of oil × $.27	= $2.97
48 pounds of meal	
(0.024 per pound × $197 per ton)	= 4.73
Total product value per bushel	$7.70
Less January soybeans per bushel	7.37
Gross crushing margin per bushel	$0.33

A processor who desires to lock in this 33 cent crushing margin on August 15 will purchase January soybeans and simultaneously sell equivalent amounts of January soybean meal and oil futures. In making this decision, the processor must forecast the buying basis for cash soybeans (the price relationship between January soybean futures and cash soybeans) that will prevail in November when soybeans will be

[5]Holbrook Working, "Hedging Reconsidered," *Selected Writings of Holbrook Working,* Chicago Board of Trade, Chicago, Ill., 1977, pp. 126–132.

purchased for crushing. Similarly, the processor must forecast the selling basis for soybean meal and oil (the price relationship between January soybean product futures and cash prices of the products) that will prevail in December when the products will be sold.

Basis forecasts are made using knowledge of historical basis patterns and personal judgments of market factors prevailing in the current year. It is easier to forecast the basis than the price level in price volatile commodities such as soybeans, soybean oil, and soybean meal. Nevertheless, after putting on the crush, the processor is still subject to basis risk. If the actual buying basis for soybeans is stronger than anticipated and/or the selling basis for soybean oil and meal are weaker than anticipated, the 33 cent margin expected from the hedge may not be realized. As cash soybeans are purchased for crushing in November, the January soybean futures are sold. When the cash products (soybean meal and soybean oil) are sold in December or January, the January soybean meal and oil futures are purchased, lifting the hedge.

Soybean processors also have opportunities to sell meal and oil on forward cash contracts to users of these products. Having established board crushing margins, as previously described, a processor may find it advantageous to sell meal and oil on forward cash contracts, in which case the futures in the products would be repurchased. Then the crush hedge would consist of long January soybean futures versus short forward cash contracts of equivalent amounts of meal and oil.

Having access to spot markets for current or forward delivery and futures markets in both soybeans and their products opens up a wide variety of trading alternatives for soybean producers.

Hedging by Agricultural Producers

Farmers can practice hedging in three principal ways. First, they can store grain when their selling basis is weak and hedge it through the sale of futures. Since the basis normally strengthens as the delivery month approaches, the farmer may earn a return on storage equal to the amount by which the basis narrows. Second, farmers can use futures to price grain in advance of production. And third, futures can be used by livestock producers to price grain for livestock feed in advance of purchase. These latter two types of hedging are called "anticipatory" hedging. The purpose of anticipatory hedging is to take advantage of the current price. In both uses of anticipatory hedging, the futures contract serves as a temporary substitute for a merchandising contract that the producer intends to make at a later time.[6]

Pricing Grain in Advance of Production.   The objective of pricing crops under production is to lock in a price in advance of harvest that will

---

[6]Holbrook Working, "New Concepts Concerning Futures Markets and Prices," *Selected Writings of Holbrook Working,* Chicago Board of Trade, 1977, Chicago, Ill., pp. 251–252.

cover production costs and allow a reasonable return. To do this requires knowledge of the normal basis, the relationship between the cash price at the farmer's local market, and the futures price in the delivery month closest to harvest. The farmer can localize the futures price by subtracting this normal basis from the futures price, which yields the "lock-in" price. The best method of determining the normal basis is to study the historical relationships between cash and futures prices.

Assume that on May 5, 1981, a farmer near Morgan, Minnesota, has planted corn and is considering using the futures market to forward price the corn which will be harvested during the last two weeks in November. On May 5, 1981, the price of December corn futures in Chicago is $3.75 per bushel. The farmer also knows that over the past three years the cash corn at the Morgan elevator during the last two weeks of November has averaged 80 cents under Chicago December corn futures. This is the normal basis, which, when subtracted from the December futures price, yields a lock-in price of $2.95 per bushel. December corn futures are then sold to set this price, assuming the farmer finds it satisfactory.

Prices for the remainder of the growing season then gradually decline; the farmer harvests corn on November 20, sells it to the Morgan elevator for $2.07, or 83 cents under the December corn future, and lifts the hedge by buying back December corn futures. The results of the hedge are shown in Table 7-6. The actual net price the farmer received was $2.92 per bushel, or 3 cents less than the lock-in price estimated on May 5. The actual selling basis was 83 cents under rather than 80 cents under, as anticipated. On a selling hedge, the realized price will be higher than the lock-in price when the actual selling basis is stronger than anticipated. Conversely, if the selling basis is weaker than anticipated, the actual price will be less than the estimated lock-in price.

If the futures price had risen between May 5 and November 20, there would have been a loss on the future, but since the cash price

Table 7-6 Examples of Using Futures to Price Corn in Advance of Production

May 5, 1981, December corn futures	$3.75
Less normal basis at harvest	0.80
(last two weeks of November)	
Lock-in-price	$2.95
(estimated cash price in November)	
May 5, 1981, Sells December corn futures	$3.75
Nov. 20, 1981, Buys December corn futures	2.90
Gain on future	$+0.85
Nov. 20, 1981, Sells cash corn	$2.07
Net corn price	$2.92

would also have risen, the lock-in price would be achieved if the selling basis on November 20 was 80 cents under the December future.

Farmers may also price grain in advance of production through a cash forward contract with their country elevator. Country elevators typically offer to purchase grain for forward delivery at a price agreed on at the time the contract is made. The country elevator then hedges to protect itself against adverse price changes.

More farmers are finding it is advantageous in marketing management to price at least some of their crops in advance of production. Each must decide which method of forward pricing is most suitable. Such forward pricing is made possible because of the futures market. The farmer can forward price grain through direct transactions in futures or through forward cash contracts, which, in effect, are indirect transactions in futures. In the latter case, such purchases are hedged in futures by country elevators or by a terminal merchant to whom the country elevator has sold grain for forward delivery.

Pricing Livestock Feed in Advance of Purchase.   This is a third way in which farmers may use futures markets for hedging. Suppose on November 6, 1980, a farmer is feeding cattle near Stewartville, Minnesota, and knows that corn will last until sometime in May at present feeding rates, but will have to buy more corn at that time. The feeder wants to lock in a favorable price for purchasing corn in May, and avoid the risk of a price increase between November and May. The futures market offers this opportunity.

In May, the July corn basis averages about 45 cents under (Figure 7-3). On November 6, 1980, the July corn futures price was $3.91. Subtracting the normal July basis in May from this price gives an estimated local corn price of $3.46. Suppose the farmer thinks this is a reasonable price, allowing a normal return on cattle feeding operation. To lock in this price, July corn futures are purchased. Later, on May 7, 1981, cash corn is purchased locally, and the corn futures are sold to lift the hedge. The results of the hedge are shown in Table 7-7.

The net price paid for the corn was $3.36, the local purchase price of $3.10 plus the 26 cent loss on the futures. This is 10 cents less than the estimated lock-in price. The actual buying basis in May was 55 cents under rather than 45 cents under, as estimated in November. A gain is made on a long hedge when the basis weakens or does not strengthen as much as anticipated. This is the exact opposite of a short hedge when gains are made on strengthening of the basis, a distinction that is an important one to remember.

Cost of Hedging

Futures contracts are bought and sold through futures commission merchants (FCMs), sometimes called "brokers" who are members of most exchanges. Their main business is to execute futures trades for

Table 7-7 Example of Using Futures to Price Livestock
Feed in Advance of Purchase

Nov. 6, 1980	July corn futures	$3.91
	Less normal July basis in May	0.45
	Lock-in price (estimated cash price in May)	$3.46
Nov. 6, 1980	Buys July corn futures	$3.91
May 7, 1981	Sells July corn futures	$3.65
	Loss on future	$−0.26
May 7, 1981	Buys cash corn	$3.10
	Net corn price	$3.36

others, such as hedgers or speculators, who are the real principals of the futures transactions. FCMs charge a commission rate for their services. The principals of futures transactions must also deposit margin money with the FCM to guarantee performance on their contracts. FCMs are required by law to keep this margin money in segregated accounts, apart from other assets of the firm as protection for their customers.

The cost of the futures transactions to the hedger consists of the futures trading commission rate, and the interest cost on the margin money on deposit with the FCM.

Table 7-8 shows the "round turn" commission rates (covering the purchase and sale of one futures contract) charged by one FCM as of October 1, 1981. The commission rate on one corn futures contract (5000 bushels) is $50, the futures commission transaction cost to the corn hedger is one cent per bushel.

Margin requirements on hedging and speculative futures transactions are also shown in Table 7-8. A corn hedger would deposit $500 per contract with an FCM and must maintain the margin at this level. For example, if the price of corn futures advances 5 cents per bushel after a hedger has sold corn futures as a hedge, the hedger must

Table 7-8 Margin Requirements and Commission Rates
on Grain Futures Contracts, One Futures Commission
Merchant, October 1, 1981 (dollars per contract)

Commodity	Hedging		Speculative		Round[a] Turn Commission
	Initial	Maintenance	Initial	Maintenance	
Wheat	750	750	1000	750	60
Corn	500	500	600	500	50
Oats	300	300	400	300	50
Soybeans	1000	1000	1500	1000	60
Soybean meal	600	600	1000	600	60
Soybean oil	400	400	600	400	60

[a]Covers the purchase and sale of one futures contract.

deposit an additional $250 per contract with the FCM to make up for the loss of equity resulting from the price increase. Hedgers must be prepared to meet these "margin calls" promptly. Otherwise, their futures positions will be liquidated by the FCM. Interest costs on margin funds represent a cost of hedging.

Initial margin requirements on speculative transactions are higher than for hedging because speculation involves more risk. But the maintenance margin on speculative accounts is lower than the initial margin and is the same as the hedging maintenance margin.

Economic Benefits of Hedging

The best known and most widely accepted economic benefit of hedging is that it reduces business risks. This, in turn, reduces marketing margins, with the result that producer prices are higher and consumer prices are lower than they would be in the absence of hedging. Hedging reduces marketing margins by enabling business firms to operate on lower margins when they can reduce the risks involved in carrying price-volatile inventories. The latter also facilitates and reduces the cost of financing. Commercial banks are willing to loan a high percentage of the value of grain inventories at prime rates when they are hedged. Huge amounts of bank credit are needed each year to finance inventories of seasonally produced annual crops such as wheat, corn, and soybeans.

A second economic benefit of hedging is that it reduces the variability in cash or spot commodity prices. This effect stems from the fact that the hedger is in a better position to judge what can be paid for the spot commodity because the futures price is a known reference point. The basis is much more meaningful to the grain merchant or processor than the flat price of the commodity. This is why basis trading is dominant in all grains that are traded on futures markets.

A third economic benefit of hedging is derived from "promoting the stockpiling, of commodities in private hands in times of surplus, inducing the economical storage of such stocks, and promoting their release for consumption at appropriate times."[7]

Hedging exerts this economic effect through the mechanism of spot-futures price relationships. In times of surplus, spot prices are at discounts to futures prices; storage prices are positive. This encourages stockpiling, as merchants have an incentive to purchase spot grain for storage and hedge it "to earn the carrying charge." Conversely, spot-futures price relationships discourage stockpiling when supplies are short. In such periods, spot prices often go to premiums over futures prices. Storage prices are then negative and, hence, merchants are induced to sell rather than store. Spot-futures price relationships

[7]Holbrook Working, "Hedging Reconsidered," *Selected Writings of Holbrook Working*, Chicago Board of Trade, Chicago, Ill., 1977, pp. 132–136.

are a highly serviceable guide to the level of inventories that merchants and processors carry.

The impact that hedging has on stockpiling in times of surplus deserves reemphasis today since the need for government reserve stock programs is receiving considerable attention by policy makers. Some people who are strong advocates of government reserve stock programs overlook the fact that the futures market mechanism, and the temporal dimension it gives to prices, provides an economic inducement for private firms to carry stocks forward when they are in surplus. This inducement also applies to carrying surplus stocks from one crop year to the next.

The Importance of Hedging to Futures Trading

There is a widespread view that futures markets are primarily speculative markets, but this is in error. In fact, "the importance of hedging is best expressed in the categorical statement that futures trading depends upon hedging."[8] Considerable empirical evidence supports this conclusion.

The strongest evidence of the dependence of futures trading on hedging is that open contracts in grain futures rise and fall with commercial stocks of the commodity. In wheat, for example, open contracts tend to rise each year as the new wheat crop is harvested, reaching a peak when commercial stocks reach their maximum. Open contracts then fall as the marketing year progresses and stocks are used. This strongly suggests that the seasonal pattern in open contracts is dictated by hedging use.

A study of the distribution of open interest (open contracts) in grain futures also shows the importance of hedging on both the long and short sides of the corn futures market.

Look at the distribution of the open contracts on the long side of the corn futures market (Figure 7-6). It shows that large hedgers (holders of a futures position of more than 200,000 bushels of grain) increased in importance from 30 percent of the open contracts in 1966/67 to nearly 80 percent in 1975/76. Some of the small traders who hold long open contracts are also hedgers, but it is not possible to ascertain how many. The larger proportion of long open contracts held by hedgers reflects the growth in corn exports during this period.

Increases in grain export sales result in an increase in long hedging because most export sales are made with cash forward contracts. This means that the grain to be delivered anywhere in from one to six months, or more, is sold and priced at the same time. If the price is fixed when these forward sales are made, the exporter assumes a price

---

[8]Roger W. Gray, "The Importance of Hedging in Futures Trading; and the Effectiveness of Futures Trading for Hedging," *Views From the Trade, Readings on Futures Markets,* Vol. III, A. E. Peck, ed., Chicago Board of Trade, Chicago, Ill., 1978, pp. 223–225.

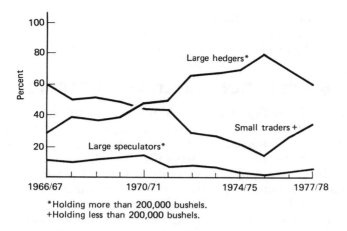

Figure 7-6.   Percent of long month-end interest corn futures held, by type of trader, 1966 to 1978 crop years. (*Source:* Commodity Futures Trading Commission.)

risk. This is the risk that the price of grain sold will increase before the exporter can purchase it. But this price risk can be lessened by purchasing futures contracts which serve as temporary substitutes for the cash grain until it is purchased. If it were not for futures markets, exporters would have to assume this risk or pass it along to the importer by charging a higher price. This substantial risk premium would reduce the volume of exports.

On the short side of the corn futures market, large hedgers have been the most important for many years (Figure 7-7). Large hedgers

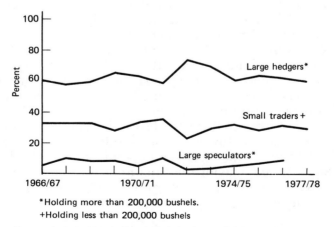

Figure 7-7.   Percent of short month-end interest corn futures held, by type of trader, 1966 to 1978 crop years. (*Source:* Commodity Futures Trading Commission.)

are mainly grain merchants and processors carrying large, unsold inventories of grain. They held 60 percent or more of the open contracts on the short side in almost every year since 1966/67.

SPECULATION FACILITATES HEDGING

Although grain futures markets depend on hedging business for their existence, futures markets that attract a large volume of speculation are better hedging markets. Speculation can be defined as the holding of a long or short position in futures for the sole purpose of profiting by correctly forecasting the movement of futures prices.

Speculators in futures perform the important economic function of facilitating hedging. Speculators stand ready to absorb the price risks that hedgers do not wish to assume. Futures markets that attract a substantial volume of speculative trade are better hedging markets for two reasons. First, speculation adds to futures market liquidity, which enables hedges to be placed and lifted with a minimum price effect. In a small, illiquid market, a large short hedger may find, for example, that the futures price may be depressed several cents by selling large quantities of futures to hedge a long position in cash grain. A liquid market, however, can absorb large trades with a much smaller price effect. The wheat market in The Chicago Board of Trade gets more speculative trade than the Kansas City or Minneapolis wheat futures markets, because Chicago has a better balance between hedging and speculative trade and can absorb larger hedging transactions at lower costs than the other two markets.

Second, futures markets that depend mainly on hedging business are frequently characterized by "imbalance."[9] In other words, they are often lopsided and tend to favor the longs or the shorts. Such lopsidedness stems from the fact that hedging is rarely balanced. Only infrequently would short hedging be equally balanced by long hedging. In the grains, for example, the futures markets must absorb large quantities of short hedges immediately after harvest when large quantities are sold by farmers and move into marketing channels. Short hedging in this period may exceed long hedging by a considerable margin. The excess of short over long hedging must be absorbed by long speculation. If speculators are not there to absorb this excess, the market may display a price bias that favors the long side. Such a price bias may appear in small futures markets that depend almost entirely on hedging trade. Such price behavior does not appear in larger futures markets such as Chicago corn, wheat, and soybeans that have a better balance between hedging and speculation.

[9]Roger W. Gray, "Why Does Futures Trading Succeed or Fail: An Analysis of Selected Commodities," *View From the Trade, Readings on Futures Markets,* Vol. III, A. E. Peck, ed., Chicago Board of Trade, Chicago, Ill., 1978, pp. 235–242.

So, even though futures markets have often been criticized as being "too speculative," research evidence supports the conclusion that futures markets that receive a large volume of speculation are the best hedging markets. Speculation facilitates hedging and, therefore, serves an important economic purpose.

REGULATION OF FUTURES TRADING

Futures trading is regulated by two principal means. First, there is self-regulation, as provided for under the rules and regulations of the exchanges or boards of trade on which the trading takes place. Second, futures trading is regulated by the federal government, under laws passed by the U.S. Congress.

The rules and regulations of each exchange constitute a code of ethics applicable to practically every aspect of futures trading. The government of the exchanges also provides a means of enforcing these rules and regulations. Enforcement begins with various committees of members who are appointed by the board of directors and charged with investigating charges and/or rumors of rule violations.

The most important committee charged with rule enforcement of futures trading is the business conduct committee, which is charged with the duty of preventing manipulation of prices. This committee also has general supervision and surveillance over all futures trading conducted by members, particularly insofar as such trading affects nonmember customers and the public.

It is in the exchanges' own best interest to have an effective mechanism of self-enforcement of their own rules and regulations. The members themselves are frequently in the best position to detect rule violations that may occur. If the exchanges do not do a good job of self-regulation, the federal government gets involved in prescribing various penalties and courses of action, as authorized by law.

Over the years, federal regulation of futures markets has broadened significantly. In 1922, Congress passed the Grain Futures Act to regulate trading in contracts for future delivery of grains and flaxseed. In 1936, Congress brought futures trading in cotton, rice, mill feeds, butter, eggs, and Irish potatoes under regulation and called the amended law the Commodity Exchange Act. This act was subsequently amended 13 times to bring additional commodities under regulation and to strengthen its provisions. The Commodity Exchange Act was designed to accomplish three principal objectives: (1) to assure that the exchanges make and enforce rules for the maintenance of competitive trading, (2) to prevent manipulation of prices, and (3) to protect the public from fraud resulting from misappropriation of funds. The latter was to be accomplished by the registration of all futures commission merchants and the requirement that all customer margin monies be kept in segregated accounts.

The Commodity Exchange Act was administered by the Commodity Exchange Authority, an agency of the USDA. There was good reason for such administrative organization because the Act regulated futures trading in agricultural commodities only. Futures trading in imported foods (such as coffee, cocoa, and sugar), metals, and several other commodities were not regulated under the Act.

From 1963 to 1973, the futures contracts traded on U.S. futures markets more than doubled from 5.8 to 11.8 million contracts. A substantial share of this increase was attributable to many new futures contracts such as frozen pork bellies, live beef cattle, live hogs, lumber, plywood, silver, and other commodities that were successfully introduced. Many of these did not come under regulation by the Commodity Exchange Authority. Futhermore, in 1972 and 1973, there was substantial increase in the volume of futures trading in the grains. World shortages in these and other commodities caused prices to more than double. Price volatility also increased as markets allocated available tight supplies among many eager buyers. Futures markets again came under public attack for poor performance and facilitating "too much speculation" in commodities. It was argued that the Commodity Exchange Authority has insufficient resources and power to effectively regulate the expanded volume of futures trading.

After holding extensive hearings on various proposals to modify and expand federal regulation of futures trading, Congress passed the Commodity Futures Trading Commission Act in 1974. This Act amended the Commodity Exchange Act of 1936. While the objectives of federal regulation, as contained in the latter, remained intact, the new legislation was designed to strengthen the regulation through three principal means.

First it created a new independent body called the Commodity Futures Trading Commission (CFTC), consisting of five commissioners to be appointed by the president of the United States. The CFTC was to be "independent" in that it was not to be a part of any existing government agency, but was to report directly to the U.S. Congress. This is in contrast to its predecessor the Commodity Exchange Authority, which was an agency of the USDA. The CFTC was also to have a larger budget, which would enable it to have a larger staff to carry out expanded regulation and surveillance of futures trading. The CFTC was designed to have the stature and regulatory power of futures trading that the Securities and Exchange Commission (SEC) has had for many years in regulating financial securities.

Second, the CFTC Act of 1974 brought all futures trading under federal regulation. Third, it broadened the authority of the new CFTC to regulate futures trading and the exchanges or boards of trade on which trading takes place. The CFTC has the authority under the Act of 1974 to go directly to the courts to obtain injunctions. It also has the authority to impose stiffer penalties or fines for violations.

The Commodity Futures Trading Commission is now in the process of implementing other provisions of the CFTC Act of 1974. It will probably take many years before many of the regulatory issues created by the legislation will be resolved.

Summary

Futures markets play an important role in the pricing and marketing of grain. They provide an efficient mechanism for price discovery and a means of shifting price risks to those willing to bear them.

The volume of futures trading in grain, soybeans, and soybean products has expanded substantially since the mid-1960s, caused by the shift to direct income payments to support farm income under government programs, and the rapid increase in U.S. grain exports during the 1970s.

Cash-futures price relationships are useful guides to successful grain marketing. Changes in the basis (the difference between cash and futures prices) are more predictable over time than changes in the level of cash prices alone. Understanding the economics of the basis and carrying charges between future delivery months is crucial to successful hedging.

The risk avoidance motive in hedging has been overemphasized. There are many different types of hedging that are motivated by economic considerations in addition to the need to shift price risks. A common element in all hedging is that futures contracts serve as temporary substitutes for intended later cash transactions. Hedging results in several important economic benefits that contribute to the efficiency of the U.S. grain marketing system. Grain marketing costs would be considerably higher in the absence of hedging on futures markets.

Grain futures markets attract a substantial volume of commercial hedging business. In fact, these markets are highly dependent on the trade of hedgers. However, futures markets that attract a substantial volume of speculative trade are also the best hedging markets, providing greater liquidity, which reduces hedging costs.

Selected References

Henneberry, Patrick and Reynold Dahl, *Cash-Futures Price Relationships, Guides to Grain Marketing*, Agricultural Experiment Station Bulletin No. 517, University of Minnesota, St. Paul, 1977.

Hieronymus, Thomas A., *Economics of Futures Trading*, 2nd ed., Commodity Research Bureau, Inc., New York, February, 1977.

Peck, A. E., ed., *Selected Writings on Futures Markets*, Vol. II, Chicago Board of Trade, Chicago, Ill., 1977.

Peck, A. E., ed., *Views From the Trade, Readings on Futures Markets,* Vol. III,Chicago Board of Trade, Chicago, Ill., 1978.

Selected Writings of Holbrook Working, Chicago Board of Trade, Chicago, Ill., 1977.

MARKET INFORMATION* CHAPTER 8

A Cleveland homemaker studies the grocery advertisement in the morning newspaper. An Illinois farmer briefly stops harvesting to telephone local grain elevators and check their cash bid price for corn. A Nebraska broker scans the video screen for news on Japanese trade negotiations before taking a position in live-cattle futures. A USDA scientist develops a sophisticated computer model to estimate winterkill in wheat in the Volga Valley of Western Russia, using satellite photographs. A radio announcer in Iowa prepares hourly updates on slaughter hog prices from terminal markets and packing houses in the area.

While the degree of sophistication varies, all of these individuals and millions of others like them are involved in the "information" business. The production of information, its dissemination to ultimate consumers, and its final use in making decisions are essential functions of marketing systems in all societies—be they private enterprise or centrally planned, developed, or less developed.

In subsistence sectors of a developing country where producer, processor, and consumer are integrated into one individual, the need for information is similar. Where are the best sources of supply? What quantity will the household need in the future? While the communication of such information may present no problem to such individuals, their very existence depends on the accuracy of the information they gather.

In the same manner, the decision-making bureau of a centrally planned economy needs information on current and anticipated supply and demand factors to devise their optimum national plan. The producer on the collective farm needs timely and accurate information describing that central plan as a guide to production efforts. In a market economy, each operator in the market searches out pertinent information on supply and demand factors, government policy, transportation conditions, current prices, etc., in order to devise a production/marketing strategy.

Buyers and sellers at all stages of the marketing channel need *technical information* on new innovations, storage practices, etc., that may indirectly affect their marketing plans. To an even greater extent, they need *market information*. Buyers need an assessment of the quan-

---

*Dean Linsenmeyer, Associate Professor, Department of Agricultural Economics, University of Nebraska, Lincoln.

tity of a commodity being supplied to the market and the level of storage stocks at the time they plan to place their bids. They also need market intelligence on the expected quantity to be offered on the market in the near future, in order to determine if it is more economical to buy now and hold for future use. In addition to supply information, buyers monitor the demands of other buyers in the market place. Buyers, other than final consumers, need market information on their own anticipated sales situation, as well as that of their competitors. Will the final demand for their product justify current purchases of inputs? Will an aggressive sales policy by a competitor effect a change in their own product design or market share?

In the same fashion, sellers need to be informed of the quantity being demanded, as well as the product specifications desired. Sellers also gather information on the sales activities of other sellers to evaluate their competition. Government policy makers, who work toward a more efficient marketing system while they protect the rights of their producing and consuming citizens, are demanding more market information. They look toward information on carry-over stocks, expected production and consumption, the market share and the returns to individual marketing firms, to guide development of public programs necessary to improve the performance of the market.

AN ESSENTIAL INGREDIENT FOR COMPETITIVE MARKETS

Information on the production and consumption of a product provides the basis for establishing a price. It is the market agent's awareness and understanding of this information that will guide decisions concerning the appropriate type and amount of the product to buy or sell, the best bid to accept as well as the best time and place to enter the market. By being aware of competing bid prices from many independent millers, exporters, feeders, and others, the grain merchandiser can be assured of the true market value of the commodity.

It is the knowledge of alternative resource suppliers, or alternative bidders for a resource, that enable inputs to flow into their most valued use. Similarly, in the product market, it is only when buyers and sellers are equally informed of the market situation that goods and services can be distributed so as to maximize the satisfaction derived by consumers.

When buyers and sellers are not adequately informed of the relative supply and demand conditions between different marketing dates or different market centers, prices may not reflect the real cost of supplying that product. To the extent that price differences are not due to differences in the product (different time, place, or form characteristics), these price differences are an indication of the lack of information or uncertainty on the part of decision makers in the market.

When traders in market X are informed of the prices in market Y, they can determine if the price differential between X and Y is greater than the cost of transferring the good between the two markets. When such is the case, the potential for profits will motivate traders to buy a commodity in one market and transfer it for sale in the other market. This practice is known as *arbitrage*. Many market agents derive successful careers from arbitrage. Transferring between markets may involve transportation (locationally distinct markets), storage (different markets over time), or processing (markets for different products). For example, a soybean trader with knowledge of crushing costs and the estimated oil content of beans will carefully monitor the price spreads between beans, oil, and meal to know when arbitrage between the three markets is profitable.

Arbitrage across markets attempts to correct unjustified price dispersion, thereby improving the market's efficiency. Arbitrage breaks down, however, if the cost of obtaining information on alternative markets is prohibitively high.

The competitiveness of the market is conditional on the many buyers and sellers being aware of the others' market activity. When access to market information becomes the possession of a select few, the potential is there for widespread misuse of the market system. Price relationships easily become distorted from their true measure of either end-use value or relative resource scarcity. Protected information concerning factors that directly affect market prices is a powerful tool for reaping windfall gains from the marketplace. Consequently, the private market agent who possesses particularly valuable information has economic incentives to suppress its release to the general public. Misinformation or unbased rumors can be purposely introduced to mislead or confuse competitors. The cost of verifying such rumors or critically analyzing misleading information, must be considered as part of the total cost of information gathering.

In order for market information to be an effective guide in planning and coordinating the market channel, it must be *accurate, adequate, understandable* for the market user, and *equally available* to all traders.

The accuracy of market information depends on the data base from which the information is derived. Average daily price quotations may be based on a large number of transactions randomly selected from an active day's trading and thus accurately represent the true mean price. However, if the particular central market was relatively inactive or handled an insignificant share of the total commodity traded, its daily price report may provide a distorted picture of actual market activity. As actual cash markets are bypassed, with more grain being shipped directly from producer to terminals, the sample base and accuracy of reports from central cash markets decrease.

A more adequate source of market information may be one that either provides more detail in its information or more timely dissemination of its information. Adequacy is determined in relation to need. Therefore, for many market agents, information on the volume of U.S. #2 HRW wheat transacted and its average sales price for the day may be adequate. However, for other buyers and sellers such as flour millers, this information is inadequate, because they need detailed information on the gluten content, protein level, and baking characteristics, in order to evaluate the price for their purposes. Farmers frequently want more detailed information on quoted prices at local elevators. While the price quoted by two elevators may be identical, the actual transaction price received by the producer may be quite different because of differences in the premium and discount factors applied against the quoted price. This extra detail determines the information's adequacy as a guide in making market choices.

Adequacy is also related to the timeliness of information. Is the information relayed to its potential user while relevant decisions are still open? The awareness of a profitable sales option is of little benefit after the commodity has been sold. Timeliness has two facets: frequency and promptness. Improved timeliness may require that information be disseminated more frequently. It may also require more rapid dissemination so that the information conveyed is a current description of the market, rather than past history. While published mailings of information are still an important source, the telephone, teletype, radio and television have become increasingly important because of their improved speed in disseminating timely information. Over 200 telephone-tape recording outlets provide market agents with instant information 24 hours per day. In addition, some 1500 radio stations and 160 television stations periodically broadcast market information each day.[1]

The third major requirement of market information is that it must be understandable by the market user in order to be effective. It must describe the structure and activity of the market, in a format that the user can quickly comprehend and relate to an immediate situation. The language of the market—its jargon and terms (bullish, bearish, basis, to-arrive, on-track, etc.,)—may render the information useless to people not directly involved in the market place yet dependent on market information to guide their own enterprises. The intelligibility of market information also suffers when too much information, either too detailed or too broad in scope, is considered in a single broadcast or publication. The final information user is not able to assimilate it in a decision framework. For example, on learning that the Soviets have experienced a 10-million metric ton shortfall in coarse grain production, most U.S. farmers are unable to incorporate that information into their optional production or marketing strategy.

[1]W. J. Manley, "Adapting to Change," paper presented to the 1977 National Marketing Service Workshop, Kansas City, Mo., March 1977.

To effectively enhance the competitiveness of the market, information must be equally accessible to all agents for whom it may have value. The more likely a bit of information is to directly impact a particular market trend, the greater the need that all agents have an equal opportunity to benefit by it. From the private trader's point of view, the more relevant the information, the greater is the incentive to tightly control its release. In this way, the individual marketer can capture a greater benefit from that person's elite position. When relevant information is not equally available, it results in commodities being underpriced or overpriced in relation to their true resource value to society. Market agents can each respond in an optimal manner when they all have equal access to the needed information; no one agent can obtain monopoly power by controlling the information flow to other agents.

It can be concluded that while the purely competitive market model assumes "perfect" knowledge by all market agents, market information in reality strives toward "relevant" knowledge equally accessible to all buyers and sellers. In fact, the perfect knowledge assumption could potentially be satisfied only in a single, completely centralized market, with a relatively small number of agents. Here, any one agent potentially could know the prices quoted by all other agents at a particular time. However, for this potential to be realized, one additional assumption must be made. Perfect knowledge implies that additional information would have no economic benefits to the user. In order for it to be economically rational for any one agent to use information when its economic benefits are nil, it must be assumed that the cost of gathering that data is zero. Only if information is a free good, with unlimited supply, will the agent choose to use the maximum amount of this input in a decision.

ECONOMICS OF INFORMATION

Market information is one of many inputs that are combined by the firm in the production process. Therefore, it may be helpful to treat market information as any other physical input in examining its production and use by market agents.

The Information Supply Industry.   As with the production of other physical inputs, scarce resources must be invested in the production of market information. Porta has estimated that the production, processing, and distribution of informational goods and services account for over a quarter of U.S. Gross National Product.[2]

---

[2]D. M. Porta, *The Information Economy,* Institute for Communication Research, Stanford University, Stanford, 1975.

Market research and data collection may take various forms depending on the type of information needed, the size of the firm involved, as well as the diversity and complexity of the commodity in question. The individual buyer or seller may have invested time and resources heavily in past experiences (i.e., trying various products or making valuable contacts with other market agents). Knowledge gained from past actions will be used by each individual, and close associates of that person, to determine which products to buy, the best time to sell, or who will offer the most favorable price.

Market intelligence gained by experience demands a high initial fixed investment in time and resources. Therefore, any one agent may only deal in a local market, where experience can be gained at a lower cost to him or her.

Larger firms commanding a greater share of the market also undertake a high fixed investment in order to produce market information but through different methods. Commodity market research departments, private meterologists, and elaborate computer facilities all are indications of the fixed resource costs incurred by major grain firms in their efforts to obtain up-to-the-minute assessments of market conditions. Not only do the larger firms command sufficient resources to acquire such data-producing technologies, they also handle sufficient volumes to spread these high fixed costs over many units. In this way they can reduce their per bushel cost components of sophisticated and expensive data gathering systems.

Once the initial investment is made, and the data are gathered, the variable costs of disseminating and incorporating this information into production or marketing decisions is relatively minor, compared to the initial investment. The combination of high fixed costs and relatively low variable costs would indicate that the information-producing industry faces economies of scale over a wide range of output. Given such economies of scale, low-volume marketing firms would operate with higher average information costs per unit of output and would be at a competitive disadvantage. With a declining average total cost curve, the information producing industry cannot remain atomistically competitive in the long-run.[3] The alternatives are either a publicly subsidized monopoly responsible for producing market information, which would then be available to all market agents, or a few large marketing firms producing large volumes of market information for their private use.

A second critical characteristic of the information supply industry is that of risk bearing. The production function for most physical inputs can be estimated with relative certainty. The proper combina-

[3]Steven Salop, "Information and Monopolistic Competition," *American Economic Review,* Vol. 66, No. 2, May 1976.

tion of metals, heat, and catalysts will produce the desired alloy. However, the production function for information cannot be predicted accurately. Any investment in market research cannot guarantee a particular outcome, or that the outcome obtained will be useful in the decision process. No insurance policy can be purchased to cover the risk of unproductive research, so private firms investing in information gathering must carry the risk themselves. Larger firms are more capable of absorbing potential losses and, therefore, are more willing to undertake specialized market research.

Another aspect of the risk involved in the production of market information is that information can be a highly perishable product. Grain supply and demand conditions are changing constantly. Consequently, the information gained in the latest monitoring of those conditions may be obsolete, or even counterproductive, before they can be disseminated to decision makers and used.

In summarizing the economics of the information supply industry for grain markets, one could expect extremely high costs per unit of information if the industry consists of small, privately operated firms competing independently for market intelligence. These high costs are frequently hidden in the total transaction cost. The risk inherent in the information production process, as well as the risk of rapid obsolescence, would further contribute to a suboptimal investment by society in market information.

The Economics of Information Use. Since market information is not a free input but is obtained with an expenditure of valuable resources, economic rationality would dictate that there is an optimal amount of information purchased by the market agent for a decision with less than perfect knowledge.

Classical economic theory indicates that the optimal amount of any input is determined where the increased value of the product derived from additional inputs equals the additional costs incurred in acquiring those inputs. Market information is used in the production of better marketing decisions. The market agent must decide between alternative actions in the marketplace—alternatives that are mutually exclusive events. Either one buys or does not buy, sells or does not sell. Before choosing one alternative, the agent attempts to evaluate the probable consequence of each alternative. What is the *expected* payoff if one buys now instead of buying later, or sells at this location rather than another? Because the agent is faced with uncertain events, information is purchased to reduce uncertainty and assist in creating the best marketing strategy. The more uncertain the outcome of a decision, the higher the value that can be attached to more information and, consequently, the higher the demand for information.

In the 1950s and 1960s large grain surpluses and relatively stable administered prices reduced price uncertainty that, therefore, reduced the need for grain market information. In the early 1970s, the demand for more and better market information increased because of increased price variability in most agricultural commodities.[4]

The consequence of one market decision is dependent on the uncertain occurrence of other events. Today's sale of grain may be judged as a "good" or "bad" decision depending on how much the price rises or falls tomorrow. What are the chances that, when one has bought from a given source, a lower offer price could have been found for the same good from a different source? Market information is frequently used to determine the probability of each result for any single market act. The sum of the various results, each weighted by their probability is the expected payoff of that marketing alternative. Therefore, the optimal course of action for the market agent is the one that yields the highest expected value. The marketer is willing to pay the cost of additional information provided it will improve the predictability of market events. Information changes uncertainty to greater certainty and, therefore, assists in more accurately identifying the expected returns from a market action. As more information becomes available, the market agent revises the probabilities attached to the different events affecting that person's decision outcome. For example, a wheat farmer whose anticipated sale price is $3.00 per bushel revises the expected price as that individual begins to collect price quotations from a sample of local elevators. As bids over $3.00 are found, sales price expectations are adjusted upward. The value of additional information equals the expected profits with the increased certainty of events minus the expected profits under the previously more uncertain conditions. If the cost of additional information is greater than the expected increase in profits derived from that information, the market agent should not invest in it.

While economic theory enables one to better understand rational decision making, it does so within a set of simplifying assumptions. Particular characteristics of market information complicate its allocation process. Production functions using fertilizer inputs in corn production can be modeled with relative certainty to determine the marginal value product per unit of fertilizer. In contrast, the marginal value product of additional information increases with uncertainty. The exact value of the information is not definable until after the information has been incorporated into the uncertain setting, and the user has taken a particular course of action in a specific decision.

Information has economic value to individual agents only if misinformation is present in the market. Misinformation may be current information inaccurately determined, and therefore misleading, or ac-

---

[4]C. H. Reimenschneider, "Economic Structure, Price Discovering Mechanisms and the Informational Content and Nature of USDA Prices," Agricultural Economics Staff Paper No. 77-19, Michigan State University, East Lansing, 1977.

curate information that is obsolete and no longer appropriate to the situation. When the information is exposed in the market, and the public can correct their expectations, then the information loses its value to the individual agent. If everyone knows that Soviet production is greater (less) than previously expected, that information loses its market power for the individual trader.

Each market agent acquires better information in anticipation of being able to identify the price dispersion and obtain a higher than average price. However, if all agents possessed the same information, price dispersion in a given market would collapse to a single average market price. Consequently, each agent would receive this average price less the cost of the information, making them in total no better off than before.[5]

. . . it is only because prices do not accurately represent the true worth of the commodity . . . that the informed are able to earn a return to compensate them for the cost associated with the acquisition of the information.[6]

Quality of market information, which distinguishes it from other private goods, is that the supplier of information cannot fully appropriate the returns from all users. Once the information is acted on by one agent in the market, it is revealed for other nonpurchasers to benefit. Consumption by one market agent does not preclude consumption of the same information by other agents. This characteristic encourages individual firms to maintain secrecy of market information, so that they may capitalize on the market advantage that it gives them.

In reviewing both the economic structure of the supply and demand of information, and the importance of open access to information in an efficient, competitive market, several qualities of market information were particularly important.

High fixed costs and economies of scale in information production have indicated that efficiencies could be gained when such market information is produced by a relatively few large-volume firms and/or public agencies. It was noted that investment in information gathering is a high-risk venture, with little certainty of the product gained. This results in a comparative advantage for large firms who can absorb the risk. The comparative advantage in access to information translates directly into a competitive advantage in the market place and greater inequality in market power between small and large firms in the long run.

Because the value of information to the industrial user increases with uncertainty in the market place and cannot be fully recovered by

[5]Robert Wilson, "Informational Economies of Scale," *The Bell Journal of Economics,* Vol. 6, No. 1, Spring 1975.
[6]Stanford Grossman and Joseph Stiglitz, "Information and Competitive Price Systems," *American Economic Review,* Vol. 66, No. 2, May 1976.

the supplier of information,[7] society would benefit by more market information being produced and used than the quantity that private interests would choose to produce. Market information has many characteristics that make it a collective (or public) commodity, with advantages to be gained by publicly supplying this good.

THE COMPONENT PART

Although it is true that no part of the world's economy operates in total isolation from the rest, some parts have a more direct impact on grain markets and therefore merit closer monitoring. Market prices are the common denominator or the grand indicator of all the world forces affecting a particular commodity. By identifying and understanding the impact of those forces on market prices, the market agent can select the components of informational input needed to improve the market decision.

Major Supply Factors. Four categories of forces that market information must address are the availability of supply, demand for the commodity, physical market constraints, and those government programs and regulations that modify the framework within which supply and demand interact. For purposes of clarity, it is convenient to categorize these forces; in reality, they are continuously interrelated and dynamic.

Information on the supply of grain, capable of coming to the market in the current planning period, is extremely important to the market agent. Since grain production in the temperate climates is a very seasonal enterprise, information on the quantity produced is crucial. This information facilitates the market's effective rationing of that supply among users until the next harvest becomes available.

The assessment of grain production begins five to six months before the crop is actually planted. Estimates of producer planting intentions provide an early indication of expected acreages of the particular crop. This allows the competitive forces of buyers and sellers to evaluate more accurately the existing supply in line with longer-term supply projections. Planting intentions are periodically revised until the figures for actual acreages planted become available shortly after planting is completed. Since the length of growing season may become a constraint on the quantity or quality of grain produced, the actual timing of the seeding is also important information. If the planting of regular season varieties is delayed, the probability increases that fall crops will be frosted prematurely. Lighter test weight and lower protein or oil content may result as well from heat damage or drought during the period when new kernels are filling out.

Throughout the season, information on crop-growing conditions

[7]The "free rider" problem associated with other collective goods is also evident in the market information industry.

help buyers and sellers revise their estimates of future supply. Temperature, relative humidity, and wind and precipitation patterns provide early warning signals to the market that particular crops may be under stress and, therefore, raise the possibility of reduced yields. Information on weather conditions is also important in projecting harvests of the current season, as well as in the succeeding season. Subsoil moisture levels are a measure of the water reserve held in the soil that next season's plants may tap. Other adverse growing conditions such as fungi, insects, blights, diseases, or winterkill are directly affected by weather patterns. Wide distribution of such information allows all buyers and sellers to revise their market decision and act accordingly. After the plant is mature, weather has an important impact on the actual bushels harvested. Crop losses increase as wind and precipitation hamper harvesting efforts. It also affects the extent of artificial drying necessary to maintain the crop in condition during storage. Major grain producers and merchandisers need information on weather and other production variables in planning their market strategy.

Available supply is composed of current-season output plus the carry-over stocks of grain in storage from earlier periods. The ability to place grain in storage and remove it in later periods of relative scarcity facilitates more uniform consumption. Accurate data on the level and location of grain stocks inform traders of the size and accessibility of these additional supplies that may be tapped if needed. So long as the anticipated increase in price more than offsets the cost of storage, stocks are withheld from the market place.

Major Demand Factors.   Information concerning the demand for grains must also be analyzed in relation to the total available supply. The demand for grain depends on its value as food for humans, as a livestock feed input, its value in industrial products, and its value productivity as seed. These sources of demand may be domestic or international. In the latter case they would be reflected in our export demand. Information reflecting increases or decreases in swine farrowings, poultry numbers, cattle-on-feed, or breeding stock is important to grain marketers as they represent changes in the intermediate and long-run demand for grain. Crucial to the use of such figures is the marketer's ability to estimate their impact on price changes for grain. Low livestock numbers and subsequent high meat prices relative to the cost of grain inputs are reflected in wider feeding margins. The wider the feeding margin, the greater the economic incentive for feedlots to feed slaughter cattle to heavier weights, thereby increasing the demand for grain. Equally important in the feed demand for grains are changes in consumers' tastes for lower-grade leaner meat cuts. Information on such changes indicates long-term adjustments in the demand of grain-fed meats, which directly affect the demand for grain.

Grains are also used as a raw material in producing a wide array of industrial products so diverse as dynamite, cosmetics, and gasohol. Technical information on new innovations in the manufacturing process carry an economic impact in grain markets. Successful technological changes may increase the marginal value product of grains, resulting in a new optimal level of grains used. Early access to accurate technical information improves the market position of the grain marketer.

Physical Marketing Constraints.   In addition to being knowledgeable of changes in supply and demand conditions, the market agent must keep abreast of physical marketing constraints. When portions of the Illinois, Ohio, or Missouri Rivers freeze over in the fall, grain destined by barge for lower Gulf ports must be sent by a different mode. Such bottlenecks in transportation depress cash bid prices in producing regions, and raises sales prices to the final user or exporter. Other market agents who do not face a particular transportation bottleneck need information in order to locate and benefit from such premium markets.

Quantitites of a particular grain supplied and demanded are seldom equal at a given location, and transportation must, therefore, be arranged to move the commodity. An accurate and adequate information source can assist the market agent in choosing the most economical mode of transportation. Grain merchandisers place a high priority on being informed of the availability and location of hopper cars, the freight structure of alternative modes to alternative destinations, and the limitations on load-carrying capacities over rail branch lines. Since grain movement is absolutely vital to being able to take advantage of any particular supply or demand source, information on the physical transportation constraints is central to any marketing strategy.

The market agent must also accurately assess other physical constraints such as the availability of storage, processing, and handling facilities. New on-farm and commercial elevator storage facilities are being built annually. Such facilities differ in their handling, drying/aeration, and storage costs. Knowing which facilities have uncommitted space and the total costs involved in utilizing each facility provide the basis for wise marketing decisions. Knowing the cash bid prices of a local milling company, soybean crushing plant, or livestock feeder facilitates greater flexibility among potential grain marketing outlets. Because such localized demands may utilize a large share of local grains, basic patterns may change frequently. Remaining aware of changes in local markets distinguishes the aggressive marketer from all others.

Information of the physical constraints at port or terminal elevators may be equally important in impacting local prices and marketing choices. As port elevators become congested, or embargoed, grains must be redirected to other ports, possibly using different modes of transportation. Knowledge of these adjustments and their relative marketing costs will soon be reflected in local cash bid prices to producers.

Government Programs and Regulations. Commodity markets always operate within the political framework of the country in which it is located, as well as being affected by the political/economic situation in other countries. Some public regulations such as antitrust laws affect the structure of the market, while others such as price support legislation affect market prices more directly. Regardless of their direct impact, they ultimately result in an alteration of supply or demand and a new market equilibrium.

As soon as it is reasonably clear that impending legislation will be passed, market agents search out information that will clarify its probable impact on their operations. Wheat and feedgrain producers contact their local ASCS office to better understand and analyze all the provisions of the set-aside or price support program. These programs restructure their marketing alternatives that they must adjust to. Each operator must assess the impact of this new framework, be it a higher import quota for red meats or a three-year grain reserve program, on the supply of and demand for grains. Knowledge of such regulations and the ability to accurately assess their impact translates into profitable market positions for those firms that can respond quickly.

Being informed early of foreign nations' policy changes is difficult for most domestic grain merchandisers. Brazil's policy to subsidize fertilizer and other structural inputs in soybean production translates directly into more market competition for U.S. soybeans. The Soviet decision to expand wheat acreage or livestock numbers has a direct economic impact on total world supply and demand for grains. The agent who gains information on such changes and can interpret their probable impact in the grain market ahead of other merchandisers can reap considerable benefits by reacting early. Such information is extremely valuable and when gathered by private operators is a carefully protected resource.

Public regulations also affect the demand for grains directly. With the passage of the Staggers Act, railroads had new flexibility to change rail rate structures or initiate unit-train rates over new routes. Consequently the purchasing pattern for grains in the affected areas was changed. Some firms benefited by such changes while others were placed at a comparative disadvantage. Being informed of current and potential changes is important in making better investments in marketing facilities.

Changes in the demand for U.S. grains and consequently price adjustments are directly affected by the presence of import restrictions into foreign countries. All major firms dealing with the export of U.S.

grains closely monitor changes in the grain import levies imposed by the EC. They must evaluate the changes and respond quickly in order to maintain their market position. Early information on the composition of bilateral grain agreements, or on exchange rate adjustments in the currency markets, can be the deciding factor in the success or failure of many grain companies. Because such information is so crucial to the life of the firm, vast amounts of private funds are expended annually to obtain accurate details before it is generally available. The more such information is readily accessible to all agents, the quicker agents can respond accordingly in their buying and selling practices, thus improving the physical and pricing efficiency of the entire system.

Sources of Market Information

The market agent seldom relies on any one source for market information. As the agent's needs vary in terms of subject matter, depth, and timing, those sources of information are selected that are most suited to that person's needs. Part of the information will come in published form such as newspapers, government circulars, radio or TV broadcasts, or commodity newsletters. Information derived from published sources will usually cover topics that are either quite general, appealing to a large audience, or topics that may be in detail but that do not become outdated quickly. These sources are useful to the agent who may not be operating daily in the market but who still needs to keep abreast of underlying market trends.

Other information will be obtained from direct-contact sources. These may be face-to-face discussions, or telephone interviews with other market agents. Direct-contact sources have an important role in disseminating information that is quite detailed or that becomes obsolete very rapidly. One grain producer may visit directly with other producers or with several grain merchandisers, in order to gain specific market information for a particular location. Here, an up-to-the minute picture of a specific market can be received. Brokers, exporters, or other large volume grain merchants who operate daily in the market place rely heavily on telephone contacts to anticipate market changes before they occur.

The direct communication lines for just one international grain trading firm are illustrated in Figure 8-1. Direct-contact monitoring of conditions in production centers, political capitals, and transportation centers allows them to keep abreast of changes in the main factors influencing their worldwide operations. For example, the trading company in this figure has direct telex channels to Halifax, Nova Scotia. While Halifax is relatively small and distant from major grain producing regions in Canada, it is one of Canada's major winter ports handling their international grain exports.

Throughout any given day a grain merchandiser may call several producers in different major producing regions for a snapshot of field

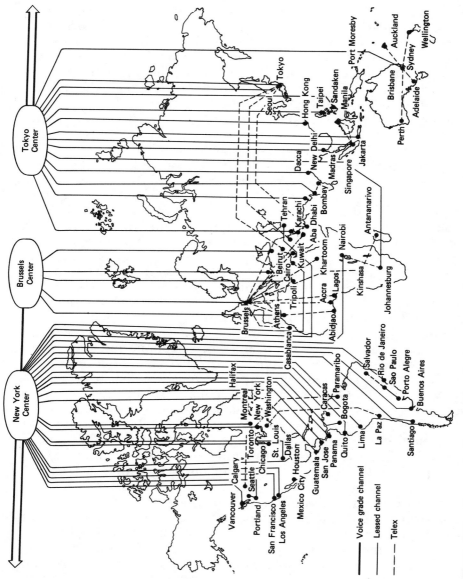

Figure 8-1. Communications system of a Japanese trading firm. (*Source: Feedstuffs*, March 13, 1978.)

228

conditions; several elevator managers to monitor prices, storage conditions, and transportation constraints; several brokers to evaluate the rumors and activity of the central markets; several major processors to analyze the strength of the demand for their products. Representatives at the port or on the trading floor will also be contacted for in-house information. Within a matter of minutes, the major factors affecting the market at that time can be pulled together from this network. The agent then proceeds with market operations and rechecks several of the more volatile factors throughout the day's trading. The accuracy of this information may be questionable at times, but the important issue is *regardless of whether it is fact or fiction, it has an immediate and direct impact on the market.* The challenge of obtaining timely information is to anticipate early what the market will do with that information when it becomes generally known.

The marketing agent must evaluate the reliability of information sources. Does the agent perceive the information as fact or fiction? Equally important is the question, "Will the market in total accept the information as fact or fiction?" The individual buyer or seller may judge the information to be a false rumor and, believing that the rest of the market will accept it as false, choose not to make a position adjustment in the market place. However, if the individual market agent perceives the information as false, but the rest of the market sees it as true, this individual may choose to enter the market place to take advantage of the market's inaccurate perception. The actual accuracy of the information may be immaterial, so long as it is perceived in the market as being accurate and reliable.

In actuality, grain market agents use both direct-contact sources to fine tune each day's strategy, and published sources, to cross check and revise their close-up estimates in light of underlying aggregate changes. Either direct-contact or published sources may be publicly or privately funded.

Public Sources. Sources supported by public funds have frequently been looked to as a means of equalizing access to accurate unbiased information for all interested market agents. This is an important role in equalizing market power among agents regardless of size and, in the process, improve the market's efficiency.

The Department of Labor releases statistics on employment and wage levels by sector. This provides some indication of changes in purchasing power. They also compute and publish the Consumers' Price Index, which measures the changes in price levels for major consumer goods, such as food. Other indexes of sales and industrial production are released by the Department of Commerce. Every five years they also undertake a "Census of Agriculture." Such publications provide an evaluation of general demand levels in the economy.

Some of the agencies of the USDA that publish information more specific to grain marketing are the Agricultural Marketing Service, the Agricultural Stabilization and Conservation Service, the Economic Research Service, Statistical Reporting Service, the World Food and Agricultural Outlook and Situation Board, and the Foreign Agricultural Service.[8] Table 8-1 illustrates some of the publications available to the public throughout the year by the Economic Research Service. The date and hour for release of figures by the Crop Reporting Board of the USDA is published ahead of time, as shown in Table 8-2. Therefore, all market agents can obtain equal access to that knowledge at exactly the same time.

Private Sources.   Private agencies also provide market information. In many respects their operations lie between the extremes of direct contact and governmental publications. For an annual or monthly subscription fee, an individual may receive a variety of informational aids. Wire services are one of the more expensive devises but provide the user with instantaneous teletype reports of news and market information from most of the major grain and livestock markets. In addition, information is transmitted on weather conditions, government programs, and other national and international forces which will affect the cash and futures markets.[9] A major advantage of instantaneous electronic news services is the speed with which market information is collected and transmitted to the potential user. Speed in delivery is extremely important because market news is a perishable, quickly obsolete product. Commodity News Service, Grain Instant News, Reuters' Economic Service, and the Associated Press are just a few of the private firms that provide wire services.

Subscribers to daily or weekly technical market reports receive an analysis of forces that determined the major trading patterns for that day, week, or month. While such reports are not as frequent, they have the advantage in that they not only provide the user with factual market happenings; they also explain and assist in analyzing the impact of various market factors. Examples of this type of private information service are the Mid-West Market Information Service, and Leslie's Market Report.

Another private source of market information is provided by brokerage and investment firms. They primarily issue market information on the futures prices of select commodities. Usually these reports will provide a summary of major market trends and a brief analysis of factors likely to affect the market in the near future. Technical Market Perspective and Commodity Weekly News Highlights by E. F. Hutton

[8]Walter G. Heid, Jr., F. Niernberger, and L. D. Schnake, *An Overview of the U.S. Wheat Industry with Emphasis on Decision Making and Information Sources,* Commodity Economics Division, Economic Research Service, USDA, Washington, D.C., May 1977.
[9]Ian M. T. Steward, *Information in the Cereals Market,* Hutchinson and Co., Ltd., London, 1970.

Table 8-1 Release Schedules for Situation Reports and Supply-Demand Estimate Reports

Report	Jan	Feb	Mar	Apr	May	June	July	Aug	Sept	Oct	Nov	Dec
Agricultural outlook	X	X	X	X		X	X	X	X	X		X
Agricultural supply and demand		X	X	X		X	X	X	X	X	X	X
Cotton and wool		X	X		X			X	X		X	
Dairy			X			X			X			X
Fats and oils		X		X			X			X		
Feed		X						X		X		
Fertilizer												X
Fruit			X				X		X		X	
Livestock and meat		X			X		X	X				
Poultry and egg		X			X		X	X				
Rice			X									
Sugar and sweetener		X			X				X			
Vegetable	X			X			X			X		
Wheat		X			X		X		X		X	
World agriculture									X			
Agricultural finance outlook								X				
Outlook for U.S. exports					X				X		X	X
Farm real estate market developments					X							X

Source: Economics, Statistics, and Cooperatives Service, *Periodicals: 1978*, USDA, Washington, D.C., January, 1978.

Table 8-2 1982 Crop Reporting Board Releases for Selected Commodities

Released at 3:00 P.M. ET Unless Noted	Jan	Feb	Mar	Apr	May	June	July	Aug	Sept	Oct	Nov	Dec
Crop production	11	10	10	12	10	10	12	11	10	12	10	10
Annual summary	14											
Field crops												
Acreage						29						
Crop values	21											
Grain stocks	25		22			22				21		
Popcorn	14											
Potatoes and sweet potatoes									28			
Potato stocks	14	12	15	15	13							15
Prospective plantings		18										
Rice stocks	25			22				19		21		
Soybean stocks									22			
Vegetables												
Celery[a]	5	4	4	6	5	4	7	3	3	5	4	3
Onion stocks	12											
Tomatoes			(Released each Tuesday during growing season from Orlando, Fla., ESCS office)									
Vegetables				9	6	7	15	5	9	8		
Annual summary	7											
Vegetable—preliminary						4						29
Livestock and products												
Cattle	29		4,22									
Cattle on feed	18	12	15	19	15	26	19	13	14	19	16	14
Hogs and pigs			19			22			22			22

Report	Jan	Feb	Mar	Apr	May	Jun	Jul	Aug	Sep	Oct	Nov	Dec
Livestock slaughter	22	19	19	23				22		22		
Annual summary		15										
Meat animals—production, disposition, and income				2								
Sheep and goats	26											
Sheep and lambs on feed	19	17										
Wool and mohair			26									
Poultry and eggs												
Broiler and hatchery report			8									
Poultry—production, disposition and income												
Egg production	5	24	25	23	21	17	15	12	9	7	4	2,29
Eggs, chickens and turkeys	28	23	23	21	21	23	23	23	23	20	23	21
Hatchery production—annual		12										1
Poultry slaughter	5	1	2	1	4	1	1	3	1	1	2	1
Turkeys	8											
Turkey hatchery report		2										
Milk and dairy products												
Dairy products		1	1			1		2			1	
Annual summary												
Milk production	15	12	11	13		16				13		
Milk production, disposition, and income			24									
Dairy reports												
Butter and American cheese production[b]												
Prices received by farmers for mfg. grade milk in Minn. and Wisc.[b]		2										
Agricultural prices												
Agricultural prices	29	26	31	30	28	30	30	31	30	29	30	30
Annual summary						30						

(Broiler and hatchery report: Released each Wednesday from 21 state ESCS offices)

(Turkey hatchery report: Released each Thursday from 9 state ESCS offices)

(Butter and American cheese production[b]: Released from Madison, Wisc., ESCS office)

(Prices received by farmers: Released each Tuesday)

[a] Celery released at 1:00 P.M. ET.

[b] Butter and American cheese released at 3:00 P.M. CT.

Source: Economic Research Service, *1982 Crop Reporting Board Calendar*, USDA, Washington, D.C., January 1982.

are examples of such information market reports issued by brokerage firms.

The Kansas City Grain Market Review is a daily publication of market information provided by grain exchanges; in this case by the Kansas City Board of Trade. The Minneapolis Grain Prices and Receipts and the Weekly Commodity Review are similar publications made available by the Minneapolis Grain Exchange and the Chicago Board of Trade respectively. Such information sources frequently cover cash or futures trading prices at the close of the market, a statement of the volumes transacted, and a record of the receipts, shipments, and stocks at other primary markets.

One additional source of market information is the commercial market advisory service. This provides the user with more specialized and detailed assistance in analyzing market forces than other private sources. In addition to a technical interpretation of daily price charts for commodities at central markets, the subscriber to this service may receive specific charting services and daily access to a toll-free telephone giving instant market reports for grains. Top Farmer Market Insight and Doane Market Watch are just two examples of a commercial advisory service.

Summary

One of the keys to the control and allocation of physical resources and the reaping of pure economic profit is the control of information. Patent laws protect the rights to *technical information* for a limited period so that the inventor may receive a return on the initial investment. However, the rights of the investor in *market information* are unprotected. The investor must limit dissemination of the product in order to obtain a return on a relatively high fixed investment.

In many respects market information possesses qualities similar to other public or collective goods. As with most collective goods, the individual optimizer cannot take into account many of the positive externalities gained from market information. Consequently, the competitive market system will not allocate adequate resources to the production of information as the broader collective interests of society would prefer. For this reason, publicly supported information-generating agencies are engaged in the producing and disseminating information at subsidized costs to buyer and seller alike.

Public agencies provide market information that is released to all interested market agents at the same time. This has the effect of helping to equalize the access to some market information and, therefore, to equalize market power.

As grain markets have become more widespread and specialized for particular grading characteristics the need for more timely and detailed information has grown. Traditional cash market reports have become more obsolete as an ever-larger share of the transactions are made through direct sales arrangements or forward contracts. Such transactions are more widely dispersed and more individually negotiated. Therefore, the burden to provide adequate, accurate, and timely market information to a broad spectrum of market agents has become more difficult.

Selected References

Alchian, Armen A., "Information Costs, Pricing and Resource Employment," *Western Economic Journal,* Vol. 7, No. 2, June 1969.

Grossman, Sanford and Joseph Stiglitz, "Information and Competitive Price Systems," *American Economic Review,* Vol. 66, No. 2, May 1976.

Hayame, Yujwo and Willis Peterson, "Social Returns to Public Information Services: Statistical Reporting of U.S. Farm Commodities," *American Economic Review,* Vol. 61, No. 1, March 1972.

Heid, W. Jr., F. Niernberger, and L. D. Schnake, *An Overview of the U.S. Wheat Industry with Emphasis on Decision Making and Information Sources,* Commodity Economics Division, Economic Research Service, USDA, Washington, D.C., May 1977.

Manley, W. J., "Adapting to Change," paper presented to the 1977 National Marketing Service Workshop, Kansas City, Mo., March 1977.

Porta, D. M., *The Information Economy,* Institute for Communication Research, Stanford University, Stanford, Cal., 1975.

Reimenschneider, C. H., "Economic Structure, Pricing Discovering Mechanisms and the Informational Content and Nature of USDA Prices," Agricultural Economics Staff Paper No. 77-19, Michigan State University, East Lansing, 1977.

Rothschild, Michael, "Models of Market Organization with Imperfect Information: A Survey," *Journal of Political Economy,* Vol. 81, No. 6, December 1973.

Salop, Steven, "Information and Monopolistic Competition," *American Economic Review,* Vol. 66, No. 2, May 1976.

Steward, Ian M. T., *Information in the Cereals Market,* Hutchinson and Co. Ltd., London, 1970.

Theil, Henri, *Economics and Information Theory,* North Holland Publishing Company, Amsterdam, 1967.

Wilson, Robert, "Informational Economies of Scale," *The Bell Journal of Economics,* Vol. 6, No. 1, Spring 1975.

WORLD GRAIN TRADE

WORLD GRAIN TRADE*   **CHAPTER 9**

International trade is vital to American agriculture. Currently, the United States exports the production from one out of every three acres of cropland. These exports generate about 30 percent of U.S. farm income. The U.S. proportion of world agricultural exports has increased from 12 percent in the early 1950s to 17 percent in the early 1980s. Much of this increase in the U.S. share of the world market has occurred in grains. U.S. exports of all agricultural products increased from $7 billion in 1970 to $44 billion in 1981.

Grains, feeds, oilseeds, and oilseed products account for nearly 68 percent of the value of U.S. agricultural exports (Table 9-1). Exports of grain and feeds increased considerably during the world food crises from 1972 to 1975, and 1979–80.

Some U.S. agricultural industries depend more heavily on the export market than do others. In 1980, the United States exported 53 percent of domestic soybean production, 68 percent of the rice crop, 65 percent of the wheat, 40 percent of the grain sorghum and 30 percent of the corn produced. From these figures, one can see how important the international market is to the grain and oilseed producers in the United States.

THE BENEFITS FROM TRADE

Basically, nations trade for the same reason that individuals trade—because of the benefits that can be obtained from so doing. Gains to nations are due to the fact that a larger total output of goods and services is possible from specialization and division of labor, which increases total national productivity. A larger output, however, is beneficial only if some of this increased output can be traded for other producers' goods and services that are more highly valued than the additional goods produced domestically. Through the process of mutual and voluntary trade, individuals and nations increase their level of living. Voluntary trade will occur only if one or more parties to the trade are made better off without making another party worse off. In general, trade allows an individual to obtain more goods and services for a given money income than could be obtained without trade.

The direct benefits from international trade are evident when analyzing the actions of importers and exporters. Importers, in order

*Gail L. Cramer, Professor, Department of Agricultural Economics, Montana State University, Bozeman.

Table 9-1   Value of U.S. Agricultural Exports, by Principal
Commodity Groups[a] (million dollars)

Commodity Group	1970	1975	1976	1980	1981[b]
Grains and feeds	2,531	11,561	11,920	17,168	20,310
Oilseeds and products	1,885	4,753	4,692	9,811	9,305
Livestock and products	829	1,666	2,207	3,771	4,115
Cotton (including linters)	328	1,055	919	3,016	2,230
Fruits, nuts, and vegetables	632	1,373	1,532	3,464	4,445
Tobacco (unmanufactured)	537	897	929	1,349	1,339
Other	215	549	560	1,902	2,044
Total exports	6,957	21,854	22,759	40,481	43,788

[a]Years beginning October 1.
[b]Preliminary.

Source: U.S. Department of Agriculture, *Agricultural Statistics,* 1982.

to maximize their profits, purchase goods from other countries if they
can be obtained at a lower price than comparable domestically produced goods. Exporters, on the other hand, sell goods to other countries if they can obtain a higher price than they could get in the domestic market. Therefore, it is *relative* prices of goods among countries that
determine what goods are imported and exported.

In order to more clearly demonstrate the benefits of trade, let's
use a simple example. Assume two countries, the United States and
Russia, each with a set of resources capable of producing two commodities—wheat and crude oil—in a competitive environment. While
this illustration involves only two nations and two commodities, the
results of our analysis readily extend to all countries and all commodities.

The amount of wheat and oil that each country can produce is
shown by its "production possibilities" (or product transformation)
curve, Figure 9-1. The production possibilities curve for the United
States (labeled *AB*) shows that, given all the resources available in the
United States and its current technology, it can either produce *OA*
bushels of wheat and no oil, *OB* barrels of oil and no wheat, or any
combination of wheat or oil on or within the boundary of the production possibilities curve, such as point *C* in the diagram. The United
States would not willingly produce at some point inside its production
possibilities curve, such as at point *E,* since that represents a production combination with unemployed resources; nor can they produce at
a point *D,* since that combination of products lies outside of the capabilities of their resources. Russia faces similar resource and technological limits to its wheat and oil production choices.

Notice that the production possibilities curve is not a straight line
but a curve that is concave to the origin. A concave production pos-

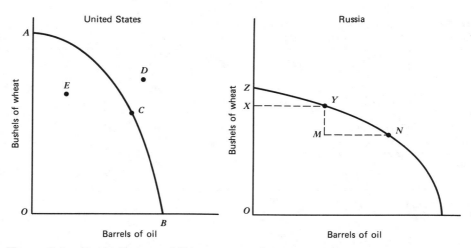

Figure 9-1. Production possibilities curves cf the United
States and Russia.

sibilities curve illustrates diminishing marginal resource productivity
(i.e., increasing opportunity costs). Resources cannot be shifted from
wheat production to oil at a constant rate, only at increasing costs. The
cost of an additional barrel of oil, in terms of wheat sacrificed, increases as additional oil is produced; more and more wheat has to be
given up to get additional barrels of oil. Some resources are better
suited to producing wheat than oil, and vice versa. As more and more
resources are shifted from wheat to oil production (or from oil to
wheat production) their productivity declines, thus the increasing cost
shape of the production possibilities curve.

The diagram for Russia, in Figure 9-1, shows that they must sacrifice ZX bushels of wheat for XY barrels of oil, if they have been producing OZ of wheat and no oil and wish to increase oil output by XY.
Further, if they are now producing OX wheat and XY oil (at point Y),
an addition to their oil output of MN will require a sacrifice of YM
wheat. The shift from point Y on their production possibilities curve to
point N requires a much greater sacrifice of wheat than would the shift
from point Z to point Y (given that $MN = XY$). The slope of the
production possibilities curve demonstrates the *marginal rate of transformation* ($MRT = \Delta W/\Delta O$). It shows how much the output of wheat must
be decreased in order to increase oil output by one barrel.

Equilibrium Before Trade. A competitive economy that is not engaged
in international trade will be in equilibrium when it produces a combination of products such that the marginal rate of transformation
($\Delta W/\Delta O$) equals the domestic price ratio for oil and wheat (P_O/P_w),
shown by the line BT at point A in Figure 9-2. At point A, this country
is producing the equilibrium quantities OW bushels of wheat and OC

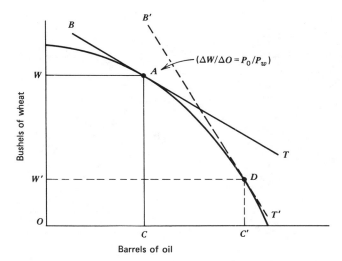

Figure 9-2. Equilibrium in a closed economy.

barrels of oil, because the cost of producing another unit of each good is just equal to the values of those goods to the consumers. If the market price of crude oil increases relative to the price of wheat, as shown by the line $B'T'$, the optimal output of oil would increase to OC' and the optimal production of wheat would fall to OW'.

Before trade opens between the United States and Russia, the United States is in equilibrium at point A, and the Soviet Union is in equilibrium at point A' (Figure 9-3). The domestic exchange ratio in the United States is two bushels of wheat for one barrel of oil, whereas the domestic exchange rate in Russia is one bushel of wheat to two barrels of oil. In the United States, the opportunity cost of one bushel of wheat is ½ barrel of oil, and in Russia, wheat and oil exchange at a 1:2 ratio. Thus, the real cost of wheat is lower in the United States than in the Soviet Union, because the amount of oil sacrificed for a bushel of wheat is less in the United States than it is in Russia. Hence, the United States has a "comparative advantage" (its greatest relative advantage) in wheat production. On the other hand, Russia has a lower opportunity cost in oil. Their opportunity cost of one barrel of oil is only ½ bushel of wheat, as compared with two bushels of wheat in the United States; thus, Russia has a comparative advantage in the production of oil. The benefits of these advantages cannot be realized, however, until trade is permitted between these two nations.

Equilibrium with Trade.   It is the price (or exchange) ratio that determines the comparative advantage for nations, and the goods that countries will produce and trade. Given free trade, the United States will emphasize the production and export of wheat to Russia; Russia will

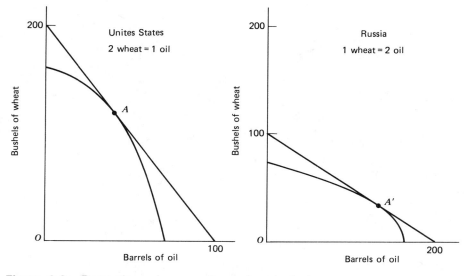

Figure 9-3.   Domestic exchange ratios before trade between nations.

produce and export its oil to the United States. Thus, it is *comparative* advantage, not *absolute* advantage, that determines what products enter international trade.

From their no trade equilibrium positions, at points A and A', respectively, assume now that the United States and Russia permit trade of wheat and oil between these two nations, at market determined prices and quantities. When these countries open trade they each will specialize at the newly determined price ratio for wheat and oil, which is the same in both countries (the slopes of AT and AT' are the same, see Figure 9-4). The new equilibrium output in the United States will be at point B, producing more wheat and less oil than would be the case without trade. Russia's new equilibrium will be at point B', with a greater oil output and a reduced level of wheat production.

Note that after trade opens, a country can consume anywhere along its price ratio line. The equilibrium point of consuming the two commodities depends on each country's intensity of demand, and its ability to exchange specific quantities of the commodities at the AT ($= AT'$) ratio of prices. Equilibrium points of consumption, with trade, are D and D'; the United States produces combination B and now is able to consume combination D, while Russia will produce at combination B' and consume at D'. The United States reaches a higher level of satisfaction (indifference curve I_2) through trade by exporting BE bushels of wheat to Russia, and importing ED barrels of oil from them. Russia also reaches a higher indifference curve (I_2') by importing $E'D'$ ($= BE$) bushels of wheat from the United States, and exporting $B'E'$ ($= ED$)

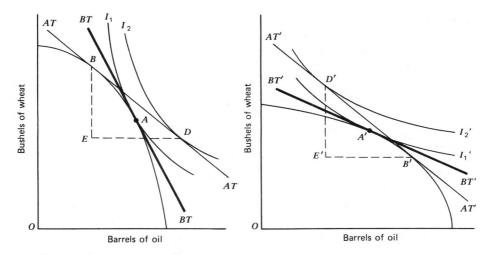

Figure 9-4. Two-nation equilibrium with trade.

barrels of oil to the United States. Consumers in both nations are better off with trade because they are able to consume wheat and oil in quantities that are beyond their individual resource base capabilities on a higher indifference curve than is possible without specialization and trade.

One can observe many examples of comparative advantage. For instance, a medical doctor may be able to type much more rapidly and accurately than the receptionist. The doctor's opportunity cost of typing is high, however, because of the greater medical practice earnings that would be sacrificed while typing. In spite of the fact that the doctor has an absolute advantage both in practicing medicine and typing, he or she has a comparative advantage only in practicing medicine; the doctor is unable to compete with the receptionist's comparative (or relative) advantage in typing.

When countries promote and engage in free trade, and each country also specializes in producing those goods and services in which it has a comparative advantage, the world's resources are used more efficiently and the world's consumers are able to share in a larger total world output, increasing their well-being. Any restraint on the volume of international trade will reduce the world's output of goods and services and cause an inefficient use of resources.

Trade Barriers

Many countries establish barriers to trade in the form of tariffs, quotas or nontariff barriers. *Tariffs* are taxes levied on a commodity when it crosses a nation's boundary. *Quotas* restrict the absolute quantity of a good that may be imported. *Nontariff barriers* are government regulations that reduce the free flow of goods in international trade. The economic effect of all such actions is to reduce the volume of trade and to increase the price of the product to domestic consumers.

As an example, suppose a small country is importing American corn, a situation depicted in Figure 9-5. That nation, with domestic demand and supply curves labeled D_d and S_d, is in equilibrium when it produces and consumes quantity q_0 at market price P_0. With trade, this country is able to purchase all the corn it wants at the international price of P_1. At price P_1, domestic corn producers will provide Oq_2 bushels of corn, and q_1q_2 corn will be imported from the United States. Total corn consumption in that country is Oq_1.

Now suppose that a tariff of x dollars per bushel of corn is imposed by that nation. The domestic price of corn will rise to $P_1 + x$. Domestic production increases from q_2 to q_4, but domestic consumption decreases from q_1 to q_3. Imports of U.S. corn drops from (q_1 to q_2) to (q_3 to q_4). With tariffs, consumers pay higher prices for their goods and services and consume less of those goods than if free trade is permitted.

As shown in the diagram, domestic producers gain from a tariff because, with a tariff, they are able to produce more at a higher market price than they could without the tariff. It is producer groups that pressure for tariffs because of the benefits they see for themselves, but it is the consumers who lose when tariffs are applied. Other methods, such as direct payments are more efficient in supporting farm incomes, if that is their goal.

Most countries have trade barriers intended to protect the incomes of their producers, but their use reduces worldwide production efficiency. Export policies, such as the variable levy system in the EC,

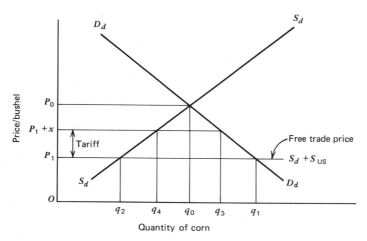

Figure 9-5. Domestic impact of an import tariff.

and the quotas and tariffs of Japan, reduce U.S. exports of agricultural commodities and depress their prices in the United States.

POLICY ISSUES

Balance of Payments.   The U.S. balance of payments is a statement that shows all international transactions between residents of the United States and all other nations. This record includes the transactions of both private and government units for a given period of time, usually one year. It is an accounting record that is useful in determining changes over time in the economic strength of the United States compared to other countries, and often is used in determining specific trade policies.

Any international trade transaction can be divided into either a *plus item* (credit) or a *negative item* (debit). Those transactions where Americans receive foreign currency (dollar inpayments) are *credit* items, whereas those transactions where foreigners receive U.S. dollars (dollar outpayments) are *debit* items. The United States has a deficit in its balance of payments when debits are greater than credits; a surplus exists when credits are greater than debits.

Under freely fluctuating exchange rates the balance of payments should come close to balancing. If the United States runs a deficit in its balance of payments its currency should depreciate, which makes U.S. goods cheaper to foreigners and foreign goods more expensive to Americans. Therefore, U.S. exports should increase and U.S. imports should decrease, with a resulting improvement in the U.S. balance of payments. The reverse would occur for a country that is running a surplus in its balance of payments.

Agricultural exports since 1971 have helped strengthen the dollar, even with large expenditures for OPEC oil. In 1981, agricultural exports exceeded imports of agricultural products by $26.6 billion. This large surplus helped offset a $56.6 billion nonagricultural deficit. Even so, the United States continues to run large balance of payments deficits, which have continued to put downward pressure on the dollar relative to other currencies. Therefore, it is important for those involved in public policy to be aware of the effects of restricting agricultural trade among nations. In fact, much more effort is needed to encourage freer international movement of grains.

Bilateral Agreements.   For many years, the USDA has used a variety of domestic agricultural policies in attempting to stabilize the production and prices of grains. With unstable foreign demand causing domestic and world prices to fluctuate, especially since 1972, the United States and importing countries have intensified their efforts to moderate the effects of variations in world production and demand.

The United States has signed long-term, bilateral agreements with several countries, including the Soviet Union, the People's Republic of China, Poland, and Mexico. By virtue of their minimum sales guarantees, such agreements temper somewhat the effects of variations in foreign demand, and aid the USDA in achieving domestic policy objectives. Importers are also assured of a more stable source of supply to meet their grain needs. At present, these bilateral agreements account for only a small proportion of total production in grain exporting countries. In normal circumstances, bilateral agreements have a relatively small impact on U.S. producers. Some economists are concerned, however, about their effects when U.S. supplies are tight or free reserves are low. During such periods, prices could be quite unstable, causing even more price variability than without those agreements.

The United States signed its first long-term grain supply agreement with the Soviet Union in October 1975. The reason for the agreement was to stabilize the price effects of their unexpectedly large purchases of U.S. grain and to encourage them to hold larger grain reserves. The first agreement was for a five-year period, and required the Soviet Union to import 6 million metric tons of wheat and corn per year. Up to 8 million tons of grain could be purchased under that agreement, but quantities greater than 8 million tons were dependent upon American grain supplies and required prior consultation with the U.S. government as well.

Despite the perceived advantages of long-term agreements, the contract with Russia has been caught up in broader U.S. foreign policy changes. Upon expiration of the original agreement, renewals have been limited to one-year extensions only, with the most recent extension being made in August 1982.

Cartels. Wheat producers in Canada and the United States have suggested the formation of a wheat cartel composed of the United States, Canada, Australia, and Argentina. Each country in the cartel would remain as separate business organizations, but these countries would jointly make decisions regarding marketings and prices of their grains.

Since the cartel would be composed of independent nations, each would have its own policies and goals, and internal conflicts between cartel members could be expected. Presently, the marketing strategies of these countries differ widely. Private grain traders in the United States adopt policies to maximize their profits. The Canadian and Australian Wheat Boards, as government and producer marketing boards, respectively, seek to maximize producer and consumer gains. Australia, however, follows a strategy of selling most of its grain crop each year because of their limited storage capacity. Argentina's objectives are to maximize their foreign exchange earnings.[1]

---

[1]Alex McCalla and Andrew Schmitz, "The World Market for Wheat," in *How Prices Are Determined for Montana Wheat*, KEEP Public Affairs Forum at Great Falls, Montana, September 1977, Montana State University, Bozeman, 1977.

Besides using different marketing approaches, each country has a different marginal cost of producing and marketing wheat. Consequently, at some point, one or more of the cartel members may find it advantageous to market individually, rather than staying with the cartel. In addition, if the cartel succeeds in increasing the world price of wheat, it must control supply within each member country in order to maintain that price. At the new, higher price, domestic and international consumption would fall, countries not in the cartel would increase their production of wheat, and other countries would intensify their efforts to develop substitute products. All such actions and efforts would weaken the cartel and threaten its effectiveness.

Embargoes.   Most nations, at one time or another, and for a variety of reasons, have embargoed the movement of goods and services to or from another country. On numerous past occasions, the United States has also utilized the embargo to achieve a specific foreign policy objective.

As a result of the massive grain and oilseed sales in 1972, the need for a better monitoring and export reporting system was recognized in order that domestic supplies of these commodities might be better maintained. On June 27, 1973, an embargo was placed on new sales of soybeans, soybean meal, and cottonseed, and previously committed sales of these commodities were reduced on a pro rata basis. On October 4, 1974, the administration temporarily suspended the sale of 3.4 million tons of grain to the Soviet Union.

Another grain embargo was placed on the Soviet Union on January 4, 1980, on all sales in excess of 8 million metric tons. This embargo was in response to the Russian invasion of Afghanistan. This suspension was a part of broader U.S. foreign policy, rather than from inadequate supplies at home. The embargo lasted 18 months, but its impact on the U.S.S.R. was small; it forced Russia to reduce its grain purchases only slightly. Russia paid somewhat higher prices for their grain, and reduced domestic meat supplies a bit, but they also developed new grain trading partners for their import supplies as a result of America's actions. The effect of the embargo within the United States was reduced corn prices through the following winter, and that impact was partially offset by CCC grain purchases and changes in the farmer-held grain reserve program.

Export reporting system.   Exporters are required to file declarations on exports with U.S. Customs at the time of shipment. Export reporting, as of October 21, 1974, is a voluntary system, asking exporters to report sales and destination options. Exporters report export sales exceeding 100,000 tons in any one day to any single country, or cumulative sales to a single foreign destination during any one week to exceed 200,000 tons, or changes in known or unknown destinations previously reported to exceed 100,000 tons in any one day, or 200,000 tons in any one week. Weekly reporting, and the export declaration, are required.

Buffer Stocks.   Buffer stocks of grain have been proposed to reduce the large fluctuations in grain prices and to provide emergency food aid. On an international basis, there is little agreement on which countries should contribute to the stocks and hold reserves. Under present conditions of plentiful supplies, importers do not want to pay the added cost of storage. Although some of the food-deficit countries have increased their stocks of food grain, producers are not advocating worldwide buffer stocks because producer prices would most likely be depressed by the existence of such reserves. The U.S. grain reserve program will act as a buffer stock, increase price stability, and provide emergency food aid.

TRADE IN FOOD GRAINS AND FEED GRAINS

Grains may be used for either food or feed. Food grains normally are considered to be wheat and rice. Feed grains (or coarse grains) include corn, barley, sorghum, oats, and rye. In the developed countries, feed grains are used primarily for livestock feeds, with lesser quantities utilized directly for human consumption, or indirectly in brewery or starch products. In many developing countries, however, coarse grains are used as a food grain, with only small amounts used in livestock feeds or for industrial purposes.

The amount of grain exported from a nation is dependent on many factors other than price. Some of the major factors are national agricultural and food policies and red meat production. Countries will export only that output in excess of domestic requirements plus carry-over. Exports are used to reduce domestic supplies in order to maintain prices and incomes for domestic producers.

Agricultural policies are particularly important in world trade, since almost all countries protect their domestic agriculture from open market forces. In fact, many countries explicitly plan the amounts of grains to be produced and to enter world trade.

Supply management is a major policy goal of many grain producing countries. Supply management is used to expand domestic production in order to achieve self-sufficiency or to reduce reliance on foreign sources of supply. It may also be used to control domestic production so that supply is balanced with demand at prices that provide adequate incomes to producers.

Governments are sensitive to consumer prices of food grains and some countries, therefore, control the wholesale and retail prices of grains. This is especially common in those centrally planned countries that subsidize grain production in order to keep consumer prices at a fairly stable level.

We take for granted the predominant role of the United States in world grain trade, but this nation has not always been in that position. As shown by Table 9-2, North America was not the leading exporter of grain until after the 1930s. Most countries were exporting to Europe at that time, with Latin America the leading exporter. More recently, the United States, Canada, and Australia have dominated food and feed grain exports.

The developing countries of the world have become large importers of grains. Cereal grain imbalances occur occasionally because of drought or other natural disasters. Imbalances in food grains are due primarily to increase in population and incomes in Asia, Africa, the Middle East, and Latin America. In Western Europe, Eastern Europe and the Soviet Union, the imbalances are in feed grains.

World Wheat Trade. Total world wheat trade amounted to 49.8 million metric tons in 1968/69, increased to 73.7 million tons in 1975/76, and totaled 101.4 million tons in 1981/82. The U.S. share of total wheat trade was 30 percent (14.8 million tons) in 1968/69, 43 percent (31.9 million tons) in 1975/76, and 50 percent (50.3 million tons) in 1981/82. About 22 percent of total world wheat production enters international trade.

The world's leading wheat exporters are the United States, Canada, EC-10, Australia, and Argentina, accounting for 96 percent of all the wheat that is exported. From 1977 through 1982, Canada exported 77 percent of its total wheat production, Australia—78 percent, the United States—64 percent, Argentina—49 percent, and EC-10 (Western Europe)—21 percent. Over this period of time, the United States accounted for 46 percent of the world's wheat trade, Canada—18 percent, Australia—13 percent, Argentina—7 percent, and Western Europe—12 percent.

Most of U.S. wheat exports go to Mexico, Brazil, Venezuela, Chile, Italy, the Netherlands, Poland, Romania, India, China, Japan, South Korea, Philippines, Algeria, Egypt, Morocco, Nigeria, and Russia.

Canada's markets are Brazil, Italy, United Kingdom, Russia, China, Japan, and Egypt. Australia exports grain to China, Indonesia, Japan, and Egypt. Argentina exports wheat to Brazil, Italy, Russia, and China. Most Western European countries are trading wheat among themselves, with some wheat being exported to Poland and to African nations, Asia, South America, and Cuba.

World Trade in Feed Grains. The major coarse grain producing countries are the United States, Russia, China, France, Canada, India, Brazil, and West Germany. World coarse grain production totaled 770 million metric tons in 1981/82. It is estimated that about 65 percent of this output was used as livestock feed. About 85 percent of world coarse grain exports are for use as livestock feed. Historically, coarse

Table 9-2 World Net Imports and Exports of Grain,[a] Selected Periods (million metric tons)

Region	1934–38	1960–63	1969–72	1972/73	1975/76	1980/81	1981/82
North America	+5	+43	+55	+91	+100	+137	+146
Latin America	+9	+1	+3	0	+1	−8	−3
Western Europe	−23	−26	−22	−18	−18	−7	−11
Eastern Europe and Russia	+4	0	−3	−27	−33	−47	−55
Africa and the Middle East	+1	−4	−9	−9	−14	−27	−32
Asia	+2	−16	−28	−35	−36	−41	−56
Oceania (Australia and New Zealand)	+3	+7	+11	+6	+12	+14	+15

[a]Net imported indicated by (−), and net exports by (+).

Source: Economic Research Service, *World Agricultural Outlook and Situation*, USDA, Washington, D.C., December 1982.

grains were traded among developed countries, but recently many middle-income countries have increased their use of grain for feed.

Corn is the most important feed grain traded, accounting for 71 percent of all coarse grains exported in 1981/82. Grain sorghum was second with 14 percent, then barley at 8 percent, and small amounts of oats and rye.

Wheat is classified as a food grain rather than a feed grain, but significant quantities of wheat are used for feed in the United States, Russia, the EC, and Eastern European countries. Most of the wheat that is diverted to feed use in these countries is either denatured or of low quality.

World coarse grain exports increased more than two and one-half times from 1968/69 to 1981/82, increasing from 37 million tons to 103.3 million tons per year. Corn, barley, sorghum, and rye exports have almost tripled, while oats trade has remained relatively stable.

The increased exports of feed grains are a result of rising world demand for meat and increasing per capita incomes around the world. The growth of feed grain exports was also a result of poor weather conditions that caused poor harvests in much of the world, especially in the Soviet Union. Other factors include the devaluation of the dollar, and detente with Russia and the People's Republic of China.

The major exporters of coarse grains are the United States, Argentina, Canada, South Africa, Western Europe, Australia, and Thailand. The United States, Argentina, South Africa, Thailand, and France are the main exporters of corn. The large barley exporters are Canada, France, the United States, and Australia. The United States and Argentina alone supply more than 86 percent of the world's grain sorghum exports.

The largest importers of corn are Italy, Russia, the United Kingdom, the Netherlands, Germany, Spain, and Japan. Russia, Germany, Italy, and Japan import most of the barley, and Japan imports most of the grain sorghum.

Overall, the United States is the largest feed grain exporter, with over 60 percent of the world market in 1981/82; other exporters have relatively small individual market shares. The major importers (Western Europe, Japan, and the Communist bloc countries), take about 75 percent of all feed grain imports.

World Rice Trade. The world's major rice producers are China, India, Bangladesh, Indonesia, Thailand, Burma, and Japan, accounting for more than 78 percent of total world production. Most of these countries produce mainly for their own consumption, exporting less than 2 percent of their production.

Of the 12 million tons of rice exported in 1981/82, 25 percent came from Thailand, 24 percent from the United States, 9 percent from Pakistan, and 6 percent each from China and Burma.

The major rice importers, with no one nation buying more than 600,000 tons, are EC-10, Indonesia, Iran, South Korea, Saudi Arabia, Hong Kong, Vietnam, Bangladesh, Russia, and Sri Lanka.

The United States shipped rice to about 70 nations in 1981, with the largest amounts going to Nigeria, Saudia Arabia, Iran, Indonesia, Iraq, and South Korea. Thailand's major markets are Indonesia, Malaysia, Singapore, Saudia Arabia, Senegal, and Hong Kong.

World Trade in Soybeans. Soybeans are the leading oilseed in world trade and dominate the world oil and meal markets. Soybean oil and meal are joint products from processing operations. Soybean oil is an edible oil used mainly in margarine, shortening, cooking, and salad oils; and soybean meal is used primarily as a high-protein feed supplement.

The world's sources of fats and oils are butter, soybean oil, sunflower, palm, olive, rapeseed, and marine oils. Meals include soybean, cottonseed, groundnut, sunflower, rapeseed, linseed, copra, palm kernel, and fish meal. These meals differ in quality and quantity of protein, so are not perfect substitutes for one another.[2]

Ninety-eight percent of the world's 1981/82 exports of soybeans, a total of 29 million tons, were obtained from the United States (80 percent of all exports), Argentina (11 percent), Brazil (5 percent), and Paraguay (2 percent).

Despite its large share of world soybean exports, the United States also is the world's largest user of soybeans and soybean products, at 28 percent of total consumption in 1981/82. Major importers of soybean meal are the EC, Eastern Europe, Mexico, and Canada. Oil importers are mainly India, EC, Iran, Peru, Colombia, and Pakistan.

Mechanics of Exporting Grain. Moving grain into the export market is similar to making domestic sales. These sales of grain are specified in a sales contract, and are priced at a "flat price" or "basis priced" through the use of futures. If grain is basis priced, price is not fixed in the contract but is established at a future time or through the exchange of futures contracts.

Exporters may sell grain in a number of ways including f.o.b. (free on board), c.i.f. (cost, insurance, and freight), or c. and f. (cost and freight). Most export sales are made on an f.o.b. basis, since the seller pays the cost of loading the grain in the ship's hold and there is less risk involved in the transaction. With c.i.f. sales, title to the grain is transferred at the ship's rail as the ship is unloaded at the foreign port, and includes the value of the grain, the cost of marine insurance, and the cost of transportation to the destination port. When sold c. and f., the

[2]James P. Houck, Mary E. Ryan, and Abraham Subotnik, *Soybeans and Their Products,* University of Minnesota Press, Minneapolis, 1972, p. 21.

seller provides the grain and all expenses except the cost of marine insurance until the grain is unloaded from the ship.

In the United States, only a few major exporters ship most (about 60 percent) of the grain. These firms include Continental Grain Company, Cargill, Inc., Garnac Grain Company, Bunge Corporation, and Louis Dreyfus, Inc. Other companies export smaller volumes of grain. These companies purchase, condition, segregate, blend, assemble, and transport grain. Some of these companies own inland and terminal elevators and shipping facilities. Some of these firms also have overseas affiliates that give them international communications and a well coordinated marketing network.

The Role of Concessional Sales.   The U.S. government has provided for concessional sales[3] of agricultural commodities, following passage of the Agricultural Trade Development and Assistance Act of 1954 (PL-480). The Act's purpose is to combat hunger and malnutrition in the world, control grain surpluses in the United States, develop export markets, and assist economic development in recipient nations.

There currently are four titles to PL-480, as amended.[4] Title I covers concessional sales; Title II, donations and relief; Title III, food for development; and Title IV, general provisions.

Title I sales are made to foreign governments or to private trade entities. These sales are dollar credit sales, or convertible local currency credit sales. In these cases, CCC finances the sale and exportation of the commodities. Credit terms range from 20 to 40 years at low interest rates.

Title II sales are commodity grants to nonprofit U.S. agencies, international organizations, disaster relief, or community development projects.

Under Title III, funds derived from the local sale of Title I commodities can be credited to repay their debt to the United States for PL-480 commodities, if those funds are used for rural development, health programs, or population planning.

Title IV covers a number of miscellaneous provisions. Some of these are farmer-to-farmer assistance programs, with a stipulation that countries receiving Title IV aid have adequate storage facilities.

Seventy-seven nations benefited from a total of $1.24 billion in aid from U.S. government-sponsored aid programs[5] in 1981. Egypt, In-

---

[3]Concessional sales are those sales in which the United States grants the buying country more favorable terms (in currency accepted, length of time for repayment, or interest rate) than they could obtain when trading on the open market.

[4]For an in-depth description, see Amalia Vellianitis and Eileen M. Manfredi, *P.L. 480 Concessional Sales,* Foreign Agricultural Economic Report No. 142, Economic Research Service, USDA, Washington, D.C., December 1977.

[5]In addition to PL-480 assistance, concessional aid has been provided under U.S. Mutual Security and AID programs. The International Development and Food Assistance Act of 1975 (amended in 1977) brought about an integration of PL-480 and AID programs.

dia, Pakistan, Indonesia, Bangladesh, and Poland were the major recipients in that year, with 56 percent of the total distributed in those nations.

STRUCTURE OF THE GRAIN EXPORT MARKET

The conditional requirements of a purely competitive market cannot be met if either governmental activities or regulations of the market prescribe decisions for individuals or firms, or if the market is dominated by a relatively few firms able to exert power in the market. The worldwide grain export system is an industry where there are many small producers whose products for export are handled by a few, large exporters (private trading firms and national marketing boards), and importers (private traders and state trading agencies) who also are few in number and might exert some market power. However, the variety of programs and policies of governments throughout the world probably have more influence on the prices of agricultural commodities than any of the firms and agencies in the industry.

When a government agency, influenced (or directed solely) by domestic policy objectives, is buying or selling grain in the international market, or when a very large multinational firm is negotiating with a buyer or seller (either an agency of government, or a private firm), chances are slight that the forces of supply and demand will be the only meaningful influence in price determination.[6]

As previously discussed, almost all countries enact internal agricultural or food policies to protect their farmers and consumers from world price fluctuations. Domestic policies in the U.S., such as the set-aside, acreage reduction, and farmer-owned reserve programs reduce international grain supplies relative to demand and enhance prices in the short run.

The EC has a high price support program that encourages production in the EC, discourages consumption, and reduces their imports from other nations. Its policy to subsidize exports of surplus commodities increases the supply in world trade, which reduces prices. The net impact of the EC variable levy system is an increase in the supplies of commodities produced within the EC, which exerts downward pressures on world prices outside the EC even though EC prices are maintained at high levels.

On the importing side of the international market, the EC variable levies and Japanese domestic pricing policies have reduced grain imports below what they would have been in those nations. Thus, the international market is one of imperfect competition, and influences prices received by U.S. producers.[7]

---

[6]Some argue, on the other hand, that trading firms are concerned only with their margins and not with the absolute prices of the commodities that are being traded. See, for instance, Richard E. Caves, "Organization, Scale, and Performance of the Grain Trade," *Food Research Institute Studies,* Vol. XVI, No. 3, Stanford University, Stanford, 1977/78.

[7]Caves, op. cit., concludes that the export grain industry "exhibits competitive behavior."

Grain Trading Firms

As the United States is the world's largest exporter of feed grains, wheat, and oilseeds, each year millions of tons move through the marketing channels from U.S. farms to foreign buyers around the world. These commodities are exported through the private sector by trading firms.

Six large trading firms account for about 60 percent of U.S. exports of grain and oilseeds. A number of smaller firms and several grain cooperatives handle the remaining 40 percent of grain and oilseed exports. The six large firms are multinational companies, three of them U.S. corporations and three foreign corporations. These firms are highly diversified businesses that maintain sales and procurement offices in a number of countries. They have access to or control of the many functions required in procuring, handling, selling, financing, and delivering commodities to buyers around the world. They compete in buying and selling commodities without respect to country of origin.

Several large cooperatives handle grain and oilseeds for export. A large proportion of their commodities is delivered to a U.S. port, then sold to one of the international trading firms to be sold to foreign buyers. There are some cooperatives, however, that maintain commodity control from the point of origin to the port in the importing country.

The internal marketing channels of importing countries differ from country to country. The large international trading firms may sell U.S. grains to private trading firms, such as those in the EC, or to government agencies such as the Japanese Food Agency, or the Soviet International Grain Trading Agency.

There are two principal ways of making an export sale. One is by private negotiation. Sales to the Soviets and China as well as to most buyers in the EC are of this type. The other type of sale is by *tender*. Under a tender system, the potential buyer issues specifications as to kind of grain, class, grade, time of shipment, destination, etc. Normally, all potential sellers must submit sealed offers by a specific time at a specified place.

Once accepted, an export transaction creates a short cash position for the exporting firm. This firm, however, may be in a net long or net short overall position, depending on the management's assessment of future grain prices and its willingness and ability to assume uncertain price risks.

Much of the price risk in such forward selling is covered by purchasing futures contracts. In hedging this grain, the firm is interested in the basis between its forward cash selling price and the price of futures. This basis is its margin.

Grain firms must be relatively secretive about their large grain sales as any informational leaks can drive up futures prices before they can purchase futures contracts to hedge the forward sale. An information leak could reduce the firm's basis and, hence, its margin on the sale. In closing this long hedge, the firm desires secrecy because any discount in cash purchasing prices versus futures prices will increase its margin and the profitability of the transaction.

A study conducted for the Secretary of Agriculture analyzed 29 large grain and soybean export sales during the years 1975 to 1978.[8] Exporters were found to be net long in futures, and in overall positions before and after export sales were reported, but there was little buying of futures during the week of the reported sale. Cash market purchases during the week of the sale exceeded futures purchases.

The futures market provides a reference price for grain, and it can be used to shift the price risk of grain ownership to speculators, if that is deemed appropriate. Such times would be when the firm's management thinks future cash prices may rise, or when there is considerable uncertainty over the direction of future price movements.

U.S. futures markets are quite competitive,[9] given the theoretical norm for competitive markets. But they must reflect the structure of the international grain market. Any international buyer can purchase futures contracts, hold them for delivery and then have the grain shipped to a foreign port. Or the buyer could purchase the cash grain at a port or inland terminal and have it shipped to the foreign destination. These actions on the part of buyers restrict the potential for margin-widening actions by multinationals or state trading agencies and boards. Sellers, similarly, are not wholly at the mercy of international buyers—multinationals, or state trading agencies—since they may simply sell futures contracts and deliver on that contract at its maturity. However, very few futures contracts are settled by making or taking commodity delivery.

ESTIMATED MARGINS IN THE EXPORT TRADE[10]

Margins on grain sales are not compiled in the United States, as they are in Canada where their Wheat Board regularly publishes the costs of moving grain throughout the entire grain marketing system. Indications of margins for f.o.b. and c.i.f. sales can be calculated from grain market reports of the Portland, Duluth, Gulf, and Rotterdam markets.

F.o.b. Sales. The Livestock and Grain Market News Branch of the USDA's Agricultural Research Service in Portland collects "15-day to arrive prices," and f.o.b. prices on a daily basis for barley, hard red

[8]Richard Heifner, Kandice Kohl, and Larry Deaton, "A Study of Relationsips Between Large Export Sales and Futures Trading," USDA, U.S. Government Printing Office, Washington, D.C., June 8, 1979.

[9]In a recent survey, it was found that four major grain exporting firms held 24 percent of the short futures contracts in corn, wheat, and soybeans, and 6 percent of the open long contracts at the major grain exchanges.

[10]Documented margins of firms in the industry are unavailable. Thus we are forced to rely on simple (unweighted) average price spreads. Until more reliable information is made available, the following margin estimates should be considered as "ball park" estimates at best.

winter wheat (HRW) of ordinary protein (OP), soft white wheat (SW), and dark northern spring wheat (DNS) with 14 percent protein. These price spreads show the simple average gross margin of exporting those grains, but the price spreads are unweighted and may not reflect the actual gross margin of a particular firm. Nominal average price spreads for Portland grain are shown in Table 9-3.

Since the estimated price spreads are annual averages, the price spread for a shorter period of time may be considerably higher or lower than shown here. The average barley margin of 29 cents, as compared with the 7 to 8 cents for wheat, reflects (in part) the smaller volume handled and the longer storage period involved in barley exports.

C.i.f. Sales.   Rather than selling grain f.o.b., such as to Russia, China, and PL-480 sales, many U.S. export sales are made c. and f., although market price quotes are c.i.f. The only grain price reported by the USDA for foreign markets is the c.i.f. Rotterdam asking price for 30-day delivery, as reported by the Hamburg Mercantile Exchange. The price spread on international sales can be calculated as the difference in prices between Rotterdam and the Gulf (or Duluth) minus the ocean freight rate, as shown in Table 9-4.

The gross margin minus ocean freight on wheat is much higher than for soybeans, sorghum, or corn. Wheat margins averaged 20 to 22 cents per bushel, sorghum and soybeans 12 cents, and corn 9 cents per bushel, with considerable variability in margins from year to year for commodities and between commodities. Given these data, it appears more advantageous to engage in c.i.f. sales than in f.o.b. sales; however, c.i.f. sales require foreign offices, much more general overhead expense, and considerably more risk.

The accuracy of simple (rather than weighted) average annual

Table 9-3   Average Annual Price Spreads Between 15-Day To-Arrive Prices and Current F.O.B. Prices at Portland, July-June Marketing Year, 1974/75 to 1978/79 (dollars per bushel)

Year	Barley	HRW(OP)	Soft White	DNS (14% protein)
1974/75	$0.36	$0.12	$0.11	NA
1975/76	0.29	0.06	0.06	NA
1976/77	0.29	0.07	0.05	NA
1977/78	0.25	0.06	0.06	$0.07
1978/79	0.27	0.09	0.08	0.08
Average	0.29	0.08	0.07	0.075

NA = not available.

Source: Data provided by the Grain Market News Branch, Agricultural Research Service, USDA, Portland.

Table 9-4   Average Annual Price Spreads at Duluth and the Gulf Between 30-Day, To-Arrive Rotterdam Prices and Current F.O.B. Prices Minus Ocean Freight Costs, July-June Marketing Year, 1974/75 to 1978/79[a] (dollars per bushel)

Year	Duluth[b] DNS 14 pct	Gulf			
		HRW[c] 13.5 pct	Corn[d] #2 Yellow	Sorghum #2 Yellow	Soybeans[d] #2 Yellow
1974/75	$0.22	$0.11	$0.11	$0.17	$0.18
1975/76	0.28	0.16	0.10	0.19	0.11
1976/77	0.25	0.27	0.10	0.06	0.11
1977/78	0.29	0.24	0.05	0.05	0.06
1978/79	0.08	0.21	0.07	0.14	0.12
Average	0.22	0.20	0.09	0.12	0.12

[a]Ocean freight rates were obtained from the Economics, Statistics, and Cooperatives Service, USDA.
[b]Lake freight and elevator cost adjustments were made from estimates obtained from the Canadian Wheat Board.
[c]Comparison is HRW 13.5 percent protein Rotterdam versus 13 percent protein at the Gulf.
[d]The corn and soybean price spread is between #3 yellow Rotterdam versus #2 yellow Gulf. These grains normally drop in grade in transit.

Source: Foreign Agricultural Service, USDA, Washington, D.C.

price spreads as indicators of average annual gross margins is diminished to the extent that different volumes of grain may be sold at different margins. Since the grain export industry is highly scheduled to coordinate all phases of the movement of grains to the final consumer, and the opportunity cost of holding grain is high, volume flows of grain are relatively stable. Another complicating factor in the use of simple averages is the differences in lead and lag times between the day an offer is made and the expected delivery date. Wide differences and variations occur in these, and bear no relationship to the time it takes for a shipload of grain to move from its U.S. shipping port to its foreign destination.[11]

Return and Cost Comparisons[12]

Estimates of the net returns per bushel of grain are developed in Table 9-5. The gross revenue per bushel is equal to the gross margin at the U.S. port plus the gross margins (excluding transportation) between U.S. ports and Rotterdam. Total cost estimates include the cost of

[11]United States Senate: Hearings before the Subcommittee on Multinational Corporations of the Committee on Foreign Relations, Part 16, U.S. Government Printing Office, Washington, D.C., 1977, p. 203.
[12]A *caveat:* Margins vary over time. Net margins in this series of years are wider than in both earlier and later years.

Table 9-5 Total Revenue (TR), Total Costs (TC), and Net Returns (NR) per Bushel in Exporting Grain, July–June Marketing Year, 1974/75 to 1978/79[a] (dollars per bushel)

Year	Wheat			Corn			Soybeans		
	TR[b]	TC[c]	NR	TR	TC[c]	NR	TR	TC[c]	NR
1974/75	$0.132	$0.074	$0.058	$0.140	$0.068	$0.072	$0.220	$0.089	$0.131
1975/76	0.194	0.072	0.122	0.170	0.067	0.103	0.210	0.078	0.132
1976/77	0.301	0.065	0.236	0.170	0.064	0.106	0.230	0.083	0.147
1977/78	0.322	0.066	0.256	0.170	0.064	0.106	0.200	0.079	0.121
1978/79	0.289	0.082	0.207	0.150	0.077	0.073	0.260	0.100	0.160
Average			0.176			0.092			0.138

[a]These are the author's estimates computed from Foreign Agricultural Service market data, rather than summaries developed from financial reports of grain exporting firms.

[b]Weighted average margin for DNS and HRW.

[c]These costs do not include a return on investment.

moving grain through an export port, the cost of ownership of that grain, plus an administrative overhead charge. The USDA has estimated port elevator costs for 1970/71, 1971/72, and 1974/75.[13] If these costs are adjusted by the GNP implicit price deflator, the cost of operating a port elevator facility has increased from about 3.3 cents per bushel in 1974/75 to 4.3 cents per bushel in 1978/79. The remaining cost element-administrative costs—is taken from Canadian Wheat Board reports and adjusted for exchange rate differences.[14]

Exported grain may be sold and resold a number of times before it is delivered to the final buyer. Thus, these net margins, ranging from about 9 cents per bushel of corn to 18 cents per bushel of wheat, cover all transactions under which grain is exported, rather than being net margins for each transaction in an export shipment.

Viewed by some as being much larger than these numbers indicate, a comparison with the price per bushel of grain shows that the net margins have averaged about 6 percent of the export price of wheat, about 3 percent for corn, and less than 2 percent of the value of a bushel of soybeans.

Summary

International trade is important both to American agriculture and the general U.S. economy as, with specialization and trade, more goods and services are obtained at a lower real cost than could be obtained without trade. Exports pay for imports, and make available many products that would otherwise be available only at high cost, if at all.

The United States is most clearly at a comparative advantage in producing several agricultural commodities, and is especially efficient in the production of grains and soybeans. These products account for more than two-thirds of the value of all U.S. agricultural exports.

Since the beginning of World War II, the United States has become the world's leading exporter of feed and food grains, and oilseeds and oilseed preparations, supplying more than one-half of the total of these commodities traded in the international markets. The United States provides 46 percent of all world wheat exports, over 60 percent of the coarse grain, 24 percent of the rice, and 80 percent of the soybean market. The developed countries rely on the United States primarily for feed grains, whereas the developing countries depend on the United States for much of their food grain supply.

Barriers to free trade include tariffs, quotas, and nontariff barriers. These devices are used to reduce a nation's volume of imports, for domestic, protective purposes, but they also reduce the gains from specialization and trade, and thus reduce the real wealth of the world community.

[13]Allen Schienbein, "Cost of Storing and Handling Grain in Commercial Elevators," Commodity Economics Division, U.S. Department of Agriculture, Washington, D.C., February 1977.
[14]Canadian Wheat Board, *Annual Report, 1978/79*, Winnipeg, Manitoba, p. 30.

Imperfect competition in markets is of concern to many people because of the market power that might be exercised by the participants. The international grain market is imperfectly competitive, with a marketing system so structured that the bulk of agricultural commodities is handled by state trading agencies and large multinational firms. With often huge quantities of grain involved in a single transactions, the market prices of those commodities may be influenced by the actions and decisions of the negotiating parties, rather than only by the forces of supply and demand. In spite of this market's structure, Caves found that there is competitive behavior among private grain exporting firms. Government imposed trade barriers, export subsidies and taxes, and a variety of domestic agricultural programs more effectively restrain competition in the grain export industry than do presently existing market imperfections.

Selected References

American Enterprise Institute, *Food and Agricultural Policy,* Washington, D.C., 1977.

Canadian Wheat Board, *Annual Report,* 1960/61 to 1978/79, Winnipeg, Manitoba.

Caves, Richard E., "Organization, Scale, and Performance in the Grain Trade," *Food Research Institute Studies,* Vol. XVI, No. 3, 1977–1978.

Caves, Richard E. and Ronald W. Jones, *World Trade and Payments,* Little, Brown, and Company, Boston, Mass., 1977.

Economics, Statistics, and Cooperatives Service, *Alternative Futures for World Food in 1985,* Foreign Agricultural Economic Report No. 146, USDA, Washington, D.C., April 1978.

Ellsworth, Paul T., *The International Economy,* 4th ed., The Macmillan Company, New York, 1969.

Heller, H. Robert, *International Trade: Theory and Empirical Evidence,* 2nd ed., Prentice-Hall, Inc., Englewood Cliffs, N.J., 1973.

Helmuth, John W., *Grain Pricing,* Economic Bulletin No. 1, Commodity Futures Trading Commission, Washington, D.C., September 1977.

Ingram, James C., *International Economic Problems,* 3rd ed., John Wiley & Sons, Inc., New York, 1978.

Kindleberger, Charles P., *International Economics,* 4th ed., R. D. Irwin, Inc., Homewood, Ill., 1968.

Kreinin, Mordechai E., *International Economics: A Policy Approach,* 2nd ed., Harcourt Brace Jovanovich, Inc., New York, 1975.

McCalla, Alex F., "A Duopoly Model of World Wheat Pricing," *Journal of Farm Economics,* Vol. 48, No. 3, Part 1, August 1966.

McCalla, Alex F. and Timothy E. Josling, eds., *Imperfect Markets in Agricultural Trade,* Allanheld, Osmun and Company, Inc., Montclair, N.J., 1981.

McCalla, Alex F. and Andrew Schmitz, "Grain Marketing Systems: The Case of the United States Versus Canada," *American Journal of Agricultural Economics*, Vol. 61, No. 2, May 1979.

Schienbein, Allen, *Cost of Storing and Handling Grain in Commercial Elevators, Projections for 1974/75,* Commodity Economics Division, Economic Research Service, USDA, Washington, D.C., February 1977.

Schmitz, Andrew, Alex F. McCalla, Donald O. Mitchell, and Colin A. Carter, *Grain Export Cartels,* Ballinger Publishing Company, Cambridge, Mass., 1981.

Shepherd, A. Ross, *International Economics: A Micro-Macro Approach,* Charles E. Merrill Publishing Company, Columbus, Ohio, 1978.

Snider, Delbert A., *Introduction to International Economics,* R. D. Irwin, Inc., Homewood, Ill., 1975.

Speaking of Trade: Its Effect on Agriculture, Special Report No. 72, University of Minnesota, Minneapolis, 1978.

Taplin, J. H., "Demand in the World Wheat Market and the Export Policies of the United States, Canada, and Australia," unpublished Ph.D. dissertation, Cornell University, Ithaca, N.Y., 1969.

Thompson, Sarahelen R. and Reynold P. Dahl, *The Economic Performance of the U.S. Grain Export Industry,* Agricultural Experiment Station Technical Bulletin No. 325, University of Minnesota, St. Paul, 1979.

United States Senate, hearings before the Subcommittee on Multinational Corporations of the Committee on Foreign Relations, Part 16, U.S. Government Printing Office, Washington, D.C., 1977.

Wexler, Imanuel, *Fundamentals of International Economics,* Random House, Inc., New York, 1968.

Wheeler, R. O., Gail L. Cramer, Kenneth B. Young, and Enrique Ospina, *The World Livestock Product, Feedstuff, and Food Grain System,* Winrock International, Morrilton, Ark., 1981.

10

GOVERNMENT POLICY

GOVERNMENT POLICY*   CHAPTER 10

The U.S. grain marketing system can be characterized as one in which private individuals and private firms perform the major functions and bear the consequences of their actions. The system is largely a free enterprise, private system in contrast to systems in many other countries. However, the U.S. system is not free of government involvement, particularly at the federal level, nor did it evolve without government efforts to shape the system into what it is today.

In addition to affecting the marketing system, the federal government affects grain prices through various programs. The government became involved in the grain marketing system in 1929 when it began programs to raise farm incomes from depressed levels. It has used a wide range of programs to influence prices and production, and has varied the types and amount of involvement in accordance with changing economic conditions.

More direct government involvement in agriculture was a part of the general trend in the early 1930s as the government became more involved in private economic activity. This involvement occurred in response to depressed economic conditions that included the failure of the general economic system to provide adequate employment opportunities to many of its citizens and adequate income to the nation's farmers.

PUBLIC DECISION MAKING

Policy Objectives. Public policy is a special kind of group action designed to achieve certain aspirations held by members of society.[1] It is distinct from private firm policy in that it involves group action by individuals who frequently have conflicting or diverse aspirations or objectives. However, an adopted policy requires at least minimal agreement on what is to be achieved. For a policy to be adopted, expected achievement must be consistent with or bear some correspondence to the values held by society.

Architects of U.S. farm policy, particularly since the late 1920s, have been guided by their attitudes toward political and social stability, economic stability, a particular type of economic organization, eco-

*Bob F. Jones, Professor, Department of Agricultural Economics, Purdue University, West Lafayette, Ind.
[1]Dale E. Hathaway, *Government and Agriculture,* The Macmillan Co., New York, 1963, p. 3.

nomic growth, equality of opportunity, and a desire to share U.S. agricultural abundance with other less fortunate people. These preferences are manifestations of values held by members of the society and play an important role in determining what it is that society wants to attain, both for the agricultural sector and the general economy.

Values correspond to society's subjective perceptions of what "ought to be." Beliefs and facts pertain to the situation as it currently is. In this context a belief pertains to a person's or group's perception of what the situation is. When "what is" does not correspond with what "ought to be," a policy problem may exist. When a policy problem arises, a decision must be made as to what to do about it. Society must decide whether to attempt to solve the problem, ignore it, or learn to live with it. Beliefs, even when factually incorrect, have an important role in policy formulation because they influence problem definition and choice among policy alternatives. Therefore, one task of policy formulation is to sort fact from belief, with emphasis on verification of the "true" situation.

President Lyndon B. Johnson's "Message on Agriculture" in 1964[2] contained representative statements of the objectives of farm policy, as perceived by the executive branch of government. That message stated that farm program objectives were "to maintain and improve farm income, strengthening the family farm in particular," and "to use our food abundance to raise the standard of living both at home and around the world."[3] The preamble of the Agriculture and Food Act of 1981 stated the objectives to be "to provide price and income protection for farmers, assure consumers an abundance of food and fiber at reasonable prices, and continue food assistance to low income households, and for other purposes."[4]

Policy Formulation. Grain production and marketing policy is established at the federal level by the House of Representatives and the Senate, and is subject to approval by the president. Policy is formulated in each legislative body after study and recommendation by the Senate Committee on Agriculture and Forestry and the House Agriculture Committee. The USDA, in addition to administering programs, contributes input to the legislative committees, often taking the lead in designing programs and serves in an advisory capacity to the committees. Farmers contribute to the process, individually, and through their farm organizations; other business groups, consumer groups, private citizens and other governmental agencies also provide input to the legislative committees.

---

[2]No president since Johnson has sent a special message on agriculture to the Congress.

[3]"President Johnson's Message on Agriculture," transmitted to the 88th Congress, 2nd Session, January 31, 1964, printed in the *Congressional Quarterly Almanac* (Congressional Quarterly Service, Inc., Washington, D.C., 20:887, 1964).

[4]Public Law 97-98, 95 Stat. 1213, 97th Congress, December 22, 1981.

Approaches to Public Policy for Agriculture. Public policy for grain production and marketing has followed two approaches. Policies are designed to make the private production and market system work more efficiently. Where it is believed noncompetitive behavior is present, policies may be designed to enforce competition. The second approach involves direct government intervention into the production and marketing processes.

Policies to promote competition. Examples of this approach include establishment of grades and standards, collection and dissemination of market information, and provision of funds for agricultural research and extension activities.

In this approach, public funds are entitled in order to make the marketing system work more efficiently and thereby lower marketing costs. Lower marketing costs can result in lower costs to consumers and/or higher prices to producers. In a competitive economy all consumers of agricultural products benefit by being able to buy food products at lower cost and stand to gain from public expenditures for these types of activities.

Consumers receive greater benefits when the system is more competitive and the benefits of lower costs are passed through to them. Regulation of railroads that began in 1887 was visualized as necessary to assure competition and equitable freight rates for shipment of grains. This type of regulation was discussed in Chapter 4. Regulation of commodity markets was believed to be necessary in order to reduce fraud and increase competition in commodity exchanges. These forms of government involvement, which affect the infrastructure within which grain marketing takes place, have evolved over time, continue in various forms today, and are subject to continual review and modification.

More direct government involvement. Depressed conditions in agriculture in the 1920s led to passage of the McNary-Haugen bills. This legislation authorized establishment of a board that would determine fair prices for agricultural products to be sold in the domestic market and would sell surpluses of wheat and seven other basic commodities abroad. The bills passed Congress twice but were vetoed by President Coolidge. They were considered to be price fixing and against the economic principles of free enterprise.

As agriculture continued to suffer from depressed economic conditions other approaches were tried. The Federal Farm Board was established by the Agricultural Adjustment Act of 1929. It was set up with a revolving fund of $500 million, had authority to make loans to cooperative associations and could buy up surplus grains.

The Board had no control over production or acreage and soon exhausted its revolving fund as wheat prices on the Chicago market dropped from $1.20 in 1929 to $0.39 a bushel in 1931.

As the general economy was severely depressed in 1932, additional approaches for agriculture were tried in the form of the Agricultural Adjustment Act of 1933. With passage of this Act, the federal government began programs to influence grain prices and farm incomes through acreage allotments, direct payments to farmers, and storage programs. These programs focused on the objective of raising farm prices by restricting production. The approach assumed demand for agricultural products was inelastic and that by reducing production, prices would rise sufficiently to increase farm income.

The Commodity Credit Corporation was created in 1933 to carry out loan and storage operations as a means of supporting prices above the level that would have prevailed in a free market. Export demand had nearly disappeared as a result of depressed world market conditions and a progressively more restricted export market as tariff walls were raised worldwide. Consumers' incomes had dropped, causing domestic demand for farm products to shrink still further. At the same time the quantity of marketable grain was increasing as tractors were replacing horses.

Restoration of purchasing power for agriculture was a key feature of the Agricultural Adjustment Act of 1933. This goal became known as parity for agriculture. The original legislation designated wheat, corn, cotton, hogs, rice, tobacco and milk as basic commodities that would be supported. It was assumed that support for a few key commodities could raise farm incomes.

The advent of World War II relieved the crisis of overproduction and low farm prices. Prices rose as stocks were used up. Concern over surpluses turned to concern over producing enough food with which to fight the war.

In part to stimulate production during the war, and also to relieve farmer concerns over a return to low farm prices that were expected to return following the end of the war, the Steagall Amendments were passed in 1941. They authorized that farm prices be supported at relatively high levels for two years following the declared cessation of hostilities. The Amendments expired on December 31, 1948.

AGRICULTURE'S CHANGING TECHNICAL AND ECONOMICAL ENVIRONMENT

World War II to 1972. Farm prosperity during and after the war enabled farmers to invest heavily in new production technology. Output expanded rapidly as new chemical, biological, and mechanical technologies were acquired in agriculture. As wartime demand declined and output expanded, grain stocks again accumulated in CCC storage. Public debate arose over whether fixed price supports were more appropriate for simultaneously supporting farm income, while facilitating resource adjustment to changing technological and market conditions, or whether flexible supports would be more appropriate.

Grains policy was considered the central element in price and income support, with the CCC loan rate a key component of the policy. Grains were considered the key because of their storability and their role in livestock production. It was believed that farm incomes could be maintained through use of the loan rate and government storage of grain.

Justification for continuing price and income programs for agriculture following World War II was based on the following lines of reasoning. Domestic demand for food had recovered as a result of general economic recovery associated with the war. Export demand had expanded during and immediately following the war but had declined following recovery in Europe. The U.S. physical plant for producing farm commodities had expanded as a result of wartime demands and was capable of producing more than could be sold at acceptable prices.

Although farm prices and incomes were significantly above the levels of the 1930s, per capita income in agriculture continued to lag behind per capita incomes in the nonfarm sector. Given the low-income elasticity of demand for food, and the tendency for farm output to continue to grow as a result of adoption of new technology, incomes were likely to continue to lag behind nonfarm incomes. Proponents of continued government support for agriculture argued that farmers needed help in making the necessary resource adjustments as new technology was being acquired. The surplus commodities tended to be looked on as temporary surpluses that would likely be needed as weather and crop conditions changed. Storage programs would enable producers to store commodities past the low-price harvest period, and if prices stayed low during the year, the CCC would acquire grain that could be disposed of in subsequent years. Thus, storage programs were considered necessary as a means of both stabilizing farm prices and raising farm incomes.

Dramatic resource adjustments were occurring in agriculture. The number of farms declined from 6.3 million in 1930 to 4.8 million by 1954. Yet the adjustments were not occurring rapidly enough to bring farm incomes up to the level of nonfarm incomes, and governmental help in the form of price supports was considered necessary.

The continued concern over equitable treatment of the farm sector, and the desire to maintain political, social, and economic stability, maintained political support for a continuation of governmental involvement in supporting farm prices. Emphasis shifted toward disposing of surplus stocks in the export market with passage of the Agricultural Trade Development and Assistance Act, better known as Public Law 480. Finally, the magnitude of excess capacity in agriculture was becoming more apparent as grain stocks accumulated and storage costs escalated.

Although greater emphasis was placed on surplus disposal with passage of PL-480 in 1954, the loan rate and storage programs continued to play a key role in price and income policy. The Feed Grain Program for 1961 included direct payments to farmers who would idle a portion of their feed grain acreage as a means of supply control. This provision represented a slight shift from dependence on price supports toward direct payments to producers as a means of income support. This trend grew in importance and eventually evolved into the target price/direct payment approach in existence with passage of the Agricultural Acts of 1973, 1977, and 1981.

After 1972. A series of events in 1972 to 1974 changed the economic and technical environment in which agriculture operates. These events dramatically affected the grain production and marketing system, as well as its participants. Two events had key roles in changing the environment—one was the large increase in exports of wheat to the Soviet Union starting in 1972, the other was the quadrupling of crude oil prices between 1972 and January 1, 1974.

As a result of adverse weather conditions in the U.S.S.R. in 1972, the Russian wheat crop was expected to be sharply reduced. Since Soviet planners had embarked on a five-year plan to increase food production, especially livestock products, they sought grain from the world market. Since the United States held large stocks of grain in government storage and was eager—in retrospect, probably too eager—to dispose of its surplus stocks, a bargain was struck. The United States would supply wheat to the U.S.S.R. at the prevailing world trading price of about $1.65 per bushel. Since prices were being supported to U.S. wheat producers above this level, export subsidies were required to move the wheat. During mid-1972 Soviet grain buyers agreed to purchase over 400 million bushels of wheat from the United States. A purchase of this magnitude enabled the CCC to unload its stocks of grain, so that by the end of 1974 the CCC held no wheat stocks under its control.

In a series of moves in 1973 the Organization of Petroleum Exporting Countries (OPEC) raised the price of crude oil from $3.01 to $11.65 per barrel.[5] The Arab-Israeli War and the Arab oil embargo dramatized to the world the dependence of many countries on imported oil. Since importing countries continued to buy oil at these prices, and were either unable or unwilling to get OPEC to lower its prices, the era of cheap energy came to an abrupt end.

A combination of the surge in exports in 1972/73, sharply reduced U.S. grain stocks, and a relatively poor corn crop in the United States in 1974, led to much higher grain prices in the United States and in world markets. Thus, supply conditions and worldwide inflation, fueled by expansionary monetary and fiscal policy in the United States, contributed to higher grain prices.

---

[5]Ronald Cotterill, *Cartel and Embargoes as Instruments of American Foreign Policy*, Agricultural Economics Report No. 373, Michigan State University, East Lansing, April 1980, p. 39.

As a result of the increase in exports and depletion of government grain stocks, no cropland was held out of production under set-aside programs in 1974 through 1977. Most of the 50 to 60 million acres of cropland that had been held out of production under various programs during the late 1960s and early 1970s came back into production.

Agriculture in the mid-1970s appeared to be more nearly in equilibrium than at any time in the previous 40 years. Growth in demand was primarily from the export market. Agricultural exports expanded from $4.5 billion in the early 1960s to over $43.8 billion in 1981. During this period of time, agricultural exports as a percent of sales of farm products increased from 14 percent to 30 percent. Clearly, agriculture had become much more dependent on the foreign market as a source of its receipts.

Conditions for the expansion of exports of U.S. agricultural products had been developing through the 1960s. The steady long-term growth is a result of rising real per capita incomes worldwide and growing world population. Poor crops in the U.S.S.R., Australia, and Brazil in 1972 contributed to the sudden growth in demand for U.S. products. Changes in the world monetary system that resulted in devaluation of the dollar relative to the currencies of Japan and several Western European countries, contributed to expansion of U.S. agricultural exports.

Labor continued to move out of agriculture during the 1960s, and the number of farms continued to decline. Most of the excess labor had been removed from agriculture. After return of set-aside land to production, additional production was possible through bringing new land into production, and through increasing productivity of existing resources. Some evidence existed to show the long-term growth in productivity of agriculture was declining.

With expanding exports, and U.S. agriculture more nearly in an equilibrium situation in the mid-1970s, the set of questions concerning consumers and policy makers changed; they became more concerned over high and unstable farm prices, and the adequacy of grain stocks. The situation of higher prices and no government stocks contributed to passage of the Agricultural Act of 1973, which brought into being the target price/direct payment approach as the principal means of income support for agriculture.

Ever since storage programs came into existence in the 1930s they have been combined with various types of programs to restrict and manage the supply of selected farm products in order to maintain prices. The amount of restriction and control over supplies have depended on the changing economic environment for agriculture. Control programs have taken the form of acreage allotments, marketing quotas, and land diversion under various names. They all represent attempts to tailor production to demand in a manner similar to that used by industrial producers.

ANALYSIS OF PRICE AND INCOME SUPPORT PROGRAMS IN A CLOSED ECONOMY

Analytical Approach.   The general impacts of government commodity programs can be analyzed using conventional supply-demand concepts, as briefly discussed in Chapter 2.[6] Programs can be categorized into those that affect demand and those that work through supply. Various forms of demand expansion have been used since the 1930s. They include commodity distribution programs (which have made surplus commodities available to persons on welfare), child nutrition programs (such as the school milk program), and donations of surplus commodities to school lunch programs. Food stamps are supplemental income to consumers and represent another form of demand expansion. Surplus distribution in the export market under authorization of PL-480 and the Mutual Security Administration has taken various forms that represent demand expansion.

The supply of farm commodities that can be marketed has been affected through marketing quotas, domestic allotments that limit the acreage planted, and soil bank or acreage set-aside programs that reduce either a specific crop or the total acreage available for the production of grain crops.

Loan and storage programs.   Assume that D in Figure 10-1 represents the demand curve for wheat that domestic consumers would buy at various possible prices in a given time period, for example, one year.[7] Assume, also, that S represents the quantity of wheat that producers would supply at various prices, and that there is no carry-over. In the absence of government intervention, price would be P_0 and quantity produced and sold would be Q_0. If the government determines that P_0 is too low to provide equitable income to producers, and further determines that price should be at P_1 and makes loans available to producers at that rate, prices will tend to rise to P_1. With price at P_1, consumers will purchase only Q_1, and the government will need to store Q_1Q_2 of wheat as a result of loan takeover.[8]

If the storage program is a voluntary one and has requirements such as a reduction in acreage planted that some producers may not

[6]Initially, the analytical approach includes only domestic consumers. It assumes all trade is domestic or that the international market is unimportant to the analysis. The international market is explicitly introduced in subsequent sections.

[7]For simplicity it is assumed all consumers demand unprocessed wheat. Introducing marketing margins and derived demands would only complicate the analysis and add little to the analysis at this point.

[8]An important feature of CCC commodity loans has been that they are nonrecourse loans to eligible producers. The producer is loaned a specified amount of money per unit of the commodity (the loan rate). At the end of the loan period, usually one year or less, the borrower must pay off the loan plus interest or forfeit the grain to the CCC. If market price is less than the loan rate the CCC considers the loan as fully paid with no further recourse to the borrower. The bulk of the grain acquired by CCC has been acquired in this manner.

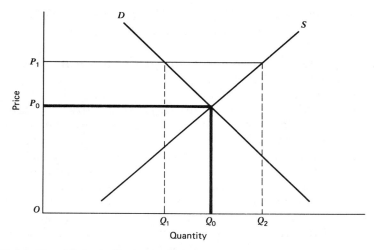

Figure 10-1. Hypothetical effects of a loan rate.

wish to meet, not all grain will be eligible for loan so market prices may drop somewhat below the loan rate. If the government places no restrictions on the amount produced or sold, producers will gain from the loan programs so long as the government is willing to continue to store grain. If technological progress is occurring that causes the supply curve to shift to the right over time, the government will be faced with the problem of acquiring larger quantities of grain each year. This tended to occur in many of the years from 1948 through the 1960s.

The Agricultural Act of 1949 provided that the CCC should not sell any storable commodity in the domestic market at less than 5 percent above the support price plus reasonable carrying charges. The Secretary of Agriculture may (and has) set a higher minimum level. For feed grains and wheat, the minimum selling price was raised 15 percent above the support price plus carrying charges for the 1974 through 1977 crops.[9] If the grain was in danger of going out of condition with continued storage, the CCC was allowed to sell grain at less than the established release price.[10]

Release policies of the CCC kept market prices near the loan rate when they had large quantities of grain in storage. As a result of large stocks and operation of the resale rules, grain prices tended to be

[9]Agricultural Stabilization and Conservation Service, *Acquisition and Disposal of Farm Commodities by CCC*, USDA, ASCS Background Information, B.I. No. 3, Washington, D.C., October 1975, p. 5.

[10]This provision sometimes generated controversy over administration of the program. Since determination of "going out of condition" requires a degree of subjective judgment, managers of the inventories were sometimes accused of using this provision to encourage participation in voluntary programs.

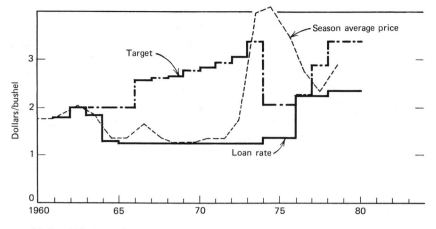

Figure 10-2. Wheat support levels and farm prices.

relatively stable from the early 1950s through 1965, at which time the drought in Southeast Asia caused world grain prices to rise (see Figures 10-2 and 10-3).

When the CCC supports the price of grain above the market price as in Figure 10-1, producers offer a larger quantity to the market. Furthermore, when technological progress is causing the supply curve to shift to the right at a more rapid rate than demand shifts (due to low-income elasticity of demand and slow population growth), the quantity that farmers wish to put under loan continues to grow over time. If the government chooses to restrict its expenditures on commodity programs it may do so with several types of restrictive devices. If it were to choose marketing quotas, specifying that a given quantity

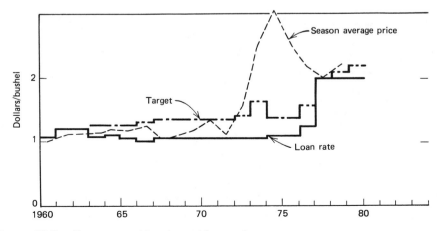

Figure 10-3. Corn support levels and farm prices.

of wheat could be marketed by producers, the situation would be as illustrated in Figure 10-4. If the marketing quota were set at Q_1, price would be maintained at P_1. Producer incomes would increase if demand for wheat were inelastic, as it was believed to be. If, on the other hand, the elasticity of demand for wheat were elastic (greater than 1), producers would gain from selling more wheat at lower prices.

Marketing quotas were used for wheat during the 1950s and early 1960s. A producer's market quota was the amount of wheat grown on the allotted acres. Acreage allotments were tied to the acres of wheat planted on the farm in previous years. An allotment of this type represents a less precise quantity than implied in Figure 10-4, because total production on a fixed allotment would vary as yield per acre increases or decreases.

Whether demand is elastic or inelastic is crucial in determining whether programs that restrict supply will benefit producers. Research evidence used in formulating policies in the 1950s and 1960s clearly indicated that demand for grains, especially wheat, was indeed inelastic in the domestic market. Evidence of demand elasticity on the foreign market was less certain, but it too was presumed to be inelastic.

When supply restrictions are imposed on one input, the supply curve tends to shift upward and to the left (e.g., S_2 in Figure 10-5). However, other inputs tend to be substituted for the input being limited. Therefore, the supply curve shifts less than might be expected. When programs have required that production of a given crop be limited to an acreage allotment, farmers have supplied more fertilizer and other variable inputs to the planted acres and have been able to increase average yield on allowable acres in the program. Slippage in

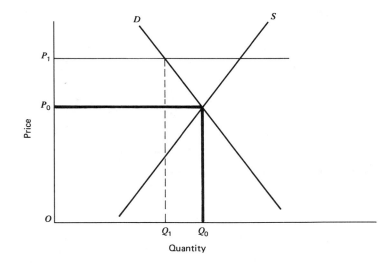

Figure 10-4. Example of quota restriction on quantity sold.

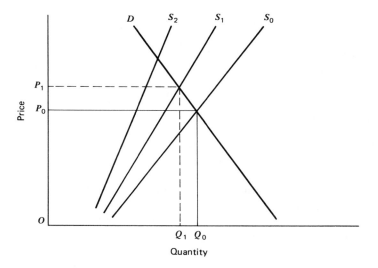

Figure 10-5.   The effect of acreage restriction on supply.

the program also occurs from another source. Since farmers tend to idle their poorer acres, the average yield on planted acres increases. Research has shown that the productivity of idled acres is about 85 percent of the cropped acres on the farm. After all adjustments, the reduction is equivalent to a leftward shift in the supply curve to S_1, as illustrated in Figure 10-5.

When grain prices are supported above the market equilibrium price, market prices tend to be higher, producers have an incentive to increase production, consumption is less, and stocks accumulate in government storage. Existence of government-owned stocks and operation of release rules tend to keep prices within a narrow range. The loan rate becomes the floor price and the ceiling price is only slightly above it. The risk of carrying stocks is largely transferred from farmers and the grain marketing system to the government. When stocks become too large greater emphasis tends to be placed on methods of expanding domestic demand and surplus disposal, even though it is at a loss to the government.

Deficiency payments plus a loan program.   The Agriculture and Consumer Protection Act of 1973 incorporated a new concept in the commodity price support system. Target prices were established for wheat and feed grains. Grain prices were allowed to be determined by market forces. Direct payments per unit of the commodity were made to eligible producers if the market price received by farmers for the first five months of the marketing year was below the target price as established by the legislation. The deficiency payment could be no larger than the difference between the target price and the loan rate. To be eligible for program benefits, participants were required to limit production by setting aside a percentage of their planted acres on which no grain or forage crop could be grown for harvest. The Secretary of Agriculture could require set-aside acres if supply-demand conditions warranted it.

The effects of this method of price support depend on the level of the loan rate and target price relative to the market equilibrium price. With the loan rate below the market equilibrium price, as in Figure 10-6, grain would not be acquired by CCC through loan forfeitures. Some farmers would place grain under loan, using the program as a source of credit rather than as a price-supporting mechanism, although the loan would keep prices from dropping below that level. Since not all farmers choose to participate in voluntary programs, prices could drop below the loan rate, as has occurred occasionally. Prices shown in Figure 10-6 indicate a deficiency payment of the difference between P_0 and P_T would be paid to eligible participants. Since program participants would receive the market price for their grain plus a deficiency payment they would tend to expand their output from Q_0 to Q_1. If a set-aside requirement were in effect, production would expand less than Q_0 to Q_1. Conceptually, the supply curve would rotate to the left as land was removed from production (as illustrated in Figure 10-5).

During the period from 1973 to 1976, market prices tended to be above both the target price and the loan rate for wheat and feed grains (Figures 10-2 and 10-3). In these cases no deficiency payments were made and the CCC did not accumulate grain as a result of loan takeover. In later years when the market price dropped below the loan rate (both target prices and loan rates were increased after 1976), some grain was acquired by the CCC as a result of loan takeover.

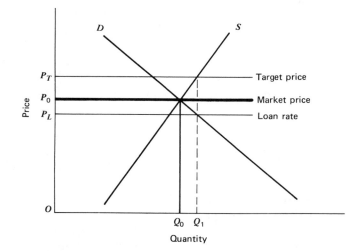

Figure 10-6. Example of target price and loan rate.

Use of the target price/loan rate approach allows market prices to vary with changing supply-demand conditions. It encourages greater consumption and export of grain as supplies increase rather than cause an accumulation of grain in government storage. This approach allows exports without export subsidies when the loan rate is equivalent to or below the world trading price for the grain.

Inventory management policy. Producers who participate in loan programs may store grain on their farm or in approved commercial facilities. In either case the producer is responsible for storage costs for the initial period of the loan (typically up to 11 months). From a national perspective, most of the wheat is stored off the farm, while corn usually is stored on the farm. If a producer decides to forfeit the grain at the end of the loan period, it must be delivered to an approved storage facility designated by the CCC. The CCC has tended to use commercial facilities close to areas of production when available and has encouraged construction of commercial storage facilities through use guarantees.

When the CCC held large stocks of grain during the 1950s and 1960s, and commercial facilities were inadequate, CCC-owned bins were erected in major grain producing areas to receive grain from loan takeover. Storage capacity on farms was increased through operation of the storage facility loan program. Credit was extended to farmers under favorable terms, and rapid write-off as an expense for calculating federal income tax liability was allowed and encouraged.

Storage programs from the 1950s through the mid-1970s required farmers to pay the costs of storing grain under loan whether stored on the farm or in commercial facilities. In some years a reseal program was offered after the initial storage period. During the reseal period farmers were paid a storage allowance. When grain was acquired by CCC, and not under reseal, storage costs were paid by the government. Since the CCC owned large stocks of grain from mid-1950 through the early 1970s the government assumed a large share of the cost of carrying the nation's grain inventory.

During the period from 1974 to 1977, when the government held almost no stocks of grain, the private sector was carrying the grain inventory. Changes in inventory management following passage of the Agricultural Act of 1977 are discussed in the section on price stabilization and food security.

EVOLUTION OF TRADE POLICIES

Foreign markets have been an important but variable source of income to U.S. farmers for almost two centuries. The abundance of rich agricultural land and a relatively small population have enabled U.S. farmers to produce more farm products than could be consumed domestically.

The quantity of agricultural products that enters into foreign markets is a function of demand conditions in other countries, the competitive position of U.S. suppliers relative to other supplying nations and importing countries, and the policies that countries follow toward regulating the flow of products in international markets. Important buyers can significantly influence the volume and terms of trade through both their domestic and trade policies. Similarly, the United States can influence the amount it sells through its domestic and trade policies. To understand changes in the volume of trade it is helpful to get some historical perspective on U.S. trade policy as it has evolved over time, especially since the turn of the century.

Pre-World War I to the Great Depression. From the end of the Civil War to World War I the United States became a major producer and exporter of grain to Europe. However, conflicts between liberal and protectionist advocates in the United States kept trade policies and tariffs fluctuating, affecting the volume of exports and imports. Tariffs reached their highest level with the Dingly Tariff of 1897.

Just prior to World War I, some reduction in U.S. tariff barriers was accomplished with passage of the Underwood-Simmons Tariff of 1913. Trade in agricultural products expanded rapidly in response to mobilization needs and to meet needs created by wartime disruptions in European grain production. Grain production increased in the United States, Canada, and Australia to meet the goal of winning the war and to supply immediate needs, not in response to long-time economic needs. Following the armistice and recovery of European agriculture, much of the export market for grain collapsed. Farmers around the world petitioned their governments for restrictions on imports. Although U.S. farmers were exporters of agricultural products and not importers, they saw their interests as coinciding with the interests of industry and called for higher tariffs against foreign imports. Congress responded in 1930 by passing the Hawley-Smoot Tariff, one of the highest in U.S. history and a watershed in U.S. tariff levels.

In retrospect, it is difficult to understand trade policies from World War I to the beginning of the Great Depression, and why farmers took the positions they did. After being a debtor nation since its founding, the United States had emerged from the war as a creditor nation. It had entered into agreements requiring that the losers in the war pay reparations to the winners. Yet the United States and other nations kept raising their tariff walls, thereby making it more difficult if not impossible for reparations to be paid, since the shipments of goods is the principal way by which one country repays its debts to another. The impossible situation that developed was a factor in the Great Depression, in the conditions leading to World War II, and in repudiation of war debts to the United States.

Reciprocal Trade Agreements, 1934. The Reciprocal Trade Agreements of 1934 represent a turning point in U.S. trade policy. The Trade Agreements Act emphasized the need to expand markets for U.S. products and authorized the President to enter into mutually advantageous bilateral trade agreements. The Act contained a "most favored nations" provision that allowed the benefits of bilateral negotiations to have a multilateral effect. Agreements were concluded with over 30 countries, which moved the United States toward freer trade in industrial products, a necessary condition for expansion of agricultural trade.

While U.S. tariffs were being lowered for industrial products, agricultural trade was being curtailed. The introduction of direct market intervention in domestic agriculture had international trade repercussions. Government support of domestic agricultural prices above world trading price levels required restrictions against entry of competing products and use of export subsidies in order to sell products abroad.

The General Agreement on Tariffs and Trade and Trade Negotiations. Passage of the Reciprocal Trade Agreements Act was a first step in a long line of activities by the U.S. government to promote freer world trade. The United States has been a participant in international organizations and multilateral negotiations that had the intent of expanding international trade, including trade in agricultural products.

Following World War II, an attempt was made to formulate a set of principles for carrying out international trade. The Charter for the International Trade Organization (ITO), drawn up in 1948, specified principles for reduction of tariffs, elimination of quotas, and creation of conditions for expansion of multilateral trade. It set up rules for international commodity agreements. The charter recognized the need for national governments to relate foreign trade policies to domestic programs. President Truman submitted the agreement to Congress for approval in April 1949. Hearings were held by the House Foreign Affairs Committee but it did not go further.[11]

The General Agreement on Tariffs and Trade (GATT). Although the ITO failed, many of the basic provisions survived on a more modest scale in the General Agreement on Tariffs and Trade (GATT) in which the United States has been a participant since its inception. This agreement contains a code of principles and rules and provides a continuing forum with a permanent staff and headquarters for periodic negotiating conferences to be called by member nations. More than 80 governments including the United States participate fully; others have associate or observer status.

[11]Robert L. Tontz, "U.S. Trade Policy: Background and Historical Trends," *U.S. Trade Policy and Agricultural Exports,* Iowa State University Press, Ames, 1973, pp. 17–41.

The GATT has five basic principles, each of which has some impact on the growth and conduct of international trade in grain.

1. Trade must be nondiscriminatory. All contracting countries receive equal treatment regarding import and export duties and charges. The original agreement allowed exceptions for less developed countries and regional trading groups.

2. Domestic industries receive protection mainly by tariffs except that agriculture was granted special treatment. For example, Article 11 permits import quotas on agricultural products if domestic production restrictions are in effect. (This authorization was critical if the United States were to retain Section 22 authority.)

3. Agreed-on tariff levels bind each country. If tariff levels are raised, compensation must be paid to injured countries.

4. Consultations are provided to settle disputes.

5. When warranted by economic or trade circumstances, principally balance of payments difficulties, GATT procedures may be waived (or escape provisions allowed) if other members agree and compensation is made.[12]

From its inception through 1980 seven major "rounds" of trade negotiations have been held under GATT auspices. Negotiations led to significant reductions of industrial tariffs. Much less has been accomplished for trade in agricultural products. The escape clause that allows exceptions when domestic agricultural programs are in effect to restrict production has permitted the retention of import quotas.

Despite the difficulties encountered when domestic and trade policies conflict, progress has been made in facilitating trade in agricultural products. The willingness of countries to negotiate and resolve differences has been a positive factor. For commodities that had no duties, agreement was reached to continue to allow duty-free entry. This is an important factor for U.S. exports of soybeans, soybean meal and certain by-product feeds to the EC. Agreement also has been reached on expansion of quotas on imports.

A thorough study of the GATT and trade negotiations is beyond the scope of this chapter. However, one needs some understanding that an international institution exists whose objective is to expand trade among nations. Trade expansion is no simple task when one recognizes the problems associated with reconciling policies of over 80 soverign nations, each with its own internal institutions, monetary systems, economic conditions, and national objectives.

ANALYSIS OF PRICE AND INCOME POLICIES IN AN OPEN ECONOMY

Analytical Approach. The preceding section in this chapter considered only the domestic market for agricultural products. This section

[12]Mary E. Ryan and Robert L. Tontz, "A Historical Review of World Trade Policies and Institutions," *Speaking of Trade: Its Effect on Agriculture,* University of Minnesota, Minneapolis, Special Report No. 72, 1978, pp. 5–19.

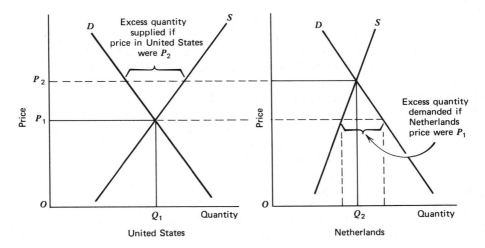

Figure 10-7.   Two-country supply and demand model without trade.

explicitly introduces the foreign market as a component of total demand for agricultural products. The modification in approach is presented in order to (1) explicitly recognize the interdependence between markets in two countries when international trade occurs and (2) develop an analytical device for determining the effects of domestic policies on international trade. The approach shows that quantities exported and imported are a function of price and not just a result of a "surplus" in the exporting country or of a "shortage" in the importing country. The model permits determination of the surplus and/or shortage. The graphical approach represents a partial equilibrium model, given the usual assumptions of a perfectly competitive model.

Assume two countries each of which produces and consumes an agricultural product, for example, wheat. Production in each country is represented by the conventional supply curve that slopes upward to the right. Similarly, demand can be represented by the conventional demand curve which slopes downward to the right. These conditions can be illustrated graphically, as in Figure 10-7.

For now, assume that these two countries are isolated from each other and that no trade between them occurs. Given these assumptions, the U.S. equilibrium price would be P_1 and consumers would demand Q_1 of wheat. Only at this price-quantity combination would both producers and consumers be satisfied. In the Netherlands consumers would demand Q_2 of wheat and would pay P_2 per unit for it. In this example, the price of wheat in the Netherlands would be significantly higher than in the United States.[13]

---

[13]An additional assumption is important for simplifying the analysis. Although each country has its own form of money—dollars and guilders—we assume the two currencies and all prices are quoted in dollars.

If the two economies are closed to trade, price can be significantly higher in the one country compared to the other. When resources are less well suited for production of a particular product, per unit cost tends to be higher. The number of people in the country and their per capita incomes tend to cause differences in demand. When these conditions cause the equilibrium price to be different in two countries, opportunities for trade exist.

If price were P_2 in the United States, an excess supply would exist (i.e., producers would be willing to supply more than U.S. consumers would purchase at that price). At price P_1, no excess supply would exist in the United States. For prices above P_1, the horizontal difference between the supply and demand curves in the United States would represent the excess supply of wheat in the United States.

If price P_1 were to exist in the Netherlands, consumers would demand more wheat than producers would be willing to supply at that price. At price P_2, no excess demand would exist in the Netherlands. Therefore, at prices below P_2, the horizontal difference between the supply and demand curves in the Netherlands would represent the excess demand curve for wheat in the Netherlands.

Now assume trade is possible between the two countries. In this case U.S. producers would like to sell at the Netherlands price, P_2. Netherland's consumers would like to buy at the U.S. price, P_1. An equilibrium trading price would lie somewhere between these two extremes. It can be determined by transferring the information in Figure 10-7 to a new set of excess supply and excess demand curves (Figure 10-8).

In Figure 10-8 the left panel represents supply and demand conditions in the United States. The right panel represents supply and demand conditions in the Netherlands. The center panel supplies the connecting link and is labeled the "world market." The excess supply curve, or export supply curve, is derived from the U.S. market. The excess demand curve, or import demand curve is derived from the Netherlands market. The intersection of the excess supply and excess

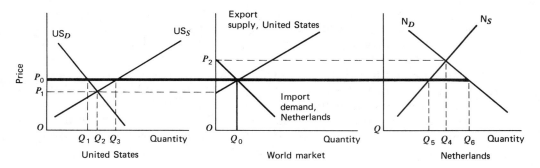

Figure 10-8. Two-country supply and demand model with trade.

demand curves in the center panel determine the world trading price for wheat, P_0. In equilibrium, the price of wheat is the same in both countries; it has increased from P_1 to P_0 in the United States, and has declined from P_2 to P_0 in the Netherlands.[14] The amount of wheat traded, OQ_0, is determined in the center panel. It is equal to the amount exported from the United States, Q_1Q_3, and the amount imported in the Netherlands, Q_5Q_6. An important lesson from this is that internal prices in the United States are determined by both domestic market conditions and world market conditions. The exportable surplus is a function of the world trading price. Similar statements pertaining to price and the shortage can be made about the Netherlands.

The model can be used to trace through the effects of technical, economic, or policy changes in the United States or the Netherlands. The important point is to start with shifting the appropriate curve. For example, unusually good weather in the United States would cause the US_S curve to shift to the right. This would cause the export supply curve to shift to the right. All other curves would be assumed to remain fixed. New prices and quantitites could be determined. In a similar manner an increase in income in the Netherlands would cause a rightward shift in the N_D curve, which generates a rightward shift in the import demand curve. Using this approach, one change at a time can be analyzed.

The model can be expanded to handle more than two countries by making the simplifying assumption that demand and supply curves can be aggregated for all importing countries into one set of curves for the importers and labeling the region the "rest of the world" (ROW). The world market, as in the center panel of Figure 10-8, becomes an analytical link between the United States and the ROW. The model then becomes a useful tool for analyzing the effects of policy changes in the United States. Both domestic policy changes and trade policy changes can be analyzed.[15]

U.S. Deficiency Payments in an Open Economy.
The Agricultural Acts of 1977 and 1981 retained the concept of a target price-deficiency payment as a means of supporting income to U.S. farmers. The effects of this program were discussed and analyzed in a previous section but did not include selling grain in the export market.

Since the export market for U.S. grain has become such an important component of total demand for U.S. grains, it is necessary to add that dimension to the analysis.

---

[14]For simplicity, transportation costs have been assumed to be zero. When transportation costs are introduced prices tend to be different in the two countries by the amount of the transportation cost per unit. Price would be lower than P_0 in the United States and higher than P_0 in the Netherlands.

[15]Only two cases are illustrated here. A larger number of policies are analyzed in "Interrelationships of Domestic Agricultural Policies and Trade Policies," by Bob F. Jones and Robert L. Thompson in *Speaking of Trade: Its Effect on Agriculture*, Special Report No. 72, University of Minnesota, Minneapolis, 1978, pp. 37–68.

When the government guarantees farmers a price above the market price for their grain, larger production is stimulated. However, with the deficiency payment approach the government does not buy grain and store it. Instead, all grain enters the market, and the government makes up the difference between the market price and the target price.

In Figure 10-9, P_0 is assumed to be the equilibrium price in the United States and the ROW before any government intervention. The price is determined by the intersection of the export supply curve and the import demand curve in the world market. Exports are OQ_0.

A deficiency payment does not cause the supply curve to shift. Instead, production moves along the supply curve. Farmers produce and sell Q_4, which is determined by price, P_1, the target price. In this case farmers receive P_2 from the market, plus P_1P_2 as deficiency payment from the government. In effect the U.S. supply curve below price P_1 is irrelevant and can be considered to be vertical below P_1. The effect of this modification is to cause the excess supply curve to become kinked at price P_1. The new excess supply curve in $ABES_{US}$. The intersection of the kinked supply curve with ED_{ROW} determines the price P_2, which exists in ROW, the world market, and in the United States. U.S. farmers get the deficiency payment in addition.

As a result of the target price being above the market price that would have prevailed, U.S. output expands, U.S. exports are larger, and price in the world market is lower. U.S. consumers buy a larger quantity, Q_1 to Q_2. Producers in the ROW receive a lower price for their production. Production in ROW is reduced but consumers buy more because of the lower price which occurs with increased imports.

To minimize government cost of the deficiency payment program and to minimize complaints from ROW producers, the United States may impose production restrictions in the form of an acreage set aside. In this case, quantity produced could be restricted so that the quantity

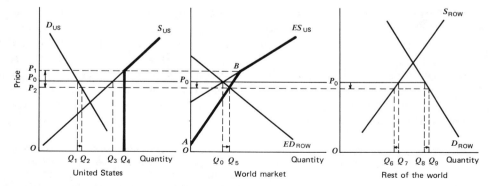

Figure 10-9. Effects in the United States and the rest of the world of a U.S. deficiency payment policy.

exported would remain at the level that existed before the deficiency payment program went into effect.

The Impact of EC Variable Levies on U.S. Exports.

Other countries frequently have domestic programs which lead to restrictions on exports of U.S. products. The Common Agricultural Policy (CAP) of the European Community is a well-known example that affects a large market for U.S. grain and oilseeds. The CAP uses a system of target prices for grain (similar to the system used in the United States since 1973) that guarantees a specific price level to producers. Market prices are maintained near that level by imposing a variable levy on imports. When the import price drops below the target price, the levy increases to offset the difference. Figure 10-10 is a graphic analysis of the effects of the variable levy on the United States as well as in the EC.

Assume the initial equilibrium price and quantity exported are P_0 and Q_0 as indicated in the center panel. When the EC sets its target price at P_1, the rest of the world would attempt to increase production and exports to Q_1. To avoid this flood of imports, the EC would charge a variable levy of P_1P_2 on each bushel of imports. The price P_2 would be determined by the intersection of the new kinked ED_{EC} import demand curve and the ES_{ROW} curve. This price would prevail in the ROW. Regardless of how low the price fell in the ROW, if, for example, the S_{ROW} shifted right, imports would not increase.

The consequences of this policy are higher prices in the EC, larger domestic production, less domestic consumption, and reduced imports. In the ROW there would be lower producer and consumer prices, reduced production, and increased consumption. How large these effects will be depends on the size of the EC market relative to its suppliers, the amount by which the target price exceeds the market price, and the elasticities of demand and supply in both the EC and the ROW. Since the United States is the world's largest supplier of both

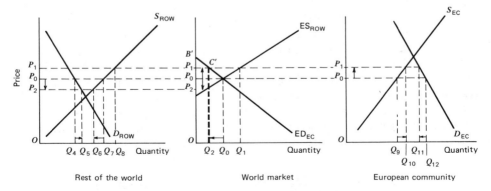

Figure 10-10. Effects in the rest of the world and the EC of a price support policy that includes a variable levy in the EC.

feed grains and wheat to the EC, a major part of the impact on ROW suppliers would fall on the United States.

Government Programs to Expand Foreign Demand for U.S. Grain. The U.S. government has participated in two types of programs to expand foreign demand for agricultural products. Public Law 480 facilitates the shipment of about $1 to $1.5 billion of agricultural products per year. Since 1954, the dollar amount shipped under PL-480 has remained relatively stable. In the mid-1950s, PL-480 shipments varied from 25 to 40 percent of all U.S. exports of agricultural products. By 1980, exports had grown to such an extent that PL-480 shipments were only about 3 to 4 percent of total shipments. About one-third of all PL-480 shipments are donations of food to charitable organizations that distribute food to very low-income people. The other two-thirds of PL-480 shipments are to countries that buy the grain using long-term credit arrangements with the United States. Credit may be extended for as many as 40 years, with interest rates of 2 or 3 percent per year.

Market development activities under PL-480. The government also participates in market development activities under PL-480 authorization. Market development typically consists of activities jointly sponsored by the government and U.S. producer groups. The United States provides market development services through its system of agricultural attachés that is a part of the U.S. foreign service stationed abroad. Examples of market development activities include introducing new products in foreign markets, provision of technical services to potential users of products, training foreign persons in use of U.S. products, and participation in school lunch programs abroad.

CCC credit for export sales. In addition to PL-480 market development activities, the United States provides a limited amount of credit for purchase of U.S. commodities. Credit is extended through the CCC under terms that are similar to those extended by commercial lenders. Money is loaned at a rate slightly above the U.S. prime rate for periods of a few months to three years. If this amount of credit—about $1 to $1.5 billion per year in the late 1970s—is truly a net addition to credit available for financing grain sales abroad, it would represent some expansion in demand for U.S. grain exports. It is an attempt to meet the competition for U.S. grain sales when U.S. competitors, primarily Canada and Australia, provide credit to facilitate their grain sales.

PRICE STABILIZATION AND FOOD SECURITY

Grain prices tend to fluctuate from day to day and over time for several basic reasons. Demand for grain tends to be both price and income inelastic. Supply tends to be inelastic in the short run. The quantity produced in any production period may be significantly changed because of weather conditions. Markets are characterized as having a large number of producers (sellers) each with no control over price.

Price Stabilization Prior to 1972.   Since the early 1930s the federal government has tried to remove some of the instability from the grain market. Usually it relied on loan programs and government purchase of grain as means of placing a floor under prices. Emphasis was on keeping prices up rather than holding them down. Although specific price stability objectives were not stated in legislation or by administrators of the legislation, the availability of grain in CCC storage served as a stabilizing factor in the market until 1972. Existence of large government stocks and resale policies adopted by CCC kept prices in a relatively narrow range (see Figures 10-2 and 10-3).

Large grain exports from the 1972 and 1973 crops, and the rapid drawdown of government stocks followed by a short U.S. corn crop in 1974, led to much greater price variability than had been encountered in the two previous decades. Policy efforts were directed toward reducing the amount of variability in U.S. grain prices. Since much of the instability originated from the foreign markets, managing grain exports became of major interest.

Embargoes and Trade Suspension.   Since the United States produces much more grain and soybeans than are consumed domestically, internal price variability could be reduced through control of exports. The United States tried this three times during the 1970s. Embargoes were placed on additional shipments of grain and/or oilseeds and were kept on for short periods of time until supply conditions became known with greater certainty. The embargoes were applied at times when grain prices had risen sharply, and caused short-run prices to fall.

The use of embargoes generated much unfavorable reaction from farmers and the grain trade. It was argued that their immediate repercussions had fallen on farmers who had been urged to expand production. Furthermore, the long-run effect would be to stifle export growth. The use of embargoes became a sensitive political issue.

Antiembargo support led to a provision in the Agricultural Act of 1977 that required that loan rates be raised to 90 percent of parity for the commodity if, based on determination of short supply, the president or any member of the executive branch suspended the commercial export sale of any named commodity. Wheat, corn, grain sorghum, soybeans, oats, rye, barley, rice, flaxseed, and cotton were included.

The January 4, 1980 suspension of sales of grain to the U.S.S.R. in response to the Russian invasion of Afghanistan was not covered by the above provision. Specifically, sales were not suspended because of "determination of short supply" but as a means of attaining foreign policy objectives.

Export Sales Reporting System. Chapter 8 noted the importance of market information to the efficient functioning of markets. Foreign purchases sometimes involve a large volume of grain purchased in a short period of time. The timing of purchases relative to the announcement of sales may cause farmers to sell before full information is available about the volume of grain purchased. The export reporting system, as modified in October 1974, requires that any sale of more than 100,000 metric tons of any one commodity in any one day to any one country, or more than 200,000 metric tons in one week, must be reported for prior U.S. approval. The USDA is obligated to act on the request within a few hours, and agrees to promptly release the information to the public. The 1974 "prior approval" requirement was dropped when it was determined that the Foreign Agricultural Service did not have such authority. Otherwise, the system has undergone only minor modifications, including the raising of minimum reportable quantities.

The effectiveness of the reporting system has been questioned and continued to be a subject of study and hearings in 1979.[16] Use of overseas subsidiaries of large U.S. grain companies makes it possible for sales to be made before knowledge becomes available through the reporting system.

U.S.-U.S.S.R. Grain Agreement. Because a major source of price instability in U.S. grain markets was believed to be a result of unpredictable sales of grain to the U.S.S.R., the United States sought to stabilize their purchases. The instability arises principally from variable import needs that are caused by variations in Russian grain production. Historically, Russia has entered world grain markets when their production was reduced below expected needs. When production recovered, imports were reduced or stopped.

The U.S.-U.S.S.R. five-year agreement, signed in 1975, called for Russia to purchase at least 6 million metric tons (mmt) of grain per year from the United States. Up to 8 mmt could be purchased without further U.S. approval. Minimum purchases were to be divided between corn and wheat and were to be spread evenly over the year. The Russian government could request to purchase larger quantities, and the United States agreed to offer more if production conditions warranted.

For the first four years under the agreement, purchases were as follows: 1976/77, 6.1 mmt; 1977/78, 14.6 mmt; 1978/79, 14.8 mmt;

[16]*Export Grain Sales,* hearing before the Subcommittee on SBA and SBIC Authority and General Small Business Problems of the Committee on Small Business, House of Representatives, 96th Congress, First Session, June 11, 1979, U.S. Government Printing Office, Washington, D.C., 1979.

and 1979/80, 7.94 mmt. Prior to the suspension of sales in 1980, the Russians had contracted to buy about 21.7 mmt. The United States had given authority for purchase of 25 mmt. As a result of the suspension, sales of 13.7 mmt were cancelled and approval of the additional sales was withdrawn.

Research to determine the impact of the agreement on U.S. grain sales used a simulation model that took into account Russian yield variability and variable import needs.[17] The research showed that the combined purchases of the U.S.S.R. and Eastern Europe would increase by 2.8 mmt of grain per year with the agreement. The research also showed the agreement would probably have no effect unless the purchase agreement between the United States and Poland remained in force. Without the latter agreement, the Russians tended to buy U.S. grain and sell it to Poland in years when Russia had crops sufficient to meet domestic needs. In those cases Polish purchases from the United States were decreased.

The Farmer-Owned Grain Reserve.   The Food and Agriculture Act of 1977 authorized a farmer-owned grain reserve. The Act provided for accumulation of grain in the reserve when prices were relatively low. Ownership of the grain was to be retained by farmers who would store grain on their farm or in commercial facilities for periods of not less than three nor more than five years. Participants would receive a non-recourse loan on the commodity from the CCC. They could enter the grain in the reserve at the end of the initial storage period or sooner if authorized by the Secretary of Agriculture. Grain would be released from the reserve as prices rose above specified levels. Farmers would receive storage payments for grain stored in the reserve. The Secretary was authorized to waive interest charges on grain in the reserve.

The legislation authorized a wheat reserve of not less than 300 million bushels nor more than 700 million bushels. The Secretary was given authority to develop a reserve of feed grains but no quantity was specified. In administering the law in 1978, he established an initial target of 17 to 19 million metric tons of feed grains.

Grain was to enter the reserve at the existing loan rate. Grain could be released from the reserve when the market price reached a specified percent of the loan level. Loans were to be called when market prices rose to a higher specified percent of the loan rate. The release level for wheat as specified in the Act was to be not less than 140 percent of the loan level nor more than 160 percent of the then current level of price support. Release and call levels for corn were set at 125 and 140 percent of the loan level.

Penalties were specified for withdrawal of grain from the reserve

[17]James H. Hilker and Bob F. Jones, *A Stochastic Simulation Analysis of the U.S.-USSR Grain Purchase Agreement,* Department of Agricultural Economics, Agricultural Experiment Station Bulletin No. 356, Purdue University, West Lafayette, December 1981.

before the price rose to the release level. A penalty of one-fourth the loan rate plus repayment of storage payments was specified. The CCC was restricted from selling any grain that it owned at less than 150 percent of the loan rate.

In 1979 and 1980 the U.S. was gaining experience from operation of the reserve. During mid-1979 grain prices rose above release levels for wheat and feed grains. When the size of the 1979 corn harvest became evident, corn prices declined below the release level. Authorization for release was withdrawn. Corn began to reenter the reserve, especially after the Secretary authorized additional incentives to get corn in the reserve. Following the 1980 suspension of sales to Russia, additional corn entered the reserve. Later, when it became apparent that the 1980 corn crop would likely be reduced because of drought and heat damage, prices again exceeded the release level and approached the call level.

Although the farmer-owned reserve appeared to be working as intended—accumulating grain during periods of low prices and feeding it back into the market during periods of higher prices—it did not have specific price stabilization objectives. In 1978, 1979, and 1980 it probably kept prices from falling as low as they would have without the reserves. The reserve does not contain sufficient grain stocks to keep prices from rising significantly if a major shortfall were to occur in world grain production. Since farmers retain control over the grain, subject to prescribed rules, grain may not be fed back into the market as prices exceed the call level. They may choose to hold for further price rises. Some analysts argue the government should have more control to require farmers to put grain on the market when prices reach the call level rather than let farmers continue to speculate. This assumes government is more capable of assessing future production and consumption than the larger number of participants in the market.

Food Security. In response to heightened world food concerns, a World Food Conference was held in Rome in 1974, under the auspices of the United Nations. Since that conference, the United States has played a more active role in efforts to achieve greater world food security. PL-480 has made it possible for the United States to pledge grain to meet the goal of 10 mmt from all nations. In 1979, the United States raised its pledge to 4.47 mmt of cereal grains as our minimal annual commitment to food aid while negotiations for a new Food Aid Convention were in progress. While this was a multilateral commitment on the part of the United States, it was intended to encourage other donor countries to implement pledges they had made earlier.

Creation of a food security reserve represents some increase in demand for wheat, at least during the time the reserve quantity is being acquired. More importantly, it provides a type of food insurance at a time when food supplies might be short. Grain could be purchased from the market, but experience shows purchases for humanitarian needs get scaled down after prices have risen sharply.

GENERAL ECONOMIC POLICY

General economic policies of the nation affect both the prices farmers receive for their grain and the incomes of grain marketing firms. Monetary and fiscal policies affect interest rates and foreign exchange rates, which in turn affect the prices farmers receive for grain.

Changes in interest rates affect prices mainly through changes in the cost of holding grain in storage. In early 1980, the prime interest rate rose from about 12 to 20 percent, as the Federal Reserve Bank sought to slow inflation by curtailing the rate of growth in the money supply. An interest rate increase of 8 percentage points would raise the interest cost for holding a bushel of soybeans (valued at $6) by 24 cents for a six-month period. This increase would cause more soybeans to be placed on the cash market and would lower prices accordingly. A similar change in interest rates would raise the six-month cost of holding a bushel of corn valued at $2.50 by 10 cents. During periods of tight credit, some farmers would probably be unable to get operating credit and would be forced to sell grain to meet expenses. This would put further downward pressure on prices.

From the Bretton Woods Conference in 1944, the United States and its major trading partners operated until 1973 with fixed exchange rates for each currency. Under this system the U.S. dollar had an important role as a major reserve currency. As a supplier of a major reserve currency, the United States ran a persistent deficit in its balance of payments.

This system worked reasonably well until inflation accelerated in the United States in the late 1960s. Gradually the U.S. dollar became overvalued at fixed exchange rates relative to other currencies. Foreigners became less willing to hold U.S. dollars at established prices.

In a 13-month period in 1972 and 1973, the United States moved to a market-determined exchange rate. With persistent high rates of inflation in the United States during the 1970s, the dollar declined in value relative to other major world currencies. Rates fluctuated relative to the German mark and Japanese yen during the 1970s, but the general trend was downward.

A declining exchange rate contributes to higher U.S. grain prices. Since a devaluation of the dollar means a revaluation of the other currency, holders of the other currency (e.g., marks) have to put up fewer units of them to buy a unit of U.S. grain. At lower prices, foreigners tend to purchase more of our grain. This leads to higher prices in dollars, especially if the supply of grain in the United States is relatively inelastic.

Monetary and fiscal policy has other diverse effects on grain prices. During inflationary periods, people seek to protect their wealth by acquiring assets that increase in value along with the rate of inflation rather than hold their wealth in money. They may buy precious metals, commodities, or land in an attempt to protect their wealth. Thus, money may move in and out of the commodity market affecting commodity prices as a result of changing monetary and fiscal policies.

Inflation affects commodity prices in other less direct ways. Although commodity prices do not necessarily advance with the rate of inflation in the short run, they tend to advance in the long run because of changes in the cost structure for producing grains. Farmers purchase over 80 percent of their inputs from the industrial sector, which operates on a cost-plus basis and is able to pass on its costs due to its form of industrial organization. As higher costs are passed on to farmers, they may be in a cost-price squeeze in the short-run since they cannot pass on higher costs. In the longer run, however, producers adjust production and/or revalue their production assets in order to cover their full costs of production. Farmers receive help from government in doing this when target prices are adjusted upward based on changes in the cost of production.

Antitrust Policy. In the introduction to this chapter it was noted that the federal government attempts to affect performance of the economy by trying to make it more competitive. Grain marketing, especially in export markets, is concentrated in the hands of a small number of firms. It has been estimated that 60 percent of all U.S. grain exports are handled by the six largest international firms. Cooperatives handle only about 7 percent of U.S. grain exports.[18]

The federal government does not have any explicit policies that deal with market structure in terms of the number, size, and location of plants and firms in the grain marketing industry.[19] Instead, it tends to be concerned over mergers and their potential impacts. In recent years, the federal government has attempted to promote competition in export grain marketing by encouraging cooperatives to increase their share of the market. These actions have been undertaken through the USDA's Farmer Cooperative Service.

POLICIES FOR ALTERNATIVE MARKETING SYSTEMS

As noted in the introduction, the U.S. grain marketing system is essentially a privately owned system, rather than a government-owned or operated system. Government influences the system through the many policies discussed in this chapter.

[18]Co-ops are involved in a large share of U.S. grain exports but not through all stages of the exporting process. The five large companies sell grain both c.i.f. and f.o.b. while the co-ops tend to sell f.o.b., leaving the final stages to the private firms.

[19]Dale C. Dahl, "Public Policy Changes Needed to Cope with Changing Structure," *American Journal of Agricultural Economics,* Vol. 57, No. 2, May 1975, pp. 206–213.

The large increase in grain exports during the 1970s and the large price variations that occurred have raised questions about the conduct and performance of the system. These questions arise, in part, because of the way the world grain marketing system is organized. The concentration of market power, and the differences among countries in the organization of their markets, raise questions about equitability of treatment of the many participants in the system, especially U.S. farmers.

Grain marketing in Canada and Australia is conducted by government-sanctioned marketing boards. The boards are jointly controlled by representatives of farmers, consumers, and governments and are given monopoly control over most domestic sales to flour mills and the export marketing of grain. Farmers pool their wheat and, in effect, turn over the marketing functions to the board. They share in proceeds from the pool after all wheat is sold. Therefore, farmers receive an average-for-the-year price for their wheat.

Many countries, such as the U.S.S.R., China, and India, have state purchasing agencies that have responsibility for purchase of all imported grain. In countries such as the U.S.S.R., the purchasing agency has at least one advantage when dealing with firms in a market economy. They have a high degree of control over information about domestic crop conditions, internal feed and food needs, and government policy decisions about imports. This may enable them to manipulate world markets and exert a degree of monopsony power in purchasing grain.

It has been estimated that as much as 90 percent of all wheat that enters world trade involves state traders or marketing boards on at least one side of the transaction. Given this large variation from the competitive model, various proposals have been made to change the U.S. system to one that would more effectively deal with state traders. These proposals include establishment of a marketing board for the United States, or turning all export marketing over to the CCC. Other proposals include joining with Canada, Australia, the EC and Argentina to form a cartel for marketing wheat.

These and other proposals will likely receive much discussion and study over the next decade. The current state of knowledge is too inadequate to determine whether U.S. producers would benefit from any of the proposals, or whether any of the proposals would be feasible in the long run.

Summary

Grain marketing in the United States is conducted by a privately owned grain marketing system. Although the system is private it has been molded by various government policies and programs. These policies affect both the system and the prices that farmers received for their grain.

Policies have been designed to attain economic, political, and social stability, economic growth and equality of opportunity for U.S. citizens. The United States has also been willing to share its argicultural abundance with other countries. The process by which the U.S. system formulates policy is a slow-moving, complex one, which tries to reconcile the diverse interests of many conflicting groups.

Agricultural policies have followed two general trends. On one hand, policies were designed to make the private production and marketing system work more efficiently. These types of policies predominated prior to the 1930s and continue today, but in a lesser role. Since the 1930s, the government has intervened directly in markets to affect both the marketing system and the prices which producers receive for their grain.

Policies have changed over time and will continue to do so in response to changing technical and economic conditions in the United States and in the world. To try to understand government policies for grain production and marketing without study of the technical and economic environment is like trying to understand the behavior of a boat in the river without observation and study of the water in which it is operating.

A graphic approach was presented for analysis of commodity programs in a closed economy. The partial equilibrium approach enables the analyst to determine the effects of a program on price, production, consumption, storage, and government costs. Inferences can be drawn about the effects of the program on the marketing system.

A brief history of trade policies in the United States points out variations in U.S. trade policies, from restricting trade to freeing up trade and back again to restricting trade. Since the mid-1930s, efforts have been made to promote freer trade even though protectionist tendencies always lurk near the surface.

Recognizing the dramatic growth of trade in agricultural products that occurred during the 1970s, the graphic approach was expanded in order to analyze programs in an open economy. This approach makes it possible to show how U.S. grain prices are determined by the interaction of supply and demand in the United States and supply and demand in importing countries. The tendency for many countries to develop domestic programs to influence farm prices and incomes within their own country has important repercussions for trade in agricultural products. Since domestic objectives generally take precedence over trade objectives, trade policies tend to be modified accordingly.

Since the export market has become such a large component of total demand for U.S. grain, U.S. prices have become more variable than they were during the 1950s and 1960s. The government has used embargoes, an export reporting system, and long term agreements with several nations to try to stabilize world and U.S. grain prices. A farmer-owned grain reserve, which accumulates grain during periods of abundance and feeds it back into the system during periods of below trend production, has been developed in the United States. The U.S. continues to contribute to food security programs for less developed countries.

General economic policy, particularly monetary and fiscal policy, affects grain marketing. Prices are influenced through changes in the interest rate and changes in foreign exchange rates.

Six multinational grain firms dominate private world trade in grain. Their ability to serve U.S. farmers' needs when facing a world characterized by national marketing boards and state trading agencies continues to be questioned and evaluated.

Selected References

Agricultural Stabilization and Conservation Service, *Acquisition and Disposal of Farm Commodities by CCC,* USDA, ASCS Background Information B.I. No. 3, Washington, D.C., October 1975.

Cotterill, Ronald, *Cartel and Embargoes as Instruments of American Foreign Policy,* Agricultural Economics Report No. 373, Michigan State University, East Lansing, April 1980.

Dahl, Dale C., "Public Policy Changes Needed to Cope with Changing Structure," *American Journal of Agricultural Economics,* Vol. 57, No. 2, May 1975.

Export Grain Sales, hearing before the Subcommittee on SBA and SBIC Authority and General Small Business Problems of the Committee on Small Business, House of Representatives, 96th Congress, First Session, June 11, 1979, U.S. Government Printing Office, Washington, D.C., 1979.

Hathaway, Dale E., *Government and Agriculture,* The Macmillan Company, New York, 1963.

Hilker, James, H. and Bob F. Jones, *A Stochastic Simulation Analysis of the U.S.-USSR Grain Purchase Agreement,* Department of Agricultural Economics, Agricultural Experiment Station Bulletin No. 356, Purdue University, West Lafayette, Ind., December 1981.

Jones, Bob F. and Robert L. Thompson, "Interrelationship of Domestic Agricultural Policies and Trade Policies," in *Speaking of Trade: Its Effect on Agriculture,* University of Minnesota, Special Report No. 72, Minneapolis, 1978.

"President Johnson's Message on Agriculture," transmitted to 88th Congress, Second Session, January 31, 1964, printed in *Congressional Quarterly Almanac,* Congressional Quarterly Service, Washington, D.C., 20:887, 1964.

Public Law 97-98, 95 Stat. 1213, 97th Congress, December 22, 1981.

Rasmussen, Wayne D. and Gladys L. Baker, *Price Support and Adjustment Programs From 1933 Through 1978: A Short History,* Economics, Statistics, and Cooperatives Service, USDA, AIB-424, Washington, D.C., February 1979.

Ryan, Mary E. and Robert L. Tontz, "A Historical Review of World Trade Policies and

Institutions," in *Speaking of Trade: Its Effects on Agriculture,* University of Minnesota, Special Report No. 72, Minneapolis, 1978.

Talbot, Ross B. and Don F. Hadwiger, *The Policy Process in American Agriculture,* Chandler Publishing Company, San Francisco, Cal., 1968.

Thurston, Stanley K., Michael J. Phillips, James E. Haskell, and David Volkin, *Improving the Export Capability of Grain Cooperatives,* Farmer Cooperative Service, USDA, FCS Research Report No. 34, Washington, D.C., June 1976.

Tontz, Robert L., "U.S. Trade Policy: Background and Historical Trends," in *U.S. Trade Policy and Agricultural Exports,* Iowa State University Press, Ames, 1937.

CANADA'S GRAIN
MARKETING SYSTEM

CANADA'S GRAIN MARKETING SYSTEM*

CHAPTER 11

Almost 90 percent of Canada's grain is produced in three western prairie provinces: Alberta, Saskatchewan, and Manitoba. Of this production, more than 50 percent is exported. Grain was the major contributor to the economic development of western Canada, and the grain industry today remains as one of Canada's most important. It ranks second, behind the lumber industry, as an earner of foreign exchange.

The development of the early system of marketing grain in Canada closely paralleled that of the United States. Because the establishment of the grain economy in Canada lagged behind that in the United States by about 40 years, it was relatively attractive for Canadians to adopt the American open market grain marketing system, one that had many of its inefficiencies already worked out.

The first export shipment of wheat from the Canadian prairies took place in 1876. From the time of this shipment until World War I the marketing was handled by private companies, as it was in the United States. Circumstances surrounding the two world wars, and the Great Depression between them, resulted in Canada taking a much different approach than the United States to the marketing of its major export commodity, grain.

The following discussion traces the origins of the present grain marketing policies and institutions in Canada and it outlines the workings of the Canadian grain marketing system. There is an intricate mixture of government, cooperative, and private enterprise in the Canadian grain markets, and for this reason it is a complicated system. Only its major characteristics and institutions are described in this chapter.

Grains are marketed in Canada through one of three channels: the Canadian Wheat Board (CWB), the dual CWB-open market system, or the open market. For some types of grain only one channel is available as a market, and for others the producers have a choice. The first section of this chapter presents the historical development of the present-day system. Each of the three markets are then discussed in the above order and, following that, the major government regulations and support programs that affect the industry are described.

*Colin A. Carter, Assistant Professor, Department of Agricultural Economics, University of Manitoba, Winnipeg.

As an aid to the following discussion, Table 11-1 presents production and export figures for the major Canadian grains. Normally, about 50 percent of Canada's seeded acreage is planted to wheat every year, making it by far the most important crop. About 90 percent of the 20 million tons of wheat produced every year is hard red spring and the remainder is mostly durum, which is used in pasta products.

Canada normally exports more than 75 percent of its wheat and it is the second largest exporter in the world, behind the United States. At one time it was the largest wheat exporter; however, during the 1960s and 1970s, its market share fell behind that of the United States. Most of the wheat produced in Canada is marketed through the CWB.

In terms of world barley production Canada ranks second behind Soviet Russia. Of the 11 million tons produced, about 4.2 million are exported, on average, making Canada the world's largest barley

Table 11-1 Canadian Grain Production and Exports, 1977/78 to 1981/82

Grain Crop	Crop Year (August 1 through July 31)					Average (1977 to 1982)
	1977/78	*1978/79·*	*1979/80*	*1980/81*	*1981/82*	
Wheat						
Production	19,862	21,145	17,184	19,158	24,360	20,342
Exports	16,041	13,085	15,888	16,260	17,200[a]	15,695[a]
Oats						
Production	4,303	3,620	2,978	3,028	3,591	3,504
Exports	91	17	103	46	90[a]	69[a]
Barley						
Production	11,799	10,388	8,460	11,259	13,317	11,045
Exports	3,589	3,862	4,147	3,574	5,800[a]	4,194[a]
Rye						
Production	406	605	525	448	959	589
Exports	263	154	397	446	500[a]	354[a]
Flaxseed						
Production	653	571	815	465	485	598
Exports	271	493	449	563	475[a]	449[a]
Rapeseed						
Production	1,973	3,497	3,411	2,483	1,991	2,671
Exports	1,014	1,721	1,743	1,372	1,300[a]	1,430[a]
Corn						
Production	4,197	4,033	4,983	5,434	6,136	4,957
Exports	325	193	345	240	240[a]	269[a]
Soybeans						
Production	580	516	671	713	631	622
Exports	64	91	54	142	142[a]	99[a]

[a]Preliminary.

Source: Canada Grains Council, *Statistical Handbook '81,* Winnipeg, Manitoba.

exporter, with France a close second. Less than one-half of the barley crop is marketed through the CWB.

Canada is the world's largest producer of rapeseed, the second largest producer of flaxseed (behind Argentina), and the major exporter of both of these oilseeds. These commodities are handled in the open market.

The majority of the oats produced in Canada is marketed for feed usage outside of the elevator system through farm-to-farm and farm-to-feedlot sales.

Approximately 4.9 million tons of corn are produced annually, primarily in eastern Canada. This is outside of the designated CWB area, and its marketing is mainly through local direct sales for feed purposes.

On an individual basis, the remaining crops of rye, soybeans, sunflowers, fababeans, lentils, and forage seeds are produced on a smaller scale.

The major structural links in the Canadian grain market are shown in Figure 11-1. This chapter is basically a discussion of the marketing flows shown in this figure.

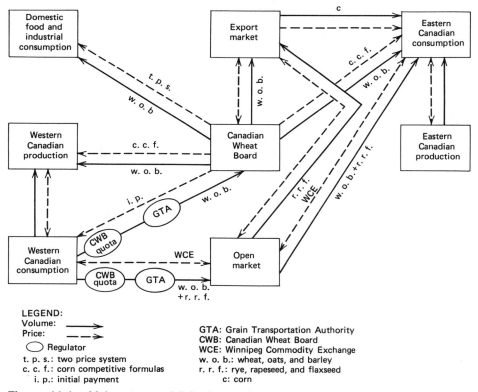

Figure 11-1. Major structural links in the Canadian grain markets.

HISTORICAL DEVELOPMENT

Prior to the turn of the twentieth century, the main marketing problems in Canada were related to grading standards and the preservation of competition at local delivery points, where railways were granting line elevator companies monopoly loading rights. The passing of the General Inspection Act (1886), the Manitoba Grain Act (1900), and the Canada Grain Act (1912), by the Canadian government, cumulatively established stringent statutory grades and provisions for the supervision of cleaning and shipping grain. This legislation corrected the early marketing problems, encouraged competition in the industry, and established a reputation for Canada as a producer of quality grain.

Price formation in the early years took place on the Winnipeg Grain and Produce Exchange, which was established in 1887. This was originally a cash grain market but, following the model of the Chicago markets, it commenced trading in wheat futures in 1904. The marketing of grain was handled by the open market until World War I broke out in 1914. The war had a major impact on the structure of the grain markets, primarily because the British government took control of grain export licenses from Canada during this period. The import purchasing agency of the British government "cornered" the wheat futures market in the spring of 1917 and as a result the market was closed. For the first time the Canadian government became directly involved in the marketing of grain through the appointment of the Board of Grain Supervisors, who were charged with selling the 1917 and 1918 wheat crops. For the entire 1919 crop the government temporarily appointed a Canadian Wheat Board. It borrowed the Australian system of pooling sales and giving producers an initial cash payment at the time of delivery and then a subsequent final payment based on net returns to the Board during the crop year. This Board was never intended as a permanent agency and consequently wheat futures trading resumed in Winnipeg in 1920. During the 1920s it became the most active wheat futures market in the world.

The farmer cooperative movement swept western Canada, in the early 1920s, as farmers placed some of the blame for low grain prices on the private grain merchants. Producers were requested to join voluntary marketing pools for a minimum of five years. The campaigning was very successful and the participation rate was high as by 1930 the Alberta, Saskatchewan, and Manitoba Pools had over 50 percent of farmers' marketings. By this time they also had control of approximately 50 percent of the total country elevator capacity. This was a tremendous feat in a short period of about seven years. Disaster struck the pools at the pinnacle of their success however. On behalf of the three prairie pools, their Central Selling Agency (CSA) marketed their grain. It advanced an initial payment to farmers at the beginning of the year and pooled returns much as the CWB had done in 1919. However, its failure to forward sell or hedge the 1929 crop resulted in massive losses as the grain prices fell drastically that year. This marked the end of farmer cooperative grain marketing on a large scale in Canada.

The federal government intervened at this point to guarantee the bank loans on the debt amassed by the pools and it was directly involved in the grain markets, controlling the operations of the CSA for the next five years. The government supported wheat futures prices by purchasing wheat futures contracts and in 1935 it reappointed the CWB. It was set up as a voluntary marketing board with a government guaranteed floor price. During World War II, the demand for grain raised prices and in 1943 the CWB was made a compulsory marketing board in order to control prices in line with the government's antiinflationary policy. The Winnipeg wheat futures market was simultaneously closed in September 1943. The compulsory board was intended to last two years at the most, but it has had sole authority over the marketing of all subsequent wheat crops. The reason the CWB was retained after the war was that most of Canada's wheat was exported to Britain under bilateral agreements and the CWB made the administration of the agreement much simpler.

In 1949 the CWB was also given the sole marketing rights for oats and barley as well as wheat, and in 1967 the passage of the Canadian Wheat Board Act made it a permanent board.

During the 1940s and 1950s, the open market with futures trading continued to operate for the merchandising of flaxseed, rye and intraprovincial feed grain sales. The CWB participated in this market to a limited extent. In the early 1960s, rapeseed production increased rapidly in western Canada and the Winnipeg Commodity Exchange initiated the open market handling of this oilseed.

The monopoly power the CWB had over domestic feed grain sales was relaxed in 1974 when the government allowed for off-board sales of feed grains interprovincially. The CWB retained its sole control over feed grain exports however.

THE CANADIAN WHEAT BOARD

The CWB is an agency of the government of Canada and is primarily a sales agency. It owns no physical facilities for the handling of grain. As set out in the Wheat Board Act of 1967, its major objectives are to the following.[1]

Market wheat, oats, and barley delivered to it in order to maximize producer returns.

Provide producers with initial payments established and guaranteed by the federal government.

[1]C.F. Wilson, *Grain Marketing in Canada,* Canadian International Grains Institute, Winnipeg, Manitoba, 1979, p. 65.

Pool selling prices for the same grain so that all producers get the same basic return for the same grain and grade delivered.

Equalize deliveries through quotas so that each producer gets a fair share of available markets.

The CWB is comprised of between three and five commissioners, who are appointed by the government and one of whom is the Chief Commissioner. The total staff of the CWB numbers approximately 600. The commissioners seek advice from an advisory committee elected by producers, but they are not responsible to them. Unlike the Australian Wheat Board, the CWB is a *government* rather than a *producer* board.

Wheat, barley, and oats are the only grains handled by the CWB, and it employs the services of both private and cooperative elevator companies to carry out the logistics of physically handling the grain that it buys and sells.

Table 11-2   Primary Elevator Receipts of Wheat, Oats, and Barley, Board and Open Market by Crop Year; Alberta, British Columbia, Manitoba, and Saskatchewan

Year and Commodity	Open Market (thousand tons)	Receipts (percent of total)	Board (thousand tons)	Percent of Total	Total (thousand tons)
1975/76					
Wheat	153.8	01	11,729.1	99	11,882.9
Oats	323.5	41	462.9	59	786.4
Barley	1,205.6	26	3,462.8	74	4,668.4
1976/77					
Wheat	350.3	03	12,955.4	97	13,305.7
Oats	316.4	38	521.1	62	837.5
Barley	872.7	15	4,902.4	85	5,775.1
1977/78					
Wheat	619.5	04	16,519.4	96	17,138.9
Oats	370.8	50	376.4	50	747.2
Barley	1,392.9	27	3,756.6	73	5,149.5
1978/79					
Wheat	907.4	07	11,913.1	93	12,820.5
Oats	295.2	88	40.4	12	335.6
Barley	1,871.9	36	3,321.6	64	5,193.5
1979/80					
Wheat	241.4	01	16,358.3	99	16,599.7
Oats	286.2	91	29.5	09	315.7
Barley	1,308.9	24	4,046.1	76	5,355.0
1980/81					
Wheat	289.4	02	14,995.9	98	15,285.3
Oats	321.7	92	26.8	08	348.5
Barley	816.6	13	5,222.7	87	6,039.3

Source: Canada Grains Council, *Domestic Feed Grain Policy Study*, Winnipeg, Manitoba, 1981.

When selling to the CWB, producers' marketing costs are deducted in two stages. Freight costs and primary elevator handling costs are deducted from the initial payment at the time of delivery. The other costs (which include interest, insurance, storage, terminal elevator handling charges, and the Board's operating costs) are later charged against the pool.

For the three grains it handles, the CWB has monopoly rights over both their exports and domestic sales for human consumption. However, a large percentage of the production of both barley and oats is marketed locally and does not even enter the elevator system. Approximately 95 percent of the wheat production enters the elevator system, in contrast to 60 percent of the barley and only 20 percent of the oats. An average of about 97 percent of the wheat that enters the elevator system is delivered to the CWB. This government agency also markets approximately 76 percent of the barley and 33 percent of the oats sold through the system. These figures are shown in Table 11-2 for the 1975/1976 through 1980/1981 crop years.

At the beginning of each crop year, which runs from August 1 through July 31, the government of Canada establishes initial producer prices. All CWB sales within a given crop year are pooled. Producers thus receive the initial payment at the time of delivery, in some years an interim payment during the crop year, and then a final payment once the pool is closed and the CWB deducts its administrative

Table 11-3 Canadian Wheat Board Prices
Paid to Producers, In-store, Thunder Bay, Ontario
(Canadian dollars per bushel)

Crop and Payment	Crop Year				
	1976/77	*1977/78*	*1978/79*	*1979/80*	*1980/81*
Wheat[a]					
Initial	3.00	3.00	3.00	3.50	4.25
Interim	0.00	0.00	0.50	0.75	1.10
Final	0.19	0.27	0.87	1.09	0.70
Oats[b]					
Initial	1.15	1.15	1.14	1.05	1.05
Interim	0.00	0.00	0.00	0.00	0.31
Final	0.15	0.00	0.17	0.00	0.57
Barley[b]					
Initial	1.75	1.75	1.65	1.75	2.70
Interim	0.00	0.00	0.08	0.20	0.15
Final	0.24	0.17	0.25	0.39	0.34

[a]No. 1 Canadian western red spring.
[b]No. 1 Feed.

Source: Canadian Wheat Board, *Annual Report (1980/81),* Winnipeg, Manitoba.

expenses from the pool. Each producer receives the same price (before freight deductions) no matter when the grain is sold to the Board during a particular crop year. The Board has five pools: one each for wheat, durum, barley, malting barley, and oats. Table 11-3 presents initial, interim and final payments for these pools between 1976/77 and 1980/81.

Domestic sales of wheat by the CWB to millers takes place at prices that are to some extent insulated from world price levels. This is referred to as the two-price wheat policy. This policy has been in effect since 1967. During the 1970s the Canadian government fixed the domestic price to mills, and thus subsidized consumers when prices were above these levels. Currently the domestic price is allowed to vary within a band of $5 to $7 per bushel (for No. 1 CWRS[2] in-store, Thunder Bay, Ontario), and the government is no longer involved in subsidizing either producers or consumers if the world price falls outside of this range. A brief description of the two price-policy, divided into eight time periods, appears in Table 11-4. The two-price system has been a controversial and complicated pricing policy. Its cost to taxpayers was estimated to be $473 million during the first 10 years it was in effect. Producers have neither gained nor lost significantly from the program and consumers have received benefits of approximately $470 million. These, uncompounded, are given in Table 11-5.

Export sales of wheat and barley by the CWB now involve mainly direct sales to national trading agencies of importing countries. These direct sales account for between 70 and 80 percent of the Board's exports. This is in sharp contrast to the practice of the CWB selling to the private grain trade in the 1950s and 1960s. The rising importance of sales to centrally planned economies and declining importance of sales to western Europe account for this major shift away from sales to intermediaries and towards direct sales.

Almost one-half of Canadian wheat exports are currently shipped under long-term agreements (LTA's) with importers. These agreements are signed for varying lengths of time and normally cover a minimum volume of trade to be carried out each year during the agreement. Separate sales contracts are negotiated under each LTA and pricing is often done on a semiannual or quarterly basis. When the LTA is initially signed, specific details such as grades or prices are not agreed on. Once the grain starts moving under the agreement these are worked out and normally a flat price applies to shipments for a three- to six-month period, after which it is renegotiated. At the present time the CWB has LTA's with 13 different countries. Table 11-6 provides details of some important LTA's between the CWB and importing nations.

----

[2]Canadian western red spring wheat.

Table 11-4   Balance Sheet for Two-Price Wheat

Period	*Program Details*
The First Six Years	
1. Aug. 1, 1967 to June 30, 1968	A minimum return to producers was established for sales on both export and domestic markets at $1.955 per bushel for No. 1 northern in-store Thunder Bay. The government paid producers the difference between this minimum return and actual sales value. The gains to producers on the domestic market are shown in Table 11-5.
2. Aug. 1, 1969 to July 31, 1972	The domestic price was fixed at $1.955 for No. 1 northern in-store Thunder Bay. When the export price fell below this level, consumers paid a higher-than-export price for their wheat, thereby subsidizing producers.
3. Aug. 1, 1972 to July 20, 1973	The government paid a subsidy (to a maximum of $1.045 per bushel) in the form of an acreage payment to producers to increase their return on domestic sales of wheat to $3.00. Domestic prices charged to mills remained at $1.955 per bushel.
4. July 20, 1973 to Sept. 11, 1973	The domestic price for wheat was allowed to vary at $1 below the export price.
The New Two-Price Wheat Policy	
5. Sept. 11, 1973 to Nov. 30, 1978	The domestic price for wheat other than durum was fixed at $3.25 per bushel, and the maximum domestic price for durum was $5.75 per bushel. The government paid a consumer subsidy (to a maximum of $1.75 per bushel) to bring producer returns to a maximum of $5.00 for wheat other than durum and $7.50 for durum. When the export price rose above these maximums, producers subsidized consumers.
6. Aug. 1, 1977 to July 31, 1978	The policy continued as in the previous period with one exception. The government paid a subsidy to producers to bring the minimum return on domestic wheat sales to $3.55 per bushel.
7. Dec. 1, 1978 to July 31, 1980	Domestic mills paid the export price for durum and wheat within a specific range set by the government. The maximum domestic price for durum was $7.50 per bushel and the maximum for other wheat was $5.00 per bushel. When the export price rose above these levels, as they did in June and July, 1979 and throughout the 1979/80 crop year, producers realized a loss of $62.2 million of which western farmers' share was $54.7 million.
8. Aug. 1, 1980 to July 31, 1981	The domestic price range for No. 1 CWRS in-store Thunder Bay is between $5.00 and $7.00 per bushel. For durum, the domestic price is a minimum of $5.00, with no maximum.

Source: Canadian Wheat Board, *Grain Matters*, Winnipeg, Manitoba, November–December 1981.

Table 11-5 Estimated Income Transfers
Under the Two-price Wheat Program, 1967 to 1980
(million Canadian dollars)

Period[a]	Producers[b] Loss	Producers[b] Gain	Consumers Loss	Consumers Gain	Government Cost
1		1.4			1.4
2		40.0	40.0		
3		70.0			70.0
4	11.3			11.3	
1967 to 1973	11.3	111.4	40.0	11.3	71.4
5	35.0			431.3	396.3
6		4.9			4.9
7	62.2			62.2	
8	4.7			4.7	
1973 to 1980	101.9	4.9		498.2	401.2
1967 to 1980	113.2	116.3	40.0	509.5	472.6

[a]See Table 11-4 for appropriate time frames.
[b]Includes eastern producers.

Source: Canadian Wheat Board, *Grain Matters,* Winnipeg, Manitoba, November–December 1981.

THE DUAL FEED GRAIN MARKET

The CWB had monopoly selling privileges for all interprovincial feed grain movement from the late 1940s until 1974. The Canadian government changed the feed grain policy in 1974 and created a dual marketing system for feed grains. This allowed for the domestic sales of feed grain either through private (e.g., Cargill, Continental, N. M. Patterson, Pioneer) and cooperative (e.g., United Grain Growers, Alberta Wheat Pool, Saskatchewan Wheat Pool, Manitoba Pool) grain companies or through the CWB. To facilitate the "open" or "non-Board" market, futures trading in feed barley, feed wheat and feed

Table 11-6 Countries with Long-Term Agreements
with Canada

Country	Date L.T.A. Came into Effect	Expiration Date	Minimum-Maximum (thousand tons)	Grain
Brazil	1/1/80	12/31/82	3,000 to 3,900	Wheat
China	8/1/79	7/31/82	8,400 to 10,500	Wheat
Jamaica	1/1/79	12/31/81	150 to 255	Wheat
Mexico	8/1/81	12/31/82	200 to 500	Wheat
Poland	1/1/80	12/31/82	3,000 to 4,500	Wheat, durum, barley, and oats
USSR	8/1/81	7/31/86	25,000 minimum	Wheat, durum, and feed grain

Source: Canadian Wheat Board, *Grain Matters,* Winnipeg, Manitoba, October 1981.

oats was started on the Winnipeg Commodity Exchange. The private and cooperative grain companies trade actively on the market, with the cooperatives being the major participants.

The 1974 radical change in market structure was brought about to correct regional feed grain price differences that greatly exceeded transportation costs. Livestock feeders outside of the prairie provinces did not have open access to low-priced western Canadian feed grains with the CWB acting as the sole supplier. The CWB's participation in the domestic feed grain market was reduced significantly with this policy change. The open market is now the major supplier of prairie feed grains to eastern Canadian and British Columbian livestock feeders. As indicated above, there also is a significant amount of feed grain sales that do not enter the elevator system. They are particularly common in Alberta where 50 percent of the feed grains produced is used locally. Over the past few years, eastern Canada has also increased its corn production to the extent it has become less and less dependent on western Canadian feed grains. Export and local markets have thus become the most important for the western feed grain producer.

After the policy change of 1974 the CWB acted primarily as a supplier of last resort to eastern livestock feeders. However, barley was selling at a premium to corn, during parts of 1974 and 1975, and Canadian livestock feeders were still dissatisfied with having to pay world prices for feed barley. As a result, since 1976 the CWB has been required to sell feed grains domestically at an administered price—the "corn competitive formula" price (c.c.f.). For livestock feeders the formula prices are alternatives to open market purchases. The c.c.f. is monitored and adjusted on a daily basis by the CWB and the Canadian Livestock Feed Board (CLFB) and there is one formula for each of feed wheat, oats, and barley. According to the formula, grain is priced in relation to its digestible energy and protein content, and the value of energy and protein are determined by the Chicago Board of Trade's prices of corn and soymeal, respectively.[3]

From the time of their inception until mid-1979, the formula prices were ineffective because they were generally above world feed grain prices. Little grain was sold at the formula prices and they did not impinge on price determination in the open market. The 1976 to 1979 period was, for the most part, a period of depressed world feed grain prices. During the 1980/81 period, world feed grain (particularly barley) prices strengthened, and the formula constrained the levels that domestic open market prices were allowed to reach.

The CWB must stand ready to sell feed grains within Canada at

---

[3]For an analysis of the shortcomings of the formula, see C.F. Carter and D. Kraft, "An Evaluation of Pricing Performance of the Canadian Feed Grains Policy: A Comment," *Canadian Journal of Agricultural Economics*, Vol. 29, No. 4, November 1981, pp. 349–354.

the c.c.f. prices. Almost all domestic sales, therefore, take place at or below this price because a domestic user would not normally bid more on the open market if he or she could buy from the CWB at the formula price. Since 1976, under the corn competitive formula, feed barley has been priced from $20 below to more than $70 above the CWB asking export price. The formula price has shown little relationship to the export price. When the formula is pricing feed grains under the export price, the opportunity loss to producers is substantial. Producers not only suffer due to the subsidy they are forced to provide through the c.c.f., but they also lose export opportunities for the feed grains as a result of the increased domestic consumption at artificially low prices.

The dual system is constrained in a number of ways and, as a result, the feed grain market has become somewhat fragmented. The corn formulas fix the CWB price, influence the open market price and, from time to time, undervalue domestic sales. Delivery quotas, which will be discussed in a later section, also apply to the open market feed grains, and prevent supply and demand from working freely in this market. Finally, the open market cannot make export sales. Therefore the dual system does not give the CWB and the open market companies the opportunity to work to the full advantage of the grain producer.

THE OPEN MARKET

As previously mentioned, the open market is made up of both farmer-owned cooperative and privately owned grain companies. These companies operate much the same as the grain companies in the United States, primarily as middlemen in the market. However, in Canada they have far more regulations and constraints to cope with.

The open market sales of feed grains are for Canadian domestic markets only. Rapeseed, flaxseed, and rye are also traded through the open market and, because these crops are not handled by the CWB, they are marketed in both domestic and international channels by the grain companies. A producer plebiscite in the early 1970s rejected the marketing of rapeseed through the CWB.

The major feed grains group, and the rye, rapeseed, and flaxseed groups, are dual and open market grains, respectively. The marketing of all six of these grains is controlled to a certain extent by the setting of their delivery quotas by the CWB. Prior to 1980, the CWB also controlled the allocation of rail cars for these grains.

The only true open market grains in Canada are, therefore, the specialty crops. These include soybeans, corn, fababeans, sunflowers, lentils, canaryseed, and forageseed. Producers of these crops generally market them through grain companies, without quota constraint. Most often these crops, except for corn and soybeans, are exported.

The majority of grain production outside of the prairies takes place in Ontario. The total nonprairie production is approximately 6.5 million tons of which 80 percent is in Ontario and 12 percent is in Quebec.

Wheat marketing in Ontario is controlled by the Ontario Wheat Producers' Marketing Board. Feed grain sales, which consist mainly of corn, are open market transactions.

Another component of open market sales is the amount of feed grain marketed outside of the elevator system. This accounts for about 30 percent of prairie grain production and represents on-farm usage, farm-to-farm, and farm-to-feedlot sales. Generally, the Winnipeg Commodity Exchange price is used as a reference point for pricing in this market.

MARKET REGULATIONS

The Canadian grain market is heavily regulated. Some of these regulations have developed to provide equity to producers, some to facilitate ease of marketing, and some to appease special interest groups. Major regulations include grain freight rates, producer delivery quotas, rail car allocation, corn formula prices, and grain licensing and grading.

Figure 11-2 shows the major grain transportation routes in Canada, from primary elevators to export ports. The bulk of the grain is moved by rail rather than truck or barge. Historically, rail rates for grain transportation have been at very low levels. These levels were essentially established in 1897 when the Canadian Pacific Railway

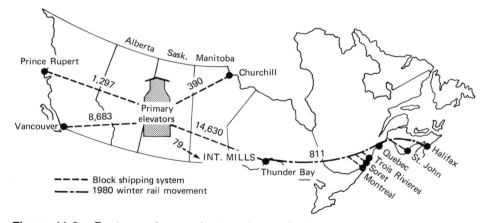

Figure 11-2. Routes and approximate volumes (in thousand tons) of Canadian grain moved by rail to export position in the 1980/81 crop year. (*Source:* Canadian International Grain Institute, *Grains and Oilseeds,* Winnipeg, Manitoba, 1982.)

(CPR) and the Canadian federal government signed the Crow's Nest Pass Agreement. As the major part of the agreement, the CPR lowered its freight rates on grain and promised to thereafter maintain the lower level. This was in return for a $3.4 million subsidy that enabled the CPR to build a rail line through the Crow's Nest Pass from southern Alberta to southern British Columbia.

These grain freight rates became the statutory rates in 1925 and they applied to grain and certain grain products moved by rail from western Canada to export position. The rates, as fixed, bore a relationship to distance from the ports (Thunder Bay, Vancouver) and averaged about 20 cents per hundredweight.

As a result of these fixed statutory rates the railways have been earning insufficient revenues. The Snavely report[4] estimated a railway shortfall of $612 million in 1981 for moving grain. This is the difference between the cost and revenues from moving grain. The grain rail system has deteriorated rapidly as a result. The CWB estimated that $1.1 billion in grain sales were either lost or deferred in the 1977 to 1979 period alone, due to inadequate and inefficient transportation services. During this period the build up of on-farm stocks of both wheat and barley was rapid in Canada, and this indicates there may have been transportation problems. The Canadian government recently initiated negotiations among the railways, farmers, and the government to rationalize the grain transportation system, and to gradually deregulate rail freight rates for grain.

For a thorough discussion of the economic impacts of the Crow's Nest rates and their removal, see Harvey.[5] His basic premise is that the Crow rates represent a direct subsidy to farmers in western Canada, paid by railway shareholders and Canadian taxpayers. Harvey believes that the rates should be changed to compensatory levels and that western grain producers should be compensated up to the net present value of the subsidized freight rates. However, he does not recognize that the rates have also been a burden on grain producers because low revenues have hampered the ability of the railway system to move Canada's grain into the export market.

Producer delivery quotas are another important set of regulations that apply to the six major grains produced in Canada (wheat, barley, oats, rye, rapeseed, and flaxseed). The CWB regulates producer deliveries to primary elevators through quotas on both Board and open market grains. Quotas have been in place since 1940, and their original purpose was to provide equitable access to markets by all producers. In the 1950s, they were also used to provide producers with equitable

[4]C. Snavely, "Costs of Transporting Grain by Rail," report prepared for Transport Canada, Washington, D.C., 1982.
[5]D.R. Harvey, *Christmas Turkey or Prairie Vulture? An Economic Analysis of the Crow's Nest Pass Grain Rates,* The Institute for Research on Public Policy, Ottawa, Ontario, 1980.

access to an elevator system that did not have sufficient capacity to handle the grain as fast as producers wished to deliver. In the 1960s and 1970s, the sales strategy of the CWB and the capacity of the transportation system began to influence quota levels and justify the continuation of the quota system. However, the quota system today is far from equitable. Grain producers are each assigned a base acreage whether the land is seeded or not. (Beginning in the 1982/83 crop year, producers who do not summerfallow heavily will receive bonus base acres.) Producers allocate their base acreage among the six different grains as they desire, and quotas are announced by the CWB as a fixed number of bushels per assigned acre for each grain. No allowance is made for varying yields across the prairies, and there has also been some concern that the delivery quotas give the CWB undue regulatory power to determine which grains are to be marketed. Quotas were particularly restrictive in the 1968 to 1971 and 1977 to 1979 periods, and farmers were forced to carry burdensome on-farm inventories.

As mentioned above, the Crow's Nest grain freight rates have contributed to an inadequate grain transportation system in Canada. Subsequent government regulation was required to provide farmers equitable access to the limited transportation service. The Grain Transportation Authority (GTA) is one of these regulatory bodies, and was formed in 1980 with the sole responsibility for the allocation of cars for the movement of grain. Figure 11-3 indicates the allocation procedure the GTA performs each week. This procedure was formerly handled by the CWB and is, therefore, not a new area of regulation.

The feed freight assistance program was developed in 1941 in order to subsidize freight costs on feed grain shipments from the prairies to eastern Canada and British Columbia. This program was truncated substantially in 1976, but it was an important factor in expanding domestic feed grain markets for prairie producers and in encouraging livestock production outside of the prairies. At the present time the feed freight assistance program costs approximately $16 million per year and applies in eastern Canada to shipments having a freight rate greater than that from Thunder Bay to Montreal. Feed grain purchasers in British Columbia also continue to receive freight assistance.

The government regulatory agency that is responsible for quality control of Canadian grain and for supervision of its handling is the Canadian Grain Commission. The Commission operates under the authority of the Canada Grain Act (1971). Among the most important of its functions are the inspection and grading of grain sold in Canada. The official inspection of grain is done on a visual basis and any new variety licensed for production must be visually distinguishable from any other variety. Canadian regulators have historically stressed the quality of grain production and this has resulted in a quality-quantity trade-off.

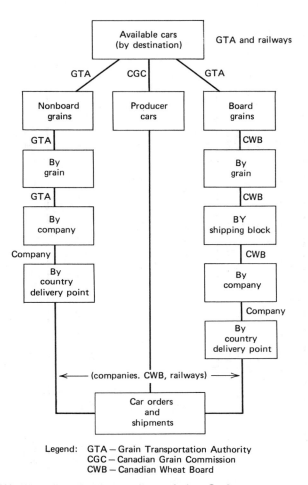

Figure 11-3. Weekly allocation procedure of the Grain Transportation Authority. (*Source:* Grain Transportation Authority, *Annual Review,* 1980/81, Winnipeg, Manitoba.)

GOVERNMENT SUPPORT

The major amount of government support in the Canadian grain industry has been in the form of transportation subsidies. The federal government has funded part of the "crow gap" that the railways have suffered as a result of moving grain at rates below cost. The feed grain freight assistance program is also financed by the government.

Unlike the U.S. government's involvement in the grain markets, Canadian policy does not involve direct income or price supports. One notable exception was the Lower Inventories for Tomorrow program in 1970, whereby farmers were paid to set aside acreage. The CWB's initial payment is guaranteed by the federal government but it has rarely acted as a support price.

Table 11-7 Level of Government Support in Canadian Wheat Production, 1965 to 1979

					Policy Transfers to Producers											
Year	Production (000 ton)	Price ($/ton)	Direct Deductions (000 $)[a]	Total Producer Value (000 $)	Two Price Wheat (000 $)	ASB Payment[b] (000 $)	Feed Freight Assistance (000 $)	Export Credit (000 $)	Western Grain Stabilization (000 $)	Corn Competitive (000 $)	Temporary Wheat Reserves Act (000 $)	Transport Subsidy (000 $)	Feed Freight Program (000 $)	Total Producer Subsidy (000 $)	Proportion Subsidy (%)	Subsidy per Unit ($/ton)
1965	17,674	73.38	102,297	1,194,621	—	—	4,105	—	—	—	33,355	66,567	—	104,027	8.71	5.88
1966	22,516	73.10	138,609	1,507,311	—	—	3,850	—	—	—	36,802	78,650	—	119,302	7.91	5.29
1967	16,137	66.65	99,340	976,191	—	—	2,753	—	—	—	46,775	60,342	—	109,870	11.25	6.80
1968	17,686	62.46	108,875	995,793	—	—	2,770	—	—	—	79,760	58,857	—	141,387	14.20	7.99
1969	18,267	61.73	112,452	1,015,170	—	—	5,573	—	—	—	53,914	61,881	—	121,368	11.96	6.64
1970	9,024	61.40	55,552	498,522	—	—	6,762	—	—	—	33,209	61,217	—	101,188	20.30	11.21
1971	14,412	58.64	88,720	756,400	—	—	5,324	2,291	—	—	25,801	87,707	—	121,123	16.01	8.40
1972	14,514	79.14	89,348	1,059,290	65,500	—	6,729	2,106	—	—	12,775	114,158	—	201,268	19.00	13.86
1973	16,159	168.21	99,475	3,618,630	118,179	—	5,190	5,996	—	—	—	102,865	—	232,230	8.87	14.37
1974	13,295	164.39	114,816	2,070,749	87,665	—	5,240	11,332	—	—	—	86,193	—	190,430	9.20	14.32
1975	17,078	156.28	156,913	2,341,257	65,422	—	3,456	9,666	—	—	—	113,634	1,387	193,565	8.27	11.33
1976	23,587	117.15	230,799	2,532,418	17,104	—	2,270	7,743	—	+1,259	—	125,871	638	154,885	6.12	6.56
1977	19,650	120.30	197,679	2,166,216	38,425	24,050	2,740	6,771	46,430	+564	—	200,579	1,180	320,735	14.81	16.32
1978	21,100	160.53	222,943	3,164,240	43,826	—	4,123	11,409	106,130	+715	—	161,015	1,171	328,389	10.38	15.56
1979	17,200	196.43	193,861	3,184,735	-54,600	16,844	3,147 est.	16,448	—	+431	—	220,890	808	203,968	6.40	11.85

[a]Direct deductions include transportation, handling, and elevation charges. These are deducted from producer revenue in order to obtain the total producer value at the farm level.

[b]Payments made by the Agricultural Stabilization Board under the Agricultural Stabilization Act.

Source: M. Glenn, C. Carter, and O. P. Tangri, "Government Support in the Grain Sector: A Canadian-U.S. Comparison," working paper, University of Manitoba, Winnipeg, 1982.

Table 11-7 provides estimates of the various levels of support provided to Canadian wheat producers from 1965 to 1979. The largest transfers occur as transportation subsidies. Over the 15-year period shown, the proportional subsidy in the wheat sector, which is the total producer subsidy as a percentage of the total producer value, averaged 11.56 percent. By comparison, the U.S. level was estimated to be 18.47 percent for the same period.[6] The U.S. level is also much more variable from year to year than the Canadian level.

Summary

This has been largely a descriptive analysis of the Canadian grain marketing system. It was shown to have many characteristics that make it substantially different from that in the United States. Unlike in the United States, there is a large degree of government involvement in Canadian grain sales, through its agency the CWB; the private grain trade is also active in Canada.

The history of the Canadian system was outlined as an introduction to a discussion of the three major marketing channels: the CWB, dual, and open markets. Government regulation and support was also described and briefly analyzed.

The Canadian and U.S. marketing systems continue to serve as interesting contrasts given that they have many similar production practices and are often competitors in foreign markets. Their grain marketing systems reflect significantly different approaches to similar marketing challenges.

Selected References

Carter, C. and D. Kraft, "Administered Versus Market Prices: An Analysis of the Canadian Feed Grain Market," working paper, University of Manitoba, Winnipeg, 1982.

Carter C. and D. Kraft, "An Evaluation of Pricing Performance of the Canadian Feed Grains Policy: A Comment," *Canadian Journal of Agricultural Economics*, Vol. 29, No. 4, November 1981.

Glenn, M., C. Carter, and O. P. Tangri, "Government Support in the Grain Sector: A Canadian-U.S. Comparison," working paper, University of Manitoba, Winnipeg, 1982.

Grains and Oilseeds: Handling, Marketing, Processing, Canadian International Grains Institute, Winnipeg, Manitoba, 1982.

Harvey, D. R., *Christmas Turkey or Prairie Vulture? An Economic Analysis of the Crow's Nest*

---

[6]M. Glenn, C. Carter, and O. P. Tangri, "Government Support in the Grain Sector: A Canadian—U.S. Comparison," working paper, University of Manitoba, Winnipeg, 1982.

Pass Grain Rates, The Institute for Research on Public Policy, Ottawa, Ontario, 1980.

McCalla, A. F. and A. Schmitz, "Grain Marketing Systems: The Case of the United States Versus Canada," *American Journal of Agricultural Economics,* Vol. 61, No. 2, May 1979.

Snavely, C., "Costs of Transporting Grain by Rail," report prepared for Transport Canada, Washington, D.C., 1982.

Storey, G. G. and S. N. Kulshreshtha, "An Evaluation of Pricing Performance of the Canadian Feed Grain Policy," *Canadian Journal of Agricultural Economics,* Vol. 29, No. 1, February 1981.

Wilson, C. F., *Grain Marketing in Canada,* Canadian International Grains Institute, Winnipeg, Manitoba, 1979.

GLOSSARY

Absolute Advantage—the ability of a nation to produce a greater amount of a good from a given set of resources than another nation can produce with a similar set of its resources.

Aeration—the practice of forcing air through bulk stored grain in order to maintain grain condition.

Agency Tariff—a tariff published by a publishing agent on behalf of two or more carriers participating in all or part of the rates and transport conditions described in the tariff.

Arbitrage—buying a commodity in one market and selling it in another because the prices in the two markets differ by more than the costs incurred in transferring that commodity from one market to the other.

Arc Elasticity of Demand—a measure of the price elasticity of demand between two points on a demand curve.

Back Haul—the use by carriers of their transport space to haul goods on the return trip rather than run empty.

Balance of Payments—a statement showing all of the transactions between residents of one country and all other nations, usually for one year.

Basis—the difference between a cash price and a specific futures price for a commodity, usually the near futures price.

Belief—our perception of "what is" in regard to the facts of a situation.

Bid—a proposal of price and other terms by a would-be buyer of a commodity.

Bilateral Agreements—agreements between an exporting and an importing country to purchase or sell a certain amount of products per year.

Blending—the systematic combining of two or more lots or kinds of grain to obtain a uniform mixture to meet a desired specification.

Booking the Basis—entering into a sales agreement that prescribes price in terms of the basis.

Buffer Stocks—reserve grain stocks that are available to handle the selling or purchase of grain in order to reduce price fluctuations in the grain market.

By-product—a secondary product that results from processing a commodity to obtain a primary product.

C. and f.—cost and freight to the designated delivery point, paid by the seller.

Canadian Wheat Board—an agency of the Canadian government with monopoly control over the export and domestic sales for human consumption of wheat, barley, and oats.

Carrying Charge Market—a market situation in which each successive future in the market is quoted at a higher price than the previous delivery month.

Carry-over—the amount of grain in inventory at the first (beginning carry-over) or last (ending carry-over) day of a designated crop year; the stock of grain available for consumption but not consumed in the year that it was produced, thus is available for consumption in a later year.

Cartel—a group of independent sellers who have joined forces in order to control the production and/or marketing of a commodity.

Cash Forward Contract—a forward contract made in the cash market as contrasted to one made in the futures market.

Cash Grain Merchant—any person or firm dealing in the buying or selling of grain.

Cash Market—a market other than the futures market, including spot markets and markets in forward contracts.

Certificate Final—a certification of the quality of a shipment of grain being exported.

Certificate of Competency—a Small Business Administration certification that a party seeking to contract with an agency of the U.S. government is qualified to fulfil the terms of the contract.

Charter Party—a contract binding ship owners and charterers of ocean freight shipments.

C.i.f.—cost, insurance, and freight to the designated delivery point, paid by the seller.

Class Rate—a freight rate based on a uniform classification of all freight hauled by rail or motor carriers.

Coarse Grains—includes feed grains (corn, barley, oats, and grain sorghum) and rye, plus millet in some foreign nations.

Commercial Storage—grain storage space that is commercially provided for a fee.

Commission Merchant—one who buys and sells grain for others on a consignment basis without taking title to the grain.

Commodity Credit Corporation (CCC)—created as an agency of the USDA in 1933 to carry out loan and storage operations as a means of supporting prices above the level that would have prevailed in a free market.

Commodity Futures Trading Commission (CFTC)—established in 1974 to take over the duties of the Commodity Exchange Authority, with emphasis on regulating and surveillance of futures trading; reports directly to the U.S. Congress.

Commodity Rate—a rate applicable to the specifically identified commodity or commodities only, and usually supersedes a class rate.

Common Agricultural Policy—a system of producer subsidies and import levies maintained by the EC (or other similar groupings of nations) to attain specific objectives supporting the agricultural industry in the 10 member nations.

Common Carrier—any person or firm licensed to transport goods, services, or people for a fee, with certain exemptions being granted motor carriers when hauling whole grain or grain products.

Complements—commodities that are used together because of the additional benefit obtained from using them in combination rather than singly. The computed cross price elasticity between such commodities is negative.

Comparative Advantage—a situation in which an individual or nation that is relatively superior at producing some goods gains by trading for other goods that another individual or nation is relatively more proficient at producing.

Concessional Sales—sales of commodities at terms more favorable to the recipient than at the going market rate; sales made or subsidized by the U.S. government.

Concurrence—an authorization for a publishing agent to issue a tariff on behalf of the carriers. A letter of concurrence constitutes a power of attorney assignment to the publishing agency in matters identified in the letter.

Conservation Reserve—a land conservation and supply control program designed to improve farm incomes by removing certain acreages of land from production. Also referred to as the Soil Bank program.

Consignment—a lot or shipment of a commodity that is placed under the control of an agent or broker for custody or sale.

Constructive Placement—placing a cargo-carrying vehicle in position for a shipper to load or unload when it cannot be placed at the elevator's rail siding.

Container Freight—freight that is shipped in sealed containers for loading on rail cars or oceangoing ships.

Corn Competitive Formula (c.c.f.)—the Canadian system of pricing grains on the basis of their digestible energy and protein content.

Country Elevator—an establishment that buys grain from farmers with facilities for receiving farmers' grains and shipping grains by truck or rail.

Country Merchandiser—is generally located in a rural area, buying grain from country elevators and selling it to terminal markets, processors, and exporters.

Crop-Fallow System—a management method that alternates the use of land between cropping and fallowing, especially in arid or semiarid areas, to improve soil moisture and fertility and control plant pests, diseases, and weeds.

Crop Year—the officially designated production and marketing year for a grain crop. For wheat, the crop year is from June 1 to May 31. For corn and soybeans, it is from October 1 to September 30.

Cross Price Elasticity of Demand—an index that measures the responsiveness of the quantity of a good X demanded to a 1 percent change in the price of another good Y, *ceteris paribus*.

Crow's Nest Pass Agreement—an agreement signed in 1897 between the government of Canada and the Canadian Pacific Railway to build a rail line through the Crow's Nest Pass between southern Alberta and southern British Columbia. The Canadian Pacific Railway agreed to maintain lower freight rates for shipping grain in return for a government subsidy to help build the rail line.

Customs Union—agreement by a group of nations, such as by the EC member nations, to eliminate tariffs and other restrictions on goods exchanged by those nations and to impose a uniform tariff policy on the exchange of goods with nonmember nations.

Deferred Payment—a payment at a prescribed (later) time after a change of ownership occurs.

Delayed Pricing—a form of cash trading used by country elevators when buying grain from farmers that provides for determining the price of the grain after ownership of the grain has been transferred.

Delivery—the act of transferring ownership or title from a seller to the buyer; it may or may not involve the physical movement of the commodity.

Demand—the quantities of a good or service that will be bought at various prices per unit of time, *ceteris paribus.*

Demand Curve—a graphic representation of the relationship between price and quantity demanded, *ceteris paribus.*

Demurrage—the dollar penalty imposed on a shipper for failing to load or unload a freight-carrying vehicle, following its constructive placement, within the time allotted by the carrier.

Diminishing Marginal Utility—the greater the number of units of any given commodity that an individual consumes, *ceteris paribus,* the less will be the amount of satisfaction (i.e., utility) added by each additional unit of the good that is consumed.

Disposable Income—the spendable income remaining to an individual after paying personal and other taxes to the government.

Disposition—the use of products. The terms utilization, consumption, and use are used interchangeably with the terms disposition and disappearance. In a broad sense, disposition may refer to domestic and export disappearance; in a narrower sense, it may refer to such specific uses as for food, feed, seed, or industrial.

Diversion and Reconsignment—the selection of alternative destinations for enroute shipments.

Diverter-Type Mechanical Sampler—an officially approved mechanical device, operated by electricity or air, that is used to obtain a representative sample (for testing and grading) from a stream of grain being moved from one location to another.

Draft—the vertical distance from waterline to keel of a waterborne vessel.

Dry Processed Products—products made without the addition of moisture, such as the milling of corn for corn meal or grits.

Dryeration—a process utilizing high speed and a high temperature to remove moisture from grain, with cooling by aeration.

Effective Demand—a phraseology occasionally used to emphasize that consumers are "willing and able" to buy the quantities indicated by the demand curve.

Elasticity of Demand—*price* elasticity of demand. An index relating the percentage change in quantity demanded in response to a 1 percent change in the price of a good or service, *ceteris paribus.*

Elasticity of Supply—a measure of the *price* elasticity of supply, identical in method to that used to measure elasticity of demand. An index relating the percentage change in quantity supplied in response to a 1 percent change in the price of a good or service, *ceteris paribus.*

Electronic Trading—the use of electronic communication equipment to enable traders at different locations to exchange bids and offers and enter into sales agreements.

Ellis Cup—an officially approved manual sampling device, designed to draw a sample from grain moving on a conveyor belt. The Ellis cup is used at domestic interior points and not at export points.

Embargo—a government-ordered suspension or prevention of trade with another nation; it may be applied to all trade with that nation, or to selected goods and services.

Engel's Curve—a graphic description of the relationship between a family's income and the quantities of goods purchased; based on Engel's law, which states that as a family's income increases, proportionately less of that income is spent on food.

European Community (EC)—a customs union with common agricultural and other policies, established in 1957 and signed by Belgium, France, Luxembourg, Italy, West Germany, and the Netherlands. The United Kingdom, Denmark, Ireland, and Greece joined later, thus, the occasional reference, "EC-10."

Equilibrium Price—the market-clearing price at which buyers will take the quantity of a good that sellers want to sell.

Exceptions—statements by individual carriers not wishing to comply with certain provisions of an otherwise governing rate tariff.

Exempt Carriage—transport not subject to regulation. Exemptions normally apply to products transported, not to the carrier. Bulk containers are generally exempt from regulation when transported by barge. Unprocessed agricultural products are exempt when transported by trucks. Private transport by truck or barge also is exempt.

Ex-Pit Transaction—a special type of trade allowed under the rules of a futures market involving the exchange of a futures contract for a cash commodity.

Exports—domestically produced goods and services that are sold abroad.

Fair Average Quality (FAQ)—the quality of a shipment of grain is at least equal to the quantity of all such grain shipped during a specified period.

Farmer-Owned Grain Reserve—a grain reserve authorized by the Food and Agriculture Act of 1977 to support farm prices. Farmers retain ownership of the grain and store it on their farms or in commercial facilities for periods of not less than three years nor more than five years.

F.a.s.—free alongside ship, specifies that the seller delivers goods to the port elevator or dock at the specified location, and the buyer pays for loading the ship and for ocean freight.

Federal Grain Inspection Service—an agency of the USDA established by the Grain Standards Act of 1976. This agency is responsible for maintaining uniform measures of grain quality and for grading grain at ports of export.

Federal Maritime Commission—an agency of the U.S. government responsible for regulating of ocean and Great Lakes shipping.

Feed Grains—grains that are used primarily for animal feed: corn, barley, oats, and grain sorghum.

First Handler—a merchant or processor who buys farm products directly from farmers.

Fixed Costs (of Storing Grain)—the costs of facilities ownership. Fixed costs include depreciation on facilities, interest on invested capital, insurance, and other costs that remain constant whether the facility is used for storing grain or is left empty.

Flagout—omission of rate changes on specific items of a class of freight for which rate changes have been authorized.

Fleeting—the assembly of barges into larger or smaller towing units in response to differing channel conditions.

F.o.b.—free on board, specifies that the seller loads the ship or other conveyance at the specified delivery point, with the buyer paying freight charges.

Food Grains—grains used primarily for (or in products for) human consumption. Wheat, rye, and rice are classified as food grains.

Formula Pricing—agreeing to set the price for a trade by using a special formula or rule usually based on a reported price to be observed in the future.

Forward Contract—a sales agreement calling for delivery during a specified future time period.

Forward Pricing—an agreement between buyer and seller that sets the price and other terms of trade and provides for the transfer of ownership at a later date.

Forward Trading—trading in forward contracts.

Fourth-Section Departure—Section 4 of the Interstate Commerce Act prohibits higher rates for a longer haul than for a shorter haul of the same commodity over the same line. Departures from this rule are allowed under certain conditions.

Free Market—an economic system in which decision makers (people and firms) are able to buy and sell in their own best interests, with a minimum of governmental restriction of their activities; also referred to as an "open" market.

Freight Forwarder—an assembler of freight shipments who arranges shipping details. Ocean container shipments are frequently arranged by a freight forwarder.

F.s.t.—free on board, stowed, and trimmed; specifies that the seller loads the ship and pays for stowing and trimming the load at the specified delivery point, while the buyer pays the ocean freight.

Fumigation—the process of exposing grain to the fumes (vapor) of a chemical agent to kill pests.

Fundamental Analysis—an effort to explain and predict price movements by using the concepts of supply and demand.

Futures Contract—a standardized forward contract that is traded under the rules of an organized exchange.

General Agreement on Tariffs and Trade (GATT)—an international code of tariffs and trade rules that became effective on January 1, 1948, following signature by the 23 participating nations, intended to foster the growth and conduct of international trade by reducing tariff barriers and eliminating import quotas and other discriminatory treatment between trading nations. GATT membership currently exceeds 80 nations.

Grain Grades and Standards—specific standards of grain quality established to maintain uniformity of grains from different lots and permit the purchase of grain without the need for visual inspection and testing by the buyer.

Grain Merchandiser—a person or firm buying and selling grain; a middleman.

Grain Reserve—stocks of grain withheld from the market and stored for use in times of critical shortages.

Grain Warehouse Receipt—a legal document by which a warehouseman formally acknowledges that grain has been received for storage.

Grits—coarsely ground cereal grain used for human consumption.

Hectare—a land area measurement of 10,000 square meters that is used in most of the world, and equal to 2.47 acres.

Hedging—buying or selling a futures contract as a temporary substitute for an anticipated cash transaction. Hedging is used to protect the firm or individual from losses caused by price fluctuations.

Horizontal Integration—occurs when a single management gains control, by voluntary agreement or ownership, over two or more firms performing similar activities at the same level or phase in the production or marketing sequence. An example is the merging of two country elevators.

Identity Preservation—seggregation of a commodity from one point to the next in the marketing system so that the initially identified commodity is delivered to the next point in the marketing system without being mixed with other units of the same commodity during handling and shipment.

Imports—purchases of foreign-produced goods and services.

Income Elasticity of Demand—an index that measures the relative response of quantity consumed to a change in income.

Integration—the economic linkage of two or more firms under a single management through voluntary agreement or ownership. Examples of such integration are *forward* (one step closer to the final marketing stage), *backward* (one step farther away from the final marketing stage), *vertical* (two or more different stages in the marketing process), and *horizontal* (two or more firms in the same stage of the marketing process).

Interstate Commerce Commission (ICC)—a federal agency, established by the Interstate Commerce Act of 1877, responsible for the economic regulation of railroads, barges, and interstate trucking.

In Transiter Stoppage—the right of a shipper, when permitted by the rate engaged, to stop a shipment of goods before it can be delivered if the one to whom the shipment is consigned is unable to pay for the goods.

Inverse Carrying Charge—distant futures are quoted at lower prices than near futures, ordinarily occurs when grain supplies are short relative to demand.

Inverted Market—a market situation for a storable commodity where the price for near-term delivery exceeds the price for later delivery during the same marketing year.

Joint Rate—a single rate involving two or more interconnecting carriers.

Land in Farms—the land area under the control of farm producers and in use or available for their use in producing agricultural products.

Land Retirement—usually refers to the removal of land from production according to the objectives of a farm program.

License—formal permit from a state or federal authority to operate a grain warehouse or other regulated business.

Line Elevator—two or more grain elevators owned by a grain company, usually located along a railroad line.

Local Tariff—a tariff describing rates and transportation conditions when all origins and destinations are served by a single carrier.

Long—an individual or firm that owns a commodity or holds fixed price agreements to buy the commodity in excess of any fixed price sales agreements.

Malthusian Theory—a theory postulated by Thomas R. Malthus that the world's population has the biological capability of increasing at a more rapid rate than food supplies can be increased.

Manifest—an invoice listing the cargo aboard ship.

Marginal Rate of Transformation—the rate at which products substitute for one another along a production possibilities curve.

Margin Pricing—in grain merchandising, the practice of setting one's bid price by subtracting a fixed amount (or margin) from a buyer's bid price.

Market—any group of buyers and sellers who have the ability to communicate with one another.

Market Channels—the agencies and institutions through which products are moved from their original producers to the final consumers.

Marketing—the performance of all the business activities that direct the flow of goods and services from producers to the final consumers.

Marketing Board—a government or quasi-government agency with exclusive marketing priveleges for a commodity.

Maturing Future—a futures contract during the last few weeks that it is traded; for example, the March corn contract between March 1 and the last day of trading in that contract.

Metric Ton—1000 kilograms of weight, equal to 2204.6 pounds.

Moisture Content—the amount of water in grain; measured by the weight of water in grain as a percentage of the total weight of that grain.

Multinational—a business firm with subsidiaries in more than one country.

Most Favored Nation—provision in a treaty between two nations that grants each signatory to the treaty the same tariff rates as the most favorable rates that either may grant to any other nation.

Near Future—for a particular commodity or exchange, the futures contract currently being traded that has the earliest maturity date.

Net Position—the amount of a commodity that a trader owns plus the amount of fixed price agreements to buy minus the amount of fixed price agreements to sell the commodity.

Nonrecourse Loan—a loan in which the lender, such as the CCC, has no recourse beyond the physical commodity itself in satisfaction of the loan.

Nontariff Barriers—government regulations that reduce the free flow of commodities in international trade.

Offer—a proposal of price and other terms of trade by a would-be seller.

Off-Farm Storage—commercially provided facility used for grain storage at a fee.

Oilseeds—seed crops including soybeans, sunflowers, rapeseed, flaxseed, peanuts, cottonseed, copra, sesameseed, safflowerseed, castor beans, and palm kernel, which are grown both for their oil and high protein meals.

On-Farm Storage—farmer-owned grain storage facilities.

Opportunity Cost—the value of a sacrificed alternative.

Organization of Petroleum Exporting Countries (OPEC)—a cartel of petroleum exporting nations, organized in 1960 to increase their oil revenues.

Parity Prices—the price that gives a unit of product the same purchasing power as it had in a specified base period.

Pelican—an officially approved sampling device that is swung or pulled through a falling stream of grain. The pelican is a leather pouch attached to a long pole, and may be used for sampling grain at domestic interior points but not at export points.

Per Capita Consumption—a simple average, derived by dividing the total amount of a good consumed by the total population.

Pink Grading Certificate—a certificate attesting only to the accuracy of the grade of a sample of grain, and not to the sampling method or that it is a representative sample of the lot from which it was taken.

Place Utility—the utility created by transporting commodities to locations where those goods are more highly valued.

Policy—a plan by which a government, firm, or individual expects to achieve a given objective by specific actions.

Port Terminal—grain handling firm with facilities to load oceangoing ships.

Price Determination—interaction of the forces of supply and demand to establish price in the marketplace.

Price Discovery—the process by which, through exchanging bids and offers, the market clearing price is found that equates supply and demand.

Probe—an officially approved sampling device (a compartmentalized metal tube, 5 to 12 feet long), designed to be pushed into a bin or load of grain and simultaneously draw a sample from several different depths in the lot. The probe is the only approved method for obtaining samples from stationary lots of grain.

Processor—individual or firm that processes a raw farm product to its desired form.

Production Possibilities Curve—a curve showing all the combinations of two goods that an individual, firm, or nation can produce during a given time period with full utilization of all of the resources and the technology available to produce those goods. When resources are subject to diminishing marginal productivity, the production possibilities curve is drawn concave to the origin to reflect increasing opportunity costs.

Projection—an extrapolation that forecasts a future situation on the basis of historical relationships.

Proportional Rate—a common or uniform balance of a through rate paid beyond a rate-break point.

Public Law 480 (PL-480)—the basic legal authority for sharing the surplus agricultural production of the United States with developing countries that have food deficits. Since its inception in July 1954, it has evolved from a temporary, surplus removal measure into a major tool in the world struggle for freedom from hunger and an effective instrument to stimulate economic development and support of U.S. foreign policy goals.

Public Policy—a special kind of group action designed to achieve certain aspirations held by members of society.

Putting on the Crush—locking-in a crushing margin, accomplished by buying soybean futures and selling equivalent amounts of soybean meal futures and soybean oil futures.

Quota—restriction on the absolute quantity of a commodity that may be imported.

Rail Tariff—a legal document published by carriers or carrier associations, showing applicable rates, rules, and regulations governing service, routings, special services, demurrage, and other related matters.

Rate-Break Point—a point in the rail rate system from which incoming rail billing applies to a shipment to qualify it for a lower (proportional) outbound rate in lieu of the higher (flat) rate.

Reciprocal Trade Agreements Act of 1934—an Act that expanded the markets for U.S. products by authorizing the president to enter into mutually advantageous, bilateral trade agreements with other nations. Freer world trade was promoted as countries agreed to lower their tariff barriers.

Round Turn—the purchase and sale of one futures contract.

Scale Ticket—written document of the weight of a load of grain that may also contain such other information as test weight, moisture, grade, and price.

Seasonality—fluctuation in price, quantity, or other variables within a year or producing season.

Short—an individual or firm holding fixed price sales agreements for a commodity that exceed the amount of the commodity owned plus the fixed price purchase agreements held.

Shrink—in grain, the loss of volume or weight that occurs during drying.

Speculation—carrying unhedged cash grain inventories; buying or selling futures (or commodities), without an opposite cash market (or futures) transaction, on the basis of anticipated price changes.

Splits—in soybeans, pieces of grain that are otherwise undamaged.

Spot Market—the market in sales contracts for immediate delivery, or delivery within a few days.

Spoutline—a vertical core of grain fines that accumulates in the spaces between grain kernels at the peak of the growing pile of grain as it is being poured into a storage bin.

Storage—the marketing function that holds grain from one time period to a later time period when the grain is more highly valued.

Substitutes—commodities that can replace one another in production or consumption. The coefficient of cross price elasticity between substitute commodities is positive.

Subterminal elevator—an establishment that buys and sells grain in large quantities, and operates facilities for receiving and shipping grain that are not located at a terminal market.

Supply—the quantity of a good or service that producers are willing to sell in the market at various prices per unit of time, *ceteris paribus*. The supply of grain in any one year includes the current year's output, plus carry-over and imports.

Target Prices—prices established in farm programs that will be supported by government assistance.

Tariffs—taxes levied on commodities as they cross a nation's boundary; also refers to the schedules of charges for warehouse services, or the schedules of rates charged by carriers.

Technical Analysis—efforts to predict short-term price movements that are based on observed regularities or patterns in a price series.

Tender—a formal written offer or proposal of price and other terms of trade by a would-be seller.

Terminal Agency—wholesale dealers, car lot receivers, commission merchants, and brokers. They facilitate the assembly and distribution of grain but do not have the physical facilities for handling grain and may or may not take title to the commodity.

Terminal Elevator—an establishment that operates facilities for receiving and shipping grain in large quantities at a terminal market.

Terminal Elevator Company—involved in cash grain merchandising and in operating terminal and subterminal elevators for storage as well as for merchandising.

Terminal Market—a major assembly and trading point for a commodity. Some of the major U.S. terminal markets for grains are Kansas City, Chicago, Minneapolis, Toledo, Portland, St. Louis, New Orleans, and Houston.

Terminal Market Merchandiser—a person or firm, located in terminal market areas, and buying grain from country positions to be shipped to terminal markets.

Terms of Trade—the specific provisions of a sales agreement, including the price, quantity, quality, time and place of delivery, and method of payment.

Test Weight—a measure of grain density determined by weighing the quantity of grain required to fill a one-quart container, and converting this to a bushel (2150.42 cubic inches) equivalent.

Time Charter—a contract between shipowner and shipper in which the shipper "rents" the ship for a specified period of time.

Time Utility—the utility created through the storage function that makes goods and services available to consumers at the time they are more intensely desired.

To Arrive—a term of sale, specifying that a commodity will be moved to its delivery point at a given time in the future.

Transit Balance—the balance of a through rate from a specific origin to a specific destination that is paid beyond a designated transit point. Differs from a proportional rate because it applies to specific origin and destination points.

Transportation—a marketing function that moves grain (or other goods and services) from one location to another.

Turning—a process of emptying a bin, elevating, rebinning, and possibly blending grain to maintain its quality. Before the advent of aeration, turning was the means used to ventilate or aerate grain.

Two-Price Plans—farm programs that attempt to take advantage of differences in the price elasticities of demand in domestic and foreign markets to increase total revenue from the sale of agricultural products.

Uniform Commercial Code—a code adopted by the American Bar Association to facilitate the easy transfer of warehouse receipts. Under the Code, a warehouse receipt is a certificate of title for agricultural products that are stored in a warehouse.

Uniform Straight Bill of Lading—a uniform shipping contract between a shipper and a for-hire common carrier. The straight bill of lading serves as a nonnegotiable receipt for goods that have been delivered to the carrier.

Unit Train—an assembled train loaded at one location by a single shipper, moving to a single consignee at a single location; used most commonly in shipping coal, grain and soybeans.

U.S. Warehouse Act—an Act passed in 1916 to protect the interests of producers and other grain owners who store commodities with public warehousemen.

Utility—the satisfaction that people derive from consuming goods and services.

Values—an individual's or group's perception of what "ought to be" regarding a situation.

Variable Costs (of Storing Grain)—costs that are incurred only if grain is stored, including insurance, taxes on the grain, interest foregone on the grain, shrinkage and quality losses, and the costs of quality maintenance.

Vertical Integration—occurs when a firm combines two or more activities that are sequentially related but different phases in the production or marketing sequence. A country elevator merging with a subterminal or terminal elevator, or a grain producer purchasing a country elevator, are examples of integrating vertically.

Voyage Charter—a contract between a shipowner and a shipper for a specific shipment or voyage.

Wet Processed Products—products that are made from soaked grain, such as starch, dextrin, and syrup from corn.

White Grading Certificate—document issued when the sampling and grading have been performed by licensed employees of an official inspection agency.

Woodside Sampler—an officially approved mechanical grain sampling device used at domestic interior points. This sampler was often used at export points prior to the invention of the diverter-type sampler.

Working Stocks—sometimes called "pipeline" stocks. The grain inventory needed to keep a plant operating efficiently throughout the year.

Yellow Grading Certificate—this certificate may be issued by the elevator if it is equipped with a diverter-type mechanical sampler that is operated by a licensed operator. The certificate indicates the accuracy of both the sampling and grading procedure, and the grain must be graded by an official agency.

INDEX